SOCIAL GEOGRAPHY OF INDIA

About the Author

Aijazuddin Ahmad—A renowned geographer and academician, was Professor at the Jawaharlal Nehru University, New Delhi for twenty-five years. Earlier he taught at Aligarh Muslim University for more than a decade. His areas of interest include arid zone research, historical, regional and social geography, geographical thought, human geography, social perspective on regional development planning, education and demography of minority groups. During his professional career, he published 15 books and numerous articles in national and international journals.

Prof. Ahmad held prominent positions in University Grants Commission, National Association of Geographers, India, International Geographical Union, National Committee of Indian National Science Academy, Council for Scientific and Industrial Research, Indian Council of Social Science Research, National Council of Educational Research and Training, and National Institute of Educational Planning and Administration. He has been involved in several interdisciplinary exercises of various councils and national institutes.

Second Revised & Enlarged Edition

Social Geography of India

Aijazuddin Ahmad

Professor of Geography (Retd.)
Centre for the Study of Regional Development,
Jawaharlal Nehru University, New Delhi, India

CONCEPT PUBLISHING COMPANY PVT. LTD.
NEW DELHI-110 059

ISBN-13 : 978-81-8069-862-0 (HB)

Second Revised and Enlarged Edition, 2012

Published and Printed by

Concept Publishing Company Pvt. Ltd.
A/15-16, Commercial Block, Mohan Garden
New Delhi-110059 (India)
T: 25351460, 25351794, *F*: 091-11-25357109
E: publishing@conceptpub.com, W: www.conceptpub.com
Editorial Office: H-13, Bali Nagar, New Delhi-110 015, India.

Cataloging in Publication Data--*Courtesy:* D.K. Agencies (P) Ltd. <docinfo@dkagencies.com>

Ahmad, Aijazuddin.
Social geography of India / Aijazuddin Ahmad. — 2nd rev. & enl. ed.
p. cm.
Includes bibliographical references (p.) and index.
ISBN 9788180698620

1. Human geography—India. 2. Social structure—India. 3. Land use—India. I.Title.

DDC 304.20954 23

In loving memory of
my parents

Preface to the Second Edition

The first edition of this book was published in November 1999. The reception of this book was so overwhelming that the author decided to revise it and update it. The contents were partially modified and brought up to date. The wonderful reception gave the author a new hope that the book in the print media can still be of value to the vast readership despite the age of computers and the internet. I thank the readers for their interest in the area of social geographic research.

The new edition takes care of the deficiencies felt by the readers, particularly scholars at the research level. Maps have been modified, so as to suit the needs of students both at the M.A. and research levels. Some maps have been deleted. A new chapter on the social fabric of the Indian republic has been added. The author's treatment of the material on social geography and the themes covered left behind an impression that tribe, caste, language and religion exist in a watertight compartment. But this is not true. These themes are inter-penetrative and inter-dependent. The fundamental principle of integration and unity cannot be by-passed. In fact, regions of India have led to regional tendencies in the polity.

The chapters included in this book present aspects of the spatial organisation of Indian society in its ethnic, tribal, caste, linguistic and religious expressions. While these elements define the parameters of socio-cultural diversity of our people, they do not express themselves in isolation. In fact, they are elements of a composite identity, intertwined and inseparable from one another. It is also evident that the Indian social identity is not pluralistic. A Tamil, for example, is a member of a language group, which in itself is a culture-world, perceived at the highest level of identity. The language binds a Tamil (or for that matter a Kannadiga, a Punjabi or a Kashmiri in similar culture-realms) to a larger ethno-lingual formation. Subsumed in the Tamil language world may be other smaller worlds, such as the Yerukala or the Toda. These dialect groups living within the over-arching unity of the Tamil language have their own spheres of communication and community-based identity and social practice. These lower-level identities divide the larger Tamil identity into smaller sets. Besides being the member of a language group a Tamil may also be a Hindu, a Muslim or a Christian at the same time. His Hindu identity is further split into caste or tribal configurations—Tamil Brahman, Tamil Visvabrahman, Arya Vaisya, Yadava or the Ayyanavar, Chakkaliyan, Adi Dravida, Holeya and the Pulayan or the Kadar, Konaga, Malasar, Mannan and the Toda. As *jatis* or *janajatis*, each of these groups, have their own social identity, defined by the caste-specific or tribe-specific religio-magical rituals, ceremonies, social practices and the communitarian mode of conduct. However, their solidarity to the Tamil language and culture is basic as it lies over and above the narrow differences based on caste and religion. These examples show the intertwined nature of social identity, which expresses itself at different levels from the *up-jati,* to the *jati* and the *bhasha, boli* and the *dharma*. It is the *bhasha* that defines the outer limit of our culture-worlds.

May 2006 **Aijazuddin Ahmad**

Preface to the First Edition

This book has grown out of my involvement in the M.A. level course on social geography with special reference to India, which I taught at the Jawaharlal Nehru University for twenty-four years at a stretch from 1972 to 1997. Many parts of this book were actually taught in the course of prolonged classroom discussions. The teaching in this course always had important inputs of research drawn from my own work conducted by me independently, sometimes as part of research projects in which I got involved, and sometimes in association with my students who joined the social geography stream at the research level. The give-and-take between the teacher and the students lasting over these years continued to enrich the course, often inducing me to accommodate new viewpoints. The ideas expressed here were in a way churned in the course of classroom lectures delivered to the successive generations of students representing all parts of India and belonging to different tribal, caste and religious groups. The actual writing, however, was done during the last three years, from the summer of 1996 to the spring of 1999. The positions taken by me on different issues relevant to the diverse themes of India's social geography may appear to be familiar, although they are also controversial in some respects. But they are based on considered opinion and may be taken as the end-product of an evolving process of thought. These opinions have, of course, been influenced by my growing knowledge of the sources and their interpretations by a whole line of scholars from F.J. Richards to Subbarao, Sankalia, Kosambi, S.M. Ali and O.H.K. Spate. On many issues a consensus has already been reached among the scholars. Divergent points of view, however, continue to persist on many other issues. I have often preferred material evidence on written record.

Not much work has been done on the spatial organisation of Indian society and its social structure as expressed in identities, such as ethnicity, tribe, caste, community, language, dialect and religion at the grass-roots level, although broad all-India outlines are discernible in stray research. The present work seems to serve two main purposes. First, it assembles together the broader outlines to construct an all-India frame, disaggregating the data wherever possible up to the regional levels. Secondly, it casts this frame into a historical mould, thus demonstrating how crucial the spatial dimension is in understanding the socio-cultural evolution of the Indian people. The enterprise of placing the various aspects of social structure in their historical context is admittedly beset with difficulties. But there is no gainsaying the fact that it is in the context of time that the data acquire their true meaning and become relevant to the contemporary generation of Indians. This work highlights the inevitability of the spatio-regional method in the implementation of the historical agenda.

In handling spatially-disaggregated data, it is important to realise the limitations of census data, in itself massive and disparate in terms of canvas, comparability and coverage. However, it is the census data that enable one to build the time-series, whatever its limitations, besides constructing the database along the horizontal scale. A census operation by its very nature is an administrative exercise. Likewise, the decision to publish the census data in a certain format is often guided by administrative concerns. The academic community may not find such a format very helpful in unravelling the social reality. Moreover, due to frequent changes in politico-administrative boundaries, particularly in cases when a new district is constituted by transferring parts of neighbouring districts, data are often rendered incomparable between two census counts. Definitions also change frequently making comparisons across time a cumbersome exercise. Additions to the list of Scheduled Castes and Scheduled Tribes lead to further complications in handling time-series data. The census authorities are sometimes under compulsion to withhold the publication of certain data categorised as 'sensitive', such as those on religion, caste or language, making meaningful socio-geographic studies almost impossible. It may, therefore, be necessary to generate primary data from the field to establish the ground truths about the caste, religious and linguistic identity of the people in selected villages and cities of India. Such an exercise may be absolutely necessary if the intention is to explore the nature of relationship between elements of social structure and the critical economic and cultural indicators, such as ownership of land, landholding size, land alienation, land transfers, occupational structure, out-migration, change of residence due to civic strife, literacy and educational levels, access to social amenities and the state of social well-being. Such monographs on selected castes and communities attempted on a regional basis will serve an important purpose in filling the research gaps.

This study by its very nature is focused on the social structure. It is evident that the Indian people, and for that matter the society as a whole, is not a static lot. They have been undergoing wide-ranging changes throughout history, although the pace of change has not been uniform in all regions or among all sections of our society. Processes, such as education, urbanisation and industrialisation, penetration of the market forces, incidence of cash economies, expansion of administration, spread of political institutions, particularly since independence, and exposure to mass media, have all induced the society towards change. The impact of these processes is neither uniform nor abiding. It is mostly fragmented. However, each development leads to a streak of change, howsoever, feeble it might be. The change is often superficial, with the result that the nature of our people has not changed much. From inside, the people are deeply religious, tied to tradition, sometimes family-specific tradition, and devoted to family gods and the lineage of priests. The influence of age-old prejudices based on caste, community, lineage and regional consciousness has remained intact despite modernisation. However, these prejudices are not generally allowed to blur the secular vision. As a people, Indians are basically secular in their orientation, tolerant to diverse faiths and diversities in cultural ethos. It may be desirable to write on the social processes, such as the spread of education and empowerment leading to the social transformation/modernisation and politicisation.

In the end, it is necessary to acknowledge with thanks the help received from different individuals, friends and students, in the course of preparation of this book, who helped me document my lectures while they were delivered in the classroom. These audiotapes provided a skeleton on which this book was developed later. The computer cartography of many maps reproduced here became possible because of the services of my students. My thanks are due to all of them.

I am also grateful to my former JNU students, who accompanied me in my hunting expeditions for archival data, and prepared several maps for the chapters on caste and religion. They also handled massive census data on computer diskettes received from the Office of the Registrar General, India. I am grateful to the librarian of the Jawaharlal Nehru University for allowing me access to the periodicals and statistical materials. My thanks are also due to M/s. Rawat Publications for meticulous handling of the first edition of the book. Lastly, I wish to place on record my deep appreciation of the generosity of my family, which emboldened me to encroach upon their time and academic resources whenever they were needed in the course of a long spell of writing, which lasted for over three years. This book is a tribute to their endurance.

November 1999 **Aijazuddin Ahmad**

Contents

List of Tables

List of Figures

List of Boxes

List of Appendices

1

Social Geography
An Introduction

This book has grown out of my involvement in the teaching of a master's level course titled 'Social Geography with special reference to India' at the Jawaharlal Nehru University (JNU), New Delhi. The course was offered by me without any break during the period from 1972 to 1996. The course was designed in 1972, after the first batch of students joined the Centre for the Study of Regional Development for their master's level course in Geography. While the then Chairperson of the Centre, the late Professor Moonis Raza who was enthusiastic about the relevance of this course, helped me in designing it, the teaching responsibility was entirely left to me. I was supposed to meet the students in four contact hours per week and evolve sessional exercises including the ones based on the data available on Indian society so as to develop an empirical basis for the theoretical problems, which the students were likely to face. Several students at the research level working either with me or with Professor Raza on problems related to social geography further helped me in developing insights into the scantily researched field of Indian social geography. While handling this course for no less than a quarter century, I came in contact with generations of students with strikingly diverse experiences of India's social reality. Teaching a sensitive course like this implied confronting viewpoints which were based on narrow sectarian or parochial ideologies, themselves arising from a limited experience of the social history. Present in my class were members of tribal communities, *viz.*, the Nagas, Khasis, Garos, Mizos, Hmars, Oraons, Hos, Bhils, Apatanis or the Minas, various castes and language groups and, of course, those representing diverse religious faiths and belief systems. In a way the classroom itself was a microcosm of India, mirroring the social and the ethnological diversity of the Indian subcontinent. This cosmopolitan nature of the audience forced me to project a balanced view without, of course, compromising with the needs of realism or scientific objectivity. Although the course teacher tried to inculcate a spirit of accommodation in the midst of conflicting ideologies, not all the ideas which were advanced in the class were received with affirmation. Many agreed with my views, some disagreed initially but converted later, others were just opposed to the message that I tried to convey through this course.

This book documents some of these ideas, particularly their practical implications as they were experimented in the midst of classroom discussions over a quarter of a century. These ideas were developed and subjected to critical evaluation and thus chiselled through discussion lasting over more than two decades before they could find a place in this book.

Seen in the context of the tradition of geographical pedagogy as received in the summer of 1972, it was felt that there was a need to develop a course of this kind in order to promote an understanding of the complex social phenomena that affected the behavioural patterns, defined the scope for social interaction, and promoted or discouraged the process of integration of the Indian people within a single 'nation'—state!

The new Indian state which experimented with the idea of federalism confronted these problems on the political as well as the administrative plane. The political solutions that were offered solved a problem here and created new problems there. While the state and the ruling party played firmly on a secular pitch, caste, community, ethnicity and linguistic parochialism or regionalism (sub-nationalism) emerged on the scene as the new political agenda. The people of India clamoured for the fulfilment of their aspirations based on their perceived identity as tribes (ethnic groups), castes (Scheduled Castes and Backward Castes) or on the ethno-lingual traits that differentiated one region (state) from the other.

It was necessary to expose the students to the social matrix and its socio-geographical interpretation which could facilitate an understanding of the social phenomena that defined India—an understanding of diversities within the larger framework of oneness that formed the basis of the Indian state.

Social Structure

The society is made up of elements drawn from diverse origins. Within the population of India are subsumed tribes—no less than three hundred ethnically differentiated communities—caste groups, language and religious groups, displaying striking differences in social organisation and cultural patterns, even material cultures. There are differences in racial strands and ethnic and cultural identities are strongly defined. Almost all religions from tribal forms of animism and totemism to Hinduism, Buddhism, Christianity, Islam and Sikhism have their followers in different proportions. The social diversity is perhaps the most powerful manifestation of Indian identity. The social groups with diverse ethnic origins, representing racial stocks from proto-Australoids and Mongoloids to the different branches of the Mediterraneans, western Brachycephalic groups and the Nordics, found a place for themselves at different points of time adapting themselves to the different ecological niches offered by the physiographic and the climatic setting of the subcontinent. There are strongly defined tribal identities based on ethnic origins. The tribal population includes within its fold hundreds of large and small ethnic groups from the Santals, Gonds and the Bhils to the Mundas, Oraons, Hos, Todas and the Apatanis, to mention only a few. The tribal India is characterised by heterogeneity of a very high order. Their geographic patterning in the Indian space in itself posed serious problems in the administration of the tribal affairs. The tribes are heavily concentrated in the northeast, in the hills and the plateau surfaces surrounding the Brahmaputra valley as well as in the mid-Indian belt from the Western Ghats to the Rajmahal hills. The tribes have been living in a world of their own, in habitats which permitted little interaction within themselves or between them and the rest of the Indian population. The mutually exclusive domains of the tribal and the non-tribal segments of population appear to have contributed to the regional differentiation of the first order. The tribal identity is thus based on ethnicity, as differentiation took place along the ethno-lingual lines. Tribalism implies allegiance to traditional values of social equality, freedom, communitarian ethos, and equality of status, including gender equality, segmentation along clan and kinship structures rather than social stratification or hierarchical order governing the status of the different sections of population. The tribal view of social order and the social law is essentially different from the rest of the society. The traditional egalitarian relations, however, underwent a change as the tribal groups were exposed to diverse influences emanating from centres of power, such as the British or Indian administrators, economic classes, such as the moneylenders and the petty traders, or the influences exerted by the peasant groups in areas of high population density who slowly spilled over the traditional tribal domains, particularly in mid-India. These exogenetic influences have helped transformation of the traditional tribal relations, with some sections acquiring the traits of an upper class society and other sections losing access to natural resources including land, and thus getting marginalised.

The organisation of space in tribal regions may thus be seen as a manifestation of the ways of adaptation to the environmental setting as determined by the historical processes of peopling of the traditional habitats by homogeneous clan and kinship groups. This primeval homogeneity originated from their common descent. Over the time, and as a result of their initial occupance of the habitats of their choice, clusters of tribal hamlets acquired the character of a monolithic tribal core region. A hill range which defined the watershed, or the channel of a river, served as a boundary separating the core region of one tribal group from the other. This illustrated the process of segmentation. The placement of tribes in spatial segments may be an outcome of a social history of contact, confrontation and contestation between the ethnically differentiated tribes and between them and the peasant groups who hastened the process of their displacement from the river valleys in the course of the colonisation of the riverine tracts.

As it would appear tribes have lived away from the river valleys ever since the colonisation of the fluvial basins by the agrarian communities. The highlands and the plateau surfaces surrounding the river valleys were not the ideal sites for the pursuit of agriculture. The tribes, although exposed to the agrarian mode, remained on the fringe of sedentary agriculture. The river valleys are occupied by peasant societies whose distinctive trait is a social hierarchical order based on the institution of caste. This hierarchical social order enshrined in the institution of caste is not a characteristic feature of the Hindu peasantry alone. All other sections of the society, whether Christian or Muslim, are also socially organised along caste lines. Caste is a social phenomenon of great relevance. In fact, caste and communal identity together define the basic parameters of the organisation of rural space. The layout and morphology of the rural settlements reflect the way different caste groups have come together to constitute the village society and have segregated in space in accordance with their function or occupation and their social ranking based on it. The spatial arrangement of caste or community groups within a village in itself is a demonstration of traditional relations based on the single criterion of caste identity. The propertied classes among these groups emerged as dominant castes, as they were owners of land—the principal means of production. Around the nucleus of landowning castes, converged a number of ancillary castes whose position in the village morphological plan reflected their status in the social hierarchy. These ancillary caste groups were subservient to the interests of the dominant castes. Since, the domains of these dominant castes were by and large mutually exclusive, the geographic patterning of the dominant caste groups also revealed the distribution pattern of social authority in rural India. The political ramifications of such a social order cannot be easily visualised.

The dominant castes wielded social power, and when democratic institutions were introduced, monopolised them as they were the ruling elites. This monopoly of democratic institutions and the developmental assets that reached the villages forced the lagging and the deprived sections of the caste society to mobilise themselves politically so as to counter the hegemony of the high castes on the political plane.

The initial process of colonisation of the river valleys from the Indus to the Brahmaputra and the Sabarmati and the Godavari to the Kaveri introduced the first level of differentiation in the ethnic content and cultural expression. The river valleys, both major and minor, provided ecological niches for the primeval groups. They might have been derived from the same stem but with distance in time and space, differences in speech form and in culture increased. The early territories which emerged in the form of *janapadas* around the middle of the first millennium B.C. reflected the onset of this process of social differentiation. Archaeologists, such as Richards and Subbarao, demonstrated how river valleys emerged as regions of attraction and acquired their own nuances of language and culture. An understanding of the cultural matrix of these so-called nuclear regions may hold the key to an appreciation of the roots of cultural diversity that the people of India demonstrated today. The peasant society based in the river valleys, with all the ramifications of caste-based hierarchy, got differentiated adapting itself to the regional ethos. The caste or *varna* system are all-India categories, but their regional expressions differ so much that no two regions are exactly comparable. The ranking of the castes and the perceptions of status within the same caste group (*e.g.*, Brahmans) varies in space, revealing an admirable correspondence with language regions.

Social Processes

Despite the fact that ethnic, tribal and caste identities are strongly defined, the Indian society has been responding to the processes of modernisation and social change with varying degrees of intensity. However, the impact of these processes is neither uniform nor all sections of population are equally responsive to change. Urbanisation, industrialisation, education, social reform movements, political awakening and the advent of democratic processes seem to have exercised an all-embracing modernising influence. Some Indian sociologists believe that the tradition itself has been modernising.[1] Urbanisation, for example, is one such process which has brought in its wake a whole series of changes leading to the transformation of traditional way of life, behavioural patterns of the people and to some extent the associated attitudes and value systems. But the impact of urbanisation is not uniform. Some regions of India are fast urbanising while others have remained predominantly rural. The impact of urbanisation is most evident in thirty-five metropolitan centres and a few hundred cities. Even the cities, particularly in the lagging regions of the country, such as Bihar, Rajasthan or Orissa, may reveal the evidence of the continuing hold of rural tradition and the effect of modernisation may only be superficial. This is true that in its developed form the urban way of life necessitates changes in the social attitudes, and more importantly, the identity of an individual is likely to be lost. Thus caste and family antecedents are not easily verifiable in a city and the individual may feel relatively free of the social constraints. Moreover, the city intensifies the struggle for survival as opportunities demand stiff competition. The aspiring sections of population acquire new skills through education and training for which cities offer an ideal environment. Paradoxically, the character of Indian urbanisation is such that it does not replace the traditional way of life. In fact, it permits the juxtaposition of the modern and the traditional. This is partly because of the continuity of traditional identities based on ethnicity, tribalism, caste, and religion, which are retained even after migration to the city.

Individuals are distinguishable on the basis of caste, religious and ethnic names which continue to be factors of social reference even in an urban setting, often leading to discriminatory behaviour. In fact, the morphology of towns itself shows the very process of settling down of different social categories in the urban space. The *mohalla, basti,* and *tola* formation within the urban centres indicates the division of the urban space between the caste, community and occupational groups.[2] Moreover, the polarisation along the communal lines accentuated since the partition of the country has resulted in the emergence of separate blocks for the two major communities. This is a common feature of the North Indian towns. This is notwithstanding the fact that the impact of urbanisation is all too pervasive, leaving its imprints on all spheres of social life.

One notices, on the one hand, that urbanisation and industrialisation have gone hand in hand generating vigorous rural-to-urban streams of migration and effecting a systematic transformation of traditional occupational structure. Urbanisation implies horizontal movement of the rural masses to the urban centres. For example, the migration to the city involves not only a change in residence but also a vertical shift from the primary to the secondary or the tertiary sector of economy. On the other hand, the process of industrialisation has been uneven in space and it has left an impact, which is spatially fragmented. Industrial complexes have emerged as enclaves revealing little linkage with their rural hinterlands. In fact, their forward linkages are stronger than their backward linkages. But industrialisation has also paved the way for a systematic transformation of the rural way of life, particularly in areas of progressive agriculture. The increasing demand for consumer goods in rural areas is an evidence of this on-going process. In sum, the transformation of agriculture and the on-going process of rural development have generated a new economic environment. This has led to an increasing degree of rural-urban interaction and a consequent loosening of the hold of traditional values.

But there is yet another side of the story. In the traditional society of India with a definite social structure, when the factory industry came, it conformed to the given occupational structure which was caste-based to a very large extent. Each caste group had a traditional association with an occupation, which was hereditary and the labour absorption in industries progressed on the same lines. Several industries attracted labour specific to its needs. The working class was, however, divided along caste-lines, trade unionism notwithstanding. Take, for example, the absorption of the *chamars* in the leather industry of Agra, Kanpur and Madras or the absorption of *dhunas* and *julahas* (castes traditionally associated with ginning of cotton, spinning and weaving) in the cotton textile industry. In fact, there were several departments of work in the cotton mill industry, where the untouchables were denied entry because their involvement in work would offend the labourers drawn from the ranks of the middle or high ranking castes.

This means that the progress in industrialisation instead of weakening the traditional caste-based hierarchical structure further reinforced it. Thus, the impact of industrialisation as a modernising process has not always been positive. In a way the caste system remained intact despite the trade unionism, which mobilised workers on the basis of class relations. Class consciousness emerged although it was not sufficient for countering effectively the overarching influence of the caste-based divisions.

The role of education in social engineering is no less significant. The British introduced a system of education which was essentially geared to their administrative needs in India. Their endeavour was really aimed at producing an educated class of Indians who could be assigned administrative responsibilities at the lower level, as lower and upper division clerks and office superintendents. The rate of expansion of British education was painstakingly slow apparently due to a general paucity of jobs in the government sector. The Indian elites drawn from the feudal and the princely houses, however, initiated their children, mostly males, into the British type of education. The scions of Indian princely houses preferred to join the prestigious institutions in England more as a status symbol than out of any economic compulsion.

This new type of education, even after the establishment of the presidency colleges at the port centres and the degree colleges at the district centres elsewhere, did not have much of an appeal to the Indian people. The masses remained outside the ambit of modern education. Even the general literacy rates remained low despite the expansion of education at various levels from the primary to the graduation. The situation did not change even after independence, and despite repeated proclamations to universalise education, it remained by and large confined to the upper echelons of society. In fact, there is no gainsaying the fact that the demand for education is intrinsically linked to the returns from education. Peasantry and the working classes which constitute, an overwhelmingly large chunk of population, did not see any value in the kind of education imparted to them ever since the days of the British Raj. Moreover, rampant unemployment further disillusioned the first-generation learners and detracted them from seeking education as jobs became scarce and competition for jobs intensified. It may be noted that today the character of higher education is basically elitist. Moreover, it has a strong urban orientation. The result is that the benefits of education have mostly accrued to the elites only comprising the upper classes and the urbanised high castes.

The expansion of education in India since independence has been widespread, although its impact has not been uniform. In fact, education has not been able to play its constructive role as a catalyst of social change. Education has also failed to weed out the traditional values based on superstition and obscurantist philosophies.

Nature of Social Geography: The Anglo-American School

The term 'social geography' carries with it an inherent confusion. In the popular perception the distinction between social and cultural geography is not very clear. The idea which has gained popularity with the geographers is that social geography is an analysis of social phenomena as expressed in space (Box 1.1). However, the term 'social phenomena', is in itself nebulous and might be interpreted in a variety of ways keeping in view the specific context of the societies at different stages of social evolution in the occidental and the oriental worlds. The term 'social phenomena' encompasses the whole framework of human interaction with environment, leading to the articulation of social space by diverse human groups in different ways. The end-product of human activity may be perceived in the spatial patterns manifest in the personality of regions; each pattern acquiring its form under the overarching influence of social structure. Besides the patterns, the way the social phenomena express themselves in space may become a cause of concern as well. This has attracted scholarly attention, particularly since 1945 when all-embracing changes in the political and economic order of the world started casting their shadows on the global society.

As compared to the other branches of geography, social geography has a certain amount of recency.[3] Eyles saw the antecedents of contemporary social geography in the development of the philosophy of possibilism in the late nineteenth century. The view of social phenomena is all-embracing and holistic, based on the totality of human interaction with environment. Eyles also visualised social geography as a continuation of the philosophy of Vidal de la Blache and Bobek:

> '... it stressed both the humanistic nature of the geographical world... and the classificatory nature of ... human geographical work...'[4]

Upto 1945, social geography was mainly concerned with the identification of different regions, themselves reflecting geographic patterns of association of social phenomena.

Box 1.1 : On Defining Social Geography

The taxonomy of a discipline, while arising out of its logical system, subsumes within itself the specificities of its intellectual tradition, whereby words and terms acquire specific connotations and nuances of meaning through large-scale usage and social acceptance. But this process of crystallisation of the classificatory scheme is greatly distorted if the same term tends to acquire different connotations or different shades of meaning tend to be expressed through the same term.

Such is unfortunately the case with that segment of geographical studies which is termed as Human or Anthropo or Social or Cultural Geography. The term "Human Geography" has a vintage value; it emerged in an embryonic state as an element in the essential dichotomy of geography during the classical period itself and acquired more definitive connotation at the hands of the great French possibilists. The term "Anthropo-Geography", on the other hand, arose within the rigid and inflexible conceptual framework of environmental determinism. The term "Social Geography" was perhaps introduced by Vallaux in 1908 through his *Geographic Sociale: La Mer* as a synonym for Human Geography and has since then remained ill-defined—its boundaries fluctuating at an alarming rate. The term "Cultural Geography" is a gift from the new world, which, while contributing a new item in geographical glossaries, has unfortunately only added to the semantic confusion. A look at some of the standard definitions of these terms would clearly bring out the prevailing lack of clarity on these questions. Monkhouse in his *A Dictionary of Geography* defines Human Geography as the "part of Geography dealing with man and human activities". In the same volume, the learned scholar states later that Social Geography "is often used simply as the equivalent of Human Geography, or in the U.S.A. as 'Cultural geography', but usually it implies studies of population, urban and rural settlements, and social activities as distinct from political and economic ones". Dudley Stamp in the *Longman's Dictionary of Geography* defines Cultural Geography as "that which emphasises human cultures and is commonly equated with human geography".

It is quite clear that definitions like the above are of no help in demarcating the areas covered by these sub-disciplines of Geography. If there is so much of connotative similarity there is a strong case for discarding two of these terms so that geographers can at least understand each other.... Alternatively two of these areas of academic work may be viewed as sub-sets of the third one.

—Moonis Raza and Aijazuddin Ahmad,

A Survey of Research in Geography 1969-72 (1979): 63-65.

In fact, during the twenties and the thirties of the twentieth century, social geography started its agenda of research with the study of population as observed in settlements, particularly urban settlements. This was understandable as population in the Anglo-Saxon and American world was overwhelmingly concentrated in the urban areas. The process of urbanisation had thrown up issues of social concern such as access to civic amenities and housing and the related socio-pathological issues, such as incidence of crime, juvenile delinquency and other expressions of mental ill-health. Socio-geographical studies of population distribution and ethnic composition in urban areas emerged as a major trend during this phase. The underlying idea was to examine the social content of the urban space which resulted from coming together of diverse ethnic groups within a city. The city with its specific functional specialisation cast these social groups in its mould, resulting in the assimilation of diverse elements into a universal (Europeanised) urban ethos. However, certain ethno-cultural identities (*e.g.*, African Americans, North Africans in France and Asians in Britain) were so strongly defined that they continued to defy the forces of assimilation. Moreover, the land market in the Anglo-Saxon and American cities further marginalised these coloured people. This resulted in their spatial segregation in ghettos with all the socio-pathological implications that follow from it. Emphasis on population characteristics remained a major preoccupation of social geographers till the fifties of this century. During the fifties, the tradition continued with social geographers mainly preoccupied with population characteristics. Social geographers differentiated between regions on the basis of dominant patterns as social phenomena, mostly based on the population characteristics. Later, under the influence of the rising tide of quantification, social geographers started employing area-specific data in order to discover spatial patterns. During this phase of development, the major focus of research remained on the analysis of the social data for the cities. Social area analysis emerged as the main tool of analysis. One inevitable consequence was that studies in this area, such as factorial ecology, made social geographic research dependent on the theories of human ecology. As against this, Emrys Jones' study of Belfast gave due consideration to the role of values, meanings and sentiments in locational activity.[5]

It may, however, be pointed out that any study of the social phenomena within the city in the context of factor analysis helped only in the identification of patterns.

It is noteworthy that the western social science was alive to the real issues in society. Social geography also could not remain unaffected by these trends. Thus, social geography in the western world developed much in response to political happenings of contemporary social relevance. For example, social change in attitudes and the perception of prevailing reality necessitated corresponding changes in the theoretical framework adopted by social scientists. The American society, for example, was overwhelmingly disturbed by the happenings in Vietnam war. A common concern was expressed on issues such as poverty and social inequality within the United States. The social relevance movement in the contemporary social sciences also affected geography and issues such as race, crime, health and poverty received an increasingly large attention.[6]

Emrys Jones and John Eyles[7] who described social geography as a group approach conceded that the attempts at defining the field represented the viewpoints of their authors to which others may not agree (Box 1.2). The progress of social geography in the decades since 1960 has taken three main paths, each cluster of research acquiring the status of a school of thought in its own way.

(a) A welfare or humanistic school mainly concerned with the state of social well-being as expressed by territorial indicators of housing, health and social pathology largely within the theoretical framework of welfare economics.

(b) A radical school which employed Marxian theory to explain the basic causes of poverty and social inequality. This school of thought related the contemporary social problems to the development of capitalism, particularly the internal contradictions of capitalism. For example, cities and the communities within the city were perceived as organised spatially in response to the class relations and the Marxian interpretation was that a welfare approach might not be helpful.

Box 1.2: Definitions

With due apologies to those omitted by oversight, the last twenty-five years or so have produced eight definitions of social geography, seven of which are provided by geographers working in the Anglo-American tradition. These are:

The identification of different regions of the earth's surface according to associations of social phenomena related to the total environment (Watson, 1957: 482)

The study of the patterns and processes (required) in understanding socially defined populations in a spatial setting (Pahl, 1965: 81)

The study of the areal (spatial) patterns and functional relations of social groups in the context of their social environment; the internal structure and external relations of the nodes of social activity, and the articulation of various channels of social communication (Buttimer, 1968: 144)

The analysis of the social patterns and processes arising from the distribution of, and access to, scarce resources and ... an examination of the societal causes of, and suggested solutions to, social and environmental problems (Eyles, 1974: 65)

The understanding of 'the patterns which arise from' the use of social groups make of space as they see it, and of the processes involved in making and changing such patterns (Jones, 1975: 7)

(It) stressed structure relations in the analysis of social problems... Analysis (is) based on interrelated material reality and the social contradictions this produces; which are seen as the motive force for change, and thus responsible for the development of problems like different level-of-living conditions (Asheim, 1979: 8)

The study of consumption, whether by individuals or by groups (Johnston, 1981: 205)

It is an interactionist perspective which aims to uncover how social structure is defined and maintained through social interaction, and which studies how social life is constituted geographically through the spatial structure of social relations (Jackson and Smith, 1984: vii)

—Courtesy: John Eyles,
Social Geography in International Perspective, 1988: 4-5.

(c) A phenomenological school which laid an extraordinary emphasis on lived experience and on the perception of space by social categories based on ethnicity, race, or religion.

It is thus obvious that contemporary social geography is in line with the theoretical development in human geography as a whole. This does not mean that the welfare or humanistic concerns or the quest for the causes of social inequality and class-based exploitation or phenomenological perceptions of space have replaced the tradition of areal differentiation or region formation. All these approaches have continued to co-exist.

Some themes have received greater attention at certain stages in the development of Anglo-American schools of geography. They may be mentioned here in brief.

References have been made to *social physics*, implying that for the analysis of human behaviour analogies can be drawn with the physical world. Around the middle of the nineteenth century Auguste Comte adopted an approach assuming that principles of physics, or mechanics, may be applicable to human society as well. The idea was revived by J.Q. Stewart in the forties of the twentieth century.[8] In association with William Warntz, the two developed the theory of social physics to create the field of 'macro geography'. Based on these concepts a gravity model was developed in human geography which tried to explain interaction between places illustrated by, for example, the movement of people and goods as products of the mass (population size, etc.). A distance factor also operated such as cost as an exponent revealing an inverse relationship. The basic idea of the gravity model also found its place in other models such as entropy maximising model and diffusion model. Other applications are found in rank-size rule and the population potential model.

These approaches were contested by many geographers who found social physics as simply mechanistic. The human society was not exactly a physical organism which could correspond to precisely defined laws.

The study of social phenomena, spatially variegated as they were, led to the identification of social areas and a *social area analysis* followed. American sociology adopted social area analysis as a technique for relating social structure with urban patterns. In this connection reference may be made to the pioneering work of two American sociologists, Eshref Shevky and Wendell Bell.[9] The two hypothesised that within a city the range and intensity of relations depends on the social rank;[10] that the process of urbanisation leads to differentiation in the functions of the households leading to changes in the family status; and that social organisation within the city leads to concentration of groups along cultural and ethnic lines.[11] Thus, the ethnic status of an individual also plays a role in social interaction. Geographers who adopted social area analysis as a method in their studies of urban social geography depended on statistics disaggregated for the micro units such as the census tracts within the city. Variables were chosen to represent the three constructs of social rank, urbanisation, and segregation in order to develop a composite index on the basis of which census tracts could be classified.

The technique was criticised for being mechanistic as there was no link between the social scaling and differentiation of population within the urban space. It was argued that the three constructs themselves were inadequate to portray the urban social reality. As a method social area analysis was abandoned in favour of what came to be known as factorial ecology.[12] Its importance, however, lies in the fact that at a certain stage in the historical development of social geography it played a highly seminal role furnishing a basis for systematic analysis of urban social space.

Western social geography, particularly the school of thought pursuing social welfare approach, attached the highest importance to the concept of social well-being.[13] It was hypothesised that well-being characterises a state in which the basic human needs of a given population are satisfied because the people have sufficient income for their basic needs. However, the concept was defined within the framework of the social system of capitalism. The high income groups organised themselves in space in such a way that their basic needs were optimally satisfied. Income played a crucial role in creating optimal conditions for the social infrastructure, such as housing, civic amenities, health, education and recreation. The underlying assumption is that the poor were not in a position to satisfy their basic needs. The state of well-being is achieved only when the income is sufficient to fulfil the basic needs, meaning thereby that the poverty has been eradicated and when the services are available to all sections of the society on a sustainable basis.

It may be noted that the western social science and social geography were alive to the real issues in society and the social scientists, including geographers, responded to political happenings and the social implications of these happenings attracted their attention. While the Indian social sciences, particularly sociology, social anthropology, political science, economics, education, social linguistics and contemporary history, have been alive to the emergent issues in the wake of political, social and economic development since independence in 1947, geographers in general and the social geographers in particular have not evinced much of an interest in the contemporary issues of national interest. The first generation of Indian geographers, *viz.*, George Kuriyan, S.P. Chatterji, S.M. Ali, C.D. Deshpande followed by V.S. Gananathan, and V.L.S. Prakasa Rao debated extensively the issues of national reconstruction, suggesting planning strategies for the optimal development of the nation and the regions by better and more efficient utilisation of natural resources. However, their debates mostly remained internal to geography, although echoes were heard in the corridors of power, *e.g.*, Planning Commission. Exceptions apart, no significant purpose was served by these debates, as a meaningful dialogue could not be conducted on a sustainable basis between geography and other social science disciplines. This thwarted the process of cross-fertilisation of ideas across the disciplines, with the result that social-geographical research suffered a major setback. Geography was not only marginalised, all possibilities enabling it to make a contribution to the critical social theory were also denied to it. Ensconced within the confines of its own academic shell, it was virtually reduced to a social isolate. In the seventies of the twentieth century, the Centre for the Study of Regional Development at the JNU emerged as a new nucleus of research with a vast potential for a dialogue with other social sciences. Issues such as tribal underdevelopment, agony of the masses hit by a syndrome of droughts, scarcities and famines, poverty, particularly rural poverty, social underdevelopment as expressed in illiteracy and levels of educational backwardness, destability in tribal areas in the wake of developmental projects, displacement of people by big river valley projects, disparities in levels of development in drought-prone, mountain and hill areas, etc., received increased research attention. This new academic environment enriched geography's adaptability to social science discourse. In a way the JNU experiment laid down a new agenda for social geographical research building systematically on the tradition of V.L.S. Prakasa Rao and his associates who focused their efforts on the problems of perspective planning for national and regional development. Social geography at the JNU paved the ground for more give-and-take between disciplines, enabling geography to find a place in the realm of Indian social science.

Social Geography in the Realm of Social Sciences

Social geography has genetic relations with other social sciences, particularly with social anthropology, sociology, social history, archaeology and socio-linguistics. Given the fact that social geography has been marked by a late arrival on the Indian academic scene, not much give-and-take has taken place across the disciplines. Unlike the western scholars, Indian social geographers were not greatly attracted by the sociological theories, nor the post-colonial, post-modern discourse influenced them much. Thus, they remained aloof to the major developments in critical social theory.

There is no gainsaying the fact that social geography in its evaluation of social structure, social processes, and social transformation cannot flourish without productive and reciprocal interaction with sister social sciences as mentioned above. Take, for example, the case of archaeology. The evolution of perennial nuclear regions and the role of the river valleys in supporting agrarian communities from Neolithic to Chalcolithic and the eventual rise of *Janapadas* in the same river valleys received extensive scholarly attention in several disciplines dealing with Indian prehistory. Archaeology furnished the basis of analysis, correlating cultural development with environment and the routes of internal migration. Archaeologists, such as F.J. Richards, B. Subbarao, Mortimer Wheeler and H.D. Sankalia, and historians, such as D.D. Kosambi, and K.M. Panikkar, evaluated the vast evidence in the form of human artefacts (tools, implements and other records of material cultures) to explore the link between cultural development and environment. Geographical accessibility, or lack of it, played a critical role in the diffusion of human cultures. Archaeologists in their turn were immensely benefited by developments in the geological science (stratigraphy, palaeontology and methods of carbon dating) as well as in palaeo-climatology. This vast fund of evidence was available to the geographers in their reconstruction of the past geographies. Of particular interest is Spate's interpretation of cultural regions as evidenced in the history of human occupance of land. S.M. Ali's reconstruction of the geography of the *Janapadas* is another example of this inter-disciplinary research. This treatise in social geography draws insights from these contributions to the prehistoric scene in India as interpreted by eminent archaeologists, historians and historical geographers.

Just as physical geography derives its basic source materials from other physical sciences, such as geology, meteorology, pedology and biology, social geography shares a common ground with social anthropology and sociology. As a field of study, anthropology is concerned with the dimension of human relationship with Nature.[14] Social geography with its emphasis on spatial variation in human interaction with Nature naturally stands face to face with anthropology. However, methodologies differ strikingly. While the latter accumulates systematic knowledge and space is only incidental to its basic logic, the former sust .ins itself through exploring and developing the evidence on the spatial correlates of social phenomena. While in the early phase the knowledge of the Indian social structure and its constituents, such as tribes, castes, rural institutions, folk customs, folk religion, social organisation and material cultures, developed through ethnographic studies, anthropological research acquired new dimensions after independence.[15] The tradition of British (and European) ethnography in India was already more than a hundred years old before the Ethnographic Survey of India was established in 1901.[16] As a result of this initiative, Indian tribes and castes, which had already been extensively studied, received an increased attention. A series of ethnographic studies on the people of India appeared in the provincial reports ı North-western Frontier Province, Punjab, United Provinces of Agra and Oudh, Central

Provinces, Bengal and Madras Presidencies and other parts of South India. These materials formed a substantial basis for cross-country comparisons in a social geographical context. Anthropologists focused their attention on questions of race and caste, cultural change among tribes, kinship, as well as on village studies. The Ethnographic Survey of India, rechristened as Anthropological Survey of India in 1946, extended this work further. Anthropologists working within the thrust areas of the Anthropological Survey of India generated valuable data on tribes and castes in the changed context of India's independence and the developmental opportunities thrown up by this political change. Foreign students of Indian society, particularly American and French scholars, also contributed to this research by analysing the institutional set-up of the rural society, tracing the impact of modern technology on these institutions and the changes coming in the wake of the community development programmes launched after independence.[17]

Studies conducted by the Anthropological Survey of India provided a vast fund of literature not only on the Indian tribes and other ethnic groups, their social characteristics and cultural change as a result of their interaction with non-tribes, but also for meaningful social-geographical interpretation. Anthropologists also studied Indian material culture in its variegated forms—settlement types, housing patterns, tools and implements, rural arts and crafts, production techniques, folk arts and dances, clothing and ornaments, and the like. The massive work done under the people of India project led by K.N. Singh is an evidence of this continuing interest. It may be noted that social geography emerged so late on the Indian scene, and its development was so retarded that much of this vast fund of literature remained unutilised, brilliant insights provided by O.H.K. Spate in his *India and Pakistan* notwithstanding. A glorious opportunity to develop models of inter-regional variation and regional integration was missed. The author in collaboration with Moonis Raza handled massive data on Indian tribes, drawn particularly from 1961 and 1971 census returns to highlight the salient features of the tribal reality. In their *Atlas of Tribal India*, which was much more than an atlas, they presented the tribal problems on maps in a spatial/regional context. However, their effort did not make much of an impact on other sister disciplines in India.[18] Another study in social geography, *viz.*, A.B. Mukerji's *Chamars of Uttar Pradesh* was also entirely based on the census data.[19]

Contributions to Indian sociology in the initial phase after independence came mainly in the area of village studies. Studies of village communities and their institutions, such as caste and religion, became the main thrust of research. Caste received an increased attention because of its role in the Indian society, particularly in the changed context. Its origin and historical development attracted the attention of many sociologists.

It may, however, be pointed out that as far as India was concerned there was no clear distinction between sociology and social anthropology. Many sociologists believed that the two disciplines were so close to each other that there was hardly any difference.[20] M.N. Srinivas believed that the nature of Indian society was such that no clear distinction could be made between sociology and social anthropology.[21] In the words of M.S.A. Rao, 'in the Indian context a sociologist can ill-afford to make any artificial distinction between the tribal and folk society and the advanced sections of the population, that is, between social anthropology and sociology, nor can he (she) confine himself (herself) to any single set of techniques. The trends of research in sociology and social anthropology in the post-independence period favoured close association between them'.[22]

The pre-independence history of development of social sciences in India also shows a close association between sociology and geography. An eminent British geographer and town planner, Patrick Geddes, was called upon to establish a department of sociology at the University of Bombay in 1919. His writings on India bridged in a big way the gap between geography and other social sciences. As a result, the sociological research also focused on urban studies and town planning.[23] A perusal of later studies shows that this glorious tradition of inter-disciplinary research did not last long. This was, however, a disturbing trend.

In the period since independence Indian sociologists and social anthropologists also focused on community development programmes, elections, communalism, *dalit* movements and the role of rural leadership. This branch of sociology, which came to be known as political sociology, tried to bridge the gap between political science and sociology. While interest in rural studies, caste and urban studies, continued, sociology diversified its area of enquiry by incorporating problems of Indian civilisation, such as social and cultural change, which were often described as Sanskritisation and Westernisation.[24]

It may be pointed out that these areas were of critical importance for a social geographical interpretation of India. These researches helped immensely in the development of socio-geographical insights and paved the way for mutual give-and-take between geography and sociology. Evidently, the underdeveloped state of social geography thwarted such a process. There was no evidence of such a give-and-take. However, geography could find a place in the Surveys of Research in Social Sciences initiated by the Indian Council of Social Science Research.[25] Academic interaction between disciplines such as social geography, social and cultural anthropology and sociology is also evident in researches conducted at the Centre for the Study of Regional Development of the Jawaharlal Nehru University[26] and at the departments of geography at several universities, such as Punjab, Pune, Mysore and the BHU.

Socio-linguists often talk of ecology of language and use ecological criteria in their attempt to understand affiliation of the people of India to a large number of spoken languages and dialects as evident in different parts of the country. Their primary interest is in the 'everyday life speech activity' as expressed in communication and institutional networks.[27] They are also concerned with the plurality of cultures and languages evident in the South Asian region. The linguists, more particularly socio-linguists, collect data on the variety of spoken languages, classifying them into groups, sub-groups, branches, sub-branches and families. Their classificatory schemes often lead to an understanding of the geographic patterning of the speech communities in India. Their studies also point out the changes which have taken place in the course of time in the geographical location of the speakers of different languages, indicating either displacement or assimilation. These changes often reveal the pattern of language maintenance or shift as well as bilingualism or multi-lingualism as a consequence of inter-communication with other groups. The linguistic plurality owes its origin to the processes, such as migration, resulting in contact and communication, as well as to the superimposition of languages through administrative mechanisms. It is thus evident that research in socio-linguistics is of direct relevance to the social geographers interested in the problem of language distribution. These studies furnish evidence of the origins of India's linguistic plurality and the communication networks of the contemporary society. In fact, contributions to linguistics and socio-linguistics have helped the development of the field of linguistic geography, sometimes referred to as geolinguistics.[28] Spatial aspects of language distribution have attracted the attention of geographers, including the Indian geographers. Research completed at the Jawaharlal Nehru University may be mentioned as an example.[29]

Linguists and socio-linguists, such as Suniti Kumar Chatterji, S.M. Katre, B.L. Sakharov, Murray B. Emaneau, L.M. Khubchandani, D.P. Pattanayak, Colin P. Masica, S.N. Mazumdar, Anvita Abbi, and E. Annamalai have made valuable contributions to our understanding of the language scene in India. Reference may also be made to the pioneering work of G.A. Grierson, particularly his *Linguistic Survey of India*. The linguists attached to the 1961 Census of India also deserve special mention. They organised the multitude of linguistic data collected during the 1961 census operations. These contributions help in understanding many crucial issues related to the language identity of the people of India. Notable among them were problems of language classification, language maintenance and language shift. Other related issues, such as geographic patterning of bilingualism and multi-lingualism, communication in the changing socio-political environment and linguistic plurality were also discussed extensively by the linguists and the socio-linguists.

As the above survey shows the field of social geography is inadequately developed in India. In fact, it is taking its roots and is likely to flourish as a major thrust area in the coming decades. Its scope and purpose will now be discussed in chapter two which presents the themes of social geography in an historical perspective, looking into the present in the mirror of the past.

NOTES AND REFERENCES

1. Yogendra Singh, *Modernisation of Indian Tradition*, Delhi: Thomson Press, 1973.
2. K.D. Sharma's study of the social morphology of the Himalayan towns substantiates this point. Sharma selected Himachal Pradesh towns of Chamba, Kullu and Kangra as case studies. There is an intrinsic relationship between the social rank and the place in the towns. There is evidence to show that all over India urban places conformed to this traditional pattern. See K.D. Sharma, 'Social Morphology of Himalayan Towns' in Aijazuddin Ahmad, *Social Structure and Regional Development: A Social Geography Perspective*, 1993, pp. 129-149.
3. John Eyles, 'Social Geography' in R.J. Johnston, *et al.* (ed.), *The Dictionary of Human Geography*, Oxford: Basil Blackwell, 1981, pp. 309-312.

4. *ibid*, p. 310.
5. Emrys Jones, *Social Geography of Belfast*, London: Oxford University Press, 1960.
6. Richard L. Morrill and E.H. Wohlenberg, *The Geography of Poverty in the United States of America*, New York: McGraw Hill, 1971; also, Richard L. Morrill, 'The Negro Ghetto,' *Geographical Review*, Vol. LV, 1965, pp. 339-361; and K.D. Harris, *The Geography of Crime and Justice*, New York: McGraw Hill, 1974.
7. Emrys Jones and John Eyles, *An Introduction to Social Geography*, Oxford and New York: Oxford University Press, 1977.
8. The paper appeared as 'The development of social physics' in the *American Journal of Physics*, Vol. XVIII, 1950, pp. 239-53. See also, G. Olsson, *Distance and Human Interaction*, Regional Science Research Institute Bibliography Series, No. 2, Philadelphia, 1965.
9. Shevky and Bell published their joint work on 'Social area analysis: theory, illustration, application and computational procedures' in 1955, Stanford: Stanford University Press.
10. The term 'social rank' was adopted by Shevky to refer to the changes in the societal scale of an individual, or a group of individuals, in the wake of economic development. Bell, however, termed this concept as economic status.
11. This coming together of groups with diverse backgrounds in culture and ethnicity is termed as 'segregation' by the authors.
12. 'Factorial ecology is an elaborate, technically sophisticated description of urban social structure in space'. See R.J. Johnston, *et al.*, *The Dictionary of Human Geography*, 1983, p. 112. In fact, *social area analysis* provided the methodological basis for factorial ecology.
13. A major contribution to this field came from David M. Smith, *A Geography of Social Well-Being in the United States*, New York: McGraw Hill, 1973. See also, David M. Smith, *Human Geography: A Welfare Approach*, London: Edward Arnold, 1977.
14. D.N. Majumdar, 'Special Report on the Teaching of Social Anthropology,' in *The Teaching of Social Sciences in India-1947-67*, Delhi: Universal Book and Stationary Co., 1968.
15. See M.S.A. Rao, 'Introduction' to *A Survey of Research in Sociology and Social Anthropology*, Vol. 1, Indian Council of Social Science Research, Bombay: Popular Prakashan, 1974, p. xxvii.
16. *ibid*, p. xxiii.
17. *ibid*, p. xxvii.
18. Moonis Raza and Aijazuddin Ahmad, *An Atlas of Tribal India*, New Delhi: Concept Publishing Company Pvt. Ltd., 1990.
19. A.B. Mukerji, *The Chamars of Uttar Pradesh: A Study in Social Geography*, New Delhi: Inter-India Publications, 1980.
20. M.S.A. Rao, *op. cit.*, p. xxiii.
21. M.N. Srinivas, 'Social Anthropology and Sociology,' *Sociological Bulletin*, Vol.1, No.2, 1952, pp. 28-37.
22. M.S.A. Rao, *op. cit.*, p. xxiii.
23. *ibid*, p. xxx.
24. See also Yogendra Singh, *Modernisation of Indian Tradition*, *op.cit*, 1973.
25. These survey series were published by the Indian Council of Social Science Research in 1972, 1979, 1984 and 1999.
26. The first M.A. level course in social geography was introduced at the Jawaharlal Nehru University in 1972. Since then, the Centre for the Study of Regional Development remains a major nucleus of research in social geography in India.
27. L.M. Khubchandani, 'India as a socio-linguistic area', in Aijazuddin Ahmad, *Social Structure and Regional Development*, *op. cit.*, 1993, p. 101.
28. Geolinguistics or the study of language as a spatial phenomenon. Studies by French, British and Canadian geographers, to mention only a few, cultivated this field. See, for example, *Discussion Papers in Geolinguistics*, published by the Department of Geography and Sociology of the North Staffordshire Polytechnic, Stafford, U.K.

29. Reference may be made to the numerous doctoral theses and M.Phil. dissertations completed under the guidance of this author at the Centre for the Study of Regional Development of Jawaharlal Nehru University, New Delhi.

SUGGESTIONS FOR FURTHER READING

Ahmad, Aijazuddin (1979): 'Language and Dialect,' in Moonis Raza (ed.), *A Survey of Research in Geography*, 1969-77, Indian Council of Social Science Research, Bombay: Allied, pp. 110-14.

Ahmad, Aijazuddin (1984): 'Social Geography' in Manzoor Alam (ed.), *A Survey of Research in Geography*, 1972-75, Indian Council of Social Science Research, New Delhi: Concept Publishing Co. Pvt. Ltd., pp. 67-84.

Ahmad, Aijazuddin (1999): 'Social Geography' in Gurudev Singh Gosal (ed.), *A Survey of Research in Social Geography*, 1976-82, Indian Council of Social Science Research, New Delhi.

Cater, John and Trevor Jones (1989): *Social Geography: An Introduction to Contemporary Issues*, London: Edward Arnold.

Eyles, John (1981): 'Social Geography' in R.J. Johnston, *et al.*, *The Dictionary of Human Geography*, Oxford: Basil Blackwell, pp. 309-12.

Eyles, John (1988): *Social Geography in International Perspective*, London and Sydney: Croom Helm. Of particular interest is the chapter ten by Robert W. Bradnock, 'Research in Social Geography: South Asia,' pp. 275-95.

Jones, E. (ed.) (1975): *Readings in Social Geography*, Oxford: Oxford University Press.

Jones, E. and John Gainless (1977): *An Introduction to Social Geography*, Oxford and New York: Oxford University Press.

Raza, Moonis (ed.) (1979): *A Survey of Research in Geography*, New Delhi: Indian Council of Social Science Research, pp. 63-65.

2

Social Geography : The Indian Context

Laying the Foundations

This book makes an approach towards a socio-geographical interpretation of India. The critical elements of the complex social phenomena that define India either today or at any other point of time in its chequered history have received scholarly attention from historians, archaeologists, sociologists, social anthropologists and socio-linguists.[1] These contributions help in understanding the dimensions of Indian social history, social structure and the ethno-lingual diversity. Historians dealing with the origin of prehistoric cultures and civilisation have also tried to correlate the rise and fall of cultures in the context of the geographical/ecological setting of the South Asian region.[2] The historians and the archaeologists have often found it necessary to interpret the unfolding of the historical forces in the context of the geographical framework of the subcontinent. A geographical interpretation of the social phenomena, such as language, tribe, caste or religion, has also not been missing.[3]

This book, however, makes an attempt to build on this body of knowledge in order to present a holistic view on the basis of a spatial interpretation of social phenomena. A systematic, or even a chorological, study of the parts does not encompass the whole which expresses itself in elements not as individual entities but in their integration in space and time. Elements, such as tribe, caste, dialect or language, or even religion-based communal identity, have always manifested themselves in a regional/spatial frame. All of them appear to have melted down in the crucible of space, leaving behind an impression of oneness, of integration.[4] The integrative process operates in a subtle manner with physical geography and its ecological correlates laying down the basis for social and cultural intermingling and cooperation as dictated by the forces of social production. Regions—cultural and social regions as such—have remained hallmarks of distinction of our people.[5] There have been phases in Indian history when empires have risen to encompass and to club together diverse regional nuclei within a single political structure. But, the regional personality has never been obliterated by such episodes of superimposed unification. It appeared as if the regions had been floating in a plastic space, and resurfaced whenever the pressure from above was released. There have been pan-Indian movements emphasising oneness of our people in the name of a dominant religious identity or a dominant cultural or racial strand. But these phases have been short-lived and transient in character. What has sustained our people is a region-specific cultural identity. Within this regional frame has emerged a social milieu, cemented together by centuries of social intercourse articulated on a geographical space furnishing material basis for survival and continuity of variegated modes of living where environment, ecology and culture intertwined in myriad ways. At a higher plane of cognition one may perceive larger, all-India, identities. But these are all-India characterisations, based on philosophies or ideological constructs. People themselves have not experienced them sociologically and have not reconciled themselves to characterisations transcendental to their own perception of the regional cultural ethos. Religions—formal religions—have played a role in defining the social milieu at the level of ritual only, although it is not the religion but the cultural heritage which has acted as a cementing force, binding together the diverse elements of social structure. It is due to this peculiar character of the society that a secular tradition is endemic to the cultural ethos and any form of religion-based fundamentalism has been unacceptable to the people. The cultural roots of the Indian secular tradition are so deep that even today, after more than half a century of independence, religious fundamentalism of any form is not acceptable to the people.

Indian state as it was born on 15th August, 1947, inherited from the British Empire in South Asia a highly disjunctive territorial structure with vast disparities in economic and social development.[6] There were hundreds of Indian princely states which were indirectly governed by the British and had a measure of autonomy in all internal matters. The people in these princely states had only been partially assimilated into the struggle for India's independence. Moreover, they carried with them a legacy of medieval political, administrative and social institutions loaded with feudal values out of tune with the times. The partition of the country which coincided with independence truncated the once unified British territories, with the eastern and the western wings of the newly-created dominion of Pakistan, separated by one thousand and six hundred kilometres of Indian territory. Partition also resulted in one of the largest migrations in history, uprooting people from their hearths and homes and pushing them into alien environments. The large-scale exodus of the Hindus and the Muslims from either side of the Indo-Pakistan borders resulted in the ethnic and cultural overlaps and intermingling on a scale unprecedented in recent history.[7] The ousted and the voluntarily out-migrating groups found themselves in new enclaves surrounded by ethno-lingual groups with whom they had little interaction in the past. The psychological hangover of the uneasy history of partition impeded further the process of cultural synthesis and emotional integration, although the degree of estrangement varied in different parts of the subcontinent. Border crossings continued despite the strong vigilance on either side leaving the ethno-lingual relations in a state of flux. Besides absorbing the streams of immigrants consisting of diverse ethnic and linguistic groups, the Indian state had to initiate a comprehensive process of integration of her territories by merging the princely states into the national territory.[8] The complexities of geography and history were so great that the unresolved problems continued to irk the relations between the three neighbouring South Asian states on a perennial basis.

In sum, at independence in 1947, the Indian state had before it a stupendous task of social reconstruction.

Agrarian and Pastoral Modes

The boundaries of the newly created state, truncated as they were after the partition, extended from Gilgit and Hunza in the north to the tip of the peninsula in Kanyakumari in the south and from Jaisalmer and Ramgarh in the west to Imphal and Churachandpur (both in Manipur) in the east. This was a vast geographical region, assuming the scale of a subcontinent, with immense diversities in physiographic, climatic and bio-geographic characteristics, accommodating a whole range of human responses to natural setting. Within the confines of this state were living a variegated lot of people with diverse ethnic origins, representing different racial strands, speaking hundreds of languages and dialects and professing diverse faiths with multiple forms of worship. On the one end of the scale were animism and totemism, while Christianity and Islam were on the other end. However, Hinduism remained the religion of the land cementing together the diverse cultural traits. The modes of living of the people, their lifestyles, material basis of culture and consumption behaviours were diverse as they were cast in the ecologically differentiated moulds, and subsequently fossilised by their dormant history and social custom. There were agrarian communities arranged all along the spectrum of social evolution from *jhuming* (shifting cultivation) of the Meghalayan type to the intensive irrigated farming of the Punjab type. There were communities whose agricultural calendar kept them busy all the year round. On the other extremity were those who raised a single *barani* crop during the rainy weather and sat idle over the rest of the year. Then, there were communities who were only partially assimilated into the agrarian mode as they were living on the fringe of the peasant agriculture and were partly dependent on the forest produce. The diverse segments of space within which the peasant communities lived had an interface with pastoralists whose nomadic, oscillatory or seasonal movements kept the sedentary agrarian groups perennially connected to an inter-regional network of linkages to ensure the circulation of surplus commodities.[9] The nomad lived on the fringe of the sedentary agriculture and was often drawn from the ranks of the marginalised peasantry whose agrarian economies were destabilised recurrently by a rhythmic cycle of drought and famine. The massive exodus that takes place from the drier regions of Marwar, Bikaner and Jaisalmer, as also from Kutch (Kachchh) and Kathiawar in Gujarat in a drought year made nomadism an essential component of the agrarian mode itself.[10] There were other types of nomads who depended almost entirely on their stock of animals—sheep, goats, camels or cattle—and remained perennially on the move. The Gujjar Bakarwals of Jammu and Kashmir[11], the Gaddis of Himachal Pradesh and the Todas of the Deccan may be mentioned as representing this type of transhumant or seasonal nomadism. In the Indian economy, the coalescence of the agrarian and the pastoral modes appeared natural and necessary. They were a product of the ecological limits set by the Asiatic monsoonal regime.[12]

The river valleys of the peninsular south and the wide open plains of the north in which the peasant communities lived in a state of dynamic equilibrium with Nature were surrounded on all sides by the tribal groups who lived in their own ecological niches outside the framework of peasant agriculture. The tribes were also exposed to the agrarian mode, although very slowly. Distinctly differentiated from the tribes, the peasant communities lived at different levels of equilibrium with Nature. The Nature in itself was so varied that it provided scope for a variety of agricultural practices and cropping patterns to emerge. The natural factors influenced human choices in two crucial areas—land and its quality and water and its availability. However, the role of temperature in determining the length of the growing season and the periodicity of agricultural work in the colder sub-Himalayan regions of the north was no less significant. The expansion of the agrarian mode over the wide, open plains and the river valleys all over the country from Indus to Brahmaputra and Krishna and Kaveri resulted in the initial occupance of the best agricultural lands. But the phenomenon did not remain confined to the first quality lands alone best suited to the agricultural pursuits. As the quest for land continued, the primeval *jungle* receded and the sown area expanded making inroads into the thin alluvial veneer flanking the upper stretches of the streams in the Himalayas and all along the slopes of the peninsular watersheds. The land was dotted with rural hamlets and nucleated villages from where the agricultural operations were carried out in consonance with the rhythmic cycle of seasons. The rivers of the North Indian Plain had carved out for themselves neatly cascaded valleys on an initial Pleistocene terrace. The interfluvial tracts which stood several metres above the bordering channels of rivers had deep deposits of older alluvium with a top layer of sandy or loamy soils while the low-lying areas closer to the river channels (riverine tracts) were recurrently fertilised by the fresh deposits of silt left behind by the annual flood. There were striking differences in the quality of land and the soil cover between these two locations. Other associated factors such as elevation and slope introduced significant variations in the fertility status of the land and the availability of water. In the relatively drier regions of western Uttar Pradesh and northern Madhya Pradesh, gully erosion by rivers in regions devoid of their vegetation cover rendered millions of hectares of land useless for agriculture. In other regions, waterlogging caused by floods, as in the Kosi plain, restricted agricultural operations to the flood-immune sites only. It may be assumed that the process of primeval occupance of land was completed in full knowledge of these local differences in the agricultural potential of land. The early streams of settlers occupied the sites of vantage marginalising the subsequent groups and pushing them towards the less productive periphery.[13] A section of these marginalised groups was, however, assimilated into the peasant agriculture for the services they offered to the cultivating groups. In fact, their services were crucial to agricultural operations themselves. However, the social system ensured that they did not have any share in land. The pre-agrarian communities, on the other hand, receded into the bordering wilderness of the hills and the *jungle* in secluded zones which guaranteed them a relative protection.[14]

Rainfall and the surface water supply acted as major constraints in determining the cycle of agricultural production, but only initially. Soon the peasant communities learnt how to divert river waters to the agricultural fields, impound surface water in reservoirs as over the plateau, or dig shallow wells to fetch groundwater from the aquifers beneath. These techniques of harnessing water ensured a relative degree of freedom from hunger but further accentuated the disparity in the social division of land and its bounty. The marginalised sections of the peasantry were systematically put to disadvantageous positions in terms of access to sources of irrigation. They remained tied down to a type of *barani* (rainfed; subsistence) agriculture which sustained them but did not free them from the clutches of hunger.

The Asiatic monsoonal regime with its characteristic vagaries in the distribution and periodicity of rainfall divided the peasant agriculture into two models. A littoral and east Indian model, where wet conditions prevailed over a longer duration in the year, demanded prolonged spell of work in the fields. In this wet region, paddy emerged as the most obvious crop. As one moved towards the west and the northwest as well as into the peninsular interior the other model could be noted. The rainfall became scantier and the dry conditions prevailed over the greater part of the year. This model was the peculiarity of the zone in which wheat, barley and a variety of coarse grains and pulses dominated the cropping cycle. These diversities in the crop ecology and the ensuing cropping pattern engendered differences in the social division of labour, in the quantum of agricultural work and leisure available to the peasant communities and the absorption of women in the agricultural labour force. On this depended social valuation of women. Exceptions apart, female labour force participation rates varied strikingly between the paddy and wheat zones.

This ecological framework which had sustained the peasant communities in India for ages registered two major changes. The first change came with the introduction of the Persian wheel in the fourteenth century.[15] The newly introduced irrigation device saved time as well as animal and human energy to a very large extent thus paving the way for the spread of irrigated agriculture over the drier regions of northwestern India. In regions where the water table was not too low the Persian wheel proved a very successful device. The second change came in the wake of canal irrigation introduced by the Muslim kings from Feroze Shah onwards and subsequently developed by the British. The Mughals introduced an elaborate canal irrigation system even in the wet regions of Bengal and Bihar. These interventions on the part of the state reduced the risk in agricultural production besides balancing the gap in agricultural yields between the wet and the dry regions. The British authorities tilted this balance when they created a massive infrastructure for canal irrigation in the dry regions (United Provinces of Agra and Oudh, Punjab and Sind) and put the irrigation system in the wet regions (Bengal Presidency and Bihar) into disuse due to sheer neglect. The peasantry in the wet regions slided into poverty as a new class of farmers emerged in the newly-created canal colonies of the dry regions, contributing to a very substantial extent, to the stability of the market-oriented agrarian economy of British India. A surplus-generating agriculture, particularly in crops such as wheat, cotton and oilseeds, helped the Raj to compete with the other food-exporting countries of the world.[16] This apparently progressive, surplus-generating, export-based economy concealed the recurring food shortages experienced over vast regions of the country. The dichotomous nature of development reduced certain regions in the peninsular interior and in eastern India into perennial food-scarcity, labour-surplus, and zones leading to the exodus of the pauperised peasantry. The port cities and the industrial nodes, such as Calcutta (now Kolkata), Bombay (now Mumbai), Kanpur, Ahmedabad and Nagpur received these migration streams of the impoverished peasantry, but could not assimilate them into the urban system fully. All possible open spaces, along the railway tracks, or under the flyovers, became the coveted sites for the settlement of the rural masses flocking to these awe-inspiring cities. The social distance between the rural village and the city was perhaps the shortest in an urban slum as the prevailing squalor, poverty and disease bridged the rural-urban gap making it almost imperceptible.

Social Organisation

The peasant communities also lived at different levels of equilibrium with society. The society in itself was constituted by an institutional frame so rigid that it operated as a major constraint on the individual human freedom. The social-institutional factors influenced the human choices in several critical spheres. But two of these spheres were most critical: access to land and its ownership pattern and the social hierarchical order which defined the status of an individual in society. The valuation of an individual in society emanated from this socially acceptable status. An individual was supposed to chart out his/her course of life in the midst of this rigid and unchanging social order.

In a vast country like India, with a variegated politico-administrative set-up through history, it was natural to expect inter-regional differences in the landownership patterns and tenurial relations. While the feudal estates (*jagirs*) remained a characteristic feature of the princely states, several forms of *zamindari* system were in practice in many parts of British India as well. In fact, the Raj policy was so designed that it recognised and accommodated multiple systems of landownership in different regions of the country depending on agro-climatology, social custom and local tradition.[17] In terms of broader framework of ownership and tenancy practices, the land systems were arranged all along the spectrum from peasant holdings of the *ryotwari* type to the communitarian ownership of village lands of the *mahalwari* type and the multiple interest, feudal ownership of the *zamindari* or the *taluqadari* type. These modes of landownership were evolved in the course of social history of land occupancy within the niches provided by agricultural ecology. But the feudal mode of ownership expanded over both the wet and fertile regions as well as the dry and less productive tracts. Feudalism recognised no ecological limits, although its burden on the tenants was variedly distributed in different eco-regions. While the land systems varied from region to region, operational rights on land granted to tenants were uniformly restricted to a class of peasants drawn from middle or high ranking castes. This resulted in a broader correspondence between the caste-based, hierarchical social order and the distribution of operational rights on land. The landed classes were always high castes. They were also drawn from the upper sections of the Muslim society.[18] This happened partly because the land grants were given to the descendants of the ruling class—Rajputs, Kayasthas, Brahmans, Sheikhs, Saiyeds and the Afghans—the feudal ownership of land remained confined to these elitist sections. Even during the British period when *zamindari* lands were freely auctioned, as in Bengal, bidders were always drawn, and understandably so, from the upper castes. When the land rights were transferred to the tenants after the abolition of *zamindari* in the early fifties of the twentieth century as part of the land reforms package, most of the landowning farmers happened to be the high or the middle ranking castes.[19] The artisan caste, the Sudras and the outcastes, on the other hand, had no access to land, although they were entirely dependent on the cultivating castes for their sustenance. An intricate *jajmani* system ensured their survival just at the level of existence. They continued to receive a share, howsoever small it might be, out of the surplus produce in lieu of the services they rendered to the propertied classes. Since land rights were hereditary and the caste-based custom of hereditary occupations did not allow large scale occupational mobility, the village communities lived in a state of forced equilibrium. No amount of oppression was sufficient enough to sow the seeds of social strife. This is not to imply that peasant unrest was uncommon or the peasant movements were not launched against the tyranny of a despotic ruler or against the oppression of a class of *zamindars*.[20] But there were hardly any revolts against the social order which nurtured and legitimised inequality. The social system accepted it as given and inevitable. Never the *dalit* castes stood up in arms against their oppressors. In rural India, social power was channelised through access to land, and the pattern of landownership conformed to the caste-based social segmentation, leading to a juxtaposition of class and caste.[21] The landless and the deprived sections reconciled to their subordinate status, as they had no other option. An unflinching faith in the divine ordination of social status (*karma*) acted as a safety mechanism. The unequal access to privilege and opportunity that ensued from it was never challenged. The social system based on the caste hierarchy prevented the subordinated masses to respond to ideas which hinted at revolutionary change.[22]

The origins of the social order based on a rigidly defined hierarchical structure may be traced in the advent of the mode of agricultural production itself which resulted in a new organisation of forces of social production in prehistoric India. The transformation of the hunting and food-gathering communities into an agricultural society was attended by a division of labour among the different constituent groups who concentrated on land. However, the division of labour was a universal phenomenon as it came with agriculture everywhere and India was no exception. What was exceptional to India was the institutionalisation of this division of labour with each group getting associated with a specific department of work on a permanent basis and that vocation becoming a hereditary trait of the family, immutable in time. Soon a social structure based on the four-fold *varna* division emerged corresponding to the broader division of labour. Each of the four *varnas* (Brahman, Kshatriya, Vaisya and Sudra) represented a vertical social division on a hierarchical basis. The lines were so drawn and enforced that crossings across the social strata were not possible and the accident of birth determined one's vocation as well as social status in a rigidly hierarchised society.[23] For example, to be a Brahman it was necessary to be born in a Brahman family and thus enjoy all the privileges of the status that flowed from it. Similarly, a child born in a Sudra family inherited all the disadvantages associated with the Sudra status and no amount of hard work, intelligence or merit could dilute the stigma attached to this status.

It may be recapitulated that the division of labour which came in the wake of the agricultural mode of production was a natural response to the emerging economic situation. As groups converging on land settled down, rural villages sprang up forming the basic settlement unit. In these pioneer settlements, cultivators constituted the nucleus of the village community. It may be imagined that initially the village communities were more or less self-sufficient groups, primarily engaged in agricultural operations, but also weaving their cloth, fabricating their pots and implements and mending their shoes. Sooner or later specialisations emerged and around the tillers of the soil gathered groups whose services were crucial to sustain the farmers in their pursuit of agriculture. Thus, the primeval village community came to be constituted by a certain number of households belonging to the cultivators as well as those specialising in the various rural arts and vocations ancillary to agriculture, such as weaving, pottery, carpentry, black smithy, shoe-making, oil-crushing and the like. These artisan groups received wages in kind in lieu of the services they rendered. All this must have happened in the rural villages that dotted the Indus basin, the North Indian plain and the valleys of peninsular rivers in prehistoric India as part of the social contract. But what differentiated the Indian society from the rest of the world society was a regimented hierarchical division of society based on these vocations. The answer to this important question lies in the origins of the *varna* system and its later ramification in the *jati* system.[24]

There is no evidence to show that with the rise of agriculture in the Indus valley in the third millennium B.C., social stratification along the *varna* lines had already taken place. Classes there were. The evidence also points to the possibility of a priestly class which exacted the people to part with a share of the surplus produce to run and manage the affairs of the society and to maintain social order.[25] An elaborately ramified occupational structure had already emerged as the Indus valley society organised itself around its primary economic functions of agriculture, artisan industry and commerce. Whether, this occupational division manifested itself along the *varna* or *jati* lines is not at all clear. The material record of the Indus valley people does not point up to any such evidence and the written record has not been deciphered yet.

It may therefore be safely concluded that the coming together of the multiple ethnic groups representing several racial strands (Proto-Australoids, Palaeo-Mediterranneans and the Nordics) resulted in the juxtaposition of the occupational classes and the social classes based on the *varna* consciousness in the Sapta-Sindhava region in the second millennium B.C. The coloured people of the Melenid, Indic and Vedic races were kept at a social distance from the fair-complexioned (Nordic) Indo-Aryans. The diffusion of the art of agriculture in the Sapta-Sindhava region was not a new phenomenon, although in the changed circumstances the social structure changed and occupational division within the village society progressed along ethnic lines. The Brahmanical class framed the social law which defined the basis of social division. The Brahmanical class also legitimised the role of Kshatriyas in enforcing the law thus enabling them to rise as a ruling class.[26] The Kshatriyas also assumed the responsibility of the defence of the territory, which was an aggregation of the rural villages. The coloured people were absorbed as Vaisyas and Sudras within the social system as they handled mundane jobs involving exchange of goods and manning sectors of work which were clean as well as not so clean. In any case these service groups were necessary for the conduct of corporate social life of the village community.

As the conjectural nature of these statements shows, the origins of the *varna* system are shrouded in mystery. However, there is no basis for any dispute so far as the historical context is concerned. The social differentiation as expressed in the four-fold *varna* division of the society started in northwestern India with the advent of the Indo-Aryans. The *jatis* which marked the progressing occupational diversification with the multiplicity of the economic functions conformed admirably to the four-fold *varna* system. Each *jati* found a place for itself within the hierarchical framework of the *varna* division.

With the passage of time, the patterns of conformity between the *jati* and the *varna* systems acquired regional nuances representing the inter-regional cultural differences as they unfolded themselves over the ethnically differentiated social space. The *varna* system served as an all-India model representing the Indian (Hindu) unity; the *jati* system which was region-specific represented the diversity of regional ethos within this overarching unity. Obviously, there were inherent operational difficulties in comparing the *jatis* across the regions. Each region, based as it was on the unity of a common medium of intra-communication (a language, *bhasha* or *boli* in itself an aggregate of local dialects), differentiated itself from the neighbouring regional systems on the same basis. Each region evolved its own *jati* system.

This is understandable in view of the vast diversity that India presented in its ethnic and agro-ecological make-up. The cultural differentiation within the geographically varied regional settings accommodated local variation while it tried to conform to the all-India framework. Thus evolution of the social system contained within it the seeds of regional differentiation.

The literary record of the diffusion of the *varna* and the *jati* systems from the Sapta-Sindhwa region to Bengal and Pragjyotis in the east and to the Andhra, Setuka and Tamil Nadu in the Dakshinapatha manifests clearly the lag in time and space which was critical to their conforming to the regional moulds. The distance in time between the *Rigveda* and the *Atharvaveda* was as important as the difference in space in their composition and the ethnic and racial implications of this change in locale. As the distance from the northwestern entry points increased, ethnic (racial) combinations changed leading to a variety of modes of correspondence of the newly emerging *jatis* to the *varna* system. Inter-regional variations in the social scale of an individual group within the *juli* system emerged in the course of time making a comparison of the hierarchical ordering of castes across regions almost impossible.

Regional differences apart, caste played a significant role in the social organisation of the peasant communities. Each caste (*jati*) had a place in the social organisation of the rural economy, performing a function which was assigned to it by social custom and tradition, and constituting a crucial link in the chain of social relations. Each caste was holding a status in accordance with its rank in the social hierarchy. It has been generally observed, particularly by western observers, that the social system based on the caste hierarchy contributed stability to the social order besides rendering it an element of timelessness.[27] The social system survived in total oblivion of the political changes that came at the apex level and was by and large resistant to social change.[28] The feudal order (*zamindari* system or its variants) adjusted with the given social hierarchical order so well that there was no need to create any extraordinary instrumentalities for the appropriation of surplus from land. The *ryot* (peasantry) performed their economic functions in accordance with the tradition of the lower ranking castes serving the *zamindari* interests as if they were the Indian prototypes of the serfs, living under them in an eternal bondage. Each village emerged as a configuration of castes, with each group contributing to the functioning of the village society in a state of complementarity. In other words, each group reinforced the process of mutual give-and-take helping the landowning castes in the transaction of the basic economic functions in strict correspondence to the hierarchical social order which defined their social status and delimited the social space within which they eked out an existence. Each village configuration, depending on the state of agro-ecology and the quantum of land available for ploughing, invited and supported a certain number of caste households from across the spectrum of occupations necessary for the cultivating castes. Sooner or later a certain principle of mutual complementarity emerged among the castes in themselves and between the cultivating and the service castes.[29] These mutually complementary caste groups functioned in a state of social equilibrium tied with what came to be known as the *jajmani* relationship. Agricultural land was generally owned and operated upon by a fixed number of caste groups in a village setting. Additions to the population of the service castes, however, resulted in recurrent outmigration which became an instrument of balancing the labour supply within the village economy. These streams of outmigration in their turn contributed regularly to the burgeoning population of cities and towns all over the country. But there were other mechanisms also to sustain the growing population of the dependent castes and to retain them within the rural world. Sometimes these castes provided their services to peasant communities in villages other than their own in the immediate neighbourhood. The *jajmani* relations which were originally confined to a particular village thus acquired territorial links leading to the social circulation of service castes within the limits of negotiable distance. Such examples were not uncommon. Even then the out-migration of the landless and the artisan castes continued ensuring a demographic equilibrium within the rural society. On the other hand, groups who moved out to the near, or the far off urban places, contributed to a peculiar pattern of social organisation. Many cities which regularly attracted these groups, such as Calcutta (now Kolkata), Bombay (now Mumbai), Kanpur, Ahmedabad, Nagpur and the like, acquired rural features defined on the basis of caste or community identity as well as linguistic and regional affinity. The *chawls* and the *katras* within these cities offered a much-needed breathing space to these in-migrant groups, who were obviously in surplus in their parent villages and were pushed out of their homes. Back at home their families missed them, although benefited from the paltry sums of money that they remitted on a regular basis.

The role of caste identity in peasant societies may be evaluated not only in the context of the environment that prevailed during the period before independence, but also after independence when caste conformed in multiple ways to the swift social, economic and political changes that came in the wake of independence. For example, in India, after independence, caste was not only relevant, but it also emerged as a powerful factor in defining, often straining, social relations. Its role in the political articulation of social forces has been no less significant.[30] For example, the institution of elections not only gave the caste system a new lease of life but also helped it acquire an element of militancy unprecedented in Indian history. An analysis of the role of caste in the peasant societies of India in the period before independence may be attempted carefully in order to evaluate its role in the contemporary Indian society.

The British observers of Indian scene, including anthropologists, administrators and others, who documented the evidence on the working of the institution of caste during the nineteenth century as well as the Indian sociologists and social anthropologists of the British period agreed that the caste system was not only rigidly hierarchical but also extremely exploitative in character.[31] The landowning castes that emerged as the dominant groups recognised no limits. The system laid down the rules of social conduct and enforced them with rigidity. Whether it was social interaction between different castes in day-to-day situations, such as personal or public meetings, receiving or giving food, collecting water, fodder or fuel, attending feasts, funerals or ceremonies, selection of the residential space within the village settlement, selection of a match in marriage, selection of the site for cremation or burial, or collective decisions in matters that affected the interests of the rural community as a whole, caste played a decisive and a deterministic role. The high and the middle ranking castes combined in alienating the lower castes from the social space shared by them. Even the site of a Sudra or the shadow cast by him was considered as a polluting effect on the high castes consisting of the Brahmans and the Kshatriyas in some regions of the country.[32] At the apex of this social hierarchical order were the landowners who owned land but did not cultivate it. They were supported by a band of mercenaries, *karindas* and *gumashtas*, who acted as managers and administrators. Both these segments were drawn from the high castes (Brahmans and Kshatriyas). In close association with them functioned the trading castes (Vaisyas) who also operated as moneylenders and bankers. This upper segment of the rural society acquired social dominance of an unchallenging nature. Under the absentee landowners (big or small *zamindars*) worked a host of cultivating castes as tenants. Their tenancy rights were defined within the general framework of the British policy on land systems. These cultivating castes included Jats (Sikh, Hindu or Muslim), Ahirs and Bhumihars in northern India and the Reddys and Khammams in the Deccan, to mention only a few. At the bottom of the social order and carrying the burden of this lop-sided social structure were the landless agricultural labourers, artisans, scavengers and water-carriers performing either clean or dirty jobs. These lower castes consisted of the *Chamars, Mahars, Meghwals* or the artisan castes, such as *Badhai* (carpenter), *Lohar* (blacksmith), *Dhuna* or *Julaha* (ginners of cotton wool or weavers of cloth) and the service castes, such as the *Kahar* (water-carriers) and *Doms* (scavengers). The social order was dependent on the rural (agrarian) economy while the economy derived its sustenance from the social order.

The British administration in India benefited immensely from this social structure, particularly from the stable nature of the social relations ensured by the institution of caste. Their administrative policies conformed admirably to this hierarchical social order which was capable of resolving its problems without much of an administrative intervention from above. The social system which recognised inequality as given and unchangeable best suited the interests of the British. The British further strengthened their grip on the masses by reinforcing the stranglehold of the landowning castes on the deprived and the downtrodden sections of the populace.

India's independence in 1947 apparently created a new environment for social change. A series of land reform measures introduced by the new government transformed the agrarian relations and paved the way for a new alignment of social forces. However, caste was not discarded as irrelevant or an anachronism, nor caste-based discrimination could be controlled fully. In fact, the institution of caste conformed to the swift social, economic and political changes that came in the wake of independence. For example, the introduction of the democratic institutions, scheduling of castes and tribes, scheduling of territories, reservation of Parliamentary/Assembly Constituencies and jobs for castes, tribes or backward classes made caste a volatile issue in Indian polity. The lower castes (*dalits*), who suffered oppression throughout history, now found an opportunity to mobilise themselves to demand their due share in the national cake. The middle ranking castes, the former tenants, who were given land rights after the abolition of the *zamindari* system, organised themselves to subdue the upper castes, thus reverting the traditional basis of social relations. The new egalitarian spirit tended to destabilise the traditional social order.[33]

The village society was socially organised along the caste lines. This implies that the social order was rigidly hierarchical. It was believed that the system was given and unchangeable. The position of an individual was determined not by merit or personal qualities but by his/her rank in the social hierarchy. The system was basically opposed to the idea of opportunity being availed on the principle of equality. The access to wealth, for example, landownership and the ownership of other resources was defined by the caste status of an individual. Traditionally, the society was divided into the privileged and the not-so-privileged sections who had remained so throughout history. Most of the agricultural land and the land under orchards belonged to the upper stratum of caste, such as Brahmans, Rajputs, Jats, Khammams, Reddys or Patels or the Sheikhs, Saiyeds or Pathans. The geographical distribution of landowning castes was generally without much of an overlap. Each landowning caste, therefore, had a sway over a tract of land of which they were the undisputed masters. Those who served under them as tenants accepted the superior status of the landed castes. The agricultural operations over these land estates were carried out by the lower segments in the caste hierarchy as well as by the untouchables. These lower segments of the village society lived in perpetual dependence on the landowning castes. They were mostly working as agricultural labourers carrying out mundane jobs on the fields and the farmsteads, tending their cattle or helping them in various ways. They were also responsible for providing the necessary social services to the community of the landowners. The lower castes were also working as artisans who supplied goods to satisfy the needs of the community.

The social framework of agriculture in the traditional rural society acquired an institutional basis for the systematic exploitation of the underprivileged sections by the landed caste elites. While the former toiled in the fields in a state of perpetual bondage to make agricultural production possible, they themselves did not derive much out of it. Their share in the surplus produce was marginal, not even sufficient to allow them to survive at the minimum existential level. Over time the institution of caste became an instrument of social exploitation, furnishing an acceptable basis for social inequality. In fact, in the caste-ridden rural society, concepts such as inequality or exploitation were unknown. The caste elites never imagined that lower castes that worked under them and whose existence was due to them would stand up to protest on the state of their deprivation. The *dalit* concept would hardly strike roots in the social ethos of the pre-independence society in India.

India's independence in 1947 and the democratic set-up that came with it brought a new awakening among the masses of their rights and privileges irrespective of their social rank and economic status. The introduction of electoral institutions accentuated further the struggle for the freedom of the individual. With this the concept of human rights acquired a political meaning. The State was conscious of the need to bring about basic changes in the agrarian structure from the very beginning. It was realised that land reforms were the first necessary steps towards these changes. As already noted, the land distribution was skewed and the system was such that it had actually denied the possibility of allowing the lower castes to have a share in land. What the state did not realise was the fact that the agrarian structure was an extension of the caste system. The two had sustained each other for ages. Changes in the agrarian structure were likely to be ineffective in transforming the social relations of production unless the state addressed the question of caste directly. Changes in the agrarian structure came but the traditional social relations of production could only be marginally modified. The caste system reinforced itself in a new and more hardened form.

The state had realised that broad-based land reforms were necessary for correcting inequality in the pattern of landownership and tenancy practices. The land reforms could abolish the class of landlords, *zamindars* and other intermediaries. The land reforms were expected to minimise the disparities in land distribution in the non-*zamindari* areas as well.[34] These interventions helped in bridging the gap between the owner-holders and the landless labourers. However, as caste-based electoral politics deepened its roots, the share of *dalits* in land remained too marginal to help them overcome their traditional deprivation. The agrarian reforms, although a remarkable achievement in themselves, failed to resolve the agrarian crisis. The land reform measures belied the expectation that the main distortions in the social and economic order in rural India would be finally removed if land relations improved.[35] The reasons for the failure were quite obvious. When social reforms are introduced in societies divided along caste lines it is difficult to change the social relations. Both the privileged and the underprivileged know fully well that they are essentially unequal. The handicapped also know that exercising their rights permissible under the law would amount to challenging the established social authority.[36] In a caste-ridden society, law carries very little meaning. What dominates is the authority of the caste, law or no law.

The experience of the rural society in India since independence shows that the developmental process could not narrow down the gap between the different segments of the caste society; it further widened it. The high castes were better equipped to avail the benefits of developmental programmes. In fact, they monopolised the developmental gains leaving little scope for a larger participation by the people. The expected filtering down could not take place as the gains were siphoned off at the top. The rural development programmes, agricultural modernisation, provision of infrastructure, such as roads, banks, etc., and health and literacy programmes, which were aimed at bridging the gap between the caste elites and the underprivileged sections, failed to bring about any transformation in the desirable direction. There were insurmountable difficulties in the wider acceptability of the egalitarian principle by an inherently unequal society. The traditional social order did not enable the lower castes to enjoy the fruits of freedom and derive the intended benefit from the programmes of social upliftment. For example, it was visualised that the abolition of the *zamindari* system would ensure an equitable distribution of land among the different sections of the society. However, this did not happen. Exceptions apart, low castes rarely benefited from the land reforms.[37] While it is true that the monopoly of the traditional landed classes, the *zamindars*, *jagirdars* and *taluqadars* weakened, their place was taken by the liberated tenants consisting of the middle ranking castes, such as Jats, Yadavas and so on. These castes emerged as a force to reckon with. As these newly-liberated caste groups accumulated land, inequality in land ownership increased. The social relations based on the traditional notion of respect for the upper castes disappeared altogether giving way to fierce competition and the resultant social conflict. The upsurge in the rank and file of intermediate castes made the village society highly volatile and violence-ridden.

Seen in this context, caste has a new political role to play in today's India. The electoral politics has not only managed to adjust itself to the caste-based social order, it has further contributed to the mobilisation of masses along caste lines. The traditional notion of 'stability' of the village society has been replaced by a state of flux. It is in this context that the geographical distribution of caste groups, their numerical strength in rural pockets and their concentration, have become important parameters in electoral politics. In fact, the geographic patterns of caste distribution furnish the very basis for political articulation by the different contending political parties in the rural constituencies. Keeping in view the electoral arithmetic, all parties bank on the dominating castes in the selection of their candidates. Thus, instead of making it redundant, the democratic process has given caste a new lease of life. While the ritualistic role of caste in social relations has weakened, caste identity has brought about further regimentation and a consequent strain in social relations. In India, today, if caste has emerged as a new symbol of identity and an instrument of social networking and political manoeuvring, a social geographical interpretation of the phenomenon would be the just necessary first step towards a better understanding.

Tribal Formation

On the periphery of the agrarian world of the caste societies live the tribes, the *adivasis* or the *janajatis*. The tribes are usually living on the fringe of the river valleys in the forested, hilly or the upland tracts. The fact that they are described as *adivasis* (aborigines) leads many to believe that they are the autochthonous population of the country. However, it is a doubtful proposition. They are certainly among the oldest groups who managed to reach India in its long history of peopling. The tribes neither belong to a single racial stock nor do their ethnic traits suggest a common origin from a single source region outside India. Archaeological as well as racial evidence corroborates the view that they came to India through the northwestern entry points as well as through the openings in the Himalayas in the north and the northeast. They came in several streams of migration and occupied the tracts closer to the entry points, till they were ousted by the subsequent waves of migration. This suggests that their early foci of convergence might have been other than the habitats with which they are associated today. This also suggests that their presence in the regions of their present concentration was an outcome of the dynamics of ethnic displacements within the country. The evidence is not lacking. The tribal folklore in all regions of the country is full of references to the history of displacement of tribes from their earlier habitats. Whatever might have been the circumstances which forced them to leave their original home-lands, the fact remains that the tribes are found today in the hilly and the forested tracts on the fringe of the river valleys. This should not have been their voluntary choice. Ecologically, these tracts are not suited to the pursuit of agriculture on an economically viable scale. And yet they are engaged in some or the other form of agriculture which is economically backward. Recent ecological history indicates that their traditional livelihood patterns have undergone significant changes, due to official measures such as earmarking the area of reserved forests as well as a systematic removal of forest cover, making it necessary for the tribes to adopt a primitive type of subsistence agriculture.

Drawn from diverse ethnic roots and characterised by distinctly different modes of living and having a variety of material cultures, the tribes have traditionally been living in ecological niches outside the framework of peasant agriculture until they were overtaken by the colonial mode of exploitation of natural resources.[38] However, their pre-agrarian status helped them to retain the traits of tribalism. For example, they were not socially stratified, and a communitarian ownership of land and its resources continued to be a distinguishing trait. With the opening up of the tribal areas—a process which was accelerated with the advent of the British Raj—these tribal traits started vanishing. It may be assumed that the tribes were already familiar with a primitive form of agriculture. This fact is further corroborated by the archaeological evidence of stone hoes found in abundance in the Chhotanagpur plateau and the northeastern region. However, the tribes were exposed to the peasant mode of production only slowly with varied degrees of intensity. Their crop husbandry was a form of adjustment with Nature. They practiced shifting cultivation (*jhuming*) or other forms of primitive agriculture to meet or replenish their requirements for food. Despite this, collection from the forest, fishing and hunting continued to be an inalienable part of the tribal livelihood pattern. Private ownership of land remained an alien concept till they became conscious of the systematic encroachment on their lands by the outsiders through the manipulation of the unscrupulous keepers of land records of the British revenue administration. Land alienation became phenomenal after independence.

All this shows that the tribes were different from the rest of the peasant society. However, this fact is not acceptable to a certain school of sociologists and social anthropologists. Some of them firmly believe that the tribes are primitive Hindus and that their tribal status is only politically defined.[39] These ideas remained controversial particularly in view of the fact that the tribes have lived outside the ambit of the caste system for the greater duration of their known history. This is not to say that the tribes were not assimilated into Hinduism as an on-going process. The phenomenon was fairly widespread in the open plateau regions of Rajasthan, Gujarat, Maharashtra and Madhya Pradesh although not so visible in the northeastern region, particularly outside the Assam valley. In fact, it is segmentation along ethnic lines, and not caste-based social stratification that distinguished the tribes from the rest of the Hindu society. There is other evidence which favours their distinctive individual identity. The tribal hamlets were essentially homogenous and not differentiated in terms of their social morphology. Their hunting and agricultural operations were collective and not individualised, thus ruling out the possibility of the emergence of any specialised division of labour. Indeed it is not to say that there were no artisans and craftsmen. But these activities did not entail a division of labour which was hereditary or implied hierarchical order. These mechanisms were in-built and inimical to the idea of rank and status flowing from the position in the division of labour. Thus, the tribal social structure was essentially different from the social structure of the caste-based Hindu society.

Contact with the peasant communities was old, much older than the advent of the British Raj in the eighteenth century. It was along this line of contact that give-and-take between the tribal and the non-tribal worlds continued through history. The peasant communities who had settled in the river valleys came in contact with the nomadic tribes who were continually on the move with their herds of cattle, sheep or goats grazing on the way while in transit between one interfluvial ridge and the other. This happened on the outskirts of the river valleys. Some of these nomadic groups also traded in commodities, exchanging salt and a variety of forest produce for goods which were in surplus with the peasants, such as the foodgrains. This highlights their role as 'bridge' communities. In other situations, the tribes also served as 'buffer' communities, forming what may be termed as shatter belts between the feudal states (kingdoms or principalities) based in the river valleys. The physical framework of the subcontinent with its mosaic of relief—river valleys alternated by river valleys—and the surrounding rim of ridges, interfluvial uplands, plateau surfaces and the hill ranges offered an ideal setting for the spatial segregation of the tribal and the non-tribal worlds.

In a nutshell, the tribes have been living in the relatively inaccessible and physically uneven tracts of land, largely unsuited to the pursuit of agriculture. Whatever might have been the original patterning of the tribal groups in the country, there is evidence to show that the expansion of the peasant mode has gradually and consistently pushed them into the interior of these inhospitable tracts. The spill over of population from the thickly populated river valleys continued to change the demographic profile within the tribal habitats.

As this study shows the tribes are heavily concentrated in a belt which girdles the middle region of India extending from the Aravallis and the Western Ghats in the west to the Chhotanagpur plateau, Rajmahal hills and the Orissa highlands in the east. The Vindhyas, Satpuras, Mahadeo and Maikala ranges, and the erosion surfaces in between, such as the Bastar plateau, are areas of tribal fastness *par excellence*. Another axis in which the tribes have concentrated lies on the southern flank of the Aravallis to the Western Ghats all the way from Maharashtra to Kerala terminating in the Annamalais and the Cardamom hills. The tribal population is not that numerous in the Eastern Ghats, apparently due to the subdued nature of relief and the open nature of the terrain. However, a major concentration is seen in the Orissa highlands overlooking the Mahanadi, Brahamani and Baitarani valleys. To the north of the peninsula, tribes are living in the upper valleys of Himachal Pradesh (Beas, Satluj, Chandra, Bhaga and Chandrabhaga rivers) and the hills in the Uttarakhand division of Uttar Pradesh as well as in Sikkim and the sub-Himalayan West Bengal. The rim of the hills and plateau surfaces in the northeast encompassing the Brahmaputra valley is another region of tribal concentration. Here, one observes a clear-cut division. The hills are inhabited by tribal groups and the valley areas by the non-tribal groups. In Manipur, for example, the surrounding hills are occupied by the Naga and Kuki-Chin tribes, while the central valley is non-tribal. The present nature of the political boundaries of the states in the northeast seems to have some conflict with the tribal view of their traditional homelands. The uneasy peace in many of these states suggests how fragile the situation is.

The Raj recognised no limits to the expansion of the colonial mode in India. With their multiple goals of controlling the territory militarily for encountering insurgency and siphoning off the natural resources—mainly minerals and forest produce—or introducing plantation agriculture in the northeast and the south, systematically transformed the tribal areas leaving a devastating impact on the tribal economies. The tea estates in the northeast and in Darjeeling, mining establishments in the Chhotanagpur region, siting river valley projects and laying down the railway tracks, reserving forests for commercial use, creating an entirely new power structure, necessary for accommodating the local princely interests in territory without disturbing the overarching British hegemony, contributed immensely to the process of displacement of tribes from their traditional homelands. The ecological basis of the tribal economic mode crumbled. The scramble for land, for example, in Chhotanagpur region, led to an unending process of land alienation and the ensuing civil strife. The displaced and the alienated tribes had meagre opportunity to survive within the limits set by the diminishing resources. As the struggle for survival intensified, Indian tribes responded to these interventions in various ways from peaceful protests to violent clashes with the British administration.

The situation registered a significant change after independence. In fact, the pattern of tribal-non-tribal interaction underwent a qualitative change with far-reaching implications. In the first place, the country entered into a phase of developmental planning in the early fifties of the twentieth century. This ushered in an era of all-round economic growth. Even though the process of development did not leave a homogenous impact on all regions of the country as regional disparities continued to be quite glaring, its impact on traditional economies in tribal areas was quite evident. The tribal regions which were lagging in economic and social development could no longer remain outside the ambit of the developmental process. The new planning strategies, laying emphasis on the development of backward regions, hilly tracts, drought-prone and agriculturally underdeveloped areas, brought within their fold peripheral areas in which the tribes had been living for centuries. More importantly, the market forces penetrated the tribal areas exposing them to the new and varied influences and drawing them into the whirlpool of economic change. For example, the moneylender who was there even before further sharpened his tools of exploitation. The expansion of the market forces integrated the tribal areas with the domestic market. With the introduction of the democratic processes, the tribes got involved into the politics of elections from the *panchayat* to the Parliamentary levels. The national and regional political parties created their own spheres of influence drawing the tribes into the arena of politics and thus making them conscious of their rights and privileges in the new India's democratic polity. The new administrative set-up created for the tribal areas was overwhelmingly constituted by elements drawn from the non-tribal segments of population. The civil servants were largely alien. So were the armed forces, stationed in tribal areas for both internal and external security.

All this shows that the assimilation of the tribes into the Indian democratic polity has not been a smooth process. The Indian constitution ensured their representation in the Central and the State Legislatures by reserving a certain number of constituencies for them in regions of tribal concentration. This did not help much in the resolution of the tribal problem.

While a large chunk of tribal population lives in the mid-Indian region from Gujarat to West Bengal, only the northeastern tribes such as the Garos, Khasis, Nagas and the Mizos were supposed to be fit for the statehood. Thus, the northeast was treated on a different footing as compared to the mid-Indian region. The major tribal groups of India—the Bhils, Gonds and the Santals—have little role to play in the political affairs of the states of their residence. In fact, each one of these groups lies divided between several States—Bhils between Rajasthan, Madhya Pradesh, Gujarat and Maharashtra; Gonds between Madhya Pradesh, Orissa, Andhra Pradesh and Maharashtra; and Santals between Bihar, West Bengal and Orissa. On the other hand, Santals living in Assam are not even treated as Scheduled Tribes and recent developments show that they are undesirable in the region. It may be concluded that the tribal question has been dealt with differently in different regions of the country. Perhaps, in the northeast, it has been treated as an adjunct of the border problem. In this sector, India has common borders with China, Myanmar, and Bangladesh and several tribes such as the Nagas, Mizos, Tripuris and the Kuki-Chins have been living all along these borders. The award of statehood to these groups was obviously a mechanism to ensure national security in a sensitive border area. But it did not help the tribes in their psychological adjustment with the new political order. In fact, the problem of tribal insurgency continued unabated.

Linguistic Heterogeneity

As the above discussion shows the Indian society is ethnically variegated and consists of numerous racial strands and a host of tribes and castes. Superimposed on this is the linguistic pluralism. In fact, the spoken languages (dialects, *bhasha, boli*) are so diverse that India is often described as a distinct socio-linguistic area.[40]

The communication network through a spoken language unifies the people into a single identity and evidently the geographical distribution of languages and dialects has contributed to a distinctive pattern of cultural regionalism. From Kashmiri and Punjabi in the north to Tamil and Malayali in the south, and from Gujarati and Marathi in the west to Bengali and Assamese in the east—all language groups have their unique cultural identity. It is commonly known that these dominant languages became the basis for state formation in India after independence. An ecological setting, a shared history, common folklore and literary tradition and a contiguous geographical territory are essential elements of this identity. Outside the framework of these major language groups and the dominant cultures represented by them lie the little worlds of minor languages from Dogri, Mewati and Bagari to Savara, Kharia and Santali or Metei, Coorgi and Yerula, to name only a few. The massive data base on mother tongues[41] and more importantly the changing affiliation of the people from one mother tongue to another shows how state patronage, or lack of it, has allowed certain languages to grow and others to die a natural death. This may lead to the conclusion that the political patronage ensured the survival of the major languages only. This inevitably helped the language-based regionalism acquire a subtle political nuance of far-reaching implications. The evidence shows that inter-regional (inter-state) conflicts sparked by such issues as the migration of population from one state to the other, or sharing of river waters by two states, have often expressed themselves through the language identity of the people. The role of language in promoting regional tendencies in the Indian polity is an issue which cannot be dismissed easily.

Communal Configuration

Included in the population of India are followers of several religions—both Indic and non-Indic. Traditionally, Hindus have been conscious of *dharma*, but they do not adhere to a regulatory religious regimen. In fact, the kind of religious orthodoxy which is commonly associated with non-Indic religions, such as Christianity and Islam, was unknown to the Hindus. Hinduism was and continues to be a way of life. There are not too many religious restrictions. In the course of time a liberal tradition developed which allowed the emergence and continuity of multiple forms of worship. Both Christianity and Islam found their followers in India because of this endemic liberalism. However, those who embraced these religions carried with them several pre-conversion (Hindu) traits. The geographic patterning of both the Christians and the Muslims shows that the two religions found niches for themselves in many parts of the subcontinent. This was, of course, due to Christian missionary and Islamic *sufi* activity.[42] However, the state patronage also influenced the spread of two religions at different points of time in history. In the course of this chequered history, India inherited a composite culture based on the essential elements derived from Hinduism and Buddhism and grafted with Christianity and Islam. Sikhism was the best example of this process of cultural and ideological synthesis. Today, the way these religious groups are distributed in India forms an interesting geographic pattern, an end-product of the history of peopling, settlement and resettlement. The geographic pattern has an implicit political meaning expressed at the level of individual consciousness as well as social behaviour in contemporary India.[43]

In the course of time, religion-based communal identity has also emerged as a social phenomenon, particularly since the British ascendency in India. The religion-based communal identity was often played up during the British Raj as a policy ploy to counter the forces of nationalist unity. In fact, communal consciousness must have emerged on the scene after the rise of Muslim power in northern India. Muslim kings often adopted policies which discriminated between the Hindu and the Muslim subjects. This is notwithstanding the fact that the rise of Muslims to power became possible only with the active support of the local chieftains of non-Muslim origin, who were holding positions of authority in civil administration as well as in the army in the newly established Muslim kingdoms. However, communal identity did not lead to any major Hindu-Muslim conflicts during the medieval period. The scene underwent a major change during the British Raj. In pre-British India, while caste identities often promoted a feeling of fraternity among the members of the same caste characterised by distinct ethnic identity (*e.g.*, Jats, Gujars, Meos) and caste-based brotherhoods (*biradri*) were common, there is no evidence to show that religion-based communal consciousness played any significant role in social behaviour.[44]

The journey from caste brotherhoods to communities must have been tortuous as well as long. Religion-based communal consciousness was not endemic to India. However, it may be considered as an extension of caste consciousness, the caste-community being a continuum. Then, there was a phase in pre-independence history when communalism played havoc. It destroyed the very edifice of Indian liberal tradition. The communal politics which resulted in the partition of the country in the name of religion converted the caste-community continuum into a divide. Partition was not the end of the road, because the seeds of strife continued to sprout ever afterwards.

It is an imperative of socio-geographical research to evaluate the expression of communal consciousness in all its facets and thus pave the way for communal harmony on a sustainable basis.

NOTES AND REFERENCES

1. Reference may be made to the pioneering contributions of F.J. Richards, *Indian Antiquary*, LXII, 1932; B. Subbarao, *The Personality of India*, 1958; Mortimer Wheeler, *Early India and Pakistan*, 1959; H.D. Sankalia, *Pre-history and Proto-history of India and Pakistan*, 1963, 1974; D.D. Kosambi, *The Culture and Civilization of Ancient India in Historical Outline*, 1970, 1972; and Fairservis, *Roots of Ancient India*, 1976.
2. Arnold Toynbee, *Between Oxus and Jumna*, 1961; M. Wheeler, *op.cit.*, (Chapter: 'The Scene'); and Sardar K.M. Panikkar, *Geographical Factors in Indian History*, 1955 are particularly valuable. Notable geographical appraisals were made by O.H.K. Spate, *India and Pakistan*, 1954 (Chapter: 'Historical Outlines'); S.M. Ali, *Geography of the Puranas*, 1966; and David E. Sopher, *An Exploration of India*, 1980.
3. Notable among these works are L.M. Khubchandani, 'India as a Sociolinguistic Area' in Aijazuddin Ahmad, *Social Structure and Regional Development*, 1993; *Plural Languages and Plural Cultures*, 1983; S.N. Mazumdar, *Marxism and the Language Problem in India*, 1970; Moonis Raza and Aijazuddin Ahmad, *An Atlas of Tribal India*, 1990; K.S. Singh, *People of India*, Vol. I, 1992; J.E. Schwartzberg, 'Caste Regions of the North Indian Plain', *Geographical Review*, Vol. LV, 1965; G.S. Gosal and A.B. Mukerji, 'The Religious Composition of India's Population', *Tijdschrift roor economische en Sociale Geografic*, Vol. LXI, No. 2, pp. 91-100, 1970; and Moonis Raza, Aijazuddin Ahmad and Nafis Ahmad Siddiqi, 'Muslims in India: Some Aspects of their Regional Demography' in Zafar Imam (ed.), *Muslims in India*, 1975.
4. Jawahar Lal Nehru, *The Discovery of India, 1961*; see also Moonis Raza and Aijazuddin Ahmad, *General Geography of India*, 1977 (Chapter: 'Unity in Diversity').
5. B. Subbarao, *The Personality of India, op.cit.* (Chapter: 'Regions and Regionalism').
6. Boudhyan Chattopadhayay and Moonis Raza following Gunder Frank and Samir Amin (*Indian Journal of Regional Science*, 1975) related the regional disparities in India to the colonial model of underdevelopment.
7. Ali Tayyeb, *Pakistan: A Political Geography*, 1965.
8. *States Reorganisation Commission Report*, 1955.
9. B.K. Roy Burman, 'Distribution of Scheduled Tribes in India: An Exploratory Geo-cultural Appraisal', in A. Chandra Shekhar (ed.), *Economic and Socio-cultural Dimension of Regionalisation*, Census Monograph, No. 7, Census of India, 1971, New Delhi, 1972, pp. 491-493.
10. Aijazuddin Ahmad, 'Human Geography of the Indian Desert', unpublished Ph. D. thesis, Aligarh Muslim University, 1962.
11. R.P. Khatana, 'Development and the Process of Sedentarization among the Gujjar Bakarwals of Jammu and Kashmir' in Aijazuddin Ahmad (ed.), *Social Structure and Regional Development*, *op.cit.*, pp. 283-307.
12. David E. Sopher, 'Indian Pastoral Caste and Livestock Ecologies: A Geographic Analysis' in L.S. Leshnik and G.D. Sontheimer (eds.), *Pastoralists and Nomads in South Asia*, 1975, pp. 183-208.

13. Partly this struggle is recorded in Rigvedic hymns. The present-day distribution of the Kolerian group of tribes shows that their original homelands were fragmented as a result of incursion of the peasant groups and their eventual settlement in the river valleys.
14. Subbarao's concept of regions of isolation and of relative isolation is relevant here. The regions of isolation were *cul-de-sac*, or refuge zones, for the groups ousted from the plains. See his *Personality of India, op.cit.*
15. Irfan Habib, Presidential address to the Medieval History Section, Indian History Congress, Patna, 1969; W.H. Moreland, *The Agrarian System of Muslim India*, 1929.
16. Jather and Beri, *Indian Economics: A Comprehensive and Critical Survey*, Vol. I, London, 1949, pp. 161-169.
17. Baden-Powell, *Land Systems of British India*, 1892.
18. *Ain-e-Akbari*, Vol. II mentioned, for example, the following Muslim Land-owning Castes (*Qaum-e-zamidaran*) in the *Subah of Agrah*: Shaikhzada, Chishti, Saiyid, Mussalaman, Afghan, Meo, Turkman, Malikzadah, Farmuli. However, their proportion in population is nowhere significant (Second edition, translation by Col. H.S. Jarrett, annotated by Jadu Nath Sarkar, Calcutta, 1949, pp. 190-206.
19. Andre Beteille, 'The Social Framework of Agriculture', in Louis Lefeber and Mrinal Dutta Chaudhury (eds.), *Regional Development Experiences and Prospects in South and Southeast Asia*, 1971; *ibid., Caste, Class and Power*, 1966.
20. A.R. Desai (ed.), *Peasant Struggles in India*, 1981.
21. M.N. Srinivas, *India: Social Structure*, 1969.
22. Andre Beteille, 1966, *op.cit.*
23. J.H. Hutton, *Caste in India: Its Nature, Functions and Origins*, 1969.
24. G.S.Ghurye, *Caste and Race in India*, 1969.
25. Stuart Piggott, *Prehistoric India*, 1952.
26. Manu Smriti, see references in G.S. Ghurye, *op.cit.*, pp. 89-93; also see *Laws of Manu* (Buhler's translation, 1886).
27. David E. Sopher, 'Indian Pastoral Castes and Livestock Ecologies', *op.cit.*; also see *An Exploration of India, op.cit.*, 1980.
28. Andre Beteille, 1966, 1971, *op.cit.*
29. Joseph E. Schwartzberg, for example, mapped the population of castes in the North Indian Plain, showing a combination of cultivating and service castes within each village surveyed by him. See 'Distribution of Castes in the North Indian Plain', *Geographical Review*, 1965; *ibid.*, in Milton Singer and Bernard S. Cohn (eds.), *Structure and Change in Indian Society*, Chicago, 1968.
30. See, for example, M.N. Srinivas, *Caste in Modern India and Other Essays*, 1962; also *ibid., Social Change in Modern India*, 1966.
31. Notable contributions came among others from J.H. Hutton, M.N. Srinivas, G.S. Ghurye and A.R. Desai.
32. 'All over India the impure castes are debarred from drawing water from the village well, which is used by the members of other castes. In the Maratha country, the Mahar —one of the untouchables, might not spit on the road lest a pure caste Hindu should be polluted by touching it with his foot, but had to carry an earthen pot, hung from his neck, in which to spit. Further he had to drag a thorny branch with him to wipe out his footprints and to lie at a distance prostrate on the ground if a Brahmin passed by, so that his foul shadow might not defile the holy Brahmin (Russel, i, pp. 72-73). In the Punjab where the restrictions regarding pollution by proximity have been far less stringent than in other parts of India, a sweeper, while walking through the streets of the larger towns, was supposed to carry a broom in his hand or under his armpit as a mark of his being a scavenger and had to shout out to the people warning them of his polluting presence (Punjab Census, 1911, p. 413). The schools, maintained at public cost, are practically closed to such impure castes as the Chamars and Mahars. 'Both

teachers and pupils in the school make it most difficult for low-caste boys to sit in the classrooms' (Buggs, p. 23), *op.cit.*, Ghurye, 1969, *op.cit.*, pp. 11-12.

33. See Bernard S. Cohn, 'The changing status of a depressed caste', D.N. Majumdar, 'Inter-caste tensions'; Hamza Alavi, 'Peasants and Revolution' in A.R. Desai, *Rural Sociology in India*, 1969, pp. 354-365; 398-402; 410-423.
34. P.C. Joshi, *Land Reforms in India: Trends and Perspectives*, Bombay, 1975.
35. Aijazuddin Ahmad, 'Integrated Rural Development in India: Social Implications of Planning since Independence', Proceedings of the Second International Symposium on Asian Studies, 1980, pp. 905-922; Andre Beteille, 1971, *op.cit.*
36. Andre Beteille, 1971, *op.cit.*
37. Lands allotted to the scheduled caste households in the Indira Gandhi *Nahar* (Canal) Project Command Area in Rajasthan were soon taken over by the (high) cultivating caste. In any case, the Scheduled Castes did not find the terms of trade in agriculture to their favour.
38. Aijazuddin Ahmad, 'Development and Redistribution of Tribal Population in India', in Kosinski and Elahi, *Development and Redistribution of Population*, 1985, pp. 65-78; Roy Burman, *op.cit.*; A.R. Desai, 'Tribes in Transition', in *Rural Sociology in India, op.cit.*, pp. 221-231; and G.S. Ghurye, *ibid*, pp. 253-268.
39. G.S. Ghurye, for example, insists that their tribal status is no more than their status as Scheduled Tribes. *The Scheduled Tribes*, 1963, pp. 404.
40. L.M. Khubchandani, 'India as a socio-linguistic area', in Aijazuddin Ahmad (ed.), *Social Structure and Regional Development, op.cit.*, pp. 101-113.
41. There were 1,652 mother tongues as recorded by the 1961 census. It may be noted that as many as 152 out of 330 districts were linguistically heterogeneous with minority speech groups having more than 20 per cent share in district population. See L.M. Khubchandani (1972), 'Mother-tongue in multi-lingual societies', in A. Chandra Shekhar (ed.), *Economic and Socio-cultural Dimensions of Regionalisation*, Census Centenary Monograph, No. 7, Census of India, 1971, pp. 427-450.
42. However, the activities of the Christian missionaries and the Islamic *sufi silsilas*, are not comparable. Their *modus operandi* is basically different.
43. The chances of the partition of the country in 1947 were largely promoted by this geographic patterning of the Muslim community.
44. The history of communal politics shows how religion was used as a divisive force in India before independence.

SUGGESTIONS FOR FURTHER READING

Desai, A.R. (1969): *Rural Sociology in India*, Bombay: Popular Prakashan.

Kosambi, D.D. (1972): *The Culture and Civilization of Ancient India in Historical Outline*, Delhi: Vikas.

Sopher, David E. (1980): *An Exploration of India: Geographical Perspectives on Society and Culture*, London: Longman.

Srinivas, M.N. (1986): *India: Social Structure*, Delhi: Hindustan Publishing Corporation.

Subbarao, B. (1958): *The Personality of India*, Baroda: M.S. University.

3

Origins
Social Differentiation and Region-formation

Indian society is characterised by glaring diversities in its social and cultural features. The roots of these diversities lie in the hoary past. Tracing the origins of social differentiation, in itself a challenging task, may be necessary in order to understand the pluralistic nature of the present-day society.

Locational Setting

From time immemorial different streams of cultures originating from western, eastern and central Asia have made incursions into the South Asian subcontinent. Being at different stages of social evolution these culture-groups found for themselves ecological niches which suited the continuation of their specific modes of living. A keen observation of the social scene in India today may help us in perceiving a broader relationship between the way the people of India passed through different stages of social evolution and the emergence of diversities in levels of cultural and social development. In the course of this chequered social history these primeval communities were distributed and redistributed in space under different situations promoting, in some areas, cultural intermingling and in others isolation in geographical space. Early incursions were made from different entry points in the Hindu Koh[1] Himalayas in the west, northwest, north and the northeast, making the northern region of the Indian subcontinent a recipient of numerous culture-groups. The physical framework of the subcontinent determined their initial routes of migration as well as their choice to remain confined to the river valleys or the interfluvial tracts as the case may be. These groups wandered freely in space over vast tracts of land, with varied ecologies which were either inviting or repulsing. Their freedom of movement was curbed by the scarcity of food as also by the natural barriers, such as rivers, hill ranges or the desert expanses. Over the wide open valleys and the undulating plains on the plateau, they could also perceive social barriers along the contact lines between different ethnic groups; and the barriers were enforced by social custom. It may be assumed that the primeval culture domains were ethnically homogenous and socially defined, as their violation invited conflict, and internecine wars followed. Initially, there was hardly any possibility of cultural overlap. Subbarao demonstrated with the help of massive archaeological evidence how this state of mutual exclusivity has best been preserved in the remote hilly and mountainous tracts, which were characterised by a certain degree of geographical inaccessibility.[2] Those occupying the open river valleys from Punjab to the deltaic region of Bengal were always under pressure, as fresh incursions were made, resulting in their ouster and eventual exodus from the scene of conflict. These groups in their own turn moved into the bordering rim-lands, characterised by hilly terrain, desert or forest landscapes.

Indian history is full of references to such episodes in which incursions were made resulting in the ouster of the groups who came earlier and their eventual migration to the interior areas, the so-called refuge zones. Each incursion marking the arrival of a fresh cultural wave ended in the displacement of an earlier culture-group which was eventually pushed into the *cul-de-sac*. These incoming culture streams left behind a pattern in space with the earliest culture-groups to be found in the isolated and the remote pockets, farthest from the entry points in the northwest, and the youngest and the newer elements in this ever-changing cultural scenario, in the fringe areas placed closest to the entry points. Those who managed to drift into the isolated and the remote parts of the subcontinent could preserve their original ethnic traits which remained by and large unaffected by the fresh waves of incursions regularly witnessed in and along the main corridor of movement connecting the Kabul valley with the North Indian plain. We may trace the origins of social differentiation and link it to this process of incoming cultural streams at different stages of social evolution and their subsequent isolation and placement in different segments of geographical space. The physical framework—relief features, altitude, climate and more importantly, water supply—supported, in a neatly defined manner, the scope for the plurality of forms of culture, with the new elements co-existing with the old, the archaic and the primitive simultaneously, and surviving over time. While the newest elements were assimilated by the groups living all along the main route of migration, the continuity of the old, the primitive and the archaic elements distinguished the isolated regions in the backyard of this arena. One cannot dismiss this historical evidence easily. The evidence suggests a tiered pattern in the spatial arrangement of cultures. Take, for example, the northwestern region of India, consisting of sharply defined eco-regions, such as the valley of Kabul in Afghanistan, the plains of Punjab from Indus to Yamuna, the upper valleys of the Punjab rivers, such as the Satluj and Beas valleys in Himachal Pradesh, or the upper valleys of the Chenab in Kishtwar and the Jhelum valley in Kashmir, and the trans-Himalayan regions in Ladakh, Baltistan, Gilgit and Hunza. The historical experiences of the people in these sharply contrasted eco-regions have been strikingly different. The process of cultural renewal has perhaps been most active in the sprawling plains from Indus to Yamuna. Social groups in the upper valleys (*e.g.*, the Chenab, Satluj, and the Beas) lived at a level of equilibrium with Nature which allowed the continuity of older traits over longer periods of time. The valley of Kashmir offered yet another example of an agrarian culture persisting over time, at a low level of technology unable to advance beyond a certain level. The surrounding rim of hills and mountains accommodated even more primitive tribal elements at a safe distance from the impact of river valley civilisations. The restless Pathans, the transhumant Gujjar-Bakarwals and the Baltis, Ladakhis, Lahaulis and the Kannauris lived in their own protected worlds in a state of stagnation, the passage of time leaving little imprint on their mode of living or the fund of recycled ideas.

A socio-geographical interpretation of this phenomenon is understandably based on an intimate knowledge of the historical processes which unfolded themselves over the millennia. Eminent archaeologists, such as F.J. Richards, Mortimer Wheeler, Fairservis, Subbarao, Allchin and Sankalia, historians such as Toynbee, K.M. Pannikar and D.D. Kosambi and geographers such as O.H.K. Spate noted a fundamental relationship between the physical and cultural regions in the Indian subcontinent.[3]

Approaches to India

The Indian subcontinent marks a southward extension of the great landmass of Asia. The peninsula tapers towards the Indian Ocean as the two flanking expanses of the sea—the Bay of Bengal and the Arabian Sea—define its long winding coastline. Before the advent of the sailing boat or the steamship, which was a much later development, the sea must have played an important barrier role. In fact, the oceanic realm kept the Indian peninsula isolated from the littoral regions in Africa, West Asia and Southeast Asia. It is this isolation promoted by the oceanic realm which appears to have contributed to the uniqueness of the Indian civilisation as it evolved through time. Likewise, the landmass on the north is girdled by a chain of high mountains and inter-montane plateaux from west to east with the mountains forming a wall-like barrier between North India and the trans-Himalayan regions in Central Asia and West Asia. The mountains have thus acted as a formidable barrier making all approaches to India difficult. However, it does not mean that the mountains were impregnable. More enterprising nomadic groups continued to wander through the high altitude passes in the Hindu-Koh Himalayas. In fact, these passes remain snow-bound during the greater part of the year and can be negotiated with great difficulty during the short summer period.

It is during these periods that the nomadic groups moved with their herds of animals and crossed the Hindu-Koh Himalayan chain. Thus the mountains on the north and the Indian Ocean on the south have both underlined the partially enclosed character of the Indian subcontinent. It is this geographical isolation of a certain degree which has contributed significantly towards the cultural homogeneity within the South Asian region.[4]

With the passage of time, the South Asian subcontinent evolved as a distinct cultural region, differentiable unmistakably from the West Asian, Central Asian and Southeast Asian cultural realms. Girdling the subcontinent on the north, the Himalayas stretch in a northwest-southeast direction for a formidable length of 2,400 km between the Indus gorge in the northwest to the Brahmaputra gorge in the northeast. The Himalayas, however, are not a single chain of mountains. The mountains actually consist of three main series of ranges running parallel to each other from south to north. They are often referred to as the sub-Himalayas, the Lesser Himalayas and the Great Himalayas or as the Outer, Middle and Inner Himalayas. These ranges, which have varied widths and differ strikingly in structure and relief features, are separated by intervening longitudinal valleys of tectonic origin and the inter-montane plateaux, being the residual erosion surfaces of the earlier cycles of denudation. The mighty streams that cut across the Himalayas, such as the Indus, the Satluj and the Brahmaputra, appear to have given the Himalayas the contours of their commonly perceived transverse sectoral divisions—Punjab Himalayas between the Indus and the Satluj, Kumaun Himalayas between the Satluj and the Kali, Nepal Himalayas between the Kali and the Tista and Assam Himalayas between the Tista and the Brahmaputra (Dihang).

To the north of the Himalayas the terrain is dominated by diversely arranged chains of mountains in the northwest, *viz.*, Karakoram, Hindu Koh, Kun Lun, Tien Shan, Pamir-Alay and Trans-Alay ranges which converged on the Pamir promontory. The Himalayas merge into these ranges imperceptibly giving the relief a complexity of a very high order. In Kashmir, the Great Himalayan range is skirted by the Ladakh and the Zanskar ranges. Further eastward they coalesce with the Kailash range which runs parallel to the Himalayas, on the outskirts of the Tibetan plateau. The surface features are further complicated by the presence of earlier erosion surfaces, such as Aksai Chin, Deosai, Depsang and the Lingzi Tang. Like Dehradun and Patli Dun, the Kashmir valley in itself is of tectonic origin—an end-product of the differential uplift during the Himalayan orogenic phase. These narrow longitudinal valleys and the river terraces bordering them, particularly in the Kashmir valley, became centres of convergence of early human cultures.

Despite the formidable nature of the mountain ramparts, there are passes all along the length which have enabled the movement of adventurous nomadic groups throughout human history.[5]

This is notwithstanding the fact that most of these passes in the north, northwest and the northeast are situated at high altitudes and are beset with great difficulties. Understandably, trans-Himalayan communication has been an adventure always. Some of these passes are well-known, *e.g.*, Gomal, Khyber and Bolan in the Sulaiman range. Khyber has served as a gateway to India throughout history. However, the pass is accessible from the Kabul valley route and once passes in the Bamiyan province of Afghanistan in the Hindu Koh range have been crossed, it is the only natural entry point. Other high-altitude passes which have served as gateways to India include Karakoram and Zojila in Jammu and Kashmir and Rohtang in Himachal Pradesh.[6] There are passes over the Barahoti plateau in Uttar Pradesh, in Nepal Himalayas, in the Chumbi valley in Sikkim and Arunachal Pradesh as well as within the Indo-Myanmar hills. The river gorges, such as Dihang, in the northeast, have also served as corridors for incursion into India. The same role has been played by the numerous streams in Baluchistan connecting the Indus region with Iran.

The Afrasian dry zone—the river valleys of West Asia (*viz.*, Tigris and Euphrates) and North Africa (*viz.*, Nile)—has been recognised by historians as 'the most important region at the dawn of civilisation'. These steppe lands of western Asia and the dry zone of North Africa including the rim of the Mediterranean became eminent centres of human dispersal. These regions were fragile from the viewpoint of human survival.

Early humans who appeared in this area faced the chronic problem of adjustment with the natural environment which was characterised by both the scarcity of water and grassland resources. Moreover, historically the region suffered from increasing aridity. This 'progressive desiccation' is believed to have resulted in a continual process of radial migration of people to the east.[7] The streams of migration brought successive human cultures to the Iranian plateau, as well as the regions lying to the south of the Caspian Sea and the Indo-Iranian borderlands in Baluchistan. By virtue of its location on the terminal end of the Eurasian landmass, India obviously became a focal point for some of the migration streams. The Indus valley and the northwestern region of Punjab as they lay closer to the entry points became centres of attraction on a perennial basis. The traffic was, however, restricted by the formidable nature of terrain dominated by the Hindu Koh Himalayan mountain chain.

The steppe lands of East Asia (*viz.*, Gobi desert and northern China) emerged in history as another centre of radial migration. From here the nomads drifted to the west taking trans-continental migration route lying to the north of the Central Asian mountain complex. The migration streams originating in North China and Gobi eventually converged on the valleys of the Oxus (Amu Darya) and the Jagxartes (Syr Darya), south and east of the Caspian Sea. These migrations, often referred to as nomadic outbursts threatened the very base of the little oasis states that emerged in the river valleys separated by the great deserts of Kara Kum and Kyzyl Kum. Thus Central Asia remained an area of instability throughout history.

As compared to this, India enjoyed a certain degree of stability rendered by its location protected by the high Hindu Koh Himalayan mountain massif and the Karakoram and the Tien Shan ranges. The trans-continental migration route connecting North China with the East European Plain remained a major line of thrust for the nomadic traffic. Somewhere in the Amu Darya and the Syr Darya interfluve, a route bifurcated from the main line of thrust. It became possible to reach the northern face of the Hindu Koh by this route. Here a high altitude opening—passes in the Bamiyan provinces of Afghanistan—was taken by wave after wave of migrating groups to reach Afghanistan on way to India.

As an entry is made throughout the Bamiyan Pass, the natural route opens up into the Kabul valley, eventually converging on where now the cities of Kabul and Jalalabad are situated. The Kabul river flows eastward, past these old nodes of power to meet the Indus near Attock, the Khyber Pass offering an easy entry into the region. Toynbee has noted that throughout history all crossings of the Indus have been made at this strategic point.[8] It is near here that the Indus debouches from the hills, and is no more a turbulent mountain torrent. Downstream the channel of the river widens with the result that fording becomes an absolute necessity. Over time Attock acquired its nodal character emerging as the most important strategic point for a passage to India.[9] From Attock traditional routes which follow a line parallel to the foothills to the Himalayas through the Punjab plains lead to Ambala-Kurukshetra region. Southern routes were beset with many difficulties, arid climate and scarcity of water being most formidable among them. From Ambala it is possible to drift on to the Kurukshetra-Thanesar (Sthaneshwara of Hsuan Tsang) and to Mathura via Indraprastha on the west bank of the Yamuna (Jumna). There has been a strong tendency to cross the Yamuna at a point where it is closer to the hills near Yamunanagar to reach the fertile region of *doab*. A crossing of the Yamuna at this point makes the Ganga-Yamuna *doab* easily accessible from the west. The natural routes then run parallel to the Ganga. The historic cities of Hastinapur, Kanyakubja and Prayaga arose along this route. Likewise, a crossing of the Yamuna near Mathura makes possible an entry into the *doab* and a passage to Kanyakubja. In this sector one is more likely to take a route parallel to the Yamuna. Historic cities, such as Chandwar, Rapti and Kosambi arose along this route. Eastwards beyond Kashi the routes end up into the Ganga-Son triangle. It was in this region that Rajagriha and Patliputra emerged as nodes of Magadhan power at different points of time in history.

The outliers of Chhotanagpur plateau in Mukameh spurs and the Rajmahal hills about the Ganga forcing the river to take an abrupt southerly bend, thus defining the partially enclosed character of the south Bihar plain. Eastward movement into Bengal was beset with difficulties partly due to the highly dissected terrain. The Rajmahal hills thus emerge as a terminal point where the North Indian plain gets lost as an acumen. The mighty Ganga on the north and the Chhotanagpur plateau on the south seem to have contributed to the region's psyche of autonomy and self-sufficiency. Astride this route from Indus to Rajmahal hills lie the historic cultural nodes from Sapta-Sindhava and Kurukshetra to Panchala, Braj, Kosala and Magadha.

From here the movement towards the south became possible via routes which passed through the Son-Narmada furrow. These routes finally open up into the Malwa plateau and converge on the old city of Ujjaini. Narmada valley route takes one further to Gujarat and the Desh region of Maharashtra. Here, the upper tributary streams of the Godavari (*e.g.*, Purna) offer convenient routes to Telengana and the littoral Andhra where the deltas of Godavari and Krishna coalesce to form an alluvial tract of great agricultural potential along the coast. The coastal plain widens here and the coastal route takes to the south up to the Kaveri delta. The Kaveri valley route takes one towards the Western Ghats and finally ends up in Malabar. Along this route from Ujjaini to Madurai (from the Narmada to the Kaveri) emerged the nodes of regions, such as Gujarat, Maharashtra, Telangana, Andhra, Chola, Pandya and Kerala.[10]

The Regional Framework

It is commonly known that the Indian Republic is a mosaic of regions. The river valleys from Indus to Kaveri have been the areas of perennial attraction, particularly for the agriculture-oriented communities. On the outskirts of these valleys lie the areas of rugged terrain consisting of hills and dissected plateaux not much suited to the agricultural mode of production. These regions have been less hospitable and more favoured by groups engaged in hunting, food-gathering or pastoral practices. These diversities in the ecological setting and the corresponding differences in human adaptation created diverse regional patterns in culture which are a distinctive trait of India.

Developing the theme of unity in diversity in the Indian subcontinent, Subbarao noted that 'significant diversities' in the different regions of the country suggested a more fundamental relationship between the physical and cultural elements which defined India's regions. In his attempt to understand Indian history and archaeology in better light, he tried to identify and analyse factors which operated behind the baffling cultural diversity.[11]

The geographic factors have helped to a certain extent in developing the understanding of the underlying cultural processes. However, in relating culture with environment one cannot overemphasise physical factors and thus follow a deterministic line. Human relationship with Nature is a complex process and the human failure to bring about homogeneous cultural (social) development cannot be attributed entirely to the environmental factors.

F.J. Richard's pioneering contribution to the interpretation of Indian history appears to have influenced archaeologists, historians and geographers alike. Spate in his reconstruction of nuclear areas from Asoka to Aurangzeb, revealing frequency of political boundaries as they evolved through time, was trying to interpret Indian history in the geographical context (Box 3.1).

Box 3.1 : The Perennial Nuclear Regions

Thus early we can also discern the emergence of some nuclear regions or bases of power which are perennially significant in Indian historical geography: Gandhara in the vale of Peshawar and Potwar, Sapta-Sindhu narrowed down to the Punjab, seven rivers to five; Kurukshetra (Sirhind), the Delhi or Satluj/Yamuna *doab*; Panchala in the Yamuna/Ganga *doab* and Rohilkhand; Saurashtra (Kathiawad) and Gujarat; the four great kingdoms already apparent in Magadhan times. In the Dravidian south the pattern is more confused, but not without some relatively permanent pieces in the dynastic kaleidoscope: the Kalinga country or Orissa; Andhra, the Telugu country; the Chola (whence Coromandel) and Pandya kingdoms in the Tamil country; Kerala or Malabar, the isolated southwest littoral. There are, of course, many smaller areas which have preserved a historic individuality, *e.g.*, Bundelkhand, Chhattisgarh, Konkan and Kanara. Some areas again have been debatable marches: such as Khandesh, between Narmada and Tapti, or the Raichur *doab* between Tungabhadra and Krishna.

—O.H.K. Spate, *India and Pakistan*, 1957:177.

The foregoing study of the space relations of India with the adjoining regions of Asia has indicated the directions from where the cultural influences percolated into the subcontinent and affected the course of historical development. The impregnable nature of the northern mountain complex (Hindu Koh Himalayas) and the location of the subcontinent as a peninsula projecting into the Indian Ocean protected the region from the upheavals that affected the Central and West Asian regions. Whatever, cultural influences managed to reach India, they were in the form of a 'backwash' from the mainline of thrust that lay to the north of the Tien Shan range in Central Asia.

While the early man (*homo sapiens*) is not traceable in India, it is widely known that 'in the subsequent periods... every new wave of people, who entered into the Indo-Gangetic plains as conquerors or fugitives very rapidly lost their own individuality in this melting pot of cultures and added their own indistinguishable element to the make-up of this culture complex'. Some of the dominant strands left their 'deep imprints' while others remained 'unidentified and unaccounted'.

The division of the country into 'wide inviting western alluvial plains' connected to the principal gateways opening into western Asia and the southern peninsular plateau with the intermediary stretches studded with hills and the tropical monsoon forest, provided ideal ecological conditions for the survival of a variety of cultural traits, enabling 'the earlier inhabitants to isolate themselves in what may be called *cul-de-sac*, or refuge zones'. The geography of India contributed to this spatial arrangement. As already pointed out, Richards and Subbarao noted the role of relief features in the horizontal expansion and segregation of cultures. 'The chief river basins of the country', wrote Subbarao, *viz.*,

> 'the Indus, Ganges, Narmada, Tapti, Godavari, Krishna and the Kaveri were in turn penetrated and exploited by large scale agricultural communities, driving the older and static people in a more primitive economy into the forested mountains, where they have survived to this day. The main river basins of the country with a rainfall between 20 and 40 inches (500-1,000 mm), which can sustain large scale agricultural communities, have been colonised or occupied again and again'.

India has evolved in its spatial segments a typology of regions, described as: (a) areas of attraction or perennial nuclear regions; (b) areas of isolation or *cul-de-sac*; and (c) areas of relative isolation lying in between.[12] This scheme of regions is closely linked to the 'trans-continental communication system' through which people and cultures have moved from the northwestern entry points to the southern tip of the peninsula (Box 3.2).

Box 3.2 : The Perennial Nuclear Regions

Now working on this system, we can easily define the regions and their foci. Bounded by the Aravallis and the desert of Rajputana in the east, and the Sulaiman and Kirthar ranges in the west, is the Indus basin, draining the Central Himalayas. This can be roughly subdivided at the points where the hills from the west and the desert in the east converge near the Bugti country, into the lower and the upper, corresponding to Sind and Punjab respectively. Beginning with Delhi, where the Aravallis converge towards the Himalayas, the Gangetic basin runs east from the narrow divide. On its southern flank lies the Vindhyan complex. The lower deltaic region of the Ganges, as it leaves the Vindhyan complex, is Bengal. The valley of the Brahmaputra is Assam. Forming, as it were, a little triangle constituted by the Aravallis in the west, and the Vindhyas running obliquely towards the Gangetic basin, is the plateau of Malwa, drained by the rivers—Chambal, Banas, Sipra, Narmada and Son. Lying south of the Vindhyas, and constituting the upper basins of the rivers Krishna and Godavari, and more or less co-extensive with the Deccan Trap area, is Maharashtra. The lower basins of these two great rivers constitute Andhra. The southern part of the Krishna basin, more or less constituting the 'rocky triangle' formed by the Eastern and the Western Ghats, *viz.*, the Mysore plateau, is Karnataka. At its southern end, it is drained by the river Kaveri. Beginning from the constriction of the Nagar hills and Pulicat lake, and running right along the east coast, is Tamilnad. The narrow coastal plain on either side of the Palghat gap in the Western Ghats, is Kerala. The valley of the Mahanadi, surrounded by hills and plateau, constitutes Orissa. The northern part of the west coast and the peninsula of Saurashtra, abutting on the desert of Rajputana, is Gujarat.

—B. Subbarao, *The Personality of India*, 1958: 16-18.

According to this view point, the difference in the cultural milieu of the first large scale agricultural communities in different regions contributed to the baffling diversity that India inherited. The movement of people and cultures through the trans-continental communication system promoted intermingling of cultural traits thus ensuring the overarching cultural unity within the diversity. Expansion of the primeval agricultural communities from the core areas of the river basins has resulted in an encroachment on the tribal cultures surviving in the surrounding rim of hills and forested tracts in the uplands. This has initiated a process of cultural assimilation or absorption of tribal traits into the dominant peasant cultures. Its natural consequences were disturbing to the tribes whose fragile economies were destabilised with these peasant inroads and could never recover from this shock. The juxtaposition of cultures observed in the regions surrounding the river basins, in the Chhotanagpur plateau, Orissa highlands, Central Vindhyan Complex, the Aravallis or the Western Ghats, is an example of this uneasy interface between the tribal and peasant modes of production in contemporary India.

It is thus evident that the geographical setting of India played a very significant role in the evolution of cultural diversity.

The Northeast

Like the rest of India the northeast also passed through the same evolutionary history. The same process of incursion of diverse cultures, their horizontal expansion and consequent displacement, contraction or isolation of earlier cultures also affected the northeast. The region is often described as a microcosm of India with its northern mountains, central plain and southern plateau. The Brahmaputra has filled its tongue-like longitudinal valley with a massive alluvial deposit of great agricultural potential. However, the valley remained a rendezvous for hunters and food-gatherers far longer and the process of sedentarisation started quite late in history. The evidence of shouldered celts (stone hoes) scattered all over the region suggests beyond any doubt that the earlier culture-groups were familiar with the art of agriculture. However, the process of sedentarisation was postponed by many centuries.

The setting was ideal for the incursion of diverse cultures and for their eventual segregation in the Brahmaputra valley and the surrounding uplands consisting of the Garo, Khasi, Jaintia, Lushai and the Naga hills. The land routes connected the Brahmaputra valley with the hills and plateau surfaces beyond Tibetan plateau, Shan plateau and the Irrawaddy valley. The Chittagong hills also remained connected with the Cape Negaris and the Malay Peninsula through the Arakan coastal route. Moreover, the numerous passes across the Himalayan range and the Indo-Myanmar hills[13] offered access to the Brahmaputra valley which became an area of convergence of diverse cultures. The Ahoms who came to the region during the thirteenth century transformed the scene completely resulting in the division of the agrarian and the pre-agrarian modes of production along topographical lines. Today, the arrangement is such that while the tribes are more or less confined to the hills, the valley is the home of peasant cultures. Manipur replicates the same arrangement on a much smaller scale.

The Brahmaputra valley emerged as the far-eastern perennial nuclear region with its central and western segments known variantly as Kamarup or Pragjyotisa. For the simple reason that the western region was geographically isolated from the rest of northern India, it enjoyed a certain amount of independence throughout history. Even though, the spill-over from the densely populated Ganga delta to Assam remained a phenomenon, particularly after the Permanent Settlement during the British period. Even the Muslim kings from Khilji to Akbar could not control the Northeast in its entirety. The region was eventually annexed by the British during the nineteenth century who set the stage for the new political order and a more comprehensive colonial exploitation of natural resources.

Spatial Arrangement of Diverse Modes

It may be recapitulated that the river valleys were more attractive to the agrarian groups. The emergence of nuclear regions was obviously a post-agricultural phenomenon. However, before the advent of agriculture, hunters and food-gatherers were not interested in the river valleys for any particular reason. They wandered from vale to vale in quest for food. India presented diversity in its ecological setting to such an extent that the tribal, agrarian and pastoral modes could survive in a neat spatial arrangement. While the agrarian mode spread horizontally in the river valleys, the inter-fluvial tracts were favoured by the nomadic pastoralists. Higher up on the plateau surfaces or in isolated hills and mountain ranges tribes lived in their own exclusive world (Fig. 3.1).

Regional Foci

As already noted, the nuclei of perennial regions were in the river valleys, big and small, from the Indus to Krishna and the Kaveri. The underlying assumption is that the river valleys were accessible by the main route of subcontinental migration. The route inter-connected them and kept them open to fresh waves of incursions time and again. Along this route emerged Gandhara (west of Indus at the end of the Kabul valley), Sapta-Sindhu (upper Indus basin), Kurukshetra (between Satluj and Yamuna), Panchala (between Yamuna and Ganga in the upper *doab* as well as trans-Ganga region), Braj (along the Yamuna), Kosala or Awadh (north of the Ganga in its middle segment), Magadha (south Bihar plain between the Son and the Ganga), Bengal over the Ganga delta (between Rajmahal Hills and the sea) and Assam (in the lower Brahmaputra valley). In Central India emerged Malwa (between the Aravallis and the Vindhyan range), Maharashtra (upper basins of Krishna and Godavari, south of the Vindhyas), Andhra (lower basins of Krishna and Godavari), Tamilnad over the eastern littoral region and Kerala (west of the Western Ghats). Other nuclear regions may be identified as Orissa (lower Mahanadi basin) and Gujarat (basins of Mahi and Sabarmati as well as Kathiawar peninsula).

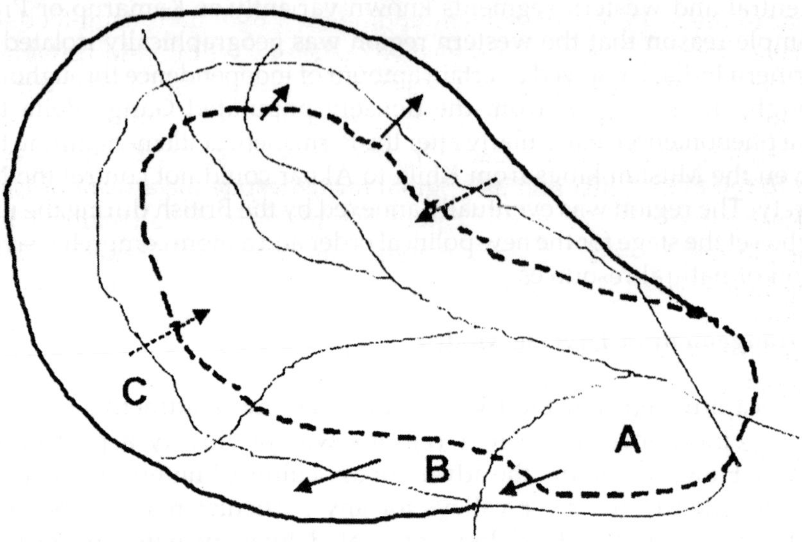

A	River Valley	Sedentary agriculture; pioneer village communities emerged along the river banks
B	Valley Slopes	Nomadic pastoralism and shifting cultivation
C	Surrounding Hills and Erosion Surfaces	Hunting and food gathering economies

——→ Reversal from agriculture to pastoralism and/or food gathering

- - -→ Assimilation of the tribal and pastoral modes into the agrarian mode

Figure 3.1: Spatial Arrangement of Tribal, Pastoral and Agrarian Modes in Diverse Ecological Niches

It may also be noted that while Orissa enjoyed a certain degree of isolation because of its location away from the main route of subcontinental migration, Gujarat remained connected to this circulation through the mid-Indian as well as the Makran coast routes. In fact, it remained in constant contact with West Asia by sea as well as land routes. Movement along the Makran coast route influenced the cultural history of Gujarat in several phases.[14]

On the outskirts of the river valleys were the so-called refuge areas—hilly, forested or arid. Foremost among these *cul-de-sacs* were Rajputana (west of the Aravallis), Gondwana (between the Son and the Mahanadi), Bastar plateau in Central India and Rajmahal hills.[15] Then there were sub-Himalayan river valleys of Chenab, Satluj and Beas in the old Punjab, as well as Kumaon and Garhwal hills. These regions served as refuge areas for both the tribal and peasant groups, particularly for the latter who were ousted from the plains of North India after each successive wave of invasion.

Scions of the displaced ruling class often found refuge in these remote hills from Dhauladhar to the Kathmandu valley founding their own little, semi-feudal states in the Himalayan retreat. Mention may also be made of Kashmir and Ladakh—regions nestled in the Himalayas and beyond. Kashmir, however, remained connected with Gandhara by the much-frequented Jhelum gorge route, even though its 'refuge area' character remained unaffected. Ladakh was away from the Kashmiri world and continued to retain Buddhism in its original form, despite the advent of Islam in the valley of Kashmir and the bordering rim of mountains from Baltistan to Chitral.

In the Northeast the bordering uplands from Arunachal Pradesh to Lushai and Chittagong hills served the role of refuge areas for the tribes ousted from the river-valleys—the tribal-non-tribal boundary runs often parallel to the 'skirts of the hills'.[16] Those who joined later such as the Kachins and Kuki-Chins, found no other place but the hills which were already partly occupied by earlier groups.

Beginnings of Cultural Differentiation

The presence of the Early Humans in the Indian subcontinent is inferred from the tools of the Old Stone Age collected by the archaeologists from countless number of sites scattered all over the region. Even though these tools provide undisputable evidence of the existence of the Early Humans, no direct evidence has yet been unearthed from any site which may throw light on the very nature of this population, their racial characteristics and physical attributes. Thus, while a multitude of tools is there all around, human skeletal remains are missing. This issue has been widely debated by archaeologists and physical anthropologists. However, it may not be a very serious problem as the tools themselves are sufficient to tell a coherent story about the evolution of Early Human cultures from the Palaeolithic (Old Stone Age) to the Neolithic (New Stone Age) and the Chalcolithic (metal using cultures) period. A socio-geographical interpretation of this evidence of the human artefacts belonging to the different pre-historic phases is important in order to understand the very process of human adaptation to the prevailing environmental conditions and the human migrations related to this adaptation. The evidence also helps in the appraisal of emergence of certain localities which were repeatedly frequented by the Early Humans in the course of geographical spread of these cultures. In fact, it is customary to recognise three types of regions, each one of them throwing up evidence of a diverse cultural history. Broadly speaking, while regions of attraction possess evidence of a complete cultural succession reflecting a remarkable continuity, the regions of isolation are different. They were not frequented so often. Their archaeological record is, therefore, discontinuous. Whatever cultural influences managed to reach there, they virtually got impounded as no new influences could percolate. In between these two extremes are the regions of relative isolation, where cultural influences were received but with breaks, thus leaving behind an archaeological record of a discontinuous nature.

The pre-historic scene in India is hazy because of the limited nature of evidence. The inadequacy of probings made into the past is an obvious explanation, although the past is a closed book unless its pages are opened systematically. This has left vast gaps in information which have often been filled with conjecture. In fact, many sites were accidentally discovered. The selection of sites for digging was also subjective. Moreover, archaeological excavations progressed in the light of assumptions; hypothesis and formulations arrived at similar diggings elsewhere in the world. The schools of European archaeology had their own models which were neatly applied to Indian data. Despite the random nature of diggings, the evidence was colossal, both in extent and content and called for rigorous analytical and interpretative exercises on a scale proportional to the size of the territory. Understandably, some sites received more attention than others and at any point of time findings based on new diggings upset the very basis of earlier conclusions. There were, however, serious limitations, both administrative and financial, which made the archaeologists' task even more difficult. Reaching the goals set by the Archaeological Survey of India was always as difficult as it is today. The archaeological record is, therefore, to be seen with care and caution.

The earliest traces of human cultures have been found in the valley of Sohan (Soan in early writings) river, a tributary of the Indus, northwest of Rawalpindi (Pakistan). The evidence collected from the terraces of the Sohan river consists of crude stone tools believed to be left behind by the ancient hunters of the Old Stone Age. These tools were found buried in the glacial as well as the fluvial terraces of the Sohan river. The terraces also presented a complete stratigraphic record of the sequence of climatic changes witnessed during the Pleistocene times. Since, the tools were found buried in the river terraces, there was a valuable stratigraphic evidence, enabling the archaeologists to determine the age of the tools with the help of strata with a certain degree of precision. In fact, it was due to this stratigraphic association of the tools that Sohan valley sprang into prominence as one of the most celebrated sites of the Lower Palaeolithic period. The Sohan valley technique of tool-making became a reference point in comparative archaeology for checking the antecedents of similar tools discovered in other parts of India. It was due to the pioneering work of De Terra and Paterson[17] that it became possible to place the whole set of evidence collected from the Sohan river terraces in its proper perspective. By correlating the human cultures with the sequence of climatic changes during the Pleistocene times, De Terra and Paterson set the stage for a meaningful study of the Palaeolithic cultures in India. The Sohan valley tools were found in four of the five terraces of the Sohan river. The lithic evidence was collected from the terraces of the second glacial, second inter-glacial and the third glacial phases.[18] In terms of evolution of tool-making techniques, archaeological studies revealed that three distinctive stages could be identified. These stages were termed as pre-Sohan, Sohan and the late-Sohan. Each successive phase revealed a technological advancement on the previous one. Thus, while the pre-Sohan tools were based on flakes, the Sohan and the late-Sohan varieties consisted of core tools. In fact, the early Sohan group, which belonged to the second inter-glacial period, consisted mostly of choppers and other scraping tools made on flat truncated pebbles.[19] Typologically, they were sub-divided into several groups ranging from Clactonian to Levalloisian.[20]

Placing the evidence in its proper environmental context, De Terra and Paterson noted a direct relationship between the climatic changes and the rise of early human cultures. It may be postulated that the tools unearthed from the terraces must have been left behind by the Early Humans over the surface in the Sohan river valley. The downward movement of the glaciers and the fluvial drift that followed the melting of snow must have displaced the tools from their original sites. Perhaps the Potwar plateau became one of the earliest sites of the diffusion of the early human cultures in the Indo-Pakistan subcontinent. The advances and retreats of glaciers implied vast fluctuations in the global temperature regimes. This must have resulted in far-reaching changes in the Earth's environment, particularly in its climate and the vegetation cover. The ancient hunters and food-gatherers must have remained on the move in the wake of these changes.

Sohan-type tools have also been found in other parts of North India. Of special interest are the sites in the terraces of the sub-Himalayan river valleys of Satluj, Beas and its tributary, Banganga, in Himachal Pradesh. Similar tools have also been found scattered on the banks of the Yamuna in Bundelkhand and along the banks of the Chambal and its tributary, Banas, in eastern Rajasthan. The pebble-based core tools (chopping choppers and scrappers) appear to have a southern limit somewhere along the 22°N Latitude, with Mayurbhanj, in Orissa, being the southern-most point where these tools have been found. Archaeologists have also found similar tools in certain stretches of the Narmada valley. Despite the widespread occurrence of these tools, no definite geographical picture of the development of Palaeolithic cultures can be reconstructed. As is generally known, the river valleys of the North Indian Plain have not yielded any tools. If any tools were left behind by the ancient hunters, they must be lying buried under the thick mantle of alluvium deposited during the successive phases of fluvial activity.

The known evidence of the Lower Palaeolithic period in Peninsular India tells a different story. Perhaps the Old Stone Age tools discovered in and around Madras (now Chennai) and other parts of Peninsular India belong to a different tool-making tradition. For one thing, the tools are not based on pebbles and mostly consist of hand axes and cleavers, made on cores and flakes. These Madras-type tools representing the 'Peninsular facies' of the Early Stone Age in India are Acheulean in typology and suggest an independent development over the region lying to the south of the Narmada. Some observers have noted similarities between the Madras hand-axes and the tools found on the East African Plateau, suggesting a possible connection. The Madras-type tools have been found in a vast area, encompassing the peninsular region. Madras is recognised as a type area where in a boulder-conglomerate bed at the site of Vadamadurai, the earliest tools were unearthed. Studies conducted by Krishnaswami and Paterson revealed that there was geological evidence to suggest that the Peninsular region experienced an alternation of wet and dry periods during the Pleistocene. These phases which were termed as pluvial and inter-pluvial left their traces in the deposits. While a direct connection with the glacial and inter-glacial cycles of Northwestern India has not been established, attempts have been made to correlate the stratigraphic and lithic evidence of the Madras region with the mid-Pleistocene fossil beds of Narmada. Other sites yielding Madras-type tools are situated in the terraces of the river Attirampakkam, near Madras and the Krishna, Godavari and Narmada basins. Tools were also collected from Nellore as well as a large number of sites along the east coast of India and the Gujarat region.

It is thus evident that the appearance of Palaeolithic hunters on the Indian scene is supported by overwhelming archaeological evidence scattered over the peri-glacial areas in the northwestern Himalayas as well as the peninsular plateau. However, the Old Stone Age sites do not lend themselves to a systematic geographical interpretation, mainly due to the incomplete nature of our knowledge. The evidence also suggests that from the upper Palaeolithic to the Neolithic there was a transitional phase which is generally referred to as Mesolithic. During the Mesolithic period, one comes across an overwhelming evidence of smaller tools known as microliths. A multitude of these tools has been collected from sites scattered all over the subcontinent. The microliths include blades, scrappers, burins, triangles, crescents and lunates. The Mesolithic period marks a change from flakes to the microlithic tradition.[21] The tools are generally made of finer varieties of rockets, such as jasper, chert, agate and quartzite. Also included in the findings are composite tools, made of stones fixed with bones or wood as well as remains of pottery. These new varieties of tools indicate sophistication in the techniques of tool making, an imperative of the multiplying human needs. Insofar as the geography of the Mesolithic sites is concerned, nothing can be said with certainty. In fact, each site was an isolated discovery and represented a type in itself. But these sites are important since they tell us the story of cultural succession from the Palaeolithic to the Neolithic. These tools are widely distributed in India, although no evidence has yet been collected from either the Ganga valley or the Himalayas. Sites have been extensively studied in western, central and southern India. In western India, tools have been found in the Mahi and the Banas river valleys of Gujarat and parts of Saurashtra, Mehasana (*e.g.*, Langhnaj), Malwa and parts of Rajasthan. A layer at Langhnaj has yielded black, red and red-and-black potsherds. Copper and iron tools have also been found at higher levels. Sites are also situated in Maharashtra, particularly in the upper Godavari valley (*e.g.*, Nevasa) and the Salsette Island and Ellora. Microliths have also been collected from sites in Singrauli basin (*e.g.*, Lekhania rock shelters in Mirzapur district). Similar tools have also been discovered from the sites in the Damodar valley (*e.g.*, Birbhanpur), Chaibasa, Chakradharpur, Santal Parganas, Durgapur, Bankura, Singhbhum, Keonjhar, Mayurbhanj and Sambalpur. Other rock shelters, such as the one at Adamgarh hill in the Narmada valley, are rich in the cultural remains of the Mesolithic period. Several sites have been excavated in parts of southern India, particularly in Chitradurga, Kurnool and Bellary districts (*e.g.*, Brahrnagiri). Not all the sites reveal a cultural continuity. For example, sites from where the hand axes were collected do not reveal a cultural succession to the Mesolithic. On the other hand, the *teri* sites in southern Tamil Nadu[22] have yielded evidence of transition from the Palaeolithic to the Neolithic cultures.

It may be concluded that the evidence of the microliths points up to a gradual transition of the Palaeolithic hunters and food-gatherers to an agriculture-based production economy. The transition from food gathering to food production was indeed a slow process involving millennia of years. Interestingly, some of the ancient hunters continued to remain with the Palaeolithic mode till very late in history. For them agriculture remained a peripheral activity, if at all. But in regions in which early crop raising became possible, the emergence and the spread of agrarian mode of production is evident. The agrarian mode eventually transformed the human society. This phase of cultural development is often referred to as Neolithic revolution. It involved a process of settling down of nomadic groups on pioneer lands reclaimed from the forest and adopting agriculture as their economic mainstay.[23]

Transition towards the Neolithic

Insofar as the South Asian subcontinent is concerned, transition towards the Neolithic appears to be somewhat confusing.[24] One general conclusion is that outside the Indus basin, the Neolithic cultures are marked by their late appearance—so late that they are mostly post-Harappan. This would mean that while the Neolithic cultures emerged in Baluchistan several millennia before, and, not only that, a civilisation took its roots in the Indus valley and the adjoining areas in Gujarat as well as in the Ghaggar (Saraswati) valley in northern Rajasthan, the rest of the subcontinent remained in the Palaeolithic age. However, some sites in other parts of India have yielded evidence of Neolithic cultures which were certainly pre-Harappan. In fact, archaeological evidence suggests that the Neolithic and the Chalcolithic cultures overlap at many places and not necessarily reveal succeeding cultural phases.[25] Sites in Baluchistan, to which a reference will be made in the subsequent paragraphs, parts of southern Deccan and the valley of Kashmir have thrown up definitive evidence of the presence of an earlier cultural phase which was unmistakably Neolithic. These Neolithic communities, although largely dependent on the use of stone, domesticated animals and practised a primitive form of agriculture. They were leading a settled life. This phase is followed by another cultural phase in which copper and subsequently bronze is associated with stone tools, thus indicating the emergence of a Chalcolithic culture. Although, Baluchistan leads in the development of the Neolithic cultural phase, there are other regions in the subcontinent in which the use of metals was quite common.

Baluchistan

The earliest village sites representative of the Neolithic cultures in the Indo-Pakistan subcontinent were dug out from the tiny river valleys of Baluchistan. That the first Neolithic communities emerged on the Indo-Iranian borderlands suggests the possibility of eastward shift of the agricultural mode from West Asia to the Indian subcontinent. The oldest village sites in West Asia are located in Turkey, Palestine and Iraq. Chronologically, they are supposed to belong to the seventh or the eighth millennium B.C. The Baluchistan cultures are, however, much younger and are dated around the middle of the fifth millennium B.C. While the time lag in this eastward shift of the Neolithic cultures is evident, their rise in Baluchistan and in other parts of the Indus valley may be seen as a remarkable development. In fact, traces of the Neolithic cultures have been found over a vast geographical area encompassing Baluchistan uplands, Indus basin and the adjoining areas in northern Rajasthan. Archaeologists agree that this Neolithic phase was pre-Harappan in its origin and must have been a major influence on the later development of the Harappan culture which developed a civilisation. Archaeological work at many of the Harappan sites has shown the presence of lower layers yielding evidence of the pre-Harappan (Neolithic) cultures. Ironically, these lower levels at many of the Harappan sites have not yet been dug out because of physical difficulties (*e.g.*, high water-table) leaving the question of Harappan-pre-Harappan connection unresolved. It belongs to the realm of conjecture.

The tiny rivers in the Baluchistan hills, Zhob, Beji, Pishin Lora, Dasht, Kel and Lora Lai, to name only a few, in their neatly carved-out valleys offered ideal conditions for the rise of primeval village settlements dependent on some form of agriculture coupled with rearing of animals. Water supply in these rivers was seasonal and permitted the sowing of crops at different levels along the river banks at a height of 1200-1600 metres above sea level. There are many sites from where the evidence of this cultural phase was collected.[26] Archaeological evidence throws light on the nature of the artefacts as well as houses and pottery traditions. Notable among these sites are Kili Gul Mohammad near Quetta, Rana·Ghundai in the Lora Lai valley, Periano Ghundai in the Zhob valley, Damb Sadaat, Togau, Siah Damb, Anjira, Nal and Amri: Kot Diji, east of the Indus, and Mundigak in the southeastern region of Afghanistan. The evidence collected from these sites shows how the food-producing mode sustained these communities. This mode eventually spread to other areas in the Indus valley and set the stage for the rise of a civilisation, the first in Indian history.

In a way these were the pre-Harappans who laid the foundations of the Indian cultural tradition, typically representative of an agrarian society. Figurines of mother goddesses (*e.g.*, Zhob goddesses) and the *pipal* leaf motifs on pottery leave much to be inferred about the origins of Indian civilisation.

Harappan Civilisation

The sites of the Harappan civilisation are scattered over a vast geographical area: from Rupar in the Punjab foothills to Lothal and Rangpur on the Gulf of Cambay and from the Makran coast to Kalibangan on the dry bed of the Ghaggar in northern Rajasthan. Alamgirpur, east of Yamuna appears to be the eastern-most outpost. The site of Bhagatrav lying on the Narmada extends the boundary of the civilisation further south. It may be inferred that its impact was even wider than what the known sites presently indicate. More sites are being discovered and it is quite possible that the currently held view about its extent and boundaries is only tentative and may be revised as new evidence is put forth. The transformation of a Neolithic culture with its modest beginnings in Kili Gul Mohammad, Rana Ghundai, Kot Diji and Kalibangan into a civilisation with a substantial food-producing economy to support an urban society predominantly engaged in the artisan goods industry and in a widespread exchange of these goods on a commercial scale, must have been a time-consuming process. The evidence suggests that the civilisation had already set in by the beginning of the third millennium B.C. The fact that it could sustain itself for one full millennium-and-a-half testifies to its ecological viability. The food-producing economy in a dry region with scanty rainfall could have been possible only in the event of rivers carrying sufficient supply of water to the agricultural fields. The Indus and its tributaries allowed the people to grow a variety of crops in the dry regions of Sind, Punjab and northern Rajasthan as these rivers carried with them a large volume of the snow-melt in the peak summer season. It appears that the surplus from agriculture was transferred to the numerous towns—Mohenjo-daro on the Indus, Harappa on the Ravi, Kalibangan on the Saraswati—to allow people necessary freedom to engage themselves in the manufacture of artisan goods. The raw materials for these industries came from far and near—a variety of minerals, particularly zinc and copper and precious stones from the Aravallis, cotton and other agricultural raw materials from Sind and the Punjab plains, wood and ivory from the surrounding forests and pearls from the sea. Trade in these goods—domestic as well as external—became a characteristic feature of the Indus valley people.[27] It was this commerce that sustained the civilisation to last so long. However, with the passage of time, no significant change came, indicating that a certain equilibrium had already been reached and the basic economic activity continued for centuries without any modification. It is believed that a priestly class managed to extract social surplus in order to maintain a semblance of law and order. The Harappan sites have not yielded any evidence of strong weapons, other than based on bronze, which could have been used to defend it from external or internal threats. The recurrent Indus floods and the inundation of the agricultural fields along the river banks must have washed away the economic base. The threats of external invasions were no less important. The end came abruptly as the Harappan mounds show a sudden break in the layers containing cultural remains. Just as the beginnings of the civilisation are obscure, little can be said about the end on the basis of the currently available archaeological data.

Neolithic in the Rest of India

As against this background, the Neolithic cultures in the rest of India, outside the Indus basin, made a late appearance, not earlier than the first half of the first millennium B.C. However, in recent years, more and more evidence has been put forward to suggest that in at least some regions of India the Neolithic cultural tradition started in the pre-Harappan times.

In this connection, one may make a special reference to Burzahom, in the valley of Kashmir, where chronologically the evidence (of Period I) goes back to the second half of the third millennium B.C. The tools dug out from the Karewa beds at Burzahom include remains of grey and black burnished pottery, stone axes and a variety of stone and bone tools. The evidence also suggests that the Burzahom culture possibly had an affinity with the Neolithic cultures of East Asia, particularly Manchuria. The practice of burying dogs with their masters was a peculiar trait common between the two regions.

The archaeological evidence collected from sites in southern Deccan (Karnataka), such as Brahmagiri, Sanganakallu, Piklihal, Maski, Tekkalakota, Hallur as well as from the ash mounds of Utnur and Kupgal, along the banks of Krishna and Godavari rivers, reveals a widespread use of ground stone axes. Domestication of animals such as goats, sheep and cattle was common. The Neolithic settlements were nestled on the granite hill slopes which were mostly terraced. The archaeological remains also include handmade pottery, a variety of grey ware. Chronologically, these cultural phases have been placed around c. 2500-1800 B.C. The cultural succession suggests a second phase (c. 1800-1500 B.C.) in which these earlier cultural traits continue along with the use of copper and bronze. A third phase has also been identified, dating back to c.1400-1050 B.C., in which the use of metals increases considerably. It has been inferred that these Neolithic communities were mainly dependent on cattle-raising, although cultivation of gram and millet was adopted as a supplementary subsistence in the third phase of cultural development. It has also been inferred that in the first phase, the Deccan Neolithic cultures were influenced, particularly in the pottery tradition by Hissar and certain sites in Baluchistan and Iran.

During the second phase, the cultural influences seem to have emanated from Malwa, and in the third phase from Maharashtra (*e.g.*, Jorwe type of pottery).

New evidence was collected from sites in Rajasthan, particularly eastern parts of the state and Malwa plateau. The archaeological remains collected from Ahar and Gilund [28] in the Banas basin in eastern Rajasthan, suggest a peculiar Banas Neolithic culture with unique characteristics—an absence of stone tools, but numerous copper axes, and a variety of black-and-red ware. It may be noted that copper was locally available.

Nagda and Navdatoli are two sites in the Malwa region which have yielded a variety of artefacts, *viz.*, stone blades, copper tools and painted black-and-red ware, indicating the emergence of the Neolithic culture. These were mainly cattle-raising communities and also domesticated sheep and goats. Chronologically, these cultural phases belong to three different periods which have been assigned dates from c. 2015 to 1380 B.C.

From the geographical spread of Neolithic cultures in the Indian subcontinent, Bridget and Raymond Allchin concluded that Saurashtra, eastern Rajasthan and Malwa appeared to have acted as centres of diffusion of post-Harappan culture in the rest of India. Locationally, these regions were situated at the junction of routes and it is likely that they became scenes of intermingling of different cultural traits—Harappan as well as West Asian. A synthesis of these traditions took place in these nodal regions from where they spread to other parts of India. This diffusion of cultural traits possibly took three routes: a southern route passing through Maharashtra and the Deccan, an eastern route passing through the Narmada and Betwa valleys and a northern route leading to the Ganga valley.

It may be assumed that the late Harappan sites of Rupar (Punjab) and Alamgirpur (Ganga-Yamuna *doab*) played a significant role in the diffusion of Harappan (and post-Harappan) influences in the Ganga valley. Sites in Maharashtra and the Deccan, on which extensive archaeological work has been done, bear testimony to this diffusion theory. Sites in the Tapti valley, *viz.*, Prakash and Bahal, as well as those in the Godavari and the Krishna valleys, *viz.*, Jorwe, Nevasa,[29] Daimabad, Chandoli, Sonegaon and Bahurupa, have yielded evidence of a stone industry in association with copper and bronze tools and pottery. These cultural phases have been dated as c. 1700-1050 B.C. The evidence collected from Eran, on the Betwa river, and Tripuri, on the Narmada, indicates the possible routes through which the Malwa influences got diffused into the central and eastern regions of India. These Chalcolithic settlements have been assigned to the period around 1500-1280 B.C. Archaeological remains also show a transition towards the Iron Age around 1040 B.C.

Reference has already been made to Rupar and Alamgirpur. The process of expansion of the post-Harappan influences over the Ganga valley may be traced along the routes connecting Alamgirpur with the rest of the region. It appears that these sites faded away soon after the Harappan phase was over. This is evident from a sudden break in cultural continuity from the late Harappan to the Iron Age. The archaeological findings of this intermediary period consist of copper hoards, dug out from the sites in the Ganga-Yamuna *doab*, other parts of the upper Ganga valley, Chhotanagpur plateau, Orissa highlands, central Vindhyan region and the Deccan.[30] The ochre-coloured pottery generally associated with the copper hoards is supposed to belong to the late Harappan and the post-Harappan phases. Later excavations at Atranjikhera in Etah district, confirmed these connections. In fact, a comparative study of the archaeological remains collected from Harappa, Rupar, Autha (Punjab), Alamgirpur, Hastinapura, Atranjikhera, Ahichhetra (*doab* and the upper Ganga valley), Noh (Indo-Gangetic divide region), Saravasti, Kosambi, Rajghat, Prahladpur, Chirand and Sonpur (middle Ganga valley) corroborate these conclusions. The different pottery types discovered at these sites help in the reconstruction of a peculiar sequence in cultural succession from ochre-coloured ware (c. 1200 B.C.), Painted Grey Ware (PGW, c. 800-600 B.C.) to the Northern Black Polished Ware (NBPW, c. 200 B.C.). At many of these sites iron tools have been found in intermediary beds around 1000-800 B.C. These phases have led Allchin to the conclusion that these Chalcolithic cultures of the Ganga valley, east of Punjab, may be assigned to an earlier stream of Aryans who reached the eastern regions prior to the arrival of the Rigvedic Aryans. In the geography of *Rigveda*, Yamuna appears to be the eastern limit. Subsequent streams of the Aryan tribes who moved eastwards are believed to have composed *Yajurveda* and *Atharvaveda* as well as the later texts in regions, lying to the east of Yamuna, from Hastinapura to Magadha.

By now the stage had already been set for the rise of states (kingdoms and republics). This was a culmination of the process of colonisation of the North Indian Plain which had been going on for centuries.

Sodasa Mahajanapadas

These states emerged as monarchies as well as republics, the latter representing a model of 'tribal democracy'. Scholars of ancient Indian history, such as Romila Thapar, have tried to trace the transition from lineage to state.[31] Thapar argued that the monarchies were a peculiarity of the fertile Ganga valley. On the other hand, the states that emerged on the northern and the southern periphery of the valley were mostly republics. This distinction owed its origin to the ecological differences as expressed in the surplus generating potential of the two types of ecological regions. Understandably, the republics must have been the first states to emerge. Gradually they were transformed into monarchies.[32] Those ousted from the monarchies continued to found new republics on the periphery of the Ganga valley. Thus monarchies and republics had an interesting geographic pattern of distribution. Moreover, the republics were generally controlled by a single tribe. However, in several cases, they were confederacies of more than one tribe. The transformation of republics into monarchies also marked a transition from the egalitarian tribal social order to a caste-based hierarchical structure. Gradually different caste groups got associated with different occupations, leading to a further augmentation of the caste-based society. Over time, caste-specific occupational specialisations also contributed to the diversification of economy on a progressive basis, with the cities emerging at nodal points as centres of trade and industry.

Angutra Nikaya, the first Buddhist text mentions the following 16 *mahajanapadas* (*sodasa mahajanapadas*): Kuru, Panchala, Kosala, Kasi, Malla, Vajji (Vrijji), Magadha, Anga, Surasena, Matsya, Chedi, Vatsa, Avanti, Asmaka, Gandhara and Kamboja (Table 3.1).

Table 3.1 : Sodasa Mahajanapadas

Mahajanapadas	*Capital City/Cities*	*Dialect/Language*
Kuru	Indraprastha/Hastinapura	Kuruvi/Khari Boli
Panchala	Ahichhetra/Kampila	
Kosala	Ayodhya/Saket	Kosali/Awadhi
Kasi	Kasi	Kosali/Awadhi
Malla	Pawa, Kusinagar	Bhojpuri
Vajji (Videha)	Mithila	Maithili
Magadha	Rajagriha	Maghai
Anga	Champanagri	Maghai
Vatsa (Vamsa)	Kosambi	
Chedi		Bundeli
Surasena	Mathura	Braj Bhasha
Matsya	Viratnagar	Bagari
Avanti	Ujjaini	Malwi
Asmaka		
Gandhara	Purushapura/Taxila	Gandhari/Pushto
Kamboja		

The later texts such as the *Digha Nikaya* and a number of *Puranas* repeat this information, although each time new *janapadas* are added to the list indicating the on-going process of colonisation of new tracts and the emergence of new territories. Sometimes, the *janapadas* are mentioned as twins (*e.g.*, Kuru-Panchala, Kosala-Kasi, Malla-Vajji, Surasena-Matsya, Chedi-Vatsa). This process of coming together of two neighbouring *janapadas* may be a political response to the over-arching authority of certain nodes of power which were emerging as empires. By the time of Buddha, Madhyadesa, or the central region of Bharatavarsa had already emerged as the major acumen of Aryan settlement outside the Indus basin. In fact, the Sapta-Sindhava region appears to have faded away as none of the 16 great *janapadas* were situated in this region. Madhyadesa, the 'Middle Country of the Epics'[33], on the other hand, had as many as 13 of the 16 *mahajanapadas*. The region encompassed the entire north-central zone of India, from the Siwaliks and the *terai* in the north to the Vindhayas and the Narmada in the south and from the banks of the Saraswati (Ghaggar) in Rajasthan-Haryana in the west to the Rajmahal hills in the east. These natural boundaries protected it and made it the most secure region, just as its rich resources of land, water and congenial climate added immensely to its agricultural potential. The mid-Indian uplands, the Chhotanagpur plateau and the Rajmahal hills defined its southern and southeastern boundary. The deltaic tract of Bengal which emerged as the core of the Vanga *janapada* was a much later development. Anga is not mentioned in the *Angutra Nikaya*. In a fertile plain like this, early Aryan settlements must have emerged on the river banks on the land reclaimed from the surrounding forest. The pioneer villages that emerged on the cultivated tracts finally got organised into territorial units, *i.e.*, clan territories, republics and kingdoms. The rivers and the forests, which occupied vast stretches of land, defined the boundaries between the *janapadas*. These were natural boundaries and they delimited the areas of influence of respective territorial entities. Cities emerged on the river banks and became the foci of political authority. Hastinapura, Ahichhetra, Kosambi, Ayodhya, Saket, Kasi, Saravasti, Vaishali, Rajagriha, Ujjaini and Taxila emerged as nodes of power attracting a large population of landed elites, artisans, warriors and administrators.

The Kuru *janapada* lay between the Saraswati and the Ganga encompassing the northern part of the Ganga-Yamuna *doab*. To its east and the southeast lay the Panchala *janapada*, between the Ganga and Saryu. It also extended between the Yamuna and the Ganga in the middle *doab*. The Kosala *janapada* extended from the Saryu to the Rapti. The Kosala also incorporated the tracts between the Gomati-Ganga and the Saryu reaching as far south as Kasi. The Kasi *janapada* was essentially a city-state based on Varanasi. But it also incorporated the tracts of land to the north of the Ganga in the Ganga-Gomati *doab*. To the east of Kosala there were four *janapadas* in the Bihar plain, two to the north of the river and two to its south. The Malla and the Vajji *janapadas* were situated in the northern plain. The former lay between the Rapti-Ganga and the Gandak and the latter between the Gandak and Kosi. Vajji also known as Videha, was a confederacy of tribes. Magadha and Anga *janapadas* were situated in the south Bihar plain. Magadha extended from the Son to the Mokameh spurs. Anga, an eastern *janapada* extended up to the Rajmahal hills.

To the west of the Yamuna the Surasena *janapada* had its focal point in Mathura. It incorporated the Bharatpur-Dholpur-Karauli region. On the south was Matsya with its core region lying in Alwar district. Further south was the Avanti *janapada*, occupying the upper reaches of the Chambal and its tributaries on the Malwa plateau and focusing on Ujjaini. To the east of Chambal and south of Yamuna was the Vatsa *janapada*. There were three other *janapadas*, lying outside the Madhyadesa. Two of them—Gandhara and Kamboja—were situated in the north-western frontier region. Gandhara occupied the lower Kabul valley. At times it served as a major link between India and central Asia. The Kamboja *janapada* occupied the valley of Kunar river on the southern slopes of the Hindu Koh. Asmaka was the southern-most among the 16 *Mahajanapadas*. It has been identified with the middle Godavari valley[34] (Fig. 3.2).

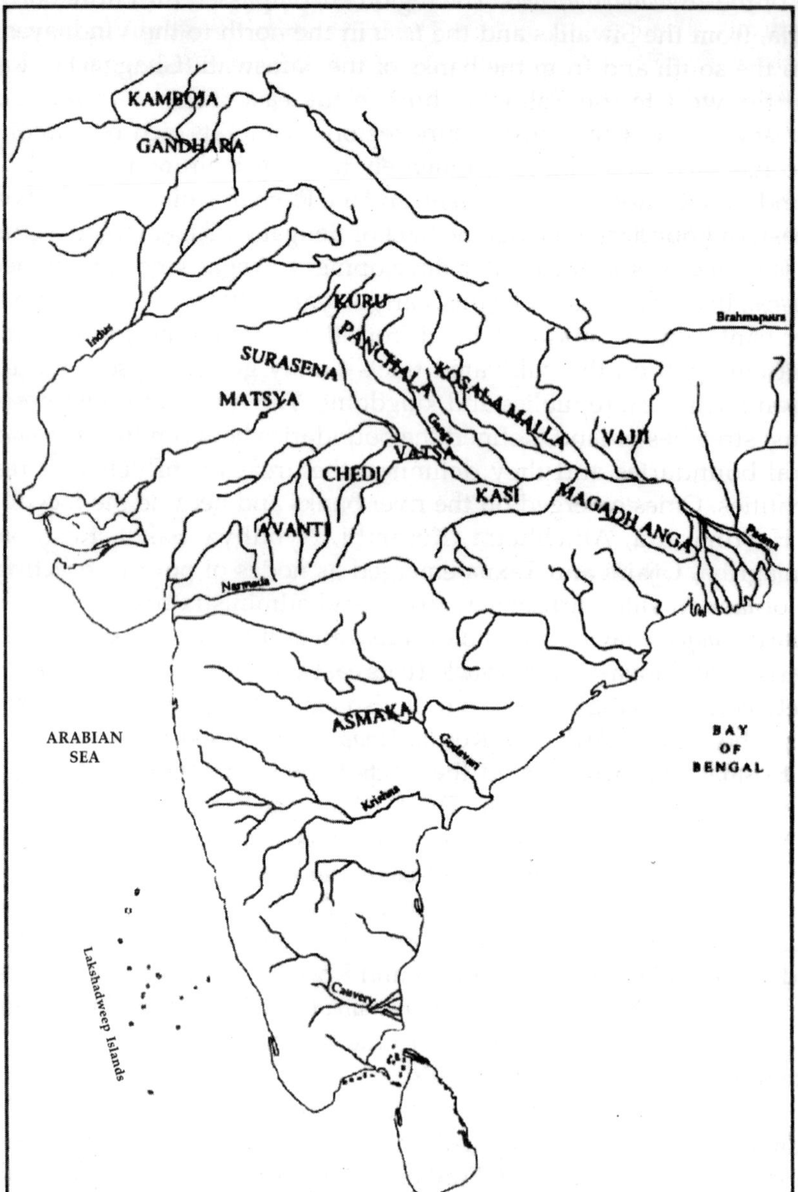

Figure 3.2 : Sixteen Mahajanapadas of Ancient India, c. 6th century B.C.

Madhyadesa became the heartland of the Ganga valley civilisation. Gradually local dialects developed with a literary tradition, in certain cases, becoming the repository of folk culture, art, religion and philosophy. This resulted in the process of cultural diversification between the *janapadas*. Each *janapada* evolved its own dialect/ language and produced its own *puranas*.

These were the beginnings of cultural regionalism that distinguished India so characteristically. These cultural regions of India are living entities and constitute the basis of regional identity. Centuries of rule from powerful *janapadas*, such as Magadha, could not wipe out this cultural regionalism.

S.M. Ali's *Geography of the Puranas* refers to many other *janapadas* in the western and southern regions of India. The evidence based on Puranic sources unravels the process of territorialisation which continued throughout the proto-historic and early historic times. Fig. 3.3 shows the major *janapadas* of the southern (Dakshinapatha) and the southwestern (Apranta) regions of India.

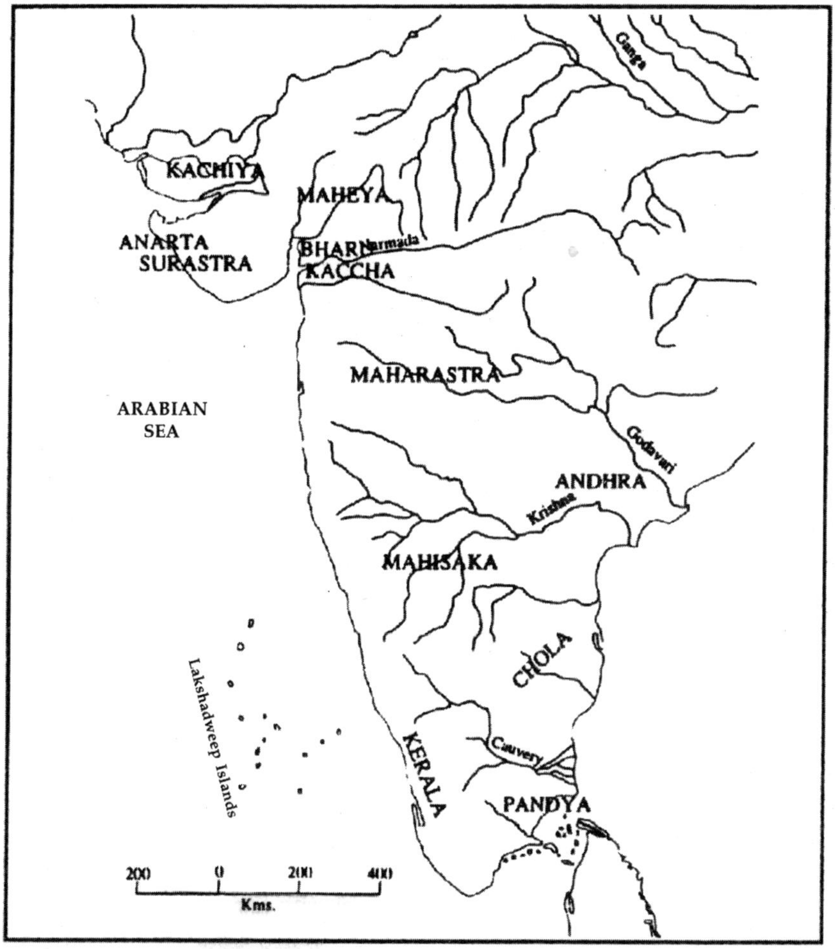

Figure 3.3: Major Janapadas of Dakshinapatha and Apranta, c. 100 B.C.

Mughal Provinces

One observes a discernible continuity from the *janapadas* to the Mughal provinces. While the political structure underwent many changes in the intervening period of two millennia, it appears that the political divisions were successively built on the legacy of cultural regions. The Mughals built their provincial structure on this very edifice.

On the authority of *Ain-e-Akbari*[35] it is possible to recognise the 12 major provinces in which Akbar's vast empire was divided. It may be recapitulated that the Mughal empire under Akbar extended from the Hindu Koh in the west to Bengal in the east and from Kashmir in the north to the river Tapti in the south. Later, as a result of consistent Mughal effort to extend the imperial frontiers towards the south, three more provinces were added to this list. The major provinces included Kabul, Lahor, Multan, Dehli, Agrah, Awadh, Illahabad, Behar, Bengalah, Malwah, Ajmere and Ahmedabad.[36] The later additions were Berar, Khandesh (renamed as Dandesh) and Ahmadnagar. Each province (*subah*)[37] was further sub-divided into *sarkars*[38] and each *Sarkar* into *mahals* or *parganahs*.[39] While the *mahals* or *parganahs* were revenue sub-divisions created for the collection of tax on land, a single *mahal*, or a cluster of *mahals*, having homogenous soil and climatic conditions was designated as a *dastur*.[40] A separate revenue code (*dastur-al-amal*) applied to each *dastur*. In a way, the *dasturs* may be seen as analogous to agricultural regions.

The regional structure of the Mughal empire may be reconstructed by tracing the extent and boundaries of the 12 major provinces (Fig. 3.4). The *subah* of Kabul extended over what is now northern and eastern Afghanistan as well as the North-Western Frontier Province of Pakistan. It also included the territories of Jammu and Kashmir, including the occupied parts of Kashmir and excluding Ladakh. The *Subah* of Lahor extended from the river Satluj to the Indus. It incorporated most of the province of Punjab, now in Pakistan, excluding the southern and the western parts. These southern and the western parts of Punjab constituted the *subah* of Multan. After the addition of Thattah (Sindh), *Subah* Multan extended from Ferozpur to the Indo-Afghan borders on the west and from the borders of Rajasthan (the territories of Jaisalmer and Bikaner) to Kachch and Mekran coast on the south.

The *subah* of Delhi lay to its east, extending from Satluj to the Yamuna near Palwal in Haryana and from Rewari to the Kumaon region of Uttar Pradesh. Virtually, Delhi incorporated almost the whole of what is now Haryana, National Capital Territory of Delhi, upper *doab*, Rohilkhand and the hilly districts of Uttar Pradesh. The *subah* of Agrah extended from Ghatampur, on the Ganga, west of Kanpur, to Palwal on the Yamuna and from Kanauj in western Uttar Pradesh to Shivpuri in Madhya Pradesh. The *subah* of Malwah, lying to the south of *subah* of Agrah, extended from Kali Sindh to the Aravallis and from Chanderi to the borders of Gujarat near Nandarbar. To the east of *subah* of Agrah lay the *subah* of Illahabad. Extending from Jaunpur, north of the Ganga, and from Kanpur, in the lower *doab*, to the borders of Behar, Illahabad incorporated the districts of the lower *doab* as well as the adjoining parts of Bundelkhand both in Uttar Pradesh and Madhya Pradesh. To its north lay

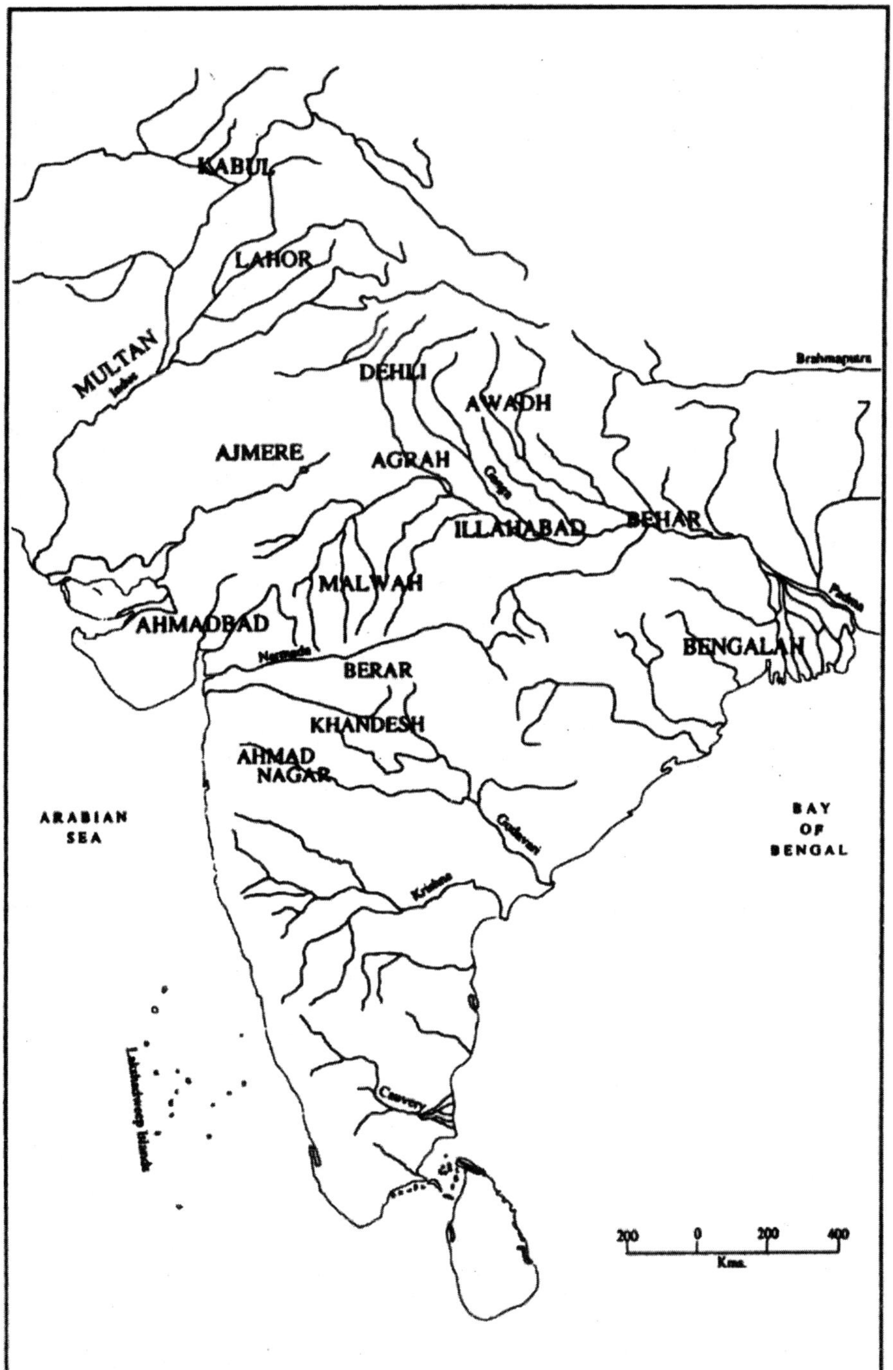

Figure 3.4 : Mughal Provinces, c. 1593 A.C.

the *Subah* of Awadh. Extending over the northern and eastern parts of the state of Uttar Pradesh, it stretched from Rohilkhand which was a part of the *Subah* of Dehli to the borders of Behar. The foothills of the Himalayas formed its northern boundary, while the southern boundary was coterminous with the *Subah* of Illahabad. The *Subah* of Behar, broadly speaking, corresponded with the present state of Bihar excluding the Chhotanagpur Plateau districts. To the east of Behar lay the *Subah* of Bengalah. It extended from Sylhet and Chittagong hills on the east to the borders of Behar in Garhi on the west and from the sea in the south to the foothills of the Himalayas in the north. The Mughal *Subah* of Bengalah thus incorporated the whole of what is now Bangladesh as well as the Indian state of West Bengal. The Province also included lowlands of Orissa incorporating the *Sarkars* of Jalesar, Bhadrak, Katak (Cuttack), Kaling Dandpat and Raj Mahendrih. *Ain* describes the land of the Tipperah tribes (now Tripura) as an adjoining territory lying to the east of the *Subah* of Bengalah.[41]

The *Subah* of Malwah comprised the western and the southern parts of the State of Madhya Pradesh. However, its eastern boundary was vaguely defined. On the east lay the Gond territory over which the Mughals had little authority. The *Subah* extended from Chanderi to Nandurbar. The *Subah* of Ahmadabad (Gujarat) extended from Burhanpur to Dwarka in Kathiawar and from Jalor to the port of Daman. Its extent and boundaries as described in the *Ain-e-Akbari* correspond admirably with the present state of Gujarat. The *Subah* of Ajmer virtually included the dependencies of Amber, Jodhpur, Bikaner, Jaisalmer and Sirohi. Its extreme limits were defined by the *Sarkar* of Ajmere in the northeast to Banswara in the southwest and from Pushkar in the east to the western boundary of Jaisalmer on the west. Mewar, comprising the *sarkars* of Chitor and Rantambhor, shown in the *Ain* as part of the *Subah* of Ajmere was, in fact, under the full control of Rajputs (Table 3.2).

Table 3.2 : Mughal Provinces and Sarkars

Subahs	*Sarkars*
Kabul	Kashmir, Pakli, Sawad (Swat), Daur-Banu-Isakhel, Qandahar, Kabul
Multan	Multan, Bhakkar, Thattah, Hajkan, Sewistan, Nasirpur, Chakarhalah
Lahor	Bet Jalandhar *doab*, Bari *doab*, Rechnau *doab*, Chenhat (Jech) *doab*, Sindh Sagar *doab*
Dehli	Dehli, Badaon, Kumaon, Sambhal, Saharanpur, Rewari, Hisar Firozah, Sirhind
Ajmere	Ajmere, Chitor, Rantambhor, Jodhpur, Sirohi, Nagor, Bikaner
Ahmedabad	Ahmedabad, Pattan, Nanded, Baroda, Broach, Champaner, Surat, Godhra, Sorath (Kathiawad)
Malwah	Ujjain, Raisin, Garha, Chanderi, Sarangpur, Bijagarh, Mando, Handiah, Nandarbar, Mandesor, Gagron, Kotri Parawa
Agrah	Agrah, Kalpi, Kanauj, Kol (Koil), Gwalior, Irij, Bayanwar, Narwar, Mandrael, Alwar, Tijarah, Narnol, Sahar
Illahabad	Illahabad (Allahabad), Ghazipur, Banaras, Jaunpur, Manikpur, Chanadah (Chanar), Bhathkhora, Kalinjar, Kurrah, Karah
Awadh	Awadh, Gorakhpur, Bahraich, Khairabad, Lakhnau
Behar	Behar, Mongher, Champaran, Hajipur, Saran, Tirhut, Rohtas
Bengalah	Udarnbar (Tanda), Jannatabad (Lakhnauti), Fathabad, Mahmudabad, Khalifatabad, Bakla, Purniyah, Tajpur, Ghoraghat, Pinjarah, Barbakabad, Bazuha, Sonargaon, Sylhet, Chittagong, Sharifabad, Sulaimanabad, Satgaon, Mandaran, Jalesar, Bhadrak, Katak (Cuttack), Kaling Dandpat, Raj Mahendrih

It may be interesting to examine the nature of correspondence between the *Janapadas* and the Mughal Provinces of the sixteenth century. While a broad concordance is there, it is understandable that the *Janapadas* expanded in space from their core areas to the periphery during the period of two millennia. The process of peopling continued with the result that the human occupence of land expanded. The extent and boundaries of the core regions also extended. In some regions, such as the Sapta Sindhva, where there were no political states as such, new territories emerged.

It may be noted that the Mughal *subah* of Dehli extended over the Kuru *janapada*. Agrah occupied the *janapadas* of Surasena and Panchala. Illahabad focused on Vatsa, and Awadh on Kosala. The *subah* of Behar was an amalgam of Malla, Vajji, Magadha and Anga *Janapadas*. The *Subah* of Bengalah represented a later extension of territory and occupied the Vanga *janapada*. However, Vanga was not mentioned in the *Angutra Nikaya*. The *subah* of Malwah occupied the Avanti *janapada*. In the northwest the *subah* of Kabul had grown out of the core *Janapadas* of Gandhara and Kamboja. The Moghul *subah* of Kabul was much larger and marked an outgrowth from the core region of Gandhara. In the process of expansion it embraced the territories of Jammu and Kashmir (Table 3.3).

Table 3.3 : Mughal Provinces and Sodasa Mahajanapadas

Subahs	*Capital City/Cities*	*Corresponding Janapada*
Kabul	Kabul	Gandhara-Kamboja
Multan	Multan	
Lahor	Lahor	
Dehli	Dehli	Kuru-Panchala
Ajmere	Ajmere	Matsya
Ahmedabad	Ahmedabad	
Malwah	Mandu	Avanti
Agrah	Agrah	Surasena-Panchala-Chedi
Illahabad	Illahabad	Vatsa-Chedi
Awadh	Faizabad/Lucknow	Kosala
Behar	Patna/Azimabad	Malla-Vajji-Magadha-Anga
Bengalah	Gaur	Vanga*
Khandesh	Burhanpur	
Berar	Daulatabad	Asmaka
Ahmadnagar	Ahmadnagar	

Note: *Vanga was not among the *sodasa mahajanapadas* as mentioned in the *Angutra Nikaya*. The colonisation of Bengal was a later development.

British Ascendency and its Impact

The British Ascendency in India which became evident with the transfer of *diwani* rights of Bengal and Bihar to the East India Company in the eighteenth century transformed the politico-administrative set-up of the country. Unlike the previous situation the British expansion started from the coastal areas thus giving the littoral region an importance unprecedented in Indian history. Initially, British power was based in the port centres, such as Bombay (now Mumbai), Madras (now Chennai) and Calcutta (now Kolkata). Of the three, Calcutta emerged like a colossus replacing the significance of traditional centres of power, such as Murshidabad, Agrah or Dehli. With the location of the capital at Calcutta started the process of concentration of political, administrative and financial institutions in and around the new port city. With this the heartland of Hindustan from Lahore to Patna and from Agra to Ujjain lost its former glory. It emerged as an hinterland of the port centre.

The impact of this process of marginalisation and underdevelopment has not yet been weakened even after half a century of independence. The British also created administrative divisions which had little relationship with the historically evolving ethno-lingual regions. They also imposed a dual administrative set-up of directly ruled provinces and the Indian princely states. Some of their provincial structures were very large. They were created in gross neglect of the ground realities.

The British Madras Presidency, for example, extended from southern Orissa to include coastal Andhra, parts of Tamil Nadu, Kerala and Coastal Karnataka. Likewise, the Bombay Presidency extended from Kathiawar and Gujarat to encompass parts of coastal and interior Maharashtra and Karnataka (Table 3.4).

Table 3.4 : British Provinces and Indian Princely States, c.1930

British Provinces	*Indian Princely States/Agencies*
Ajmer—Merwara	Rajputana Agency
Andaman and Nicobar Islands	
Assam	Assam
Baluchistan	Baluchistan States
Bengal Presidency	Bengal States
Bihar and Orissa	Bihar and Orissa States
Bombay Presidency	Bombay States
Burma	
Central Provinces and Berar	Central Provinces States, Central India Agency
Coorg	
Delhi	
Madras Presidency	Madras States Agency
North-west Frontier Province	North-West Frontier Province Agencies
Punjab	Punjab States, Punjab States Agency
United Provinces of Agra and Oudh	United Provinces States
	Gwalior State
	Hyderabad State
	Jammu and Kashmir State
	Mysore State
	Sikkim State
	Western India States Agency
	Baroda State

The National Government in India after independence was confronted with the colossal task of reorganisation of states on the ethno-lingual principle (Figs. 3.5a and 3.5b). However, the task of reorganisation of states is still incomplete. The ethno-lingual principle may be taken to its logical conclusion to satisfy the aspirations of minority language groups.

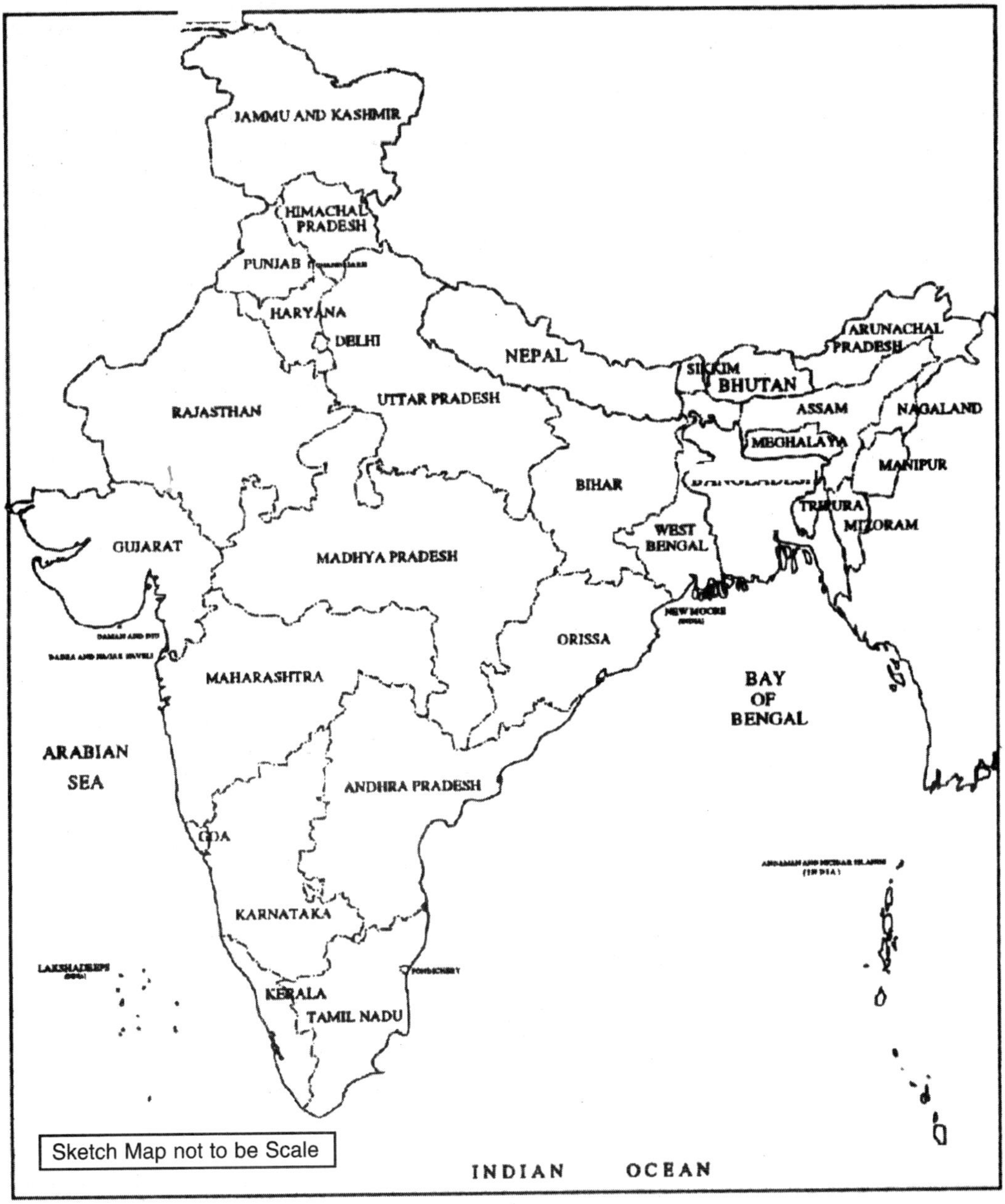

Figure 3.5a : States of the Indian Union, c. 1991

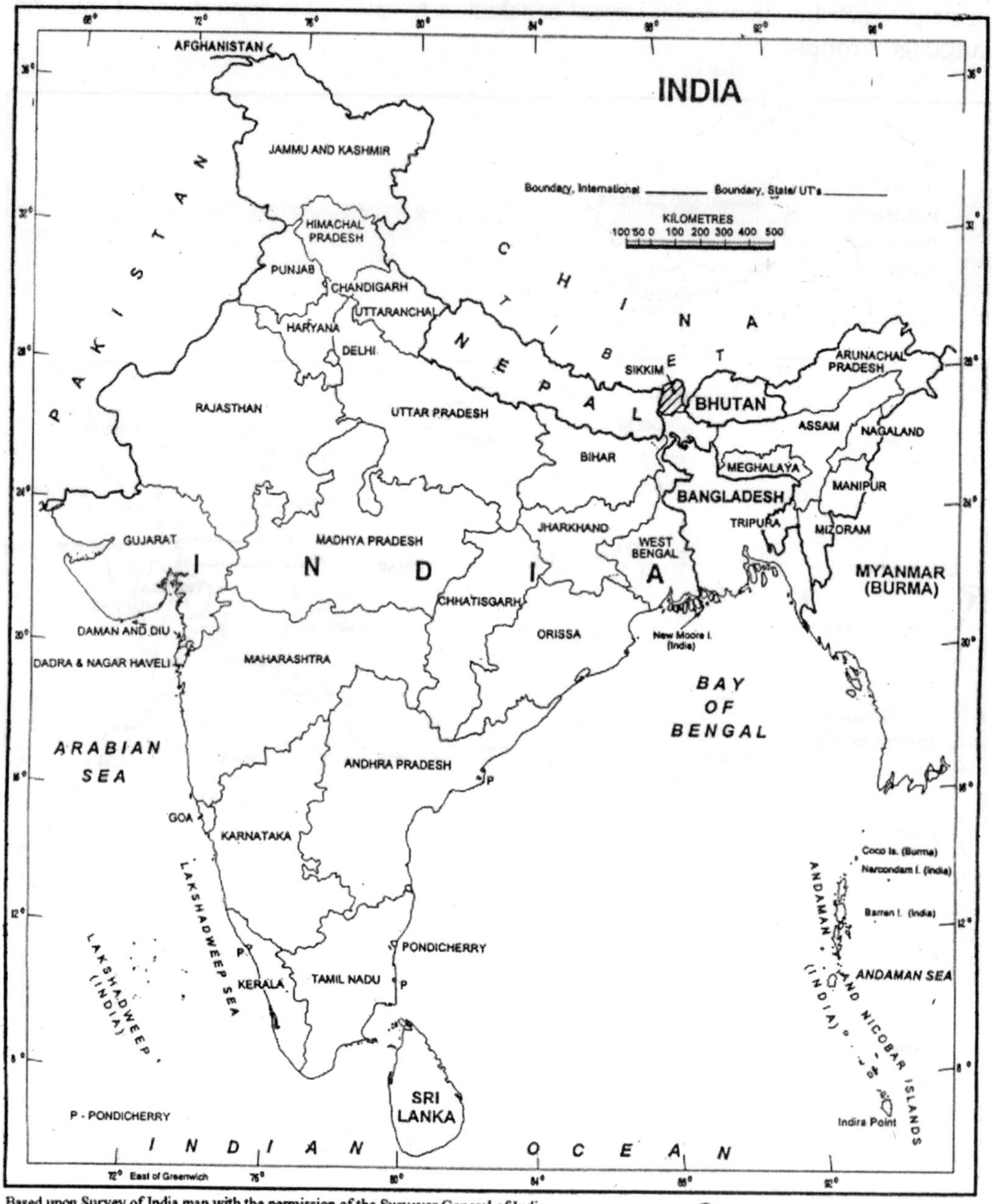

Based upon Survey of India map with the permission of the Surveyor General of India.

The territorial waters of India extend into the sea to a distance of twelve nautical miles measured from the appropriate base line.

The interstate boundaries between Arunachal Pradesh, Assam and Meghalaya shown on this map are as interpreted from the North-Eastern Areas (Reorganisation) Act, 1971 but have yet to be verified.

Figure 3.5b : States of the Indian Union, c. 2001

NOTES AND REFERENCES

1. An interesting aspect is the name of an imposing mountain range known as Hindu Kush. The very name is somewhat naive. The question is why this name? This mountain range of Afghanistan is the most challenging one for the travellers across the range. We looked for some historical records in order to trace its origin on the authority of Abul Fazal Allami. Its original name was Hindu Koh. This Mughal chronicle settles the issue of the derogatory nature of the name Hindu Kush. It appears that the travellers across the range have felt the nature of its nomenclature. Why is it known as Hindu Kush? My view is that the original name—Hindu Koh—was modified by the travellers and invaders who crossed the mountain range in their zest for conquering India changed the name to Hindu Kush. In my view it is high time the geographers and map makers adopt its original name which is Hindu Koh. The Survey of India should be asked to change the name in publications of maps, atlases and topographical sheets.
2. B. Subbarao, *The Personality of India*, Baroda: Oriental Institute, 1958, pp. 8-35.
3. F.J. Richards, 'Geographic Factors in Indian Archaeology', *Indian Antiquary*, Vol. LXII, 1933, pp. 231-43; R.E. Mortimer Wheeler, *Early India and Pakistan*; Walter A. Fairservis, *Roots of Ancient India*; B. Subbarao, *The Personality of India, op.cit.*; H.D. Sankalia, *Pre-and Proto-History of India and Pakistan, op. cit.*; Arnold J. Toynbee, *Between Oxus and Jumna*; K.M. Panikkar, *Geographical Factors in Indian History*, Bombay, 1955, *ibid., India and the Indian Ocean*, London, 1951; D.D. Kosambi, *The Culture and Civilization of Ancient India in Historical Outline*, 1972; also see, Bernard Cohn, 'India as a racial, linguistic and cultural area,' in *Introducing India in Liberal Education*, Chicago, 1957; and Lucien Febvre, *Geographical Introduction to History*, 1925.
4. See also Spate, *India and Pakistan*, p. 4; Spate described India as 'an intelligible isolate' geographically.
5. Spate noted that 'from a human point of view the values of the mountain wall are often determined as much by what lies beyond as by its own topography', *ibid.*, p. 4.
6. Holdich, *Gates of India*. See also Bridget and Raymond Allchin, *The Birth of Indian Civilization*, pp. 35-36.
7. B. Subbarao, *The Personality of India, op.cit.*, pp. 9-10.
8. Arnold J. Toynbee, *Between Oxus and Jumna, op.cit.*
9. It was not without reason that Akbar built a formidable fort at Attock.
10. The layout of this trans-continental migration route was first described by F.J. Richards, *op.cit.*
11. Subbarao, *op.cit.*, pp. 10-18.
12. 'Accepting this fundamental concept of areas of attraction, relative isolation and isolation, the whole pattern of development of material cultures in India may be defined as one of the horizontal expansion of the higher cultures, leading to a displacement, contraction and isolation of the lower cultures, in different parts of the country, and at different cultural levels', *ibid.*, p. 18. There are, however, serious difficulties in accepting such value-loaded terms as higher cultures and lower cultures. Although the context in which such differentiation is made is understandable.
13. For example, Bum La, Tse La and Tunga across the Himalayan range; Diphu, Kumjawng, Hpungan, Chaukam, Pangsau and More-Tamu across the Patkai range; An and Taungup across the Arakan Yoma (*cit.* M.Taher in Aijazuddin Ahmad (ed.), *Social Structure and Regional Development, op.cit.*, p. 201).
14. See also Sankalia, *Pre-history and Proto-history of India and Pakistan, op.cit.*
15. '... nuclear regions clearly represent the major agricultural areas, for the most part alluvial; intersecting them are arid, broken or jungly refuge areas...These are still the homes of the aboriginal tribes, and until the mergers of 1948 the great belt of country between Rajputana and Orissa as a major shatter-zone, a congeries of scores of semi-feudal states'. Spate, *op.cit.*, p. 178.

16. The boundary between Bangladesh and Tripura and Meghalaya follows the same principle. See also, Spate, *op.cit.*, pp. 178-79.
17. De terra and Paterson, *Ice Age in the Himalayas and the Associated Human Cultures*, 1939.
18. Subbarao, *op.cit.*; studies in the Alps helped the geologists to recognise four Ice Ages, *viz.*, Ginz, Mindel, Riss, and Wurm. The same model was largely applicable to the Himalayas, although Indian geologists suggested other glacial phases.
19. Subbarao, Sankalia, Allchin, *op.cit.*
20. The four types of tools are referred to as Abbevellian, Acheulean, Clactonian and Levalloisian after European archaeology.
21. Bridget and Raymond Allchin, *The Birth of Indian Civilization*, p. 78.
22. The word *teri* means a sanddune formed as a result of wind deposition in the coastal areas.
23. 'The Late Stone Age or Mesolithic industries of India must be associated with people much like the modern 'tribal' groups in more remote regions who live (or lived until less than a century ago) primarily by hunting and gathering, only sometimes augmenting this by trading with more advanced communities or by going out to work for them', Allchin, *op. cit.*, p. 95.
24. Even though the first Neolith—a ground or polished stone implement—was found as far back as 1842, even after 100 years we do not know much about the Neolithic culture or cultures of India, Allchin, *op. cit.*
25. Allchin, *op.cit.*, pp. 28-29.
26. S. Subbarao, *op.cit.*, p. 85.
27. Shereen Ratnagar, *Encounters: The Westerly Trade of the Harappan Civilization*, Delhi: Oxford University Press, 1981.
28. Gilund Culture, Sankalia, p. 194.
29. Sankalia, *op.cit.*, p. 203.
30. For the distribution of copper hoards in India, see Fig. 110 in Sankalia, *op. cit.*, p. 226.
31. Romila Thapar, *From Lineage to State*, Social Formations in the Mid-First Millennium B.C. in the Ganga Valley, Delhi: Oxford University Press, 1990.
32. Romila Thapar, *A History of India*, Vol. 1, Penguin Books, 1977, p. 50.
33. S.M. Ali, *The Geography of the Puranas*, Delhi: People's Publishing House, 1969, p. 134.
34. S.M. Ali, *op.cit.*
35. *Ain-e-Akbari*, Vol. II, Translated by Col. H.S. Jarrett and annotated by Sir Jadu Nath Sarkar, Calcutta: Royal Asiatic Society of Bengal, 1949.
36. Most of the Mughal provinces were named after the principal cities.
37. *Subah* or a province was the major administrative unit of the Mughals.
38. *Sarkar* was a sub-division of the *subah* and was comparable to the British districts. However, in many cases Mughal *sarkars* were larger than the British districts.
39. *Parganahs* were revenue sub-divisions. A *sarkar* consisted of several *parganahs*. It is interesting to note that while administrative changes came during the British period, the *parganah* as a basic revenue unit was retained as such. It continues to be the same even today.
40. The word *dastur* refers to a revenue sub-division broadly comparable to a *tahsil* or an aggregate of blocks.
41. *Ain-e-Akbari, op.cit.*, p. 130.

SUGGESTIONS FOR FURTHER READING

Ali, S.M. (1969): *The Geography of the Puranas*, Delhi: People's Publishing House.

Allchin, Bridget and Raymond (1968): *The Birth of Indian Civilization*, Penguin Books.

Panikkar, K.M. (1955): *Geographical Factors in Indian History*, Bombay.

Sankalia, H.D. (1962): *Pre-history and Proto-history of India and Pakistan*, Bombay: University of Bombay.

Subbarao, B. (1958): *The Personality of India*, Baroda: Oriental Institute.

Thapar, Romila (1977): *A History of India*, Vol. 1, Penguin Books.

4

Tribal Formation

From Tribe to Proletariat

Indian tribes have been living between two worlds: their own tribal world which is in transition and the new social order which opens up vistas for their transformation.

India today displays a very high degree of social and ethnic diversity. The population of India subsumes within it a multitude of caste and tribal groups representing different stages in the social evolution of the human kind. The social differentiation within each of these groups is no less impressive. Broadly speaking, the contemporary Indian society may be seen as comprising two mutually exclusive and differentiated social categories—a caste-based social order with an implicit social hierarchy, and a tribal segment by and large unstratified and egalitarian in both appearance and content. While centuries of shared history have facilitated and promoted interaction between the caste-based peasant society and the tribes in forms which are myriad, the two have retained their intrinsic characteristics, best manifested in ethnic consciousness, social organisation and modes of production. The word *tribe* in the Indian context, however, conveys a sense of meaning which evades clarity. Generally, it refers to a state of tribalism which is *ethnic* (ethnically defined) as well as *political* (revealing their definitional status as *Scheduled Tribes*). The underlying ambiguity and the adhocism of the scheduling policy through which a certain number of ethnically differentiated communities have been brought under the purview of a particular schedule of the Indian Constitution notwithstanding, the Indian tribes today appear to have reconciled themselves to the political reality of their times. In other words, there is a broad consensus among them on the issue of their identity as scheduled tribes.

Whatever may be the nature of the perceived reality, the issue of their definition as tribes remains an open question. Do the Indian *janajatis*—or the Scheduled Tribes as they are popularly referred to—conform to a set of scientifically defined criteria recognised by the anthropologists all over the world as the distinctive traits of a tribal social formation? There is no easy answer to this question. Perhaps there is no general agreement on the definition of tribe itself, although more agreeable position would be that they are *ethnic* tribes more than anything else. Most of them, if not all, have moved up from the state of primordial tribalism in the course of centuries of social evolution, punctuated by cultural contacts with peasant communities, themselves former tribes, who were gradually assimilated into the agrarian mode of production.

The numerical strength of the population of the Scheduled Tribes is highly impressive—84.33 millions—according to the latest census count in 2001. At the 2001 census the tribal population accounted for 8.2 per cent of the country's population. The tribal segment registered an increase during the 1991-2001 decade improving its share in the country's population from 7.95 per cent in 1991 to 8.2 per cent in 2001.[1] A population of 84.33 millions distributed over most of the states and the union territories is an immensity in itself. The tribes are far from homogenous in cultural traits, social organisation and modes of living. Not all segments of the population of Scheduled Tribes have been equally exposed to the dominant cultures of the regions in which they are living today. Furthermore, their responses to the processes of acculturation, modernisation or initiation into the democratic polity through the electoral process of public mobilisation have been far from homogenous. In fact, they reveal the highly heterogeneous character of the tribal segment itself.

On the theoretical plane it may be necessary to distinguish between the *tribes* as a category perceived on the basis of a classical tribal paradigm and the Scheduled Tribes of the modern Indian state. Developing the definition of a tribe according to the classical paradigm may also be necessary to remove some of the misgivings which are likely to exist on this subject. More so, because the induction of these groups into the schedule of the Indian Constitution creates situations which are grossly anomalous.

Tribe: A Social Formation

A few points may be highlighted here in order to develop some clarity on the basic issue of definition. It may be posited that the earliest social formation was a tribal formation. The Early Humans were dependent on their immediate surroundings. The environment offered them a variety of choices—food in the form of foliage, seeds, fruits, tubers and roots, and in the form of animals and the fish by and large. Their survival depended on food gathering and collection from the forest which was by and large bountiful although food surplus dwindled with the change of seasons. This necessitated a rhythmic movement of the food-gathering groups from one part of the territory to the other, depending on the natural cycles of reproduction. Recurrent scarcities of water and the forest fires also forced these groups to remain on the move all the time. They were organically linked to their environment and lived in complete harmony with Nature. The physical features of the terrain—rivers, hill ranges and the plateau spurs or escarpments—sometimes imposed natural limits on their movement. Gradually, their long stay in an area resulted in their association with it and slowly they developed a consciousness about their social domain, howsoever vaguely defined the domain was. Incursions, or even organised infiltration into the domain of neighbouring groups, often led to internecine wars, which further reinforced the idea of a social domain with a boundary, howsoever vaguely defined it was. Time and again random movements of stronger groups in search of food and new lands led to the violation of boundaries and resulted in clashes. The weaker groups were driven away or taken over by stronger groups. These internecine, inter-tribal, conflicts must have led to the need for an effective control of the territory on which the group subsisted.

The ancient hunters and the food-gatherers organised themselves in groups based on the extended kinship principle. As it happens in such situations, age commanded respect. Being the children of a remote ancestor, they were related to each other in blood. An elderly person, often a male, enjoyed authority over the rest of the group—men and women—and this promoted a semblance of internal cohesion. There were no gender differences as there was no division of labour as such and the group functioned on the basis of natural instincts. Women and children were collectively looked after and the old and the sick must have been exempted from the daily rigmarole of food collection. With growth in population the group expanded in size and with it the territory expanded and the tribal chief became an important instrument in maintaining internal cohesion (social order) and harmony, and in organising effective defence in the midst of external threats. It may be postulated that despite the commanding status, the institution of tribal chief did not disturb the egalitarian character of the group. Living in the midst of the forest and at a level of equilibrium with Nature, it was necessary for the group to survive with limited needs. Since, the group did not generate any wealth, no inequality in its distribution could be imagined. Emergence of the private family and the gender-based division of labour must have been later developments in history.

The tribes evolved a simple technology to deal with the natural situations. Tools for digging, cutting and chopping were the immediate needs and stone hand-axes, chopper-chopping tools and cleavers helped them wage their struggle for survival. Spears with stone blades and bow and arrow would have been the natural response to a situation in which they became more and more dependent on animals and birds for their food requirements. They crossed the rivers on rafts and caught fish with straw nets. Anthropologists have discovered evidence of the primitive tools and techniques which were commonly employed by the ancient hunters in their studies of the modern tribes in Africa, Latin America and South and Southeast Asia. Sophistication in tool-making techniques came as the struggle for survival intensified, and the transition from food gathering to food production economies progressed at the snail's pace.

The primitive tools, based on stone cores or flakes, unitary or composite when stone was combined with wood or bones of animals, constituted the material culture of this tribal society. Since settlement on land was not necessitated by circumstances, huts must have emerged much later and only when pioneer villages dotted the level plains in the beginning of the Neolithic revolution. Witch-craft, magical forms, spirit worship and group-dancing became necessary elements of early tribal cultures. Of course, propitiation of spirits was a common ritual practice. Spirits of the remote or the immediate ancestors were recalled and worshipped to obviate the impact of evil spirits. A system of magic and ritualistic group dancing was closely associated with these practices which were often related to birth, death, celebration of victory or commemorating occasions of collective achievement and pride. Drums which were used for driving wild animals to a vantage point were concomitant to such ritual exercises. Many societies which were not familiar with bow and arrow could not develop stringed musical instruments, and only drums sufficed their needs. In societies where stringed instruments came early, diverse forms of folk music were widely developed.

This social formation has certain basic distinguishing traits. The social organisation is simple, without any stratified or hierarchical social order. Wealth and its private ownership is an alien concept. Land and its resources are shared collectively and operations to appropriate them are collective and not individual. This gave birth to the communitarian mode of ownership of resources, including land. There were social mechanisms of defence against external and internal threats. Hunting expeditions and internecine wars were collectively organised. The tribal headman, a chieftain, played a commanding role in such operations and in forging internal cohesion and harmony. With a primitive technology on its command, the group could survive at a low level of equilibrium with Nature. The blind forces of Nature which were cruel and unpredictable often filled the heart with fear for the unknown and the invisible. Magic and propitiation of spirits seemed to be the only recourse. The group sought strength from its totems, both animal and floral, and guarded them zealously.

Obviously, no society could afford to stay at that level of equilibrium with Nature forever. An upward mobility along the ladder of social evolution was as natural as anything else crucial to their existence. However, in terms of social evolution, tribal groups did not display a uniform pattern anywhere in the world. In fact, change was often painstakingly slow. There were phases when change was endogenous and so much so that it transformed the social groups. Equally importantly, there were phases when contact with other cultures (out-groups) opened up the tribal societies and paved the way for their social and cultural transformation. Such episodes of exogenetic change appear to be more numerous and all-embracing in their impact.

Evolving a Definition

While evolving a definition of the term tribe, Andre Beteille noted the conventional lack of interest of the sociologists and social anthropologists in a clear definition. They were more concerned with 'facts' which were relevant to a discussion on tribes rather than in a definition. In his view, a rigid and clear-cut definition was a fruitless exercise. However, he argued that a 'clarity of concepts' was a necessary step towards a scientific study of the tribes.[2]

What are the elements of a scientific definition? Conventional anthropology treated all people as tribes who were *backward* in one sense or the other, lived in the remote, inaccessible areas—backward areas as such—and were pre-literates (not familiar with the art of writing). Anthropologists' encounters with such people (who could be easily differentiated from other people in relatively advanced areas) such as Australians, Malenesian and North American aborigines also helped them discover other traits—that they were racially different and lived through history in a state of isolation. Evidently, such a description did not fully encompass the tribal communities of Africa and India. These groups, although perceived as tribes, did not correspond to the traits of a paradigmatic tribal identity. Moreover, their links with other people, different from them, had deep historical roots and they shared with them a cultural heritage which displayed a remarkable fusion of traits—tribal as well as not-so-tribal. Most of these groups, particularly in India, lived in close proximity to other groups not identified as tribes. The Indian situation, therefore, complicated further the problem of defining a tribe (Box 4.1).

Box 4.1 : Definition of Tribe

We have described the tribe as a society with a political, linguistic, and a somewhat vaguely-defined cultural boundary; further, as a society based upon kinship, where social stratification is absent. Now it has to be emphasised that like so many definitions of social categories, this also is the definition of an ideal type. If we make a classification of societies, they will arrange themselves in a continuum. In many of these, stratification and differentiation will be present, but only in an incipient manner. The exact point along which one should draw the line between tribal and more advanced societies will, in a sense, have to be arbitrarily decided... In India, we cannot have a readymade definition with which one can go into the field and locate a tribe. The greatest emphasis has to be placed on a historical perspective. The process by which tribes have been transformed is a historical process. And only by going into the antecedents of a group can we say with any confidence whether or not it should be considered as a tribe.

—Andre Beteille, *Tribe, Caste and Religion*, 1977: 13-14.

Andre Beteille thought that a definition, if at all to be evolved on the theoretical level, should take into account "a particular mode of human grouping" in which many tribes were living in different parts. This empirical world reality was an important consideration. According to him *mode of human grouping* reminiscent of a *stage in social evolution* appeared to be the two essential elements in a definition.

'A tribe is in an ideal state, a self-contained unit. It constitutes a society in itself.'[3]

In defining a society he followed Nadel's conceptualisation: a society is constituted by people who belong to it or do not belong to it and by virtue of this belonging they bind themselves together to a code or rules, regulations, social practices and norms which determine their actions affecting their life and the life of others in the same group. By implication, societies have *boundaries* within which economic and social interaction may be most frequent and common. These boundaries have often been defined on the basis of political, linguistic and cultural criteria. The concept of political organisation is, however, confusing as tribal view of a *government* and a *territory* is often at variance with the common view.[4]

Nomenclature[5]

India's tribal world is diverse and ethnically differentiated. A careful perusal of the tribal lists published by the official agencies shows that there are at least 285 different communities living in different regions of the country in their own specific ecosystems. The tribal communities are not generally familiar with each other, except those living in the immediate neighbourhood. Seen in this context, the term 'scheduled tribe' is a generalisation. It glosses over the underlying heterogeneity. It is an imperative of social geographical research to take stock of the existing tribal communities, and place them in their proper spatial/regional context. To begin with, let us review the multiplicity of tribal names as in vogue in different regions of the country today to be able to reach the minimum clarity.

Anthropological perceptions differ and it is not easy to establish the ground truth about the names by which tribes are known in different parts of India[6]. Official lists published by the census commissioners in different states add to the already prevailing confusion. While it is understandable that the census commissioners who were assigned with the task of enumerating the tribes in their states collected and compiled data according to their own perception of the tribal nomenclature as perceived in the linguistic context of their state, there was no reason why they should not have been asked to exercise caution in checking the veracity of the lists and avoid repetition. In many cases sub-tribes have been given an equal status, thus adding to the multiplicity of tribes endlessly. For example, the Madhya Pradesh list mentions Bhil under the following categories: (a) Bhils, (b) Bhilala, (c) Bhils and Bhilalas including Barela, Patelia and other sub-tribes, and (d) Bhil-Mina. If the list itself is so confusing, how can one expect that the census investigators would be recording the information correctly without mixing up the categories provided to them in the official lists?

The story is no different in Maharashtra, Gujarat and Rajasthan. A comparative view is presented in Table 4.1 below:

Table 4.1 : Sub-tribes listed under the Bhils

Madhya Pradesh	*Maharashtra*	*Rajasthan*
(a) Bhil	(a) Bhil	(a) Bhil
(b) Bhilala	(b) Bhil including Bhil-Garasia, Dholi-Bhil, Mewasi-Bhil, Rawal-Bhil, Tadvi-Bhil, Bhagalia, Bhilala, Pawra, Vasava and Vasave	(b) Bhil including Bhil-Garasia, Dholi-Bhil, Dungri-Garasia, Mewasi Bhil Rawal-Bhil, Tadvi-Bhil, Bhagalia, Bhilala Pawra, Vasava and Vasave
(c) Bhils and Bhilalas including Barela, Patelia and other sub-tribes		
(d) Bhil-Mina		

Source: Table compiled by the author.

Likewise, the Rajasthan list mentions Garasias separately including Rajput-Garasias. On the other hand, the Maharashtra list mentions Vasava and Vasave separately who have been bracketed with Gamit or Gamta or Gavit including Mavchi, Padvi, Vasava, Vasave or Valvi. When Rajasthan, Gujarat and Maharashtra lists show Tadvi, Tetaria and Valvi along with the Dhankas as separate ethnic groups, the confusion is further confounded.

The West Bengal list shows Mahli and Mahali as separate categories. The Orissa list shows Munda as well as Mundari separately; other sub-tribes such as Munda-Lohara or Munda-Mahali are also bracketed with Munda. The Tamil Nadu list shows Muthuvan and Muduvan separately, while they are the same tribe.

Language Variations

Much of the confusion arises from the language variations. Tribes belong to different language worlds and their names are naturally differently pronounced in different states. Similarly, their names as pronounced in tribal dialects vastly differ. A few examples given in Table 4.2 below illustrate this point:

Table 4.2 : Language Variations in Tribal Names

Tribes	*State*	*Tribes*	*State*
Arandan	Kerala	Arandan	Tamil Nadu
Binjhia	Bihar	Binjhia or Binjhoa	Orissa
Chenchu	Andhra Pradesh	Chenchwar[1]	Karnataka
Chero	Bihar and West Bengal	Chiru	Manipur
Karku	Madhya Pradesh	Korku[2]	Maharashtra
Korwa	Bihar	Korua	Orissa
Kuruba	Karnataka	Kurumba	Kerala
Munda	Bihar	Munda or Munda Lohara or Munda Mahalis	Orissa
Saharia[3]			
Sawar[4]			
Waghri[5]			

Source: Table compiled by the author.

Notes:
1. Not mentioned in the Orissa list.
2. Korku includes Bopchi, Mouasi, Nihal or Nahul, and Bondhi or Bondeya. Nihal is listed as a separate tribe in Maharashtra.
3. Also spelt as Saharia, Seheria, Sosia, Sor, Seharia.
4. There are other variants such as Saora, Savara, Savar, Saura, Sawar, Sawara.
5. Also spelt as Wagri.

There is no dearth of such examples and one can cite many such anomalies in tribal lists. However, these inter-state variations in nomenclature and classification have serious policy implications. Moreover, they lead to serious distortions in understanding the tribal reality.

Scheduling Anomalies

Tribal communities have been scheduled under varied contexts. This has resulted in serious anomalies. Many a times the states have treated Scheduled Tribes and Scheduled Castes as mutually interchangeable categories. A few examples given in Appendix IV.2 reveal the regional implications of such anomalies in scheduling (*see* also Appendix IV.3).

Geographical Distribution by States and Union Territories

Since the tribes display a high tendency of clustering and concentration in the hilly and the forested tracts of the country, they are highly unevenly distributed. On the basis of relief, the States and the Union Territories may be grouped into two categories: (a) those characterised by rugged topography, and (b) those with an open relief, (plains and river valleys). The tribes are heavily concentrated in the former and not in the latter. For example, Punjab, Haryana, Chandigarh, Delhi and Uttar Pradesh, which lie over the Indo-Gangetic Plain and have a rich agricultural base, belong to the second category. They have either no tribal population or else the numerical strength of tribal population is negligible. The tribes are mostly concentrated in the hilly districts of Uttaranchal. Likewise, the tribes are either non-existent or their population is negligible over the plains of Bihar and West Bengal. On the other hand, tribes have a strong presence in the plateau region of southern Bihar, now known as Jharkhand. They are also predominant in the hilly districts of northern West Bengal as well as over the plateau districts of the state bordering Bihar and Jharkhand. Assam, despite being an extension of the North Indian Plain, supports a large chunk of tribal population. In fact, every eighth Assamese is a tribal. The southern states of Kerala, Karnataka, Tamil Nadu and Andhra Pradesh lie mostly in the plateau region and yet the population of tribes in these states is not very large. It varies from 1 per cent in Tamil Nadu to 6.6 per cent in Andhra Pradesh. The tribes are, however, numerically strong in the central Indian states from Gujarat and Maharashtra to Orissa, Chhattisgarh and Jharkhand. Among them Chhattisgarh has the highest proportion of tribal population, *i.e.*, 31.87 per cent of the state's population followed by Jharkhand (26.3 per cent), Gujarat (14.8 per cent), Rajasthan (12.6 per cent) and West Bengal (5.5 per cent).[7]

The Indian tribes display a very high degree of ethnic diversity both in their racial composition and the dialectal and linguistic affinity. The fact that the Scheduled Tribes include as many as 285 different communities is an important index of their ethnic diversity. No less impressive is the pattern of their spatial distribution. It has been commonly observed that the tribes reveal strong tendencies of clustering and concentration in the hilly, forested and the geographically inaccessible tracts of the country. This leads to the following two broad generalisations:

(a) either the tribes have generally preferred to live in areas which are by and large unfavourable to sedentary agriculture; or
(b) they have been pushed into these enclaves by the peasant groups. Today their way of life, including mode of economy, is intrinsically linked with the ecological base of their present habitat.

The northeastern states stand out as a category in themselves as the population in these states is predominantly tribal, although the numerical strength of tribes is not very large. Tribal proportion is particularly high in Mizoram, Nagaland and Meghalaya (85 to 95 per cent) and significantly high in Arunachal Pradesh (64 per cent). On the other hand, about one-third of the population in Tripura and Manipur consists of tribes. The share of tribal population is overwhelmingly large in certain Union Territories, such as Dadra and Nagar Haveli and Lakshadweep. On the contrary, the proportion of tribes in the population of Andaman and Nicobar Islands is insignificant (Tables 4.3a and 4.3b).

Evidently, tribal communities have either by their own choice favoured concentration in inhospitable environment, or conversely the peasant societies have pushed them and confined them to these enclaves thus having free access to the potentially rich land suited pre-eminently to the agricultural pursuits. This, by and large, mutual exclusivity of the tribal and the peasant modes is an important attribute of spatial distribution of social categories in India.

Table 4.3a : Distribution of Scheduled Tribes, 1991

State/Union Territory	*Tribal Population*	*Rank*	*Tribal Percentage*	*Rank*
India	**67,758, 380**		**8.01**	
States				
Andhra Pradesh	4,199,481	7	6.31	19
Arunachal Pradesh	550,351	17	63.66	6
Assam	2,874,441	9	12.82	17
Bihar	6,616,914	4	7.66	18
Goa	376	—	0.03	27
Gujarat	6,161,775	5	14.92	13
Haryana*	—	—	—	—
Himachal Pradesh	218,349	20	4.22	23
Karnataka	1,915,691	10	4.26	22
Kerala	320,967	18	1.10	24
Madhya Pradesh	15,399,034	1	23.27	9
Maharashtra	7,318,281	2	9.27	16
Manipur	632,173	15	34.41	7
Meghalaya	1,517,927	11	85.53	4
Mizoram	653,565	14	94.75	1
Nagaland	1,060,822	12	87.73	3
Orissa	7,032,214	3	22.21	11
Punjab*	—	—	—	—
Rajasthan	5,474,881	6	12.44	12
Sikkim	90,901	22	22.36	10
Tamil Nadu	574,194	16	1.03	25
Tripura	853,345	13	30.95	8
Uttar Pradesh	287,901	19	0.21	26
West Bengal	3,808,760	8	5.60	20
Union Territories				
Andaman & Nicobar Islands	26,770	24	9.54	15
Chandigarh*	—	—	—	—
Dadra and Nagar Haveli	109,380	21	78.99	5
Daman and Diu	11,724	25	11.54	14
Delhi*	—	—	—	—
Lakshadweep	48,163	23	93.15	2
Pondicherry*	—	—	—	—

Source: Computed by the author; Census of India, 1991, Series-1, India, Part II-B (i), Vol. 1, *Primary Census Abstract, General Population.*

Note: * No tribal Population.

Table 4.3b : Distribution of Scheduled Tribes, 2001

State/Union Territory	*Tribal Population*	*Proportion of ST Population (%)*
India	**84,326,240**	**8.2**
States		
Andhra Pradesh	5,024,104	6.6
Arunachal Pradesh	705,158	64.2
Assam	3,308,570	12.4
Bihar	758,351	0.9
Chhattisgarh	6,616,596	31.8
Goa	566	0.0
Gujarat	7,481,160	14.8
Haryana	—	—
Himachal Pradesh	244,587	4.0
Jammu and Kashmir	1,105,979	7.6
Jharkhand	7,087,068	26.3
Karnataka	3,463,986	6.6
Kerala	364,189	1.1
Madhya Pradesh	12,233,474	20.3
Maharashtra	8,577,276	8.9
Manipur	741,141	34.2
Meghalaya	1,992,862	85.9
Mizoram	839,310	94.5
Nagaland	1,774,026	89.1
Orissa	8,145,081	22.1
Punjab	—	—
Rajasthan	7,097,706	12.6
Sikkim	111,405	20.6
Tamil Nadu	651,321	1.0
Tripura	993,426	31.1
Uttaranchal	256,129	3.0
Uttar Pradesh	107,963	0.1
West Bengal	4,406,794	5.5
Union Territories		
Andaman and Nicobar Islands	29,469	8.3
Chandigarh	—	—
Dadra and Nagar Haveli	137,225	62.2
Daman and Diu	13,997	8.8
Delhi	—	—
Lakshadweep	57,321	94.5
Pondicherry	—	—

Source: Census of India, 2001, Series 1, *Primary Census Abstract, Total Population*, Table A-5.

District-level Distribution

In order to explore the question further one may look into the distribution of tribal population at the level of the district. While the district is not an adequate unit to analyse the spatial patterns of clustering and concentration of tribal population, there is no gainsaying the fact that it is the most significant reference unit from the viewpoint of political administration and policy implementation. However, the inadequacy of the district as a unit of reference arises from the following grounds: First, the British administration created the districts on an *ad hoc* basis, giving highest consideration to strategic factors and ignoring the ground realities, such as the terrain features, distribution of natural resources and the concentration of ethnic and cultural groups. The district boundaries were even more unrealistic in the hilly and the forested tracts of the mid-Indian region where the tribes were heavily concentrated. Secondly, the districts were created as a result of a policy of political bargaining between the British and the local claimants to power who cooperated with the British in their expansionist policy and whom they wanted to reward for their services. The directly-administered British districts and the territories of princely states were interspersed in a confusing manner.

The tribes were heavily concentrated in the hilly tracts while the intervening valleys were occupied by the peasants of non-tribal origin through a process of systematic spill-over. Thirdly, the Indian administration after independence did not alter the district boundaries much, despite the states reorganisation, implying the merger of the princely states with the larger state structures that were created in the mid-fifties.

The net result is that the reality of tribal distribution is suppressed unless the unit of reference is lower than the district; say a *tahsil, taluka* or an *anchal*. However, as noted earlier, whatever the limitations of this exercise, a district-level study of the distribution of tribal population cannot be dismissed as futile. While considering the proportion of tribal population in the total district population, it was noted by Raza and Ahmad[8] that the following percentage categories were statistically critical for grouping the data:

80-100 per cent	:	Dominant
50-80	:	Highly Important
20-50	:	Important
10-20	:	Significant
1-10	:	Unimportant
Below 1 per cent	:	Negligible

This interpretation of the district-level patterns is based on the census data. The fact that the tribes reveal a very strong tendency of concentration and clustering in enclaves in which they are in absolute majority is further borne out by the district-level data (Figs. 4.1a and 4.1b). It may be noted that more than a quarter of the total tribal population lives in 51 districts in which they have an absolute majority (Fig. 4.2). These districts have within their confines as many as 18.33 million tribes. Another 23.35 million tribes are bracketed in the 20-50 per cent category distributed over 47 districts. This category of districts alone accounts for 34.46 per cent of the tribal population. On the other end of the scale are 266 districts in which tribal presence is statistically insignificant, *i.e.*, it is below 10 per cent (Fig. 4.3). Some 13 million tribes live in districts in which the district administration, exceptions apart, may not be particularly conscious of their presence (Tables 4.4a and 4.4b).

Table 4.4a : Tribal Population as Percentage of District Population, 1991 : A Synoptic All-India View

Status	*% Category*	*No. of Districts*	*Tribal Population in the Category*	*% of All-India Tribal Population*	*Cumulative Tribal Population*	*Cumulative Percentage*
Nil		36	Nil	—	—	—
Negligible	less than 1	136	620,533	0.916	620,533	0.916
Unimportant	1-5	87	5,476,040	8.082	6,096,573	8.097
	5-10	43	7,266,074	10.723	13,362,647	19.721
Significant	10-20	52	12,705,931	18.752	26,068,578	38.473
Important	20-50	47	23,353,572	34.466	49,422,150	72.939
Highly Important	50-80	27	14,021,329	20.693	63,443,479	93.632
Dominant	80-100	24	4,314,901	6.368	67,758,380	100.000
Total		452	67,758,380	100.000	—	—

Source: Based on the 1991 Census.

Table 4.4b : Districts Classified by Proportion of Tribal Population, 2001

Percentage Category	*No. of Districts*
60.01and Above	57
40.01-60.00	31
20.01-40.00	52
10.01-20.00	69
0.01-10.00	323
Negligible	11
No Scheduled Tribes	50
Total	593

Source: Census of India, 2001, *Primary Census Abstract, Total Population*, Series 1, Table A-5.
Notes: (i) Classification of data for all 593 districts of India.
(ii) No tribes have been scheduled for Haryana, Punjab, Chandigarh and Pondicherry.

It may be observed that the tribes are conspicuous by their absence in 36 districts mostly lying over the North Indian Plain. As noted earlier, the states of Punjab, Haryana, and the Union Territory of Chandigarh as well as the National Capital Territory of Delhi have no Scheduled Tribes as such. This is anomalous. They may be found there as in migrants but not recognised as Scheduled Tribes. The other states of the North Indian Plain, *viz.*, Uttar Pradesh, northern and central parts of Bihar generally follow the same pattern with tribal share in population being negligible — less than 1 per cent.

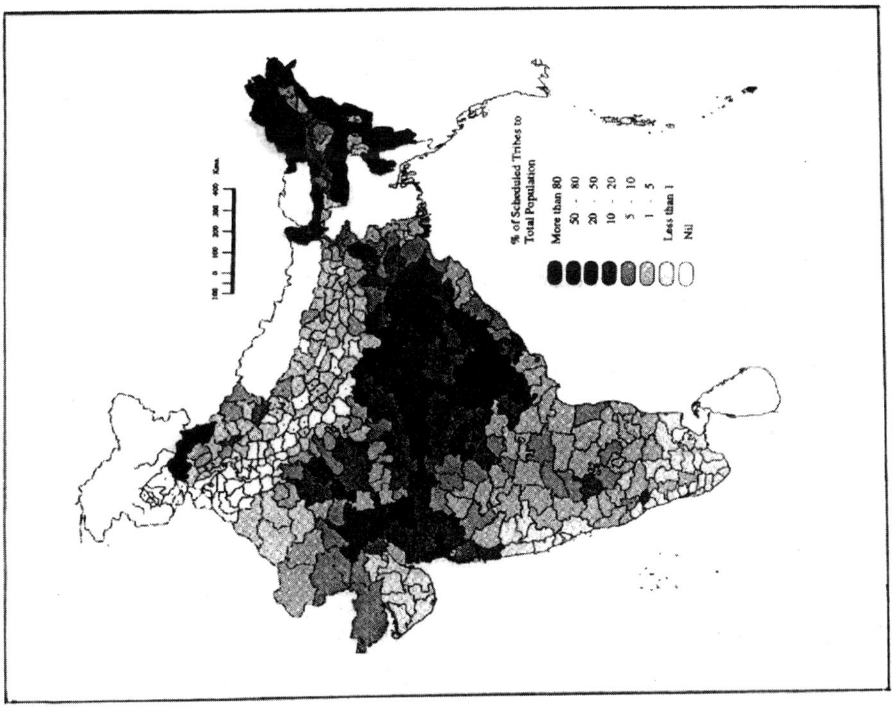

Figure 4.1 a : Scheduled Tribes, 1991
(district-level distribution patterns)

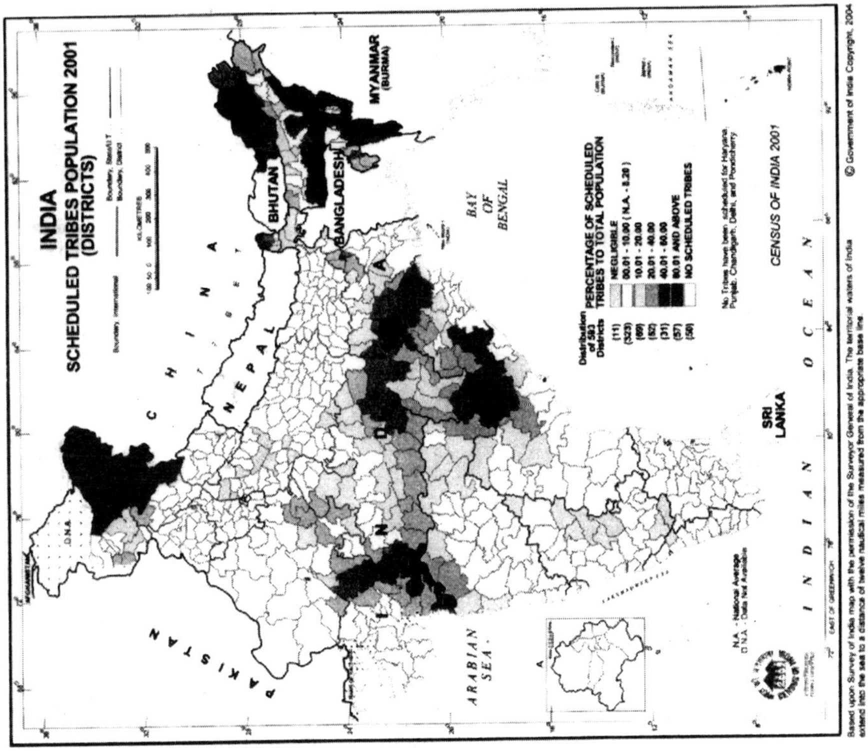

Figure 4.1b : Scheduled Tribes, 2001
(district-level distribution patterns)

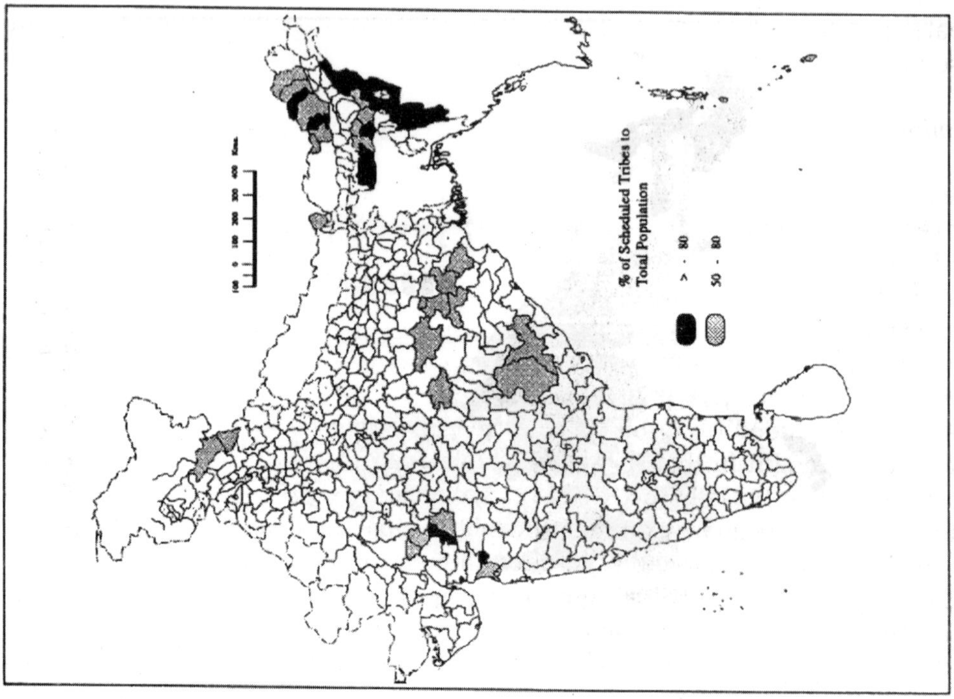

Figure 4.2 : Scheduled Tribes, 1991 (Location of districts in which the tribal proportion is more than 50 %)

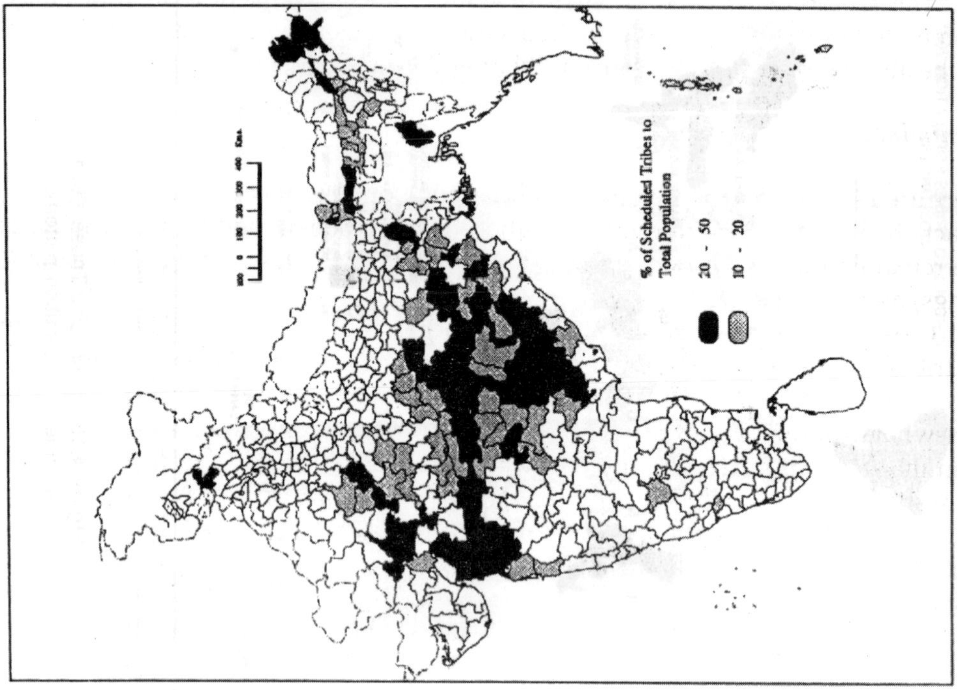

Figure 4.3 : Scheduled Tribes, 1991 (Location of districts in which the tribal constitute 10-50 % of the district population)

This would mean that over most of Uttar Pradesh groups or individuals may be enumerated as tribes, even though their status may be of in migrants. This is also true for the alluvial plains of the states of Bihar and West Bengal.

Dominance and Dispersion

There are 24 districts in which the tribal share in population is overwhelmingly large; in fact, the tribes are in a dominant position. Twenty-one of them lie in the northeast. The remaining three districts are situated in Madhya Pradesh (Jhabua), Gujarat (the Dangs) and Lakshadweep.

Closer to these districts of high dominance is another set of 27 districts in which the tribes have a majority in the district population, *i.e.*, 50-80 per cent. Many of them are contiguous to the districts of the first category. The geographical distribution is somewhat different. For example, 14 of them are situated outside the northeast. They lie in the states of Bihar, Orissa, Madhya Pradesh, Rajasthan, Gujarat and Himachal Pradesh as well as in the Union Territories of Dadra and Nagar Haveli and the Andaman and Nicobar Islands. These districts include Dadra and Nagar Haveli (UT), Lahaul and Spiti (Himachal Pradesh), Banswara (Rajasthan), Gumla (Jharkhand), Bastar (Chhattisgarh), Dungarpur (Rajasthan), Nicobars (UT), Mandla (Madhya Pradesh), Mayurbhanj (Orissa), Lohardaga (Jharkhand), Kinnaur (Himachal Pradesh), Pashchimi Singhbhum (Jharkhand), Valsad (Gujarat), Koraput (Orissa), Sarguja (Chhattisgarh), Dhar (Madhya Pradesh) and Sundargarh (Orissa).

Together these 51 districts share among themselves 27 per cent of the country's tribal population. These tribal majority districts outside the tribal states of the northeast deserve special reference.

Dominance and State Formation

The spatial patterns of concentration lead to interesting conclusions. More than 80 per cent of the country's tribal population is concentrated in the mid-Indian states of Madhya Pradesh, Chhattisgarh, Jharkhand, Orissa, West Bengal, Rajasthan, Gujarat, Maharashtra and Andhra Pradesh. None of these states has any special provision for the tribal participation in the politico-administrative set-up. As compared to this, the seven north-eastern states of Assam, Meghalaya, Arunachal Pradesh, Nagaland, Manipur, Mizoram and Tripura have just 12 per cent of the country's tribal population. If Assam is excluded from this list, we are left with just 7.7 per cent of the country's total tribal strength in the remaining six states of the northeast. The north-eastern tribes, other than those living in Assam, enjoy political power as states were created in the North-east primarily on the principle of tribal dominance. The national policy, it appears, helped substantially in the fulfilment of the tribal aspiration to political authority. However, the tribal right to participate in governance was often treated as an adjunct of the border problem. Understandably, it was difficult to delink it from the larger question of national security in a sensitive border area. On the other hand, a majority of the Indian tribes who live in the mid-Indian states did not enjoy this privilege. In fact, three major tribal groups *viz.*, the Santals, Gonds and the Bhils, lie divided among the several states of the mid-Indian region, with the state boundaries cutting across the traditional tribal territories. For example, the Santals lie divided between Jharkhand, West Bengal and Orissa; the Gonds between Madhya Pradesh, Chhattisgarh, Orissa, Andhra Pradesh and Maharashtra; and the Bhils between Rajasthan, Madhya Pradesh, Chhattisgarh, Gujarat and Maharashtra. As the things stand today there is no case for statehood for the Gonds, Bhils and the Santals.

Rural-urban Composition

Tribes are mostly a rural phenomenon. This is evident from the fact that about 93 per cent of the tribal population lives in rural areas as in 1991. Jharkhand is closest to this national average. States which lie above the national average include Uttar Pradesh, Arunachal Pradesh, Orissa, West Bengal, Madhya Pradesh, Chhattisgarh, Rajasthan, Kerala, Assam, Himachal Pradesh and Tripura. The tribes of Tripura are almost wholly rural as 98 per cent of their population is concentrated in villages. This high rural proportion shows that the tribes are mostly engaged in primary economic activity and they are naturally located in the rural areas. On the other end of the scale is Mizoram with only about one-half of its tribal population being rural. The tribal population in Tamil Nadu, Nagaland, Maharashtra, Meghalaya and Karnataka is largely rural with the rural proportion ranging between 85 and 87 per cent. It is only in Mizoram that the tribes have been significantly drawn into the urban way of life.

Even though the proportion of urbanised tribes is low in general, their numerical strength is sizeable — more than five million as in 1991. About one-half of this population was living in the cities and towns of Maharashtra, Madhya Pradesh, Chhattisgarh, Gujarat and Jharkhand alone.

In terms of the numerical strength of urban tribes, Maharashtra holds the first rank, followed by Madhya Pradesh, Chhattisgarh, Gujarat and Jharkhand. Then, there is the case of northeastern states where, as in Mizoram, the urban proportion is high, although the absolute urban population is low in comparison to the mid-Indian states. Tribal urbanisation may be seen as an example of rural push rather than urban pull. Mizoram, of course, is an exception. In other states of the country like their non-tribal counterparts, the tribes have been pushed into the urban domain by largely unfavourable conditions prevailing in the home villages. These include deteriorating man-land ratio, caused by land alienation, stringent forest policies denying the tribes their natural right to the forest, location of big or small river valley/industrial projects in tribal areas leading to displacement and the emergence of contractorship in the tribal labour market. Thus, a chunk of the urbanised tribes in an Indian city may consist of contractual labourers as well as those ousted from the development project sites. There is evidence to show that the urban economies have accommodated the tribes only marginally. They are mostly unskilled labourers engaged in low-paid jobs and living in squatter colonies. In the city they are perhaps the poorest among the poor (Tables 4.5a and 4.5b). The towns in the northeast may be an exception to this generalisation.

Table 4.5a : Rural-urban Composition of Tribal Population, 1991

States	*Urban Proportion (%)*	*Rural Proportion (%)*
Mizoram	45.18	54.82
Karnataka	14.93	85.07
Meghalaya	13.57	86.43
Maharashtra	12.46	87.54
Nagaland	12.06	87.94
Tamil Nadu	12.02	87.98
Manipur	8.38	91.62
Gujarat	8.08	91.92
Andhra Pradesh	7.59	92.41
Bihar	6.99	93.01
Uttar Pradesh	5.90	94.10
Arunachal Pradesh	5.81	94.19
Orissa	5.14	94.86
West Bengal	5.14	94.86
Madhya Pradesh	4.84	95.16
Rajasthan	4.64	95.36
Kerala	3.42	96.57
Assam	3.37	96.63
Himachal Pradesh	2.29	97.71
Tripura	1.64	98.36

Source: Computed by the author, see Census of India, 1991, Series-1, India, Part II-B. (i), Vol. 1, *Primary Census Abstract, General Population.*

Note: States arranged in a descending order according to the proportion of urban population as in 1991.

Distribution of Selected Tribal Communities

While the distribution of aggregative population of the Scheduled Tribes may be of great interest to the reader, it is also necessary to examine the geographic patterns in the distribution of individual tribal communities. This exercise is, however, confined to the selected tribal communities of the mid-Indian region as well as the North-east. While the Gonds, Bhils and the Santals have been chosen from the mid-Indian region, the Garos, Khasis, Nagas, and the Mizos represent the North-east.

The habitat of the mid-Indian tribes has been the scene of intensive developmental activity, particularly since the days of the British raj. The developmental activity has been further intensified after India entered the planning era in the early fifties. However, the developmental process has not affected all the tribes to the same extent, although its overall impact has been negative on all of them.

Table 4.5b : Rural-urban Composition of Tribal Population, 2001

States/Union Territory	*Urban Proportion (%)*	*Rural Proportion (%)*
India	**8.30**	**91.71**
States		
Andhra Pradesh	7.50	92.50
Arunachal Pradesh	14.02	85.97
Assam	4.65	95.34
Bihar	5.36	94.64
Chhattisgarh	5.31	94.68
Goa	66.41	33.56
Gujarat	8.21	91.78
Haryana	—	—
Himachal Pradesh	3.07	96.92
Jammu and Kashmir	4.65	95.34
Jharkhand	8.28	91.71
Karnataka	15.28	84.71
Kerala	3.89	96.10
Madhya Pradesh	6.43	93.56
Maharashtra	12.71	87.28
Manipur	4.75	95.24
Meghalaya	15.56	84.43
Mizoram	48.66	51.33
Nagaland	12.96	87.03
Orissa	5.48	94.51
Punjab	—	—
Rajasthan	5.30	94.64
Sikkim	8.52	91.47
Tamil Nadu	15.38	84.61
Tripura	2.56	97.44
Uttranchal	6.21	93.78
Uttar Pradesh	11.24	88.76
West Bengal	6.13	93.86
Union Territories		
Andaman and Nicobar Islands	3.43	96.56
Chandigarh	—	—
Dadra and Nagar Haveli	7.15	92.84
Daman and Diu	20.06	79.93
Delhi	—	—
Lakshadweep	43.80	56.19
Pondicherry	—	—

Source: Census of India, 2001, Series 1, *Primary Census Abstract, Total Population,* Table A-5.

The Gonds

Gonds are one of the three most numerous tribal groups of India. Their habitat extends over the northeastern flank of the Indian plateau. Despite their presence in the region where Indo-Aryan languages are widely spoken, the traditional dialect of the Gonds continues to be Gondi which is a variant of the central branch of the Dravidian. Historical evidence shows that the rise and fall of empires in northern and central

India did not affect much the traditional Gond territory. For example, on the authority of *Ain-e-Akbari*[9] one may conclude that the southern boundary of the *subah* of Illahabad and the eastern and the southeastern boundaries of the *subahs* of Agrah and Malwa were not clearly defined. It was a region of Gond concentration and it appears that the Mughals were not interested in encroaching upon the Gond territory.

Evidently, Gonds have been living through the ages in a vast region in the peninsular interior not much affected by the rise and fall of empires. However, several Rajput principalities were also established in the Gond region. Gonds were partners in these ventures. Today, their major concentration is seen in the Bastar plateau and the dissected hills in the upper reaches of the Narmada, Godavari and the Mahanadi rivers. The environmental diversity within this vast region has led to varied ecological responses with the result that the Gonds are found engaged in economies ranging from food gathering to sedentary agriculture. Raza and Ahmad,[10] in their study of cores and peripheries of the major tribes, noted that the Gond core had been fragmented as a result of incursion of the non-tribal groups. However, the Gond periphery is still intact. The impact of non-tribal incursions in the Gond heartland is evident from the fact that the Gond core consists of five fragments, each separated by pockets of non-tribal settlement. The largest of these segments lies in the Bastar and Raipur districts of Madhya Pradesh. Other fragments of the core extend over three *talukas* of Mandla district and one *taluka* each of Bilaspur, Chhindwara, Mandla, Betul, and Chandrapur districts (Table 4.6). Unlike the core, the Gond periphery is compact and extends over 43 *talukas* situated across several districts of Madhya Pradesh, Maharashtra and Orissa.

Table 4.6 : Tahsils/Talukas in which the Gonds were predominant in 1961

States	*Tahsils/Talukas*
Madhya Pradesh	Kanker, Narayanpur, Kondagaon, Bijapur, Dantewara, Jagdalpur (Bastar), Niwas, Dindori, Mandla (Mandla), Bilaspur (Bilaspur), Chhindwara (Chhindwara), Betul (Betul)
Maharashtra	Sironcha (Chanda)

Notes: (i) Administrative units as in 1961.
(ii) These units constituted the core region of the Gonds.

The Gonds are spread over 181 districts in eight states of the mid-Indian region. The 1981 census enumerated the Gonds in all the districts of Madhya Pradesh, Orissa, Maharashtra and Karnataka; 21 districts of Andhra Pradesh; 29 districts of Bihar; 13 districts of Gujarat; and 15 districts of West Bengal (Appendix IV.4). The region of enumeration extends over middle India from Gujarat in the west to West Bengal in the east and Bihar in the north to Karnataka in the south (Fig. 4.4). The distribution is, however, uneven. The Gonds account for more than 80 per cent of the tribal population in seven districts of Madhya Pradesh, four districts of Bihar and one district of Karnataka (Table 4.7). The Gonds are in a dominant status in a cluster of districts in Madhya Pradesh namely, Damoh, Narsimhapur, Mandla, Chhindwara, Seoni and Balaghat (Fig. 4.5).

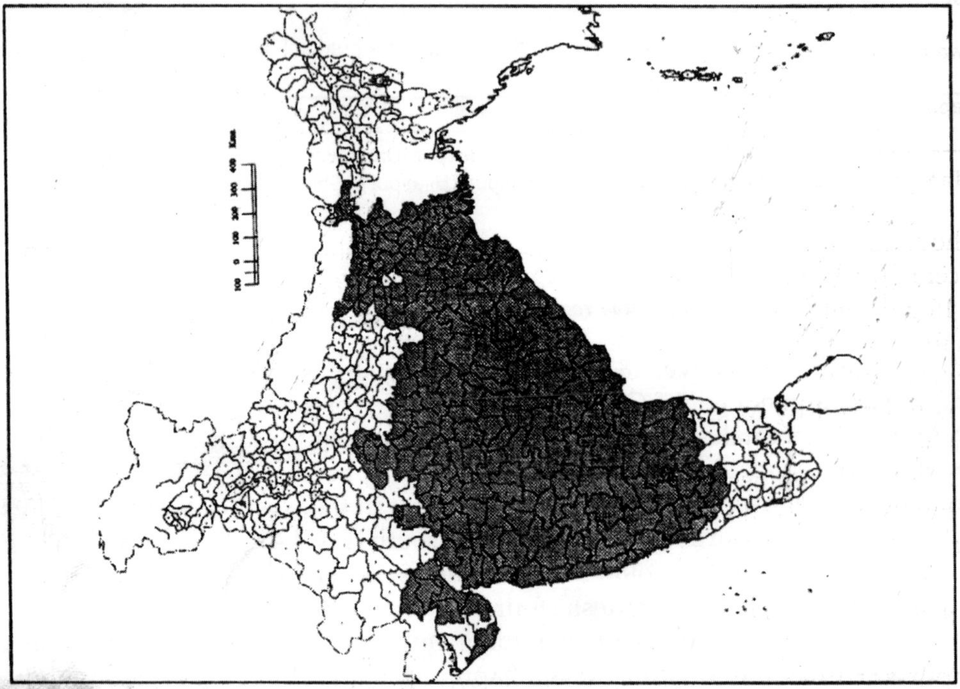

Figure 4.4 : Districts in which Gonds were enumerated in 1981

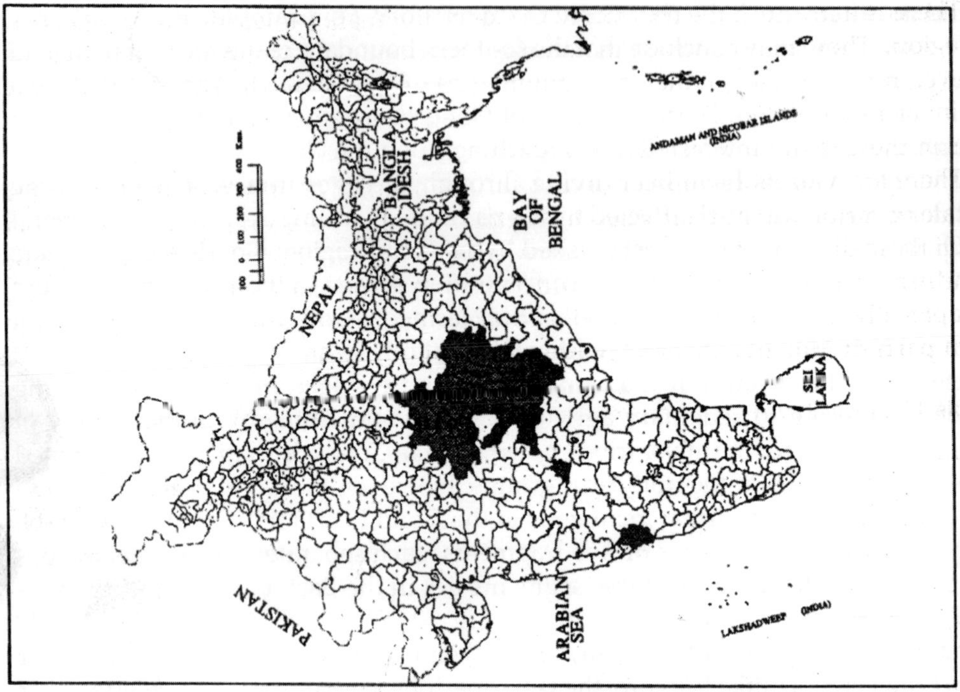

Figure 4.5 : Districts in which Gonds constituted more than 50 per cent of the Tribal Population

There is a break in the continuity of Gond dominance towards the southeast of this region. They again emerge as the most predominant group in Bastar district. However, it may be worthwhile to mention that in some of the districts, such as those lying in the Bihar plain, the tribal population itself is too small. The high proportion of Gonds in these districts is, therefore, a statistical anomaly.

There are a sizeable number of districts, numbering 29, in which the Gonds are in a state of majority, *i.e.*, their share in the total tribal population is more than 50 per cent. Of these districts, 17 are situated in Madhya Pradesh, three in Maharashtra, one in Andhra Pradesh, six in Bihar and two in Karnataka (Table 4.7). This is a geographically contiguous belt, extending over south-eastern parts of Madhya Pradesh, eastern parts of Maharashtra and northern Andhra Pradesh (Fig. 4.6).

Table 4.7 : Districts where the share of Gonds in the Tribal Population is more than 50 per cent

District	*Gond Percentage*	*District*	*Gond Percentage*
Bidar	90.83	Wardha	67.05
Seoni	90.45	Rajnandgaon	66.98
Saran	89.70	Raipur	66.46
Gopalganj	89.49	Bhandara	63.99
Narsimhapur	89.37	Bhojpur	62.76
Damoh	85.59	Uttar Kannad	61.48
Mandla	84.14	Panna	56.18
Bastar	84.10	Durg	55.64
Balaghat	83.89	Sagar	55.60
Siwan	83.22	Hoshangabad	52.81
Chhindwara	80.62	Adilabad	50.80
Raisen	79.78	Jabalpur	50.34
Chandrapur	79.14	Bilaspur	50.23
Betul	72.30		

Source: Table generated by the author; based on 1981 census.

The spatial pattern of concentration is evident from the fact that at the state level 72 per cent of the country's total Gond population is found in Madhya Pradesh alone. About 16 per cent of the Gonds live in Maharashtra, while Orissa accounts for 8 per cent of the country's Gond population. Another striking feature is that about 14 per cent of the country's Gond population lives in Bastar district of Madhya Pradesh alone. Bastar is followed by Mandla and Chandrapur — the respective share of the two districts being 7 per cent and 6 per cent. There is a fairly high concentration of Gond population over a number of districts in Madhya Pradesh. The values of concentration index range between 3 and 5 per cent over Shahdol, Betul, Chhindwara, Seoni, Surguja, Bilaspur and Raipur districts (Appendix IV.5).

Growth and Redistribution

It is important to examine the patterns of growth and redistribution of Gond population. For this study, 1961 census has been taken as the base and the growth in

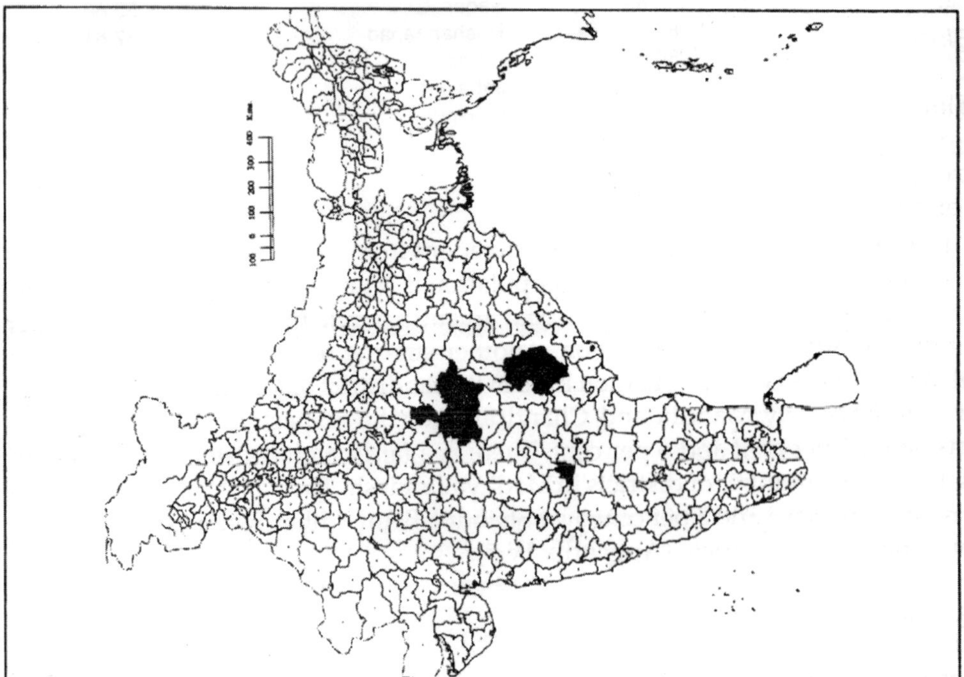

Figure 4.6 : Districts in which Gonds accounted for more than 80 per cent of the Tribal Population.

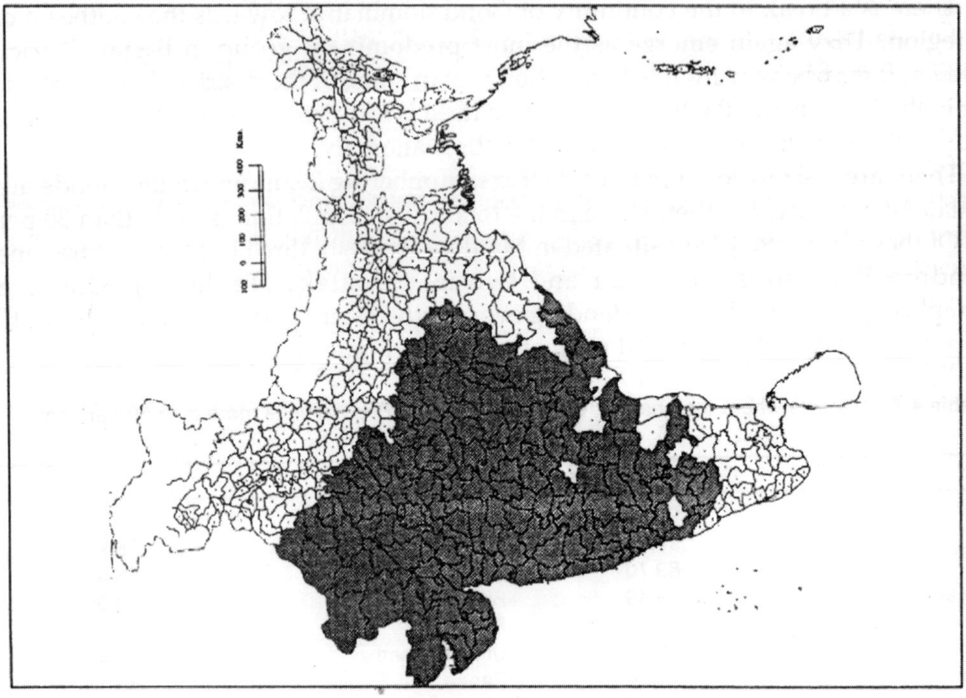

Figure 4.7 : Districts in which Bhils were enumerated in 1981

Gond population has been computed over the period of two decades ending with 1981. Gonds registered an increase of 109.77 per cent during the two decades—the average annual growth rate being 5.48 per cent. However, the picture at the district level is quite diverse. Several striking features emerge from the district-level study. First, most of the districts with a heavy concentration of Gonds experienced a growth rate of 45-50 per cent over the period 1961-81. This relatively low growth rate itself suggests a tendency of out-migration. Secondly, Raipur and Bilaspur districts stand out prominently as they recorded a high positive growth rate of 88.32 and 70.62 per cent respectively. Thirdly, Gonds registered very high positive growth rate (200 per cent or so) in Jabalpur district. Balaghat district with a growth rate of 177.36 per cent, Durg with 175.70 per cent and Chandrapur with 163.55 per cent fall in the same category. Fourthly, during the same period, the Gond population doubled in the districts of Chhattarpur, Panna, East Nimar and Hoshangabad, all in Madhya Pradesh (Appendix IV.5). Lastly, Warangal and Khammam districts of Andhra Pradesh and Balasore district of Orissa recorded a negative growth. The loss was quite significant, *i.e.*, -59.34 per cent in Warangal and -77.17 per cent in Khammam.

The dynamics of population growth and the causes behind it may be ascertained with the help of field studies, although not much research has been done so far. The developmental programmes launched in the Gond region since independence might have affected the process of growth and redistribution. There is a need to establish whether the Gonds ousted from their homes have been rehabilitated properly. It is an open question as to how the districts of inmigration have accommodated these tribes.

The Bhils

The Bhils and the Gonds have an area of overlap in the mid-Indian region. While the Bhils occupy the western flank of the central Indian plateau, the Gonds occupy its eastern flank. Like Gonds, Bhils are also fairly widespread in territorial extent. Their area of enumeration extends over the states of Rajasthan, Gujarat, Maharashtra, Madhya Pradesh, Andhra Pradesh and Karnataka (Appendix IV.6).

The present state of the Bhil society reflects the social and economic backwardness from which they have been suffering. However, historical evidence shows that they were holding sway over certain parts of central and western Rajasthan in not too distant a past. In fact, James Tod has cited some evidence which indicates that they were displaced from sites in Marwar in the wake of Rajput incursion in the thirteenth century. Bhils continued to live within the Rajput principalities. The Rajput dynasties, particularly in Amber, even involved Bhil chieftains in the ritual connected with the coronation of a new incumbent to the throne.

The sixteenth century Mughal sources mentioned the administrative organisation of the *subahs* of Ajmer, Ahmedabad and Malwah which indicate that while Bhils were living in these regions they were not controlling territory. All these examples show that the Bhils never enjoyed a state of isolation comparable to that of Gonds. This is further corroborated by the fact that linguistically Bhili is treated as a branch of Rajasthani, itself a variant of the Indo-Aryan family of languages. Linguists recognise three major groupings of the Bhili, *viz.*, Bhilali, Bhilodi and Kokna/Kokni or Kukna (Fig. 4.7).

At the 1981 census the Bhils were enumerated over a vast area extending over the states of Rajasthan, Gujarat, Maharashtra, Madhya Pradesh, Andhra Pradesh and Karnataka, encompassing 150 districts in all. However, they are mainly concentrated in the hilly and plateau regions on the southern flank of the Aravallis in Rajasthan and Gujarat as well as in the neighbouring Madhya Pradesh and Maharashtra. It may be noted that both the core and periphery of the Bhils are compact. The core extends over 18 *talukas/tahsils* in Madhya Pradesh, Maharashtra, Gujarat and Rajasthan. The Bhil periphery, on the other hand, extends over 49 *talukas/tahsils* in the same states. The compact nature of the core and periphery may be attributed to the rugged character of the region. The undulating and the dissected character of the highlands appears to have discouraged the non-tribal peasants from penetrating into the Bhil region (Table 4.8). Wherever the highlands give way to level plains, mainly along the banks of the rivers, the Bhils become conspicuous by their absence.

Table 4.8 : Tahsils/Talukas in which the Bhils were predominant, 1961

States	*Tahsils/Talukas*
Madhya Pradesh	Saliana (*Ratlam*), Thandla, Jhabua, Jobat, Alirajpur (*Jhabua*), Kukshi, Manawar (*Dhar*), Barwaha, Rajpur, Sendhwa, Khargone (*West Nimar*)
Maharashtra	Akrani Mahal (*Dhule*)
Gujarat	Santrampur, Jahalod, Dohad (*Panch Mahals*), Jhagadia, Dediapada (*Bharuch*)
Rajasthan	Dungarpur (*Dungarpur*)

Notes: (i) Administrative units as in 1961.
(ii) These units constituted the core region of the Bhils.

The process of the spill-over of the peasant communities from the densely-populated agricultural tracts to the marginal and the sub-marginal lands, so characteristic of the other tribal areas, seems to have been hampered by the adverse environmental factors of the Bhil region. This has helped the Bhils to retain their unique character.[11]

As noted earlier, the Bhils reveal a strong tendency of clustering and concentration in a few districts. For example, in Sabar Kantha, Jhabua, Dhar, Ratlam and West Nimar districts, 97-100 per cent of the tribal population is comprised by Bhils. The Bhil proportion is also very high (above 80 per cent) in Indore, Banswara, Shajapur, Mahesana and Rajgarh (Table 4.9). There are three pockets in which Bhil proportion is above 80 per cent: one lies over the districts of Banas Kantha, Sabar Kantha and Mahesana; the second encompasses Banswara, Jhabua, Dhar, Ratlam and West Nimar districts; and the third extends over the districts of Jaisalmer and Jodhpur (Fig. 4.8). The Bhils account for more than one-half of the tribal population in 26 districts. The belt in which Bhils are in clear majority extends over western Rajasthan, northern Gujarat and south-western Madhya Pradesh as well as adjoining parts of Maharashtra (Table 4.9; Fig. 4.9). Another significant aspect is the pattern of spatial concentration. About one-third of the total Bhil population of the country is concentrated in Madhya

Pradesh, a little above one-fourth in Gujarat, about one-fourth in Rajasthan and about one-eighth in Maharashtra. The index of concentration is as high as 9 in districts such as Jhabua, West Nimar and Panch Mahals. The index values range between 5 and 8 in Dhar, Bharuch, Dhule, Udaipur and Banswara. The index ranges between 1 and 5 over Ratlam, East Nimar, Banas Kantha, Sabar Kantha, Vadodra, Nashik, Jalgaon, Barmer, Dungarpur and Chittorgarh (Appendix IV.7).

Table 4.9 : Districts where Share of Bhils in Tribal Population is more than 50 per cent

District	*Bhil Percentage*	*District*	*Bhil Percentage*
Sabar Kantha	100.00	Bhavnagar	80.04
Jhabua	99.73	Bharuch	79.03
Dhar	99.31	Kheda	78.95
Jaisalmer	98.61	Jalor	78.92
Ratlam	98.18	Dungarpur	75.42
Jodhpur	98.09	Panch Mahals	73.46
Banas Kantha	97.96	Rajkot	71.97
West Nimar	97.10	Gandhinagar	70.45
Shajapur	96.50	Jalgaon	65.53
Banswara	90.48	Dhule	63.91
Indore	90.40	Ahmedabad	62.97
Mandsaur	89.50	Bhilwara	56.80
Rajgarh	86.55	Ajmer	54.71
Mahesana	86.42		

Source: Table compiled by the author; based on 1981 census.

Growth and Redistribution

The Bhils registered significant changes in population growth and redistribution during the two decades ending with 1981. The Bhil population almost doubled in Madhya Pradesh; it increased by 96.27 per cent in Rajasthan, 80.73 per cent in Gujarat and 72.70 per cent in Maharashtra. At the all-India level, the increase was of the order of 93.97 per cent. The average annual growth rate remained at 4.69 per cent. Several districts registered significant increases during 1961-81. Notable among them were Banswara, Jodhpur, Barmer, Bundi, Kota, Ahmadabad, Kheda, Surat, Ratlam, Sehore, Nanded and Pune.

The dynamics of population growth can perhaps be understood in the context of the circumstances leading to the mobility of the Bhils. Their outmigration from the core regions of their traditional homeland has been forced on them. This partially explains why their growth rates have been low in Jhabua, Dhar, West Nimar, Nashik and Dhule. On the other hand, their growth rates have been phenomenally high in regions outside their traditional habitat. They have been spreading out to these regions in search of new opportunities for survival. With development the struggle for survival has further intensified.

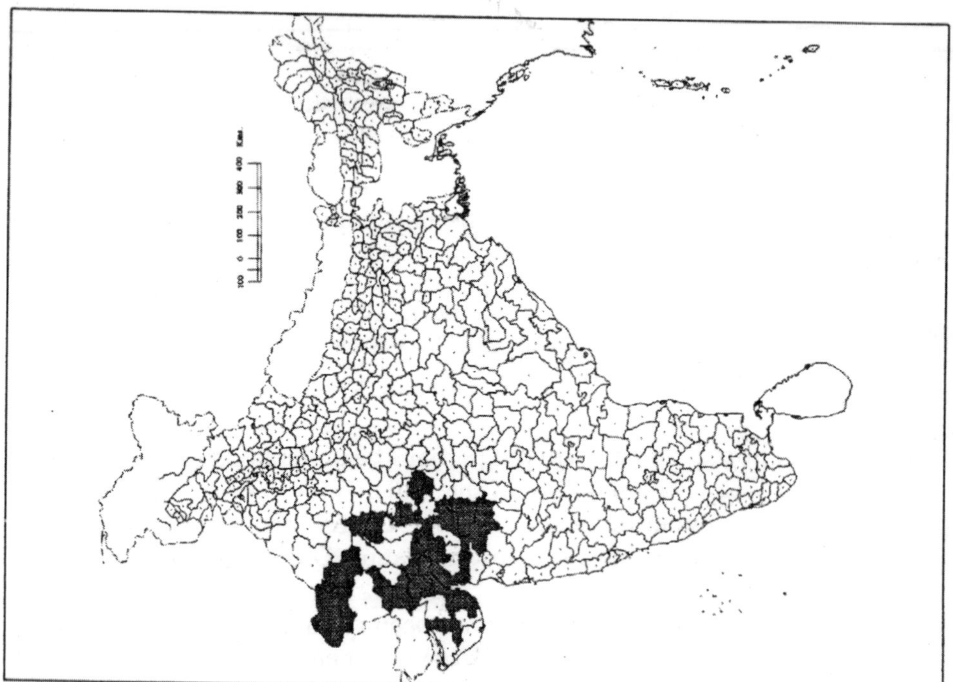

Figure 4.8 : Districts in which Bhils constituted more than 50 per cent of the Tribal Population, 1981

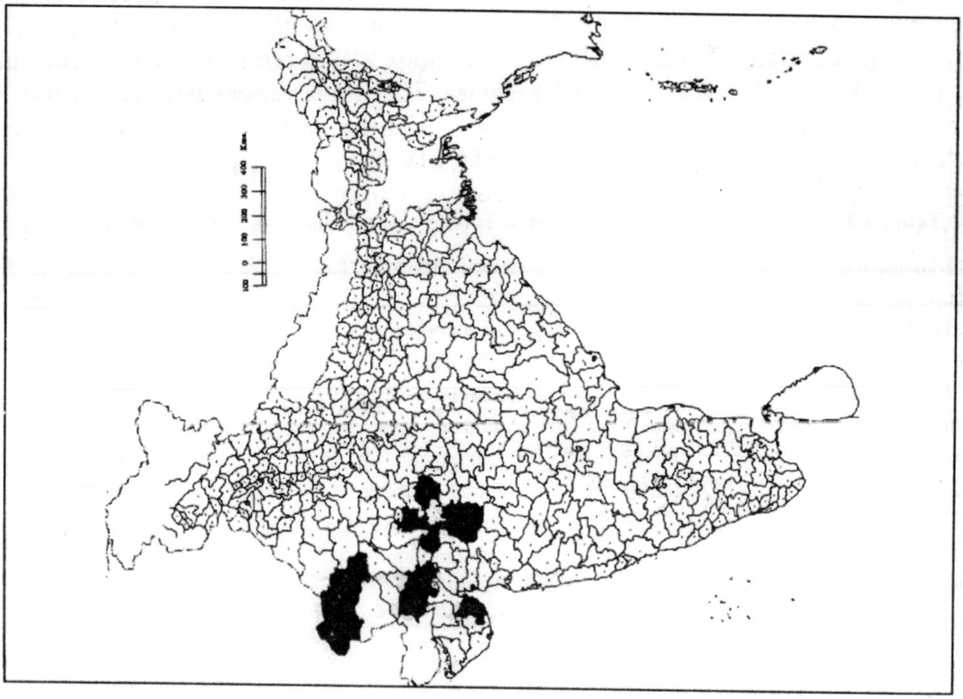

Figure 4.9 : Districts in which Bhils accounted for more than 80 per cent of the Tribal Population, 1981

The Santals

The Santals have been mainly living in the Rajmahal hills and the Chhotanagpur plateau. Having lived in the thickly forested hills and the plateau surfaces, the Santals have enjoyed a certain degree of isolation. It has been noted that the Santal habitat has been penetrated by non-tribal communities only on a limited scale. There are two segments of the Santal core—one lies in the Santal Parganas district of Bihar and the other in Mayurbhanj district of Orissa. The Santal periphery extends over one *anchal* each of Bhagalpur and Purnea, and two *anchals* each of Santal Parganas, Hazaribagh, Dhanbad and Singhbhum (Table 4.10). The periphery also encompasses a dozen *thana* circles in the districts of West Dinajpur, Birbhum, Maldah, Burdwan, Hugli, Midnapore and Purulia.[12]

Table 4.10 : *Anchals/Thana* Circles in which the Santals were predominant, 1961

	State	*Anchals/Thana Circles*
A	Bihar	Dumka, Jamtara, Rajmahal, Pakaur (*Santal Parganas*)
	Orissa	Mayurbhanj, Ramanghati, Kaptipada (*Mayurbhanj*)
B	Bihar	Godda, Deogarh (*Santal Parganas*), Araria (*Purnea*), Banka (*Bhagalpur*), Hazaribagh, Giridih (*Hazaribagh*), Dhanbad, Baghmara (*Dhanbad*), Dhalbhumgarh, Seraikela (*Singhbhum*)
	West Bengal	Balurghat, Raiganj (*West Dinajpur*), Rampurhat, Sadar (*Birbhum*), Malda (*Malda*) Katwa, Kalna, Burdwan (*Burdwan*), Sadar (*Hoogly*), Midnapore, Jhargram (*Midnapore*), Purulia Muffassil (*Purulia*)

Notes: (i) Administrative units as in 1961.
(ii) Units mentioned in (A) constituted the core region of the Santals. Units mentioned in (B) constituted the periphery of the core region of the Santals.

As compared to the Gonds and the Bhils, the Santals have a smaller territorial extent. At the 1981 census they were enumerated in 60 districts in the three states of Bihar, West Bengal and Orissa. However, they were also listed as Scheduled Tribes in Tripura. Their presence in Assam is well known, although there are no data to show either their numerical strength or geographical spread. The state-wise break-up of the districts in which Santals were enumerated in 1981 is shown in Fig. 4.10 and Appendix IV.8. There are only five districts in which the Santals account for more than 80 per cent of the total population, *viz.*, Santal Parganas, Giridih, Bankura, Bardhman and Birbhum (Table 4.11). However, there is a wider region in which the Santals live in a state of majority, *i.e.*, their share in the total tribal population of the districts being 50 per cent or more.

There are 16 districts in Bihar and West Bengal in which the Santals have a clear majority (Table 4.11; Figs. 4.11 and 4.12).

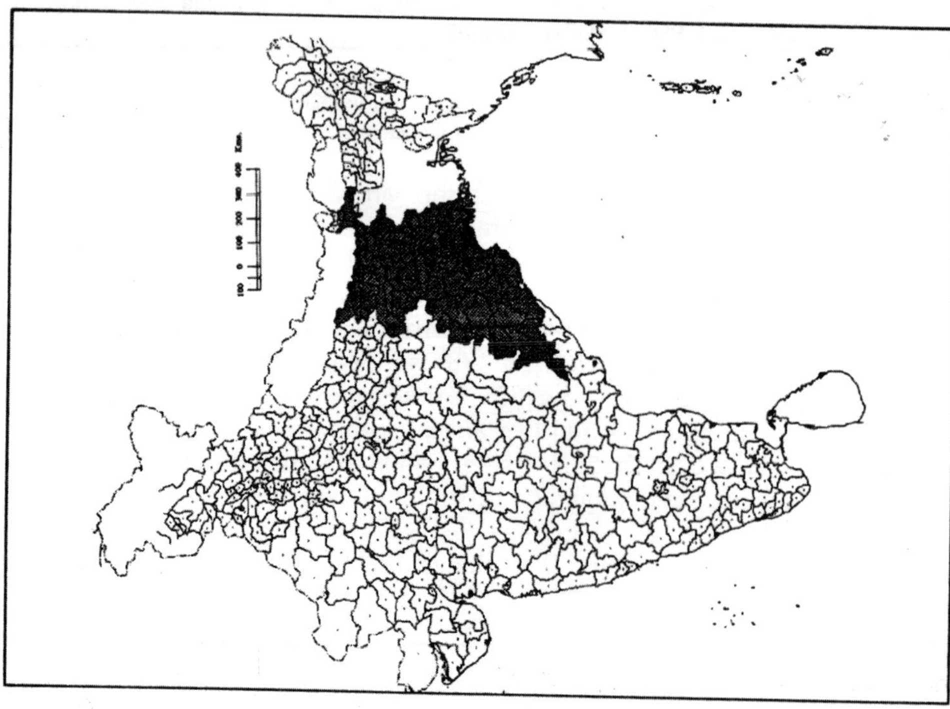

Figure 4.10: Districts in which Santals were enumerated in 1981

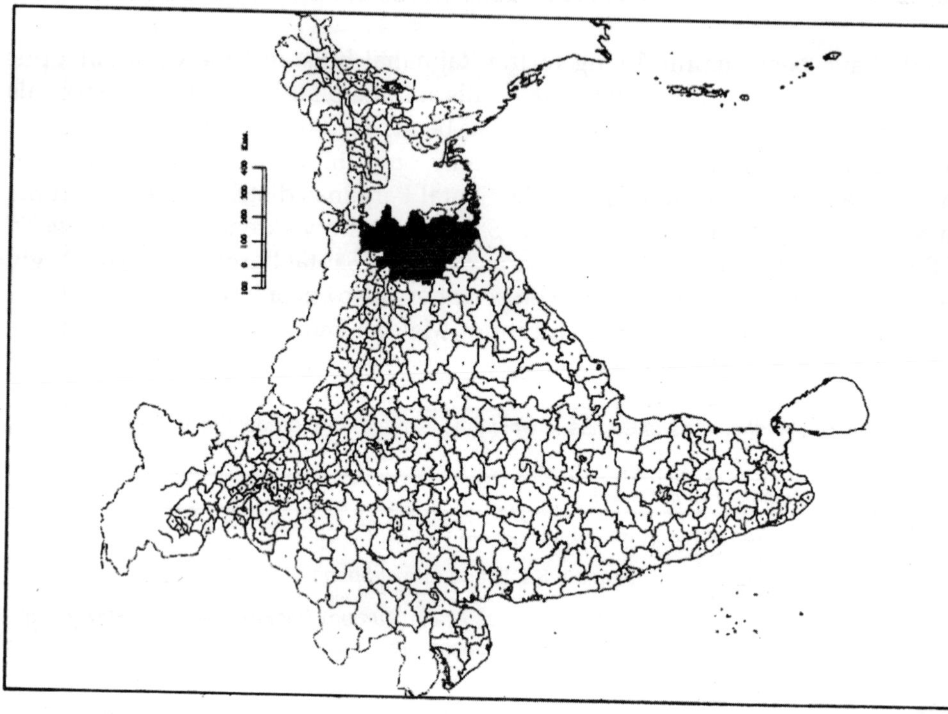

Figure 4.11 : Districts in which Santals constituted more than 50 per cent of the Tribal Population, 1981

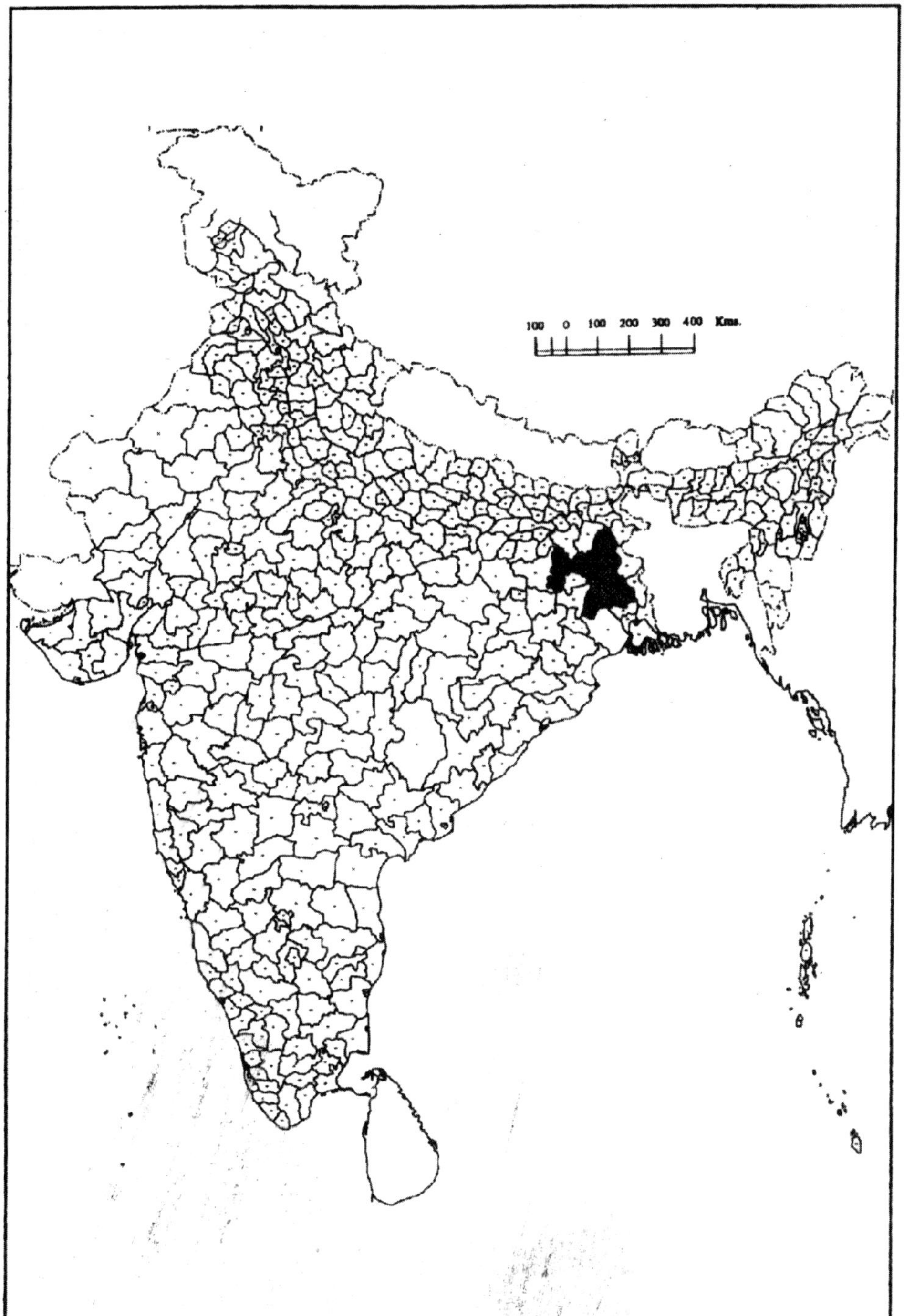

Figure 4.12 : Districts in which Santals accounted for more than 80 per cent of the Tribal Population, 1981

Table 4.11 : Districts where the Share of Santal in Tribal Population is more than 50 per cent

District	*Santal Percentage*	*District*	*Santal Percentage*
Birbhum	89.91	Hoogli	74.24
Giridih	85.62	West Dinajpur	71.60
Bardhman	83.55	Purnea	70.41
Bankura	83.12	Murshidabad	67.81
Santal Parganas	80.64	Medinipur	65.93
Munger	79.88	Purulia	64.32
Maldah	79.81	Bhagalpur	63.81
Dhanbad	79.80	Katihar	56.81

Source: Table compiled by the author; based on 1981 census.

The spatial pattern of concentration shows that about one-half of the total Santal population is found in Bihar and about two-fifths in West Bengal. They are heavily concentrated in the district named after them, *viz.*, Santal Parganas—the value of the index of concentration being 25.89 per cent. The index values are also quite high for Birbhum (12.45 per cent), Medinipur (8.33 per cent), Mayurbhanj (9.46 per cent) and Singhbhum (7.20 per cent) (Appendix IV.9).

Growth and Redistribution

In general the Santals have registered a low growth rate during the two decades (1961-81) for which data were analysed. At the national aggregative level, their population increased by 35 per cent over the 20-year period, registering an average annual growth rate of 1.75 per cent. In the absence of data on fertility and mortality for any sizeable section of Santal population, it is not possible to identify the reasons for such a low growth rate. The Santals registered a growth rate of 1.68 per cent per annum in Bihar and 1.94 per cent per annum in West Bengal. The growth rate was as low as 1.45 per cent per annum in Orissa (Appendix IV.9).

These variations in the dynamics of growth are partly due to redistribution of population in space. It may be assumed that developmental processes initiated since 1950, coupled with the state interventions in the tribal situation, have forced the tribes to remain on the move. Their own economies have been transformed to such an extent that they are no longer sustainable. This has inevitably led to inter-state and inter-district migrations. Their outmigration to such states of India where they are not recognised as Scheduled Tribes may also be an important factor in their growth dynamics.

At the district level it may be noted that there are several districts in Orissa and at least one district in West Bengal where the Santal population has increased by 5-15 per cent per annum. On the other hand, the population of Santals has significantly declined in Nadia, Jalpaiguri and Coochbehar during the same period. However, none of the districts of Orissa or Bihar registered negative growth.

The Garos, Khasis, Nagas and the Mizos

This study is restricted to the major tribal groups of the North-east *viz.*, the Garos, the Khasis, the Nagas and the Mizos. The geographical distribution of these tribes is, however, simple: they are confined to the states created for them. Of the four, Nagas appear to be the most widely spread. More than 94 per cent of the Garo population is concentrated in Meghalaya. They were also enumerated, although in small numbers, in the neighbouring states of Assam, Nagaland, Tripura and West Bengal. Like the Garos, the Khasis are also mostly confined to the state of Meghalaya. As much as 98 per cent of their population is found in Meghalaya. Over the years they have also migrated to other states in the neighbourhood, *e.g.*, Assam and Tripura. Nagaland is the domain of the Nagas, although their population is also sizeable in Manipur. The Naga sub-tribes, such as the Angami, Kabui, Kacha, Mao, Maram, Maring, Sema and the Tangkhul are all found in Manipur living in the midst of Kuki-Chin tribes. About 72 per cent of the Naga population is, however, concentrated in Nagaland. The Mizo population is concentrated in Mizoram (as much as 94 per cent). They are also found in Tripura, Manipur, Assam and Meghalaya.

The North-eastern tribes listed under the Naga group are the most numerous followed by the Khasis, Garos and the Mizos. The Garos, the Khasis and the Mizos registered an average growth rate of about 40 per cent during the decade 1981-91. The Naga growth rate was, on the other hand, much higher—more than 63 per cent.

Developmental Impact

The programmes of regional development launched in India since the beginning of the planning era have left their impact on the tribal society. While there is no gainsaying the fact that the tribes have to be drawn into the vortex of development, encounters with modernisation have produced devastating results on the tribal society. Writers on the tribal problems in the central Indian regions have often noted the autonomous status of the tribal society and economy prior to the introduction of developmental programmes. In fact, there is little evidence to show frequent interaction between the tribes and the non-tribes. It has been noted that outside contact has only been a source of disturbance to the otherwise self-contained tribal social world.[13] With the opening up of tribal areas, a process which started in the third decade of the twentieth century, the tribal society registered two major impacts: (a) an influx of non-tribal peasantry, and (b) transformation of subsistence tribal agriculture into a cash cropping economy. The tribes were drawn into the cash economy without much understanding of the processes involved therein. Obviously, this resulted in the emergence of the moneylenders and the tribal indebtedness increased phenomenally. Shift of area from food crops to market-oriented commercial crops further aggravated the problem of indebtedness as the tribes became dependent on the market for their food requirements. Indebtedness also paved the way for the transfer of land from the tribes to the moneylenders as well as to the non-tribal peasantry. In the meantime new forest policies were launched which led to greater regulations on the tribal access to the forest land. The imposition of these restrictions eventually resulted in curbing the tribal freedom of residence within the forest or movement over the forest land in pursuit of shifting cultivation practices. Inevitably, what followed was shrinkage in the area of the tribal habitat and a transformation of the tribal way of life.

Urmila Pingle's studies of the Raj Gonds, Maria Gonds (Chanda district, now Chandrapur) and the Koyas (Adilabad district) illustrated the devastating effects of non-tribal penetration on these communities. While the Maria Gonds were found to be mainly subsistence cultivators, the Raj Gonds displayed evidence of a change to cotton cultivation over substantive chunks of their land. The Koyas were worst off as about one-half of their population was virtually reduced to landless agricultural labourers. Pingle believed that the experiences of the Maria Gonds and the Raj Gonds were not going to be different from those of the Koyas (Box 4.2).

Box 4.2: Development and Change

Observations over a decade from 1972 ... proved this prediction to be only too true in the case of Raj Gonds who are faced with the ... problems of land alienation. Commercial centres have grown in the midst of tribal areas for procuring cotton. The non-tribal order ... has thrown (its) net wide open into the most interior villages where small shops have been set up to procure ... cotton .... In this way the whole of cotton production is in the hands of traders. The composition of villages has completely changed, villages which were wholly of tribal composition along the roadside (have been) displaced by non-tribals. The deep black soils are now in the possession of the non-tribals and the ... tribes are being pushed up on to the hill slopes. From a sorghum-growing area previously, the whole area has now become a continuous belt of cotton, so much so that sorghum is being imported into the area.... All the profit of the cash economy is in the hands of non-tribal, who has obviously prospered at the expense of the Gond who is daily becoming more impoverished. The Maria Gonds remained more or less static, with hardly any development scheme reaching them through the government agencies. However, their situation is much better than that of the Raj Gonds or the Koyas, as they do not have to face the onslaught of migrant population. The situation of the Koyas has reached a plateau where the change for the worst has already occurred.

—Urmila Pingle, *Demography of Tribal Development*, 1990: 165.

As noted earlier, the Indian tribes are mostly concentrated in the hilly and the forested tracts of the country. As a consequence they have not received outside influences which could transform their economies on a perceptible scale. This, to a very large extent, explains the underdeveloped state of their economies. However, with the gradual opening up of the tribal areas, the traditional modes of economy and the resultant relations of production started responding to qualitatively new changes. These influences were mostly negative and the tribes did not gain much from such exposures. For one thing, the transfer of technology to the tribal areas has been very slow. Developmental activities launched in the tribal areas were superimposed and had no linkage with the local tribal economies. In fact, as a result of the location of these activities, tribes were displaced from their land and reduced to labourers. Traditionally, tribes are pre-literates and their responses to education have not been generally encouraging, although there are notable exceptions to this generalisation.

Marking a significant departure from the example set by the British, developmental planning since independence aimed at the transformation of tribal regions by helping the tribes to overcome their economic backwardness. While developmental activity has been initiated, such as tribal area developmental projects, tribes have only been marginally affected by these processes of growth. The restricted nature of interaction between the tribes and the more developed non-tribes has allowed the continuation of the old tribal order uninterruptedly, thus denying the tribes the chance of benefiting from the on-going process of development. The official agencies in India since independence were quite familiar with the British model of intervention in the tribal situation. The new policy remained mostly a continuation of the old model. There were two main planks of the British policy. First, tribes were drawn into contact with the missionaries who introduced welfare activities in the tribal areas, such as health services and schools, and won over their confidence. The missionaries were quite influential in North-eastern India as well as in some parts of the mid-Indian region. The contact with the missionaries eventually brought some of the tribes to the fold of Christianity, besides exposing them to an overarching modernising influence. The Khasis, for example, got Europeanised. The English language which they picked up served the much useful purpose of inter-tribal communication. The Nagas and the Mizos also responded to similar influences. Secondly, the British obviously got interested in the natural resources of the Chhotanagpur region just as they were interested in the plantation agriculture in north Bengal and Assam. The location of plantation and mining establishments within the tribal areas connected the regional economies to the external trade nexus. The mineral-bearing Chhotanagpur region became the hub of mining and industrial activity. The twin processes of industrialisation and urbanisation introduced non-tribal elements into this tribal region on an unprecedented scale leading to a chain of developments. There is evidence to show that this non-tribal influx accelerated ecological changes with far-reaching implications. Such interventions disrupted their traditional mode of economy. The spill-over of peasants from the thickly populated parts of the central Bihar plains led to the process of land alienation. The alienated tribes were gradually reduced to agricultural labourers. However, encroachments on tribal lands had started much earlier as the history of tribal movements in the Chhotanagpur region shows. These resistance movements acquired proportions which were quite dangerous to the state authority during the British period.[14]

India entered into the era of planned economic growth in the early fifties. In fact, independence brought a new consciousness of the tribal rights and privileges. However, the new environment did not in any way prove beneficial to the tribes. Non-tribal encroachments on tribal lands continued. While the Christian Missionary activity came to a decline, indigenous non-Christian Missionaries started operating in many tribal areas. The colonial economic order came to a grinding halt. But the story did not end there. The old model was replaced by neo-colonial forms of extraction of natural resources from the tribal regions. The integration of the domestic market induced the market forces to penetrate into the tribal regions drawing the backward economies into the whirlpool of an external market. Inevitably, Chhotanagpur and other parts of the mid-Indian tribal region became a focal point of developmental activity on an unprecedented scale. These developments resulted in structural changes in the tribal economies. Several aspects of this impact deserve special mention. First, tribes were displaced from their lands, or deprived of access to the forests, but they were not satisfactorily rehabilitated. Location of industry, mining establishments, river valley projects and fencing of reserved forests accelerated the process of displacement further. Secondly, the influx of the non-tribal elements led to a notable demographic change in the tribal hamlets surrounding the industrial complexes. Thirdly, voluntary or involuntary eviction of tribals from the lands traditionally under their control caused occupational changes. In several situations payment of compensation to the ousted tribals resulted in increased flow of money and changes in consumption behaviour followed. The north-eastern flank of the peninsular plateau, particularly Bastar and Koraput districts, became the scene of yet another intervention. The idea was to resettle the displaced persons from the erstwhile East Pakistan in this relatively open and sparsely populated area. However, the plan was conceived in total disregard to the tribal interests. The peasant communities who came to settle down on lands reclaimed from the forest in the Dandakaranya project areas were experienced in intensive paddy cultivation. The Gonds were no match to them. This penetration of the peasant mode further accelerated the process of marginalisation of tribes.

Box 4.3: Dandakaranya: Agrarian-Resettlement Intervention Model

The agrarian resettlement model (of Dandakaranya) was unique in its *modus operandi*. The project aimed at resettling a sizeable population of displaced persons (from the erstwhile East Pakistan) in this relatively open and sparsely populated area. However, the resettlement policy was such that it destroyed the tribal, social and economic (order) without replacing (it) by a viable alternative basis for their rehabilitation. The very choice of the area in the heart of a traditional, tribal homeland betrayed lack of understanding of the tribal social reality....It was assumed that the process of settling down of peasant communities, well-versed in irrigated paddy culture, would have a demonstration effect on the primitive tribal economies....The location of an agrarian infrastructure and other social services would benefit the peasant settlers as well as the tribals. However, these assumptions ignored the inherently contradictory nature of the tribal and peasant outlooks. The peasants had a vested interest in land....Soon they encroached on the tribal lands and succeeded in driving the tribals out. The little tribal world of Dandakaranya had escaped centuries of social development so characteristic of the perennial nuclear regions of the subcontinent, and had survived as a partially closed ecosystem. The ridges and the spurs of the wooded Eastern Ghats and the Orissa hills protected it from the onslaught of civilisation.

—Aijazuddin Ahmad, *Development and Redistribution of Population*, 1985: 73.

Studies conducted in the Paralkote and the Malkangiri zones reveal the impact of this resettlement programme on the tribal communities. The resettlement scheme was introduced in the Umarkote, Malkangiri (Koraput district of Orissa), Paralkot and Kondagaon (Bastar district of Madhya Pradesh) zones. Studies conducted by this author in Paralkot and Malkangiri zones with the help of secondary data reveal several striking features. For example, the tribal hamlets in these sub-divisions registered a drastic demographic change. The non-tribal component in the population increased and consequently the tribal share declined. These changes in the traditional, ethnic territorial structure have affected adversely the tribal social and economic order.[15] It may be interesting to examine the social consequences of these developments. The on-going emphasis on tribal development should not miss the point that tribes cannot benefit from these programmes unless tribal interests are protected by themselves through their own induction in the cadres entrusted with the task of the execution of such plans (Box 4.3).

Tribal responses to the developmental processes may be examined in two crucial areas: First, structural changes in the agricultural workforce; and secondly, the shift of tribes from preliterate to literate status. The Gonds, the Bhils and the Santals have been selected as case studies for this enquiry. Understandably, these tribes have been living in several states whose performance is not comparable insofar as the implementation of plans is concerned. The state of the tribal society in these states today reflects these differences glaringly.

Changes in Agrarian Structure

Tribal assimilation into the peasant mode of production is a tortuous process. It is well known that the Indian tribes picked up the art of agriculture quite early in history, although tribal agriculture remained mostly subsistence in character. The British revenue administration in the nineteenth century found the communitarian mode of land ownership still intact in many tribal areas. However, the practice did not continue for long. Functionaries in the land records department succumbed to pressure from the vested interests and gradually lands were transferred to non-tribal peasants clandestinely. This process of land alienation affected the tribes all over the mid-Indian region.

The Gonds have undergone a significant change in their agrarian structure during the sixties and the seventies of the twentieth century. The year 1961 has been taken as the base in view of the fact that by this time the impact of developmental planning was somewhat visible on many tribal regions of India. Moreover, this is also the point of time for which the relevant data started becoming available. The 20-year period following 1961 witnessed all-embracing changes in the tribal economy, leading to the transformation of the tribal mode of production. One significant finding is that the proportion of cultivators in the agricultural workforce has declined. Moreover, the share of cultivators declined in all the districts in which the Gonds were significantly concentrated. This decline was very significant—more than 15 per cent points in as many as 14 districts mostly situated in Madhya Pradesh and Maharashtra. The change was negative but small—less than 15 per cent points—in the rest of the region. These findings are based on the census data and the implication is that during these two decades tribes have been systematically deprived of their land rights and reduced to a landless agricultural labour-force. Obviously, the state has witnessed these developments helplessly. Barring the example of Chhattarpur and Vidisha, the remaining 43 districts of this sample region witnessed a positive change in the proportion of agricultural labourers. The change was the highest in Amravati, *i.e.*, 43.11 per cent points. Among the districts where the Gonds are numerically strong the increase in the proportion of agricultural labourers was very high. It was above 20 per cent points in Raisen, Hoshangabad and Narsimhapur. The change was high—10-20 per cent points—in Shahdol, Betul, Jabalpur, Chhindwara, Seoni, Balaghat and Raigarh (Appendix IV.10).

Likewise, the Bhils experienced the same process of land alienation, although with varying degrees of intensity. The 20-year period registered a widespread decline in the proportion of cultivators and a consequent increase in the proportion of agricultural labourers. The only districts in which the proportion of Bhil cultivators increased were Jaisalmer and Aurangabad. However, the Bhils were in-migrants in these districts. In the remaining 36 districts the proportion of cultivators declined. The decline was very significant in Ratlam (26.37 per cent points) and Kota (21.45 per cent points). The decline was also significant in Sabar Kantha, Surat, Dungarpur, Banas Kantha and Sehore (between 10 and 20 per cent points).

As a consequence of this decline the proportion of agricultural labourers increased. The increase in the proportion of agricultural labourers remained very high (between 20 and 40 per cent points) in Ahmedabad, Banaskantha and Ratlam. On the other hand, Pali, Jalor, Nashik and Pune districts recorded an increase of 10-15 per cent points (Appendix IV.11).

Agricultural labourers accounted for more than 30 per cent of the Bhil agricultural workforce in a very large number of districts in Maharashtra, Gujarat and Rajasthan. In fact, almost the whole agricultural workforce was enumerated as agricultural labourers in Kheda, Ahmedabad, Valsad, Pune, Ahmadnagar and Bid districts. These findings are disturbing as they reveal a serious dimension of tribal deprivation.

The Santals also underwent a similar history. The proportion of cultivators declined considerably in all the districts of the Santal region. However, the highest decline was reported from Twenty-Four Parganas (-34.18 per cent points), followed by Darjeeling (-30.40 per cent points), Maldah (-25.79 per cent points) and West Dinajpur (-22.23 per cent points). Even the districts in which the Santals are mainly concentrated, *viz.*, Santal Parganas and Singhbhum, the proportion of cultivators declined. The other part of the story is told by the increasing proportion of agricultural labourers. The share of agricultural labourers increased phenomenally in Haora, Koch Bihar, Barddhaman, Darjeeling and Bhagalpur districts. Obviously, the Santals were working mainly as agricultural labourers in these districts. Even in Santal Parganas the increase in the share of agricultural labourers was of the order of 12.16 per cent points during 1961-81 (Appendix IV.12).

Literacy Status

Tribal responses to the programmes of literacy and education vary significantly from state to state.[16] While some sections of the tribal society have enthusiastically responded to education/literacy programmes, others have just remained outside the ambit of education. This process of transformation from pre-literate to literate status has been examined in the case of the Gonds, the Bhils and the Santals. The literacy data have been disaggregated for the male and female components for 1961 and 1981 and the gender disparity in literacy attainments and the changes registered over the two decades have been examined.

Table 4.12 : Gonds: Change in Male Literacy, 1961-81

Positive Change (per cent points)	*District*
Less than 5	Karimnagar (Andhra Pradesh), Chhatarpur, Rewa, Jabalpur, Mandla (Madhya Pradesh)
5-10	Guna, Panna, Satna, Shahdol, Sidhi, Dewas, Vidisha, Sehore, Raisen, Hoshangabad, Betul (Madhya Pradesh), Adilabad, Khammam, Warangal (Andhra Pradesh), Kalahandi, Koraput (Orissa)
10-20	Narsimhapur, Chhindwara, Seoni, Bilaspur, Raigarh, Durg, Bastar, East Nimar (Madhya Pradesh)
	Amravati, Yeotmal, Chandrapur (Maharashtra), Sambalpur, Bolangir, Boudh-Khondmals, Dhenkanal, Mayurbhanj (Orissa)
20-30	Surguja (Chhattisgarh), Nanded (Maharashtra), Keonjhar (Orissa)
Negative Change (per cent points)	
Less than 5	Balaghat (Madhya Pradesh)
10-20	Raipur (Chhattisgarh)

The Gonds display a striking male-female disparity in literacy rates. Male literacy rates were generally high in Orissa. The two states of Madhya Pradesh and Maharashtra presented a mixed picture with some districts (particularly Raipur, Durg and Balaghat) reporting male literacy rates around 15-20 per cent. In other districts literacy rates were generally below 10 per cent. On the other hand, female literacy rates were low all over the Gond region (less than 2 per cent). The only exceptions were Dhenkanal, Keonjhar and Mayurbhanj districts where 3-5 per cent of females were reported as literate. During the 20-year period male literacy rates improved very significantly in Maharashtra, Orissa and certain parts of Madhya Pradesh, although the Gond response to literacy was more spectacular in Maharashtra and Orissa than in other parts of the region. Male literacy rates were significantly high (above 30 per cent) in all the districts of Maharashtra and in at least two districts of Madhya Pradesh and four districts of Orissa. Female literacy rates were well above 10 per cent over most of the districts of Maharashtra and in at least one district of Madhya Pradesh and four districts of Orissa. Changes in male literacy during the two decades do not reveal any significant geographic pattern, although a number of districts experienced impressive increases in the proportion of male literates (Appendix IV.13; Tables 4.12 and 4.13).

Table 4.13 : Gonds: Change in Female Literacy, 1961-81

Positive Change (per cent points)	*District*
Less than 1	Guna, Chhatarpur, Panna, Rewa, Sidhi, Dewas, Vidisha, Sehore, Raisen (Madhya Pradesh), Adilabad, Karimnagar, Khammam (Andhra Pradesh), Kalahandi, Koraput (Orissa)
1-5	Shahdol, East Nimar, Hoshangabad, Betul, Jabalpur, Narsimhapur, Mandla, Chhindwara, Surguja, Bilaspur, Raigarh, Durg, Bastar (Madhya Pradesh), Warangal (Andhra Pradesh)
5-10	Seoni (Madhya Pradesh), Nanded, Chanda (Maharashtra), Sambalpur, Dhenkanal, Mayurbhanj (Orissa)
Above 10	Amravati, Yeotmal (Maharashra), Keonjhar (Orissa)
Negative Change (per cent points)	
Less than 1	Satna, Balaghat, Raipur (Madhya Pradesh)

It is evident from Appendix IV.14 that the Bhils, in general have not been responsive to the literacy programmes launched by the state. In fact, the Bhil society has been exposed to school education only nominally. However, there are striking inter-state differences in literacy rates, indicating differences in state policy on tribal education and its implementation. Bhils are better off in Gujarat and Maharashtra as compared to Rajasthan and Madhya Pradesh. Even the male literacy rates are low. Taking 1981 as the latest census year for which disaggregated data on literacy for individual tribal communities are available, one observes that the state average male literacy rate is the highest in Gujarat (27 per cent), followed by Maharashtra (19 per cent). The other two States of Rajasthan and Madhya Pradesh are trailing behind—the respective averages being 12 per cent and 9 per cent. As compared to this, female literacy rates are abysmally low even in the otherwise developed states—8 per cent in Gujarat and 4 per cent in Maharashtra. The data for Rajasthan and Madhya Pradesh with female literacy rates of 0.72 per cent and 1.12 per cent seem to paint a grim picture.

Table 4.14 : Bhils: Change in Male Literacy, 1961-81

Positive Change (per cent points)	*District*
Less than 2	Ajmer, Barmer, Jalor, Bundi, Bhilwara (Rajasthan), Ahmedabad, Kheda (Gujarat)
2-5	Tonk, Jaisalmer, Jodhpur, Pali, Sirohi, Chittorgarh, Kota (Rajasthan), Jhabua (Madhya Pradesh), Pune (Maharashtra)
5-10	Udaipur, Banswara, Jhalawar (Rajasthan), Banaskantha, Vadodra, Surat (Gujarat), Ratlam, Dhar, West Nimar (Madhya Pradesh), Bid, Ahmadnagar, Jalgaon, Dhule, Nashik (Maharashtra)
10-20	Dungarpur (Rajasthan), Sabarkantha, Panch Mahals, Bharuch (Gujarat), Aurangabad, Nanded (Maharashra)
Above 20	The Dangs (Gujarat)
Negative Change (per cent points)	
Less than 5	Sehore (Madhya Pradesh)

Insofar as male literacy is concerned inter-district variations are quite pronounced. In Gujarat, for example, the Dangs district with 45 per cent of the males returned as literate holds the first rank. Banas Kantha, on the other hand, with a literacy rate of 13 per cent, is at the bottom. The range of variation within Maharashtra is narrow. Nanded, with a literacy rate of 24.6 per cent, holds the first rank. Bid (literacy rate: 13 per cent) lies at the bottom. Among the districts of Madhya Pradesh, Jhabua is most backward (6 per cent). On the other hand, West Nimar and Dhar, with literacy rates of 10 and 9 per cent respectively, are slightly better off. Bhils in Dungarpur, Banswara and Jhalawar districts of Rajasthan have attained higher literacy rates. The lowest literacy rate of 3.2 per cent was reported from Bundi district.

A painful realisation is that not much has happened on the front of female literacy, although the Dangs, Sabar Kantha, Bharuch and Vadodra districts of Gujarat have a better record to show (Table 4.14).

Keeping this scenario in view the change in male literacy during 1961-81 may not reveal any dramatic developments. Even the ranking of states remains the same, with Gujarat registering a positive change of 11 per cent points, followed by Maharashtra (8 per cent points), Rajasthan (7 per cent points) and Madhya Pradesh (5 per cent points). These states apart from some districts have performed well. If one considers the districts in which Bhils have a notable concentration, one may note that the performance of The Dangs district has been just spectacular. It has been a quantum jump from a literacy rate of 5.5 per cent in 1961 to 44.9 per cent in 1981. In other districts of Gujarat (*viz.*, Sabarkantha, Panch Mahals and Bharuch) the change has been of the order of 10-20 per cent points. The Dungarpur district of Rajasthan also falls in the same category. A moderate change of 5-10 per cent points has been reported from Banaskantha and Vadodra districts of Gujarat; Dhule, Nashik and Jalgaon districts of Maharashtra; Udaipur and Banswara districts of Rajasthan; and Ratlam, Dhar and West Nimar districts of Madhya Pradesh. On the other hand, the change has been quite unimpressive in Jhabua (4 per cent points) and Barmer (less than 2 per cent points).

The decennial trends in female literacy are as depressing as the female literacy rates for 1981 census. It was again in The Dangs district that female literacy rates improved dramatically—from 0.8 per cent in 1961 to 12.8 per cent in 1981. Sabar Kantha and Bharuch also reported increases of 5-10 per cent points during the two decades. There was an increase of 1-5 per cent points in a number of districts, including Dungarpur, Banaskantha, Panch Mahals, Vadodra, West Nimar, Nashik, Dhule and Jalgaon. Other districts have nothing much to report. The two decades passed without leaving an imprint on the Bhil girl child by way of social development.

The Santals have been drawn into the ambit of education fairly well. In fact, there are no regional disparities in the Santal literacy rates. This is true at least for the male segment of the Santal population as reported by the 1981 census. The three states of Bihar, West Bengal and Orissa do not reveal any diversity as the male literacy rates remained at 20, 20 and 21 per cent respectively (Table 4.15). Of course, some districts within these states performed better as far as the male literacy was concerned. For example, Singhbhum (Bihar), Bankura, Medinipur and Purulia (West Bengal),

Mayurbhanj and Balasore (Orissa) are well above the average of their respective states. There are other districts, such as Purnea, Hazaribagh (Bihar), Maldah, Murshidabad, Barddhaman and Birbhum (West Bengal), which have been trailing behind in male literacy. The male bias is evident equally significantly: barring a few districts of West Bengal, female literacy rates generally remain below 5 per cent.

Table 4.15 : Bhils: Change in Female Literacy, 1961-81

Positive Change (per cent points)	*District*
Less than 1	Tonk, Jaisalmer, Jodhpur, Pali, Jalor, Bhilwara, Udaipur, Chittorgarh, Banswara, Bundi, Kota, Jhalawar (Rajasthan), Ratlam, Jhabua, Dhar (Madhya Pradesh), Pune (Maharashtra)
1-5	Dungarpur (Rajasthan), Banaskantha, Kheda, Panch Mahals, Ahmedabad, Vadodra (Gujarat), West Nimar (Madhya Pradesh), Nashik, Dhule, Jalgaon, Ahmadnagar, Aurangabad, Bid, Nanded (Maharashtra)
5-10	Sabarkantha, Bharuch, Surat (Gujarat)
Above 10	The Dangs (Gujarat)
Negative Change (per cent points)	
Less than 1	Ajmer, Barmer, Sirohi (Rajasthan), Sehore (Madhya Pradesh)

A study of time-series data shows that the progress in male literacy has been quite impressive in Jalpaiguri, Nadia, Bankura, Medinipur and Purulia (West Bengal), Singhbhum (Bihar), Keonjhar, Mayurbhanj and Balasore districts (Orissa), (Table 4.16). No significant change has been reported from other districts in the region (Appendix IV.15). There has been no progress in female literacy as such. There are two districts of West Bengal (*viz.*, Jalpaiguri and Bankura) where a positive increase of more than 4 per cent points has been recorded. On the other hand, there are districts in Orissa, such as Keonjhar and Balasore, where the Santal women have been further pushed into the mire of illiteracy (Table 4.17). These districts have reported a negative growth in female literacy over the period of two decades under study.

Table 4.16 : Santals: Change in Male Literacy, 1961-81

Positive Change (per cent points)	*District*
Less than 5	Bhagalpur, Purnea, Hazaribagh (Bihar), Cuttack (Orissa)
5-10	Munger, Santal Parganas, Dhanbad (Bihar), Darjeeling, West Dinajpur, Maldah, Murshidabad, Twenty-Four Parganas, Haora, Barddhman, Birbhum (West Bengal)
10-20	Jalpaiguri, Nadia, Hoogly, Bankura, Medinipur, Purulia (West Bengal), Saharsa, Singhbhum (Bihar), Dhenkanal, Keonjhar, Mayurbhanj, Balasore (Orissa)
Above 20	Koch Bihar (West Bengal)

It may be concluded that official intervention in the tribal areas of the country has not affected the tribes much. They have lived in their own enclaves with national planning ventures by-passing them. They have been ruthlessly exploited throughout history. They have faced difficult situations in their life. Their natural habitat has been destroyed systematically. Forests have been reserved and the factories, or mining establishments, or irrigation projects, have been located in various parts of the country. The raw materials have been allowed to flow out of the regions in which they live by the petty village-level traders. Their march from tribalism to proletariat has been very swift and painful.

Table 4.17 : Santals: Change in Female Literacy, 1961-81

Positive Change (per cent points)	*District*
Less than 1	Munger, Purnea, Hazaribagh, Dhanbad, Singhbhum (Bihar)
1-5	Saharsa, Santal Parganas (Bihar), Darjeeling, Jalpaiguri, West Dinajpur, Maldah, Murshidabad, Nadia, 24-Parganas, Hoogly, Barddhaman, Birbhum, Bankura, Medinipur, Purulia (West Bengal), Dhenkanal, Mayurbhanj (Orissa)
Above 5	Koch Bihar, Howrah (West Bengal)
Negative Change (Per cent Points)	
Less than 1	Bhagalpur (Bihar), Keonjhar, Cuttack, Balasore (Orissa)

We have chosen some cases of this phenomenon of tribal deprivation. The case of the Gonds, the Bhils and the Santals has been cited just for illustration. A comprehensive study of the tribal situation in India today is absolutely necessary. If we want to help them we should have to do research to enable them to fight for their own cause.

NOTES AND REFERENCES

1. The 2001census enumerated 84,326,240 persons as Scheduled Tribes. There was a net addition of 16.57 million persons to this population during 1991-2001, implying a decennial growth rate of 24.45 per cent. This may, however, be compared with the growth rate of India's aggregative population which was 21.53 per cent. It may be noted that such a high growth rate was also due to the recognition of certain groups as Scheduled Tribes during the same period.
2. Andre Beteille, 'The definition of a tribe' in Romesh Thapar, *Tribe, Caste and Religion*, p.7.
3. *ibid*, p.8.
4. Nadel, cit., *ibid.*, p. 8. Nadel was quoted by Andre Beteille without any reference.
5. This study has been attempted on the basis of the classification of the Scheduled Tribes as published in paper No. 1 of 1975, *Scheduled Castes and Scheduled Tribes*, Census of India, 1971.This is, however, a state-wise list. This author has compiled an all-India integrated list eliminating repetition of names in the state lists and smoothening out the linguistic differences in nomenclature. An attempt has also been made to follow a taxonomic order by re-grouping the sub-tribes under the major tribes.
6. K.S. Singh, *The People of India: An Introduction*,Vol. I, Anthropological Survey of India, Calcutta, 1992.
7. See census of India, 1991, Series I, India, Part II-B (i), Vols. I, and II, *Primary Census Abstract, General Population*, Office of the Registrar General and Census Commissioner, India, Ministry of Home Affairs, New Delhi, 1994; and Census of India, 2001, *Primary Census Abstract, Total Population*.

8. Moonis Raza and Aijazuddin Ahmad, *An Atlas of Tribal India*, Concept Publishing Company Pvt. Ltd., New Delhi, 1990, p. 28.
9. Abul Fazal Allami, *Ain-e-Akbari*, translated by Col. H.S. Jarrett and annotated by Sir Jadu Nath Sarkar, Royal Asiatic Society of Bengal, Calcutta,1949.
10. *An Atlas of Tribal India, op.cit.*, p. 36. The cores and peripheries were delineated on the basis of data on individual tribal communities by *tahsils, talukas, anchals* or *thana* circles derived from the Census of India, 1961. The analytical procedure is described on p. 35 of the Atlas.
11. *ibid.*, p. 36.
12. *ibid.*, p. 74.
13. Urmila Pingle, 'Central Indian tribal societies under stress of modernisation strategies to face the challenge', in Ashish Bose *et al.* (ed.), *Demography of Tribal Development*, B.R. Publishing Corporation, New Delhi, 1990, pp. 151-70. See also Christoph Von Furer-Haimendorf, *Tribes of India: The Struggle for Survival*, Oxford University Press, New Delhi,1982.
14. V.R. Raghavaiah, *'Background of Tribal Struggles in India'*, pp. 12-22, *ibid.*, 'Tribal Revolts in Chronological Order, 1778-1971', pp. 23-27; L. Natrajan, 'The Santhal Insurrection: 1855-56', pp. 136-47, in A.R. Desai (ed.) *Peasant Struggles in India*, Oxford University Press, Delhi, Paperback Edition, 1981.
15. Aijazuddin Ahmad, 'Regional Development Process and Redistribution of Tribal Population', in L.A. Kosinski and K.M. Elahi (eds.), *Population Redistribution and Development in South Asia*, 1985, pp. 65-78.
16. Moonis Raza, Aijazuddin Ahmad and S.C. Nuna, 'Spatial Pattern of Tribal Literacy in India', in Ashish Bose *et al., op.cit.*, pp. 273-96.

SUGGESTIONS FOR FURTHER READING

Furer-Haimendorf, Christoph Von (1982): *Tribes of India: The Struggle for Survival*, New Delhi: Oxford University Press.

Ghurye, G.S. (1963): *The Scheduled Tribes*, Bombay: Popular Prakashan.

Raza, Moonis and Aijazuddin Ahmad (1990): *An Atlas of Tribal India*, New Delhi: Concept Publishing Company Pvt. Ltd., New Delhi.

Singh, K.S. (ed., 1972): *Tribal Situation in India*, Shimla: Indian Institute of Advanced Study.

Thapar, Romesh (ed., 1977): *Tribe, Caste and Religion*, Delhi: The Macmillan Company of India Ltd.

5

Caste

In Time and Space

Caste is a basic attribute of the Indian social structure. For centuries it has served as a major reference point in social interaction and continues to do so in some form or the other even today. Social hierarchy is based on caste and it is this philosophical vision that determines the behaviour of millions of Indian people in whichever walk of life they are. This is not to say that the caste attitudes are not undergoing changes as a result of education, economic development and social and political reform movements. The impact of these movements has been particularly significant since independence. Caste rigidities have weakened with time in the course of economic development, urbanisation, weakening of feudal values and more importantly, in the process of building a secular, democratic polity. Land reforms coupled with other legislative measures to rehabilitate the socially deprived and the underprivileged sections of population, have helped transform the traditional view of caste. Urbanisation and industrialisation in many regions of the country have resulted in occupational diversification thus changing the traditional inter-caste relations drastically. Migration has created a new climate for change with people adopting new occupations and leaving behind their home villages and traditional occupations, which were caste-specific. In cities, like Delhi or Calcutta, the caste antecedents of an individual are not immediately known and cannot be easily ascertained. This does not mean that with all these changes caste as an institution has died out or its hold on the society has been loosened. On the contrary, the introduction of democratic institutions, people's representation in elected bodies from the *gram panchayats, zila parishads*, municipalities, and state assemblies to the national Parliament, have given a new meaning to the caste identity. The geographic patterning of the caste groups is such that in some constituencies some castes are preponderant. This obviously gives them an upper hand in electoral politics as evident in the fielding of candidates of the same caste by all political parties. This results in the mobilisation of votes along caste lines. Land reforms introduced after independence brought about a new equation between the castes. Those castes, which had remained traditional owners of land by and large, lost their monopoly on land. The land rights were transferred to their tenants who were mostly middle ranking castes. This naturally resulted in the dilution of the supremacy of the traditional landed elites. They had to face new challenges from sections of population who had been subservient to their interests so far and had been living under their perpetual hegemony. The state also adopted a policy of scheduling certain socially deprived castes. These castes of the scheduled category enjoyed certain privileges. For example, State and Parliamentary Constituencies were earmarked and reserved for them, they had a quota in government jobs and scholarships were instituted for them to enable them to join schools and higher institutions of learning. These opportunities were new to them and were intended to help them overcome their traditional drawbacks. However, this also disturbed the social equilibrium, which had sustained the Indian society through ages. Higher castes and the middle ranking castes were generally wary of these reforms and openly contested these policy initiatives. Thus caste in independent India became a volatile issue. The area of inter-caste struggles widened and the violence that followed was a new phenomenon unprecedented in Indian history.

It may be necessary to examine these issues at some length and map out the socio-geographical outlines of the caste phenomena in contemporary Indian society. The changing role of caste in politics, economy, education, social networking and bureaucracy may be probed in order to comprehend the existing social reality.

Traditionally, the Indian society has been governed by the institution of caste. This institutional frame has operated through history as a constraint on the freedom of an individual. The position of an individual in society and his/her sphere of social interaction and code of conduct were determined by his/her caste, that is to say the accident of birth in a family. Caste, therefore, operated as an instrument of social ordering. Each individual was supposed to lead a life in accordance with the socially accepted norms imposed by this rigid and unchanging social order defined by the caste. The concept of caste should be evaluated in this historical backdrop.

Tracing the Origins

It is generally believed that as a phenomenon caste is unique and a specificity of the Indian society.[1] Tracing its origins may, therefore, be necessary to understand the social mechanics that led to the emergence of a hierarchised social order based on caste. The origins of the caste system are, of course, shrouded in mystery, although there is a general agreement that the beginnings were made in the Vedic Age. It all began as a part of the process of peopling of the Sapta-Sindhva region by the Indo-Aryans after the decline of the Indus valley civilisation. The racial composition of population seems to be important. While the Palaeo-Mediterraneans and the Proto-Austroloids were already there, a new ethnic element that was introduced in the population was that of the Nordics (Indo-Aryans).[2] As the mode of agriculture took its roots and expanded in space it resulted in a new organisation of social forces of production. The expansion of agricultural mode implied assimilation of hunting and food gathering as well as pastoral communities into an agricultural society. This process of transformation was attended by a simple division of labour among the different constituent groups who came together to live in the pioneer villages. Understandably, the colour of the skin became the primary basis of this social division. The Indo-Aryans asserted their superiority by creating a four-fold division of the society which came to be known as *Chatur Varnaya*, and placing themselves in the upper strata of the Brahman and Kshatriya ranks. The Indus valley people and the tribes who lived on the periphery were assigned a lower status of Vaisyas and Sudras, or even treated as outcastes. The Indo-Aryans emerged as the custodians of knowledge (Brahmans) and defenders of territory (Kshatriyas). On the other hand, the Indus valley people were assigned mundane jobs such as cultivating the fields or exchanging and manufacturing artisan goods. There were other unclean jobs, such as treating the dead bodies or removing the skins of the dead animals. These jobs were handled by the lower strata of the society, sometimes described as the 'exterior' castes.

It may be interesting to note that while a similar division of labour emerged in all other agrarian societies in the world, an elaborate caste system emerged only in India. Why India is an exception to this rule? What led to the institutionalisation of this division of labour, which became so rigid that it could not be altered or challenged? Each caste group became associated with a specific department of work, so much so that a particular vocation became a hereditary trait of the family, immutable in time. It is generally known that initially a four-fold *Varna* division emerged in the Vedic Age. These four *Varnas* were Brahman, Kshatriya, Vaisya and Sudra. These groups constituted a hierarchical social division with Brahmans at the top and Sudras at the bottom. Within each group, particularly among the two upper segments of the *Varna* system, individual families started getting differentiated on the basis of clan or *gotra*. These divisions became institutionalised, as marriages were permissible within the same *Varna*. On the other hand, it was not customary to marry within the same *gotra*. This gradually led to the emergence of a social practice of *Varna* endogamy and *gotra* exogamy.

Varnas were also differentiable from one another on the basis of rituals performed on occasions such as birth, marriage and death. The details of these rituals were prescribed in the scriptures (*Brahamanas* and *Smritis*).

For all practical purposes *Varna* acquired all the characteristic features of a class division. In the social system of *Varna* the Brahman and the Kshatriya emerged as the upper classes. The Brahmanical class monopolised knowledge and imparted it to the children of the upper classes on a selective basis. The Brahmanical class also legitimised the role of Kshatriya in enforcing the law, thus enabling them to rise as a ruling class. The Kshatriyas naturally assumed their role as defenders of the territory. The Brahmanical interpretation was that the Kshatriya was a legitimate *raja*, and more importantly, a divine incarnation.

Later on, as economy diversified and a section of population concentrated in large settlements, occupations also diversified. Eventually, the *Varna* divisions ramified in accordance with this process of economic diversification into the *jati* divisions. The *jatis*, however, were hereditarily associated with certain occupations, which defined their ritual status and the rank in society. The *jati pratha* was broadly in conformity with the *Varna* system. This means that each *jati* corresponded to a particular *Varna*. The ranking of the *jatis* was relative to one another and in accordance with the *Varna* order. The *Varna-jati* system was also specific to the cultural regions and inter-regional comparisons were futile. It may be concluded that the *Varna* system acted as an all-India model representing the Indian unity. The *jati* system, on the other hand, was a regional specificity. The question of relations of one caste with the other caste and the relations with the members of the same caste can perhaps be understood in the context of regions. The *jati* system, thus, represented the diversity of the regional ethos within the over-arching all-India unity. It may be noted that the process of cultural differentiation expressed itself over a domain of language, implying that each cultural region was in reality a language/dialect region. Each region was differentiable from neighbouring regions on the basis of spoken language. A particular *jati* strictly corresponded to a language area. The *jatis* in Bengal are not comparable with the *jatis* in Karnataka, or for that matter, in Maharashtra. This is not to say that migration from one region to the other have not been common. In fact, migrations were a common phenomenon. They did result in a mechanism of preservation of cultural traits. Each emigrant group in a city found it more convenient to function as a brotherhood. This promoted intra-group interaction. The immigrant groups, divorced as they were from their traditional homelands, evolved a system, which kept them as a closely-knit community, rooted in their cultural tradition and yet living in an alien environment. It was this mechanism that made inter-regional (cross-cultural) marriages a rare phenomenon. With the passage of time sub-castes, which were splinter groups from the major castes, came into being. While initially, they were sub-divisions of a caste, gradually each sub-caste started functioning as a caste in itself. Within the sub-castes a system emerged which imposed restrictions on marriage, commensal practices and communal behaviour (Figs. 5.1 and 5.2).

Varna	Class	Deity Worshipped
Brahman	Priests, Interpreters of Dharma	Agni
Kshatriya	Warriors, Rulers	Indra
Vaisya	Commoners, Cattle herders	Visvedeva
Sudra	Peasants, Workers, Servants	

Figure 5.1 : Classical Varna Model based on Division of Labour

Note: Rigveda mentioned only the first three *Varnas*. Sudra was a later addition.

Varna	Jati	Up-Jati
Brahman	Kanyakubja, Saryupari, Gaur	Shrimali, Pushkarna
Kshatriya	Rajput	
Vaisya	Agarwal, Oswal	Disa, Bisa
Sudra	Chamar, Dom, Kalwar	

Figure 5.2 : A Generalised Model showing *Varna-Jati-up-Jati* Connection

The sociological literature on caste is voluminous.[3] Studies on caste cover a vast area in Indological, social anthropological and sociological research. Obviously, the approaches vastly differ. It may be pertinent to refer here to the differing viewpoints on the origins of *Varna-jati* system. Briefly, three major viewpoints can be highlighted here. First, caste is viewed as a product of the division of labour. Secondly, it is viewed as a cultural phenomenon and operates as an institution. Thirdly, caste is viewed as social stratification leading to institutionalisation of social inequality. It is this vision of social inequality ingrained in the Indian mind that confronts with the principles of democratic polity introduced since independence.

For all practical purposes membership of a caste is hereditary and cannot be acquired. Membership of a certain caste also determines the marriage field, as all caste groups are endogamous. It also determines the pattern of social interaction and commensal relations (whether one can accept or cannot accept cooked or uncooked food or water from a member of a certain caste).

Caste and the Morphology of Settlements

The pioneer villages that emerged in the Sapta-Sindhva region initially and the Ganga and the peninsular river valleys later evolved a social division based on the caste system. In fact, the members of the different caste groups came together in a certain proportion depending on the area of the cultivated land, productivity of soil and a certain mix of crops. As caste groups converged on land reclaimed from the forest, the territory was dotted with pioneer villages of different lineage groups. Understandably, the cultivators constituted the nucleus of the village community. The cultivating castes might have been self-sufficient in the beginning. But as the process of agricultural intensification progressed, they needed other people who could help them in agricultural operations or provide services, such as those of a potter, a carpenter, a barber, a weaver, a shoe-maker and the like. These groups who came together in a village setting specialised in specific rural arts. Their number was, however, determined by the demand for their services felt by the cultivating caste. In a typical village setting, there were weavers, potters, carpenters, blacksmiths, shoemakers, oilmen as well as those who treated the dead bodies at the cremation ground or treated the skins of the dead animals for making leather. They formed a ring of settlements around the nucleus of the cultivating castes. As is evident, these services were not, and could not be, treated as of equal rank. These groups were arranged along the vertical scale with an implicit hierarchy. Each one of them constituted a *jati* based on a specific occupation with which it had a traditional association. Those who handled unclean and polluted jobs were drawn from the Sudra ranks, and were mostly treated as untouchable. It may be true to say that this model was applicable to the pioneer villages that emerged in the first millennium B.C. in the Ganga Valley and a little later in the valleys of Krishna, Godavari and Kaveri in South India.

The village mirrors the intricacies of the caste-based Indian society. The ritual hierarchy of castes expresses in space in the residential patterning of different castes within a rural settlement in whatever region of India it is located. In fact, the social morphology of rural villages in India is a spatial surrogate of the ritual hierarchical social order based on caste. What happened was that the most favourable sites within the village settlement (*abadi*) were occupied by the cultivating caste, the dominant caste. The Brahman houses were located in their neighbourhood. Separated by lanes were the quarters in which the middle ranking castes lived. The outer periphery of this agglomerated settlement unit was occupied by other service castes that generally performed clean services. There was yet another periphery in which the unclean castes, or the untouchables, holding the lowest rank in caste hierarchy, were living. Depending on relief as in Rajasthan, or if the settlements were perched on mounds as in parts of Uttar Pradesh, the central promontory was occupied by the main cultivating caste, say Rajputs, Jats and Ahirs. At the lower level were other middle ranking castes and the low castes were situated on the outer periphery which was generally a low-lying area. Thus an altitudinal zonation based on caste hierarchy characterised the rural settlements all over the country. This model was universal and represented a type in itself. If Muslims, *e.g.*, Sheikhs, Julahas and Fakirs, were a component of rural population, they also followed a zonal distribution pattern similar to that of the Hindu castes (Figs. 5.3a, 5.3b and 5.4).

O.H.K. Spate noted that an Indian village did not follow a definite layout plan. However, 'within the seemingly chaotic agglomeration there is, as a rule, a strong internal differential, that of the separate quarters for various castes'.[4] His study of Aminbhavi, a village situated to the north-northeast of Dharwar in Karnataka, although randomly chosen was a typical example of the way caste factor operated in the residential patterning of different communities in a village. Based on a pioneering survey undertaken by C.D. Deshpande and his students and with subsequent inputs from L.S. Bhat, Spate's study can serve as a model.[5] The village population consisted of Lingayats, an agricultural caste of Karnataka (64.54 per cent), Muslims (13.40 per cent), Jains (6.09 per cent) and Brahmans (1.83 per cent). The members of each caste occupied a solid block of contiguous houses in a lane named after the caste. The village population also included Talwars (7.31 per cent), Harijans (4.87 per cent)[6], Wadars, Shikalgars and washermen. On the periphery of the village lived the low castes. The occupational structure, as in other parts of India, is caste-based. For example, Lingayats are mostly tenant farmers whereas Talwars and Harijans are generally agricultural labourers. Members of other castes are carpenters, smiths, cobblers, washermen, barbers, etc. Despite the changes in Aminbhavi, the residential patterning continues to be the same.

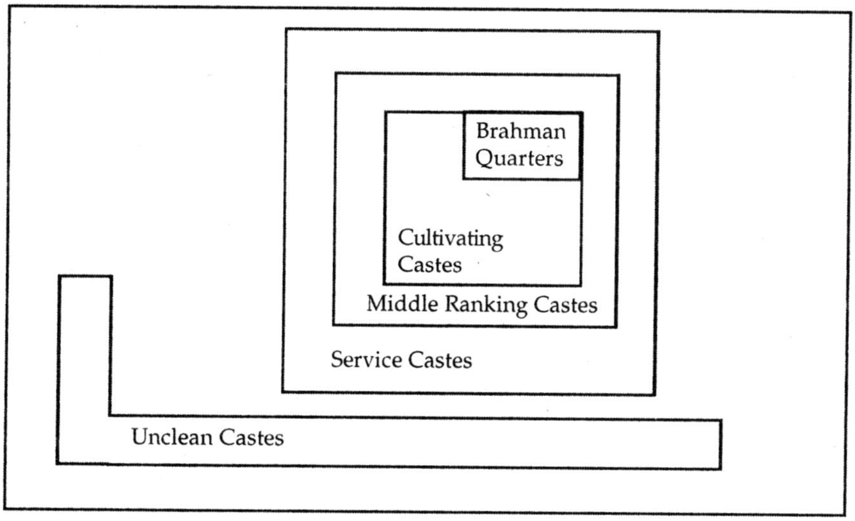

Figure 5.3a : Residential Patterning of Caste Groups in a Rural Village: Schematic

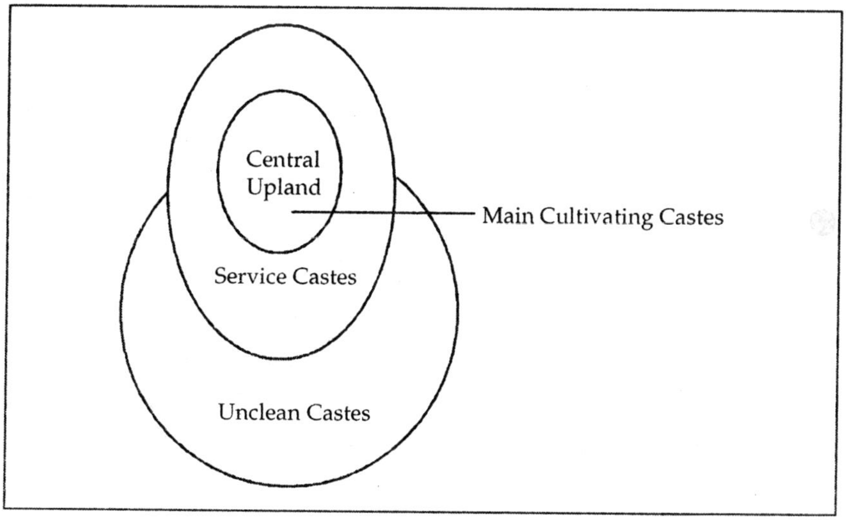

Figure 5.3b : Residential Patterning of Caste Groups in a Rural Village Located on a Mound: Schematic

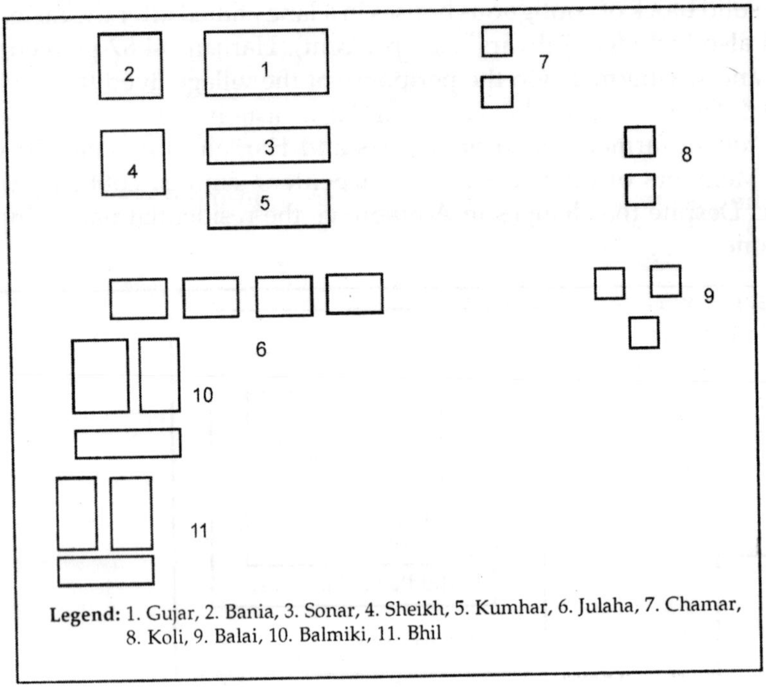

Figure 5.4 : Spatial Arrangement of Separate Caste Quarters in a Rural Village: Schematic

While caste-based residential segregation is universal, the village in south (India) presents an extreme form of spatial segregation.

'The general emphasis on caste in south (India) takes social fragmentation, allied with spatial separation, to the extreme, segregating the untouchable in outlying *cheris* or sub-villages, sometimes located several hundred yards from the main villages of which they are service-components. This is indeed a climax of geographical differentiation; apartheid'.[7] (Box 5.1).

Box 5.1 : A Typical Cheri

A typical *cheri* may consist of two rows of huts with a narrow central 'street'; in the middle this widens to make room for a tiny temple. The huts have thick mud walls, roofed with palmyra thatch, and low mud porches scrupulously swept. To enter one must bend double; the only light comes from the door and from under the caves, and furniture consists of a few pots and pans, a couple of wooden chests, and the essential paddy bin, ... raised from the ground to escape the rats and built up of hoops of mud. Poor as they are, these dwellings are yet homes, and obviously loved as such: their cleanliness, the surrounding mangoes, coconut and palmyra palms, redeem them from utter squalor. The nadir is reached in the *bustees* of Calcutta and the revolting camps of casual tribal labour found on the outskirts of the larger towns: shelters (they cannot be called even huts) of matting, of rags, of petrol tins beaten flat, on the waste spaces open to the sun and racking with filth.

—O.H.K. Spate, *India and Pakistan*, 1957: 203-04.

Andre Betielle's study of Sripuram village of Tanjore district in Tamil Nadu shows that:

> 'people who are close to each other in the social system tend to live side by side; people whose social positions are widely different live apart. The *agraharam*, for instance, is not only a cluster of habitations but also the centre of social life for the Brahmins...to the Brahmins, the *agraharam*, in more ways than one, is the village'.[8]

In the same way the *pallacheri* is not just another quarter of the village. It is a place in which the entry of the Brahmans is forbidden by social custom. They just cannot enter the *pallacheri* since the concept of pollution and purity applies to places also. It is not just interpersonal.

Caste in Urban Neighbourhoods

The residential housing in urban neighbourhoods is a continuation of the rural model—separate quarters for different castes. Take, for example, the towns of western Uttar Pradesh, such as Mathura, Aligarh, Bulandshahr, Meerut, Moradabad, Bareilly, Badaun and Firozabad. There are separate *mohallas* for different Hindu castes. And this pattern is valid for all regions of India. If there are Muslims in these towns they live in separate *mohallas, katras* or *bustees*. In the towns of British India there were mixed localities as well in which Hindu castes lived in the midst of Muslims or *vice versa*. However, segregation has increased with time and in many north Indian towns different communities live in separate blocks.

In a traditional set-up, there are separate residential quarters for Brahmans (*e.g.*, *mohalla* Chauban in Firozabad), Vaisyas, *lohars* (blacksmiths), weavers, *dhobis*, tailors and other artisan castes. The low castes such as the sweepers and the *kanjars* generally live on the periphery of the town. There is an association between the *mohalla* name and the castes that live in them. This is true for Muslim *mohallas* as well. There are separate quarters for separate castes (such as *katra* Sonaran, *katra* Pathanan, *mohalla* Shishgaran, *mohalla* Bahelian, *mohalla* Naalbandan in Firozabad; *mohalla* Churiwallan in old Delhi). With development these towns have grown into large cities with new outgrowths mushrooming on the periphery but the caste-based segregation is still intact and the community-based segregation has further widened. It may be noted that in the new Muslim residential colonies caste-based segregation is generally missing. However, propinquity between the houses of a Pathan and a Julaha in a new colony does not necessarily mean that there is an enhanced social interaction between the two families or a drastic behavioural change in the social attitude towards each other.

The neighbourhoods in the Mughal town of Shahjahanabad presented yet another example of caste-based residential segregation. In the beginning, while the royalty lived in the fort located on the banks of the Jumuna (Yamuna), there were the *mohallas* in the neighbourhood of the fort for the nobility in the area between the fort and the

Jama Masjid. This building complex was razed to the ground after the uprising of 1857. Around the Jama Masjid were arranged the *mohallas* of the service castes, as well as those of ethnic groups such as *mohalla* Punjabian, Kashmiri *mohalla*, *kucha* Pandit, Bara Hindurao and so on. Shahjahanabad continues to have the same pattern of neighbourhoods even today. There are *mohallas* with occupational distinction, such as Ballimaran, Suiwalan, Churigaran, *kucha* Chelan, Gali Rajan, etc. After the Partition of the country in 1947, Shahjahanabad changed a lot but the traditional *mohalla* structure is still intact.

Studies of the Himalayan towns such as Chamba, Kangra and Kullu reveal a close relationship between *mohalla* names and the caste/ethnic groups associated with them. In fact, the *mohalla* formation was essentially based on the principle of caste/class segregation. The capital towns of the princely states also indicated a clear impact of the feudal social order. The royalty and nobility chose for themselves the most advantageous sites, close to the fortress or the palace, followed by *mohallas* in which the elite groups (courtiers, officers, religious leaders) lived; next were the *mohallas* of artisan and trading castes (metal and stone workers, weavers, carpenters, masons, perfume workers), etc. Adjacent to them were the *mohallas* of service castes, both ritually pure (water carriers, domestic servants, cattle keepers, shepherds) as well as impure castes (sweepers, cobblers, butchers).[9] In a hilly town, an added dimension is that the caste hierarchy expresses itself in the altitudinal zonation of *mohallas*: the higher the position in caste rank, the higher the location in the town, other things remaining the same. *Mohallas* of Chamba such as Bansi Gopal, Nand and Drobhi have traditional habitations of the Brahman, Mahajan and the Rajput families. Julahas (weavers) are concentrated in a *mohalla* called Julakri, smiths in Sapdi and butchers in Kasakra. The general pattern is that the *mohallas* of high status castes are surrounded by castes which have a lower rank in ritual hierarchy. On the periphery are the *mohallas* of the low castes.[10]

Caste and Clan Territories

As already noted, rural settlements in India have largely been influenced in their residential patterning by the caste and the clan/lineage structures. In fact, the caste influences in subtle ways both the behavioural attitudes of the people as well as the social values that determine them. As is generally known, the Indian village is a complex entity. While its evolutionary history has left its imprints on the layout of habitations, even the direction in which the houses of certain caste groups are situated and the daily movement patterns of the people from their homes to the fields and the market place are all determined by caste factors. Moreover, caste does not function alone. It creates a network of relationships based on economic/functional inter-dependencies, ritual and religious customs and the feudal social order. Every settlement in India is in a way a mosaic where people live in their own exclusive social worlds despite the fact that they meet members of other castes in different situations—secular as well as religious.[11] The traditional way of life and the spatial organisation of habitations continue without much of a change. However, democratic institutions to which the rural population has been exposed since independence and the impact of planned development including creation of social infrastructure within the villages (*e.g.*, schools, dispensaries, seed depots, banks, etc.) have added new elements to the traditional settlement morphology. These developments notwithstanding, the traditional order based on caste structure is still intact.

Studies conducted by Indian and foreign scholars in different parts of India confirm the all-embracing role of caste and *jati* identities in the settlement morphology. The roots of this relationship between caste and settlement morphology have been traced in the early colonization of the Ganga valley and the emergence of territorial units (*janapadas*) in ancient India. Such a complex social system as the caste/*jati* structure and its diverse regional facets was bound to have its expression in the social organisation of rural villages and the territorial organisation based on clan/lineage connections that arose out of it. Members of the same caste/*jati* tended to live together in the rural space out of necessity and the character of the locality came to be defined by the day-to-day cooperation between them emanating from the principles of common descent and economic bondage. Thus the common descent and the common residence were associated in space. The situation continues to be the same even today.

Naturally, the kinship ties have expanded in space. Initially, they were localised, that is to say confined to the same village, but eventually they have gone beyond the village and have resulted in the emergence of caste or clan territories, loosely defined but firmly asserted by the lineage groups. The kinship ties which also operate through marriage networks further reinforce the kinship feeling. Thus, a spatial structure of great social and functional relevance based on lineage is created. K.N. Singh has cited the case of Rajputs, Jats, Bhumihars, Ahirs, Kurmis and Kansar Pathans living in the North Indian Plain who are known to have established a chain of clan territories through their patrilineal kin bodies.[12]

> 'Territorial organization and colonization normally proceed through the hegemony and control of dominant classes... which tend to earn through time great amount of political... power... from regional authorities without and social and territorial control within on a local level such as clan territories'.[13]

Over the clan territories lineage groups of dominant *jatis* wield great social authority. These clans enjoy a kind of territorial suzerainty, since they are the landed castes and their land ownership is a great factor in contributing to their social authority. This is not to deny the fact that the population composition within the supposed clan territory is heterogeneous. In fact, several castes/*jatis* live together and their population is often larger than that of the dominant caste. These territories generally encompass a certain number of villages. In popular imagination these units are generally recognised as consisting of a cluster of villages. This cluster may consist of 96 villages (*chhanbe*), 94 villages (*chauranbe*), 60 villages (*sathi*), 42 villages (*biayalisi*), 24 villages (*chaubisi*), or 20 villages (*bisi*).[14] Evidently, the extent of the territory as popularly perceived may be a function of the initial settlement of a dominant caste in a given region and its subsequent expansion in space. This historical fact acquires great significance in defining the functional authority of a caste over a territory. It has its own behavioural implications.

It may be concluded that the residential rural space in India has evolved through history within the over-arching influence of caste relations. The distinction between castes expresses itself in the segregation of population of different castes in different *dhanis, puras* or *purwas*. The dispersal of population of different castes in the *dhanis* of villages in Rajasthan is an example of caste-based residential patterning. In fact, the general principle is: the lower the rank in ritual hierarchy, the farther the location of that caste from the centre of the settlement. By the same logic, the outcastes are supposed to live in separate quarters outside the main village. This is not to deny the fact that the different caste-groups have been attracted by the dominant castes for the services they render and their social interaction and the daily give-and-take that goes on between them on a routine basis is based by and large on economic and religious factors.

Caste and Land Ownership

Historically, the factor of caste has operated as a major determinant of social status in many critical spheres of life. One such critical area was the access to land, the main productive asset in an agrarian society, such as India. As noted above, caste groups were surrogate classes and a division between those who owned land and those who did not could easily be perceived along caste lines. The upper castes invariably emerged as the landed elites. On the other hand, those in the lower rungs of the caste society were largely landless, working on the land estates of the ownership farmers. It is understandable that in a vast country like India with diverse agro-climatic conditions there were regional differences in the types of land ownership and the tenurial relations. It is also understandable that land systems of British India, such as those described as the *Ryotwari*, *Mahalwari* or the *Zamindari*, came in response to the diverse agro-ecological conditions, and the regionally diverse socio-political structures. In the course of time on the *Zamindari* lands, an Indian form of feudalism emerged. The landed elites were the high castes while the labour supply came from the low castes who were treated no better than the serfs.[15]

Exceptions apart, there was, therefore, a broader correspondence between the ritual hierarchy of caste and the distribution of ownership rights on land. The landed elites emerged as *dominant* castes (Box 5.2).

They were drawn from among the ranks of the Hindu high castes, such as the Rajputs, Kayasthas and the Brahmans as well as upper castes among the Muslims. The Mughal policy of land grants to the high castes among the Hindus and to the upper sections of the Muslim society, *i.e.*, *Ashraf*, comprising Sheikhs, Saiyids and Afghans, was apparently aimed at creating a broad-based ruling class through which the surplus from land could be appropriated (Fig. 5.5). The British retained the system as such. In fact, they further strengthened it turning it into a rigorous exploitative mechanism to serve the best interests of the colonial state. The growing accumulation of land in the hands of the members of the high castes eventually reduced the artisans, Sudras and the other sections of the outcastes to the level of paupers. In fact, all chances of their having access to land were blocked by the dominant castes. Their marginalisation acquired a form, which contributed immensely to the Indian poverty.[16]

Box 5.2 : Dominant Castes

In many parts of rural India there exist castes which are locally numerically preponderant, own the bulk of the arable land, occupy a fairly high position in the ritual hierarchy, and wield power over the other castes. Examples of such castes are Jats, Ahirs and Rajputs in the north, Patidars in Gujarat, Marathas in Maharashtra, Kamma and Reddi in Andhra Pradesh, Lingayat and Okkaliga (Vakkaliga) in Mysore, Vellala and Gounder in Madras and Nayar in Kerala. Sometimes the dominance of a caste is decisive, all types of power being concentrated in it. At other times, however, the different elements of dominance may be distributed among several castes. In the first instance, the dominant caste wields great power over the others, while in the second there is likely to be a balance of power among the powerful castes.... the maintenance of law and order in rural areas even now depends to some extent upon the leaders of the dominant caste. They are the people who can punish errant individuals and ensure the maintenance of the caste codes. When a caste is politically and economically dominant, its religious position tends to fall in line with its secular position.

—M.N. Srinivas, *India: Social Structure*, 1986: 19.

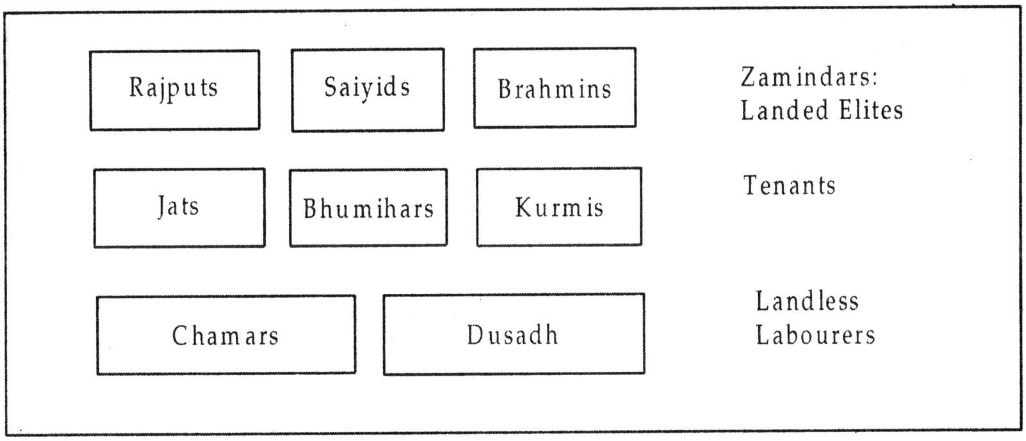

Figure 5.5 : Caste and Land Relations in Traditional Agriculture in British India, Examples from United Provinces of Agrah, Oudh and Bihar: Schematic

The Scene in the 16th and 17th Centuries

The Mughal chronicle, *Ain-i-Akbari,* mentions the names of the land-owning castes (*qaum-e-zamindaran*) in each of the *mahals* of the Mughal provinces. On the basis of this information it is possible to infer the nature of relationship between caste and land ownership. Using these data it is also possible to know the geographical distribution of the landed castes in different parts of the Mughal Empire. This study is, however, restricted to 13 *sarkars* chosen randomly from the seven provinces of India under

Akbar. The *sarkars* chosen include Agrah, Kalpi and Alwar (Subah Agrah), Awadh, Lakhnau (Subah Awadh), Dehli, Saharanpur (Subah Dehli), Rechnau Doab (Subah Lahor), Bhakkar (Subah Multan), Behar (Subah Behar), Ujjain, Garha and Chanderi (Subah Malwah).

Sarkar Agrah

Landowning castes included Gaur (a branch of Rajputs), Jat, Lodh, Chauhan Rajputs, Bhadoriya (a branch of Chauhan Rajputs), Thatthar Rajputs (Gujars converted to Islam), Brahman, Sheikhzadah, Ahir, Panwar Rajputs, Sikarwar (a branch of the Badgujar Rajputs), Sheikhzadah Chishti, Saiyid and Badgujar. However, despite this diversity of landed castes most of the land was owned by the different clans of Rajputs. Brahmans and Sheikhzadahs are mentioned in two *parganahs* only. Jats are mentioned in three *parganahs* and Saiyid in one only.

Sarkar Kalpi

Landowning castes include Rajputs, Kachhwaha Rajputs, Sengar Rajputs (a branch of the Agnibansi Rajputs) and Rajput Kumbi, Bais, Sheikhzadah, Malikzadah, Brahman, Afghan and Turkoman. The names of the Rajput clans are mentioned repeatedly thus indicating that most of the land was under the possession of Rajput clans who were the dominant caste. The names of Sheikhzadah, Brahman, Afghan and Turkoman are mentioned in one *parganah* each.

Sarkar Alwar

Castes mentioned include Khanzadah (a Meo sub-caste), Kachhwaha, Badgujar and Chauhan Rajputs, other Meo sub-castes, Mina, Jat and Abbasi. However, land was mostly owned by the Khanzadahs, Meos of other *gotras* and the Rajputs. Mina, Saiyid, Baqqal, Abbasi and the Jat are mentioned in one *parganah* each.

Sarkar Dehli

Castes mentioned include the Rajputs, Chauhan Rajputs, Badgujar Rajputs, Chhokar, Ahir, Afghan, Gujar, Ranghar, Jat, Brahman, Taga and Saiyid. While different Rajput clans are the main landed caste, there were many other caste-groups who were holding land in different parts of the *sarkar* of Dehli.

Sarkar Saharanpur

Landowning castes mentioned include the Ranghar, Taga, Jat, Gujar, Ahir, Brahman, Afghan, Turkoman and Saiyid. Apparently, there were several caste-groups who were equally dominant in this *sarkar*.

Sarkar Awadh

Brahman, different Rajput clans, such as the Kumbi, Chauhan, Ghelot, Gaikwar, and the Sombansi, Bais (newly converted to Islam) and the Ansari are the castes listed in the *Ain*. Evidently, most of the land was held by the different Rajput clans including those who were recent converts to Islam. Ansaris are mentioned only in one *parganah*.

Sarkar Lakhnau

Castes mentioned include Rajputs and their different clans such as Chauhan, Chandel, Ghelot, and the Bachgoti. Other castes mentioned include the Brahman, Saiyid, Jat, Afghan, Sheikhzadah and Ansari.

In fact, Rajputs were the main land-owning caste followed by the Brahmans, Sheikhzadahs and the Bais. Afghan and Saiyid are mentioned only in one *parganah* each.

Sarkar Behar

Afghan, Brahman, Kayath (Kayastha), Sheikhzadah and Rajput were the major landowning castes. All the five caste-groups are listed under the different *parganahs,* thus indicating a diversity of landed castes.

Sarkar Chanderi

Bagri, Baqqal, Khati, Dangi, Ahir, Brahman, Rajput Bundela, Kayath, Musalman, Khichi, Dingi, Makhati, and Khatri were the main landowning castes. However, the data do not indicate dominance of any particular caste. Thus the region shows a fairly large diversity of dominant castes.

Sarkar Garha

Gonds (a well-known tribe) are shown as the only landowning community.

Sarkar Ujjain

Among the main landowning castes are the Ujjainia, Rathor, Soriah, Magwar (Meghwal), Deora (Rajput), Bais and Jadon (Yadu,Yadava). Different Rajput clans were the dominant caste over most of the area.

Sarkar Rechnau doab

Bhatti, Khokhar, Chimah, Jat, Manhas, Balawariah, Bhutiyalah, Taral, Brahman, Sanawal, Langah, Gujar and the Hatiyalah were the landowning castes in the different *parganahs* of this *sarkar*. However, it appears that the Jats and their different clans were the most dominant over most of the Rechnau (Ravi-Chenab) Doab region.

Sarkar Bhakkar

Castes mentioned include the Dharejah, Mehar, Rahar, Jahna, Bhatti, Sahejah, Harejah and Jaman. Insofar as the caste dominance is concerned the picture is quite diverse.

It is thus obvious that historically land relations in India conformed to the social reality of the caste. The *Ain*'s data further confirm this view.

The British Period

The character of Indian feudalism/quasi-feudalism underwent a major change under the British. In fact, the British created multiple interests in land and the number of intermediaries which increased as the *zamindari* system took its roots, particularly in Bengal and Oudh, added a new dimension to the exploitative processes of the *ryot*. The caste system, which was a manifestation of the social hierarchical order, conformed to this pattern of absentee landlordism admirably. Caste-groups of various ranks took positions of vintage in this pyramid of feudal exploitation (Table 5.1).

Table 5.1 : Multiple Interests in Land: Examples from British India

One Interest	*Two Interests*	*Three Interests*	*Four Interests*	
• The government	• The government	• The government	• The government	• The government
	• The *ryot*[1]	• A landlord[2]	• A landlord	• An overlord
		• Actual holders[3]	• Tenure holders[4]	• A landlord
			• The *ryot*	• Actual holder

Source: B.H. Baden-Powell, *Land Revenue and Tenure in British India.*

Notes: 1. An occupant with a definite title, not a tenant.
2. A *zamindar, talukadar* or a village body as in the *mahalwari* system.
3. May be a co-sharer.
4. A sub-proprietor.

India at independence inherited this pattern of land relations. The Indian National Congress, which struggled for India's independence, always pleaded for drastic land reforms in order to ensure a better deal for the oppressed sections of the rural society. The *zamindari* abolition in the early fifties of the twentieth century was a part of the land reforms package introduced by the National Government under Nehru.[17]

The Scene in Contemporary India

One may conclude that the relationship between caste and land ownership is not simple. The fact that among the landless are included most of the low castes, designated as Scheduled Castes, and most of the land is in the hands of the privileged sections of the caste society, speaks volumes about the social forces that operate at the village level. This question of economic rehabilitation of the oppressed sections has received attention in many sociological and anthropological studies conducted at the village level[18] (Box 5.3).

Box 5.3 : The Changing Village

Caste itself is relatively unimpaired. Every one, including the Ganjam DISTILLERS and the Boad OUTCASTES, 'believes in caste'. They observe the rules of endogamy and inter-dining. Caste usages affect every aspect of their lives. The solidarity of caste-groups has not lessened.

But the local structure is undergoing a fundamental change. It is losing its politico-economic function. This function rested on the fact that productive resources were allotted according to caste, and control of these resources was organised by a localised structure of caste-group. In one case the structure has adjusted itself successfully to the new economy. But in other cases it has failed. The new economy is widespread: caste-group organisation is appropriate to a localised economy. The new economy demands social mobility: but untouchability is at once a cornerstone of caste and an insuperable obstacle to mobility. Localisation and untouchability are the rocks against which beats the tide of the new economy.

The men of Bisipara today derived their right to a share in the resources of production not by membership of a caste but as citizens of India. In the village the hierarchy of caste-groups is no longer a complete reflection of economic realities, nor an adequate means of ordering political relations. Under pressure of economic change the political functions of caste are beginning to be taken over, as one might expect, by the ultimate political authority, the Government of India.

—F.G. Bailey, *Caste and the Economic Frontier*, 1972: 275.

Few geographers have ventured in this area. Reference may, however, be made to the pioneering work of S.M. Mandavdhare who investigated the question of caste and land relations empirically by selecting a sample of fifty villages from the Marathwada region of Maharashtra. His data based on individual caste households show a broad conformity between the status of a caste-group and the proportionate share of land it holds. The data were collected for all the castes living in the sample villages. The sample included the major agricultural castes of Marathwada, such as the Maratha, Wanjari, Mali and Lingayat as well as the Scheduled Castes, such as the Mangs, Mahars and Chambhars (local name for Chamars).[19] Marathwada, as this study shows, presented a case in which the number of marginal and small farmers is quite high. The proportion of large farmers among the Scheduled Castes is very low. The study further shows that land inequality among the castes is significantly high in villages lying in the rainfall scarcity zone. Similarly, in villages where the Scheduled Castes are politically organised, inter-caste inequality has considerably reduced. This shows that, other things remaining the same, political mobilisation may help the oppressed sections in their economic rehabilitation.

Broadly speaking, an understanding of the social status of a caste group and its share in the village land cannot be properly developed without linking it to the *jajmani* system and its local variants which formed the basis of inter-dependent relationship between the landowning and the landless castes.[20] The caste-based production relations in rural India thus reveal features of class-like formations where caste actually acts as a surrogate class. As actual tillers on land are very often the low castes who neither own land nor have a just share in the surplus generated by them, agrarian relations have remained ridden with conflicts.[21]

Distribution of Caste-Groups

There is no data base available to enable one to analyse either the numerical strength or the geographic distribution pattern of different caste-groups living in India today. The successive censuses conducted in India since independence happily opted to discontinue the earlier practice of collecting and publishing data on caste. However, data were and are still collected during all the censuses on the scheduled category of population—castes as well as the tribes. Understandably, these data are partial and not enough as they tell us only a part of the story. The data are grossly inadequate insofar as the question of the caste identity of the people of India is concerned in the context of today. In a country where the affairs of the state have been influenced by caste and community identities, non-availability of geographically disaggregated quantitative data on caste may be a serious handicap to social science research. For example, a socio-geographic interpretation of caste is not possible in the absence of such crucial data. There is no gainsaying the fact that geographical distribution of caste-groups helps in understanding the character of ethno-lingual regions as well as the implicit meaning of the ongoing dynamics of social change in different parts of the country. Caste is a social reality. Its role in society and its politics cannot be minimised by suppressing data. The levels of social development reached by different caste-groups are an important indicator of their progress and the place in society. The relations between different castes, as the contemporary evidence shows, are becoming increasingly competitive. This is largely due to the skewed distribution of wealth. Hidden behind these conflicts is the basic question of social justice.[22] Moreover, caste identity is an important factor in politics. No political party can be oblivious of the presence or otherwise of numerically strong caste-groups in a certain region. This information is crucially important in chalking out the electoral strategy at a given point of time. In the absence of updated data on caste no social science debate on the role of caste in electoral politics, economic development and education can be meaningful.

It may be interesting to examine the geographic patterns of distribution of different caste-groups in British India. As is generally known, the last point of time when comprehensive data on caste was collected, was during 1931 census, almost 80 years from now. The 1941 census was sketchy due to the impact of War on census operations. The 1931 census of India collected data for all the caste-groups living in the country in the British districts as well as the princely states, adopting not a very satisfactory scheme of classification, but nonetheless trying to capture the prevailing social reality of caste identities. The massive data generated during the census operations were published along with the Reports of the 1931 census under various heads. For example, tables were titled as 'territorial distribution of principal communities' (Madras Presidency), 'caste, tribe or race' (Assam), 'race, tribe or caste' (United Provinces of Agrah and Oudh), and so on. Population was classified into Brahmanic Hindu, non-Brahmanic Hindu and Muslim castes. Tribal groups were mixed up with castes. They were further cross-classified by religious persuasions. Using the district-level data of 1931 census, one can broadly identify the geographic patterns in the distribution of different caste-groups. This will perhaps serve as a benchmark. It may be noted that certain caste-groups have been very mobile in space. Moreover, the partition of the country in 1947 resulted in far-reaching changes in population composition in different parts of India. Urbanisation, migration for employment and industrialisation, among other things, have contributed to this spatial mobility. This study is, therefore, no more than of historic significance. Admittedly, a comprehensive study of 1931 data on caste-groups calls for an independent exercise at the all-India scale, and may not be feasible within the scope of this work. This study is, therefore, by choice restricted to the three British provinces, *viz.*, United Provinces of Agrah and Oudh, Madras Presidency and Assam, as in 1931. However, the political map of India has also changed since then. While the United Provinces of Agrah and Oudh, now known as Uttar Pradesh, have not registered any change in the outer boundary, the Madras Presidency and Assam have changed drastically. The British Presidency of Madras incorporated parts of southern Orissa, coastal Andhra Pradesh, Tamil Nadu and parts of Kerala and Karnataka. Similarly, several states have been carved out of the British Province of Assam.

United Provinces of Agrah and Oudh

The British province consisted of 48 districts directly administered by the British and three princely states of Rampur, Tehri-Garhwal and Benares. These princely states have since then been merged with Uttar Pradesh. Several British districts have also been bifurcated. The other significant change was the merger of the several tiny princely states of the erstwhile Central India Agency with the Bundelkhand districts of the present state of Uttar Pradesh. Despite these politico-administrative changes within the state, the outer boundary has remained by and large unchanged.

Classification

Castes are often classified into three main groups: (a) functional or occupational castes, (b) racial or ethnic castes, and (c) sectarian castes. Included among the occupational category are the priestly castes of the Brahmans, and trading castes, such as the Baniya or Vaishya, Khattri of Punjab, Aggarwal and Oswal of Rajasthan, etc. In fact, there are innumerable caste-groups belonging to the category of occupational castes. They include the whole range of artisans from weavers and carpenters to potters, goldsmiths, barbers, washermen, and so on. Also included in this category are astrologers, oilmen, cattle-breeders, musicians, folk-dancers, acrobats, snake-charmers, and so on.

The racial and ethnic castes vary regionally. There are, for example, Rajbansis and Chandals in Bengal and Bihar; Rajbhar and Chero in Uttar Pradesh and Bihar; Jats, Gujars and Meos in Punjab, Haryana and Rajasthan; Koli and Mahar in Maharashtra; Nair (Nayar).in Kerala; Paraiyan in Tamil Nadu and Kerala.

Lingayats appear to be the best example of a sectarian caste. In fact, they originated from a religious sect. In Tamil Nadu, Andhra Pradesh and Karnataka the different groups of Brahmans, such as Telugu Brahmans, Kanarese Brahmans and Oriya

Brahmans reflect the differences perceived in language, cultural tradition and regional identity. Tamil Visvabrahmans and Telugu Visvabrahmans are other examples of regional variations in caste identity. This confirms the view that caste is relevant within a language domain only. It is in the linguistic context that the origins of a particular lineage group can be traced.

The data on caste-groups in the United Provinces of Agrah and Oudh show a vast variety. Subsumed within the castes are occupational groups, ethnic groups and others with distinctly different origins. No distinction has been made between the castes and the tribes. Thus the list of castes also includes several tribes such as the Bhil, Bhoksa, Gond and the Tharu.

Numerical Strength

The 1931 census enumerated 99 castes under the Brahmanic Hindu category in the United Provinces of Agrah and Oudh. Besides, there were other categories such as *'no caste'* and *'caste unspecified'*. The total population of Brahmanic Hindu castes was around 41.5 million persons. In order to understand the pattern of distribution, 99 caste-groups have been classified into major, medium, minor and insignificant categories (Table 5.2). It may be noted that there were 10 caste-groups in the major category with population ranging between 1 and 6 million. Their cumulative strength was about 25.8 million. There were 46 caste-groups in the medium category with population ranging between 50,000 and 1 million, their cumulative population being 14.5 million. Under the minor category were 25 castes with a population ranging between 1,000 and 50,000. Their total strength was 0.48 million only. There were 18 castes in the insignificant category with population ranging between 1 and 1,000 persons. Their cumulative population was just 5,000. Moreover, a total population of about 5,000 could not declare their caste, while the caste of another 2,000 persons remained unspecified. The major castes accounted for 62.3 per cent of the Brahamanic Hindu population. The castes of the medium category constituted about 35 per cent of the population, while the share of the minor castes was as small as 1 per cent (Table 5.2).

Table 5.2 : United Provinces of Agrah and Oudh: Numerical Ordering of Caste Groups, 1931

Category	*Range of Population*	*Number of Caste Groups*	*Total Population*	*Percentage to Total of the Brahmanic Hindus*
Major	1,000,000 +	10	25,880,042	62.31
Medium	50,000-1,000,000	46	14,495,448	34.90
Minor	1,000-50,000	25	478,685	1.15
Insignificant	1-1,000	18	5,040	0.01
No caste	—	—	4,698	0.01
Caste unspecified	—	—	1,919	0.00

Included in the category of major castes were Chamar, Brahaman, Ahir, Rajput, Kurmi, Pasi, Vaishya, Kahar, Lodh and Gadariya groups. The medium category included some well-known castes such as the Jats, Gujars, and the Kayasthas as well as common occupational castes, such as *Kumhar* (potter), *Lohar* (blacksmith), *Teli* (oilmen), *Mehtar* (scavanger), *Mallah* and *Kewat* (boatmen), *Sonar* (goldsmith), *Barahi* (carpenter), *Baghban* (gardener), *Darzi* (tailor), *Khatik* (butcher) and *Halwai* (confectioner). The category of minor castes included occupational groups, such as *Mochi* (cobbler), *Faqir* (beggar), *Nat* (acrobat), *Beldar* (construction labourer) and *Bahelia* (bird trapper). Included in this category were also castes, such as the Khatri, Khangar and the Saharia.

Spatial Distribution

In order to understand the patterns of spatial distribution 17 caste-groups have been selected. Their population as well as percentage share are given in Table 5.3. It is evident that eight caste-groups were numerically very strong as their population exceeded one million persons each. There were nine caste-groups among the 17 castes under study whose population ranged between 1 lakh and 7.5 lakhs. Together these selected castes accounted for 66.68 per cent of the Brahmanic Hindu population. The selected castes include occupational groups such as Brahman, Vaishya, *Teli, Nai, Mehtar, Mallah* and *Khatik*. They also include ethnic castes such as Rajput, Jat, Gujar, Ahir and Dom. In terms of numerical strength, Chamars were holding the first rank. They outnumbered all other castes. Brahmans with a population of 4.5 million followed the numerical strength.

Table 5.3 : United Provinces of Agrah and Oudh: Population of Selected Brahmanic Castes, 1931

Caste	*Population*	*Per cent of all Brahmanic Hindus*
Chamar	6,292,338	15.15
Brahman	4,525,893	10.90
Ahir	3,886,045	9.36
Rajput	3,538,054	8.52
Kurmi	1,750,557	4.21
Pasi	1,459,940	3.51
Vaishya	1,169,914	2.82
Lodh	1,095,793	2.64
Teli	751,648	1.81
Jat	712,803	1.72
Nai	659,430	1.59
Mehtar	482,718	1.16
Kayastha	467,088	1.12
Mallah	295,673	0.71
Gujar	287,615	0.69
Khatik	209,668	0.50
Dom	109,906	0.26
Total Population	27,695,083	66.68
All Brahmanic Hindus	41,534,981	
Total Hindu Population	41,856,310	

Source: Census of India, 1931, Vol. XVIII, United Provinces of Agrah and Oudh, Part II—*Imperial and Provincial Tables*, Table XVII, *Race, Tribe or Caste*, pp. 500-19.

Note: Castes arranged in descending order by numerical strength.

It may be noted that many of these caste-groups are ubiquitous (*e.g., Chamar*, Brahman, Vaishya, *Teli, Nai, Mehtar* and *Khatik*). Similarly, Ahirs and the Rajputs are fairly widespread, although they display a tendency of concentration in a few districts. On the other hand, castes, such as the Gujar, Jat, Lodh, Kurmi and the Dom display a high degree of concentration in certain parts of the province.

Chamar: At the provincial level Chamars constituted 15 per cent of the Brahmanic Hindu population. However, there were several districts in which their proportion was much higher than the provincial average (Fig. 5.6). Notable among these districts were Saharanpur (33.5 per cent), Bijnor (27.7 per cent), Moradabad (23.3 per cent), Muzaffarnagar (22.6 per cent) and Azamgarh (22.3 per cent). On the other hand, there were districts in the Kumaon division in which their share was less than 1 per cent, Nainital being an exception. Percentages were also low in Bahraich (9.3 per cent), Pilibhit (8.2 per cent) and Gonda (3.9 per cent).

Brahman: Brahmans constituted some 11 per cent of population at the provincial level. However, there were several districts in which Brahmans were more preponderant (Fig. 5.7). For example, in the hilly districts of Uttar Pradesh, such as Nainital, Almora and Garhwal as well as the princely state of Tehri-Garhwal their proportion ranged between 20 and 24 per cent. Likewise, the proportion of Brahmans was larger in Muttra and Cawnpore—the respective percentages being 17.6 and 15.2. The districts where the proportionate share of Brahmans was much lower than the provincial average included Muzaffarnagar and Etah (both 6.6 per cent), Mainpuri (6.1 per cent), Saharanpur (5.6 per cent), Moradabad (5.3 per cent), Bijnor (4.5 per cent) and Rampur (4.2 per cent). Understandably, the proportionate share of Brahmans among the Hindus was low in districts with high Muslim population.

Ahir: Ahirs accounted for 9.4 per cent of the Brahmanic Hindu population of the United Provinces. They were largely an insignificant component of population in the Meerut as well as Rohilkhand divisions (Fig. 5.8). Likewise, their proportion was generally low in Muttra and Agrah. They, however, displayed a tendency of clustering in many districts of Allahabad division, their proportionate share being far above the provincial average. Ahirs accounted for about 20 per cent of Brahmanic Hindu population in Azamgarh and 18 per cent in Jaunpur. On the other hand, in Kumaon division they were conspicuous by their absence.

Rajput: Rajputs were fairly widespread in the United Provinces (Fig. 5.9). However, their proportionate share remained around 6 to 8 per cent, the provincial average being 8.5 per cent. It is interesting to note that in the hilly districts of United Provinces, Rajputs constituted a high proportion of the Brahmanic Hindu population. In Garhwal, for example, their proportion was as high as 56.5 per cent. Similarly, in the princely state of Tehri-Garhwal their proportion was even higher *i.e.,* 59.9 per cent. The other hilly districts of Almora, Dehra Dun and Nainital also had large proportions of Rajputs, the respective percentages being 49.7, 29.2 and 27.5. This strong presence of Rajputs in the hilly districts was an outcome of migration from the southern plains after the Rajputs lost power in the plains during the medieval period. There were 2 districts with a high percentage of Rajputs in the plains of United Provinces.

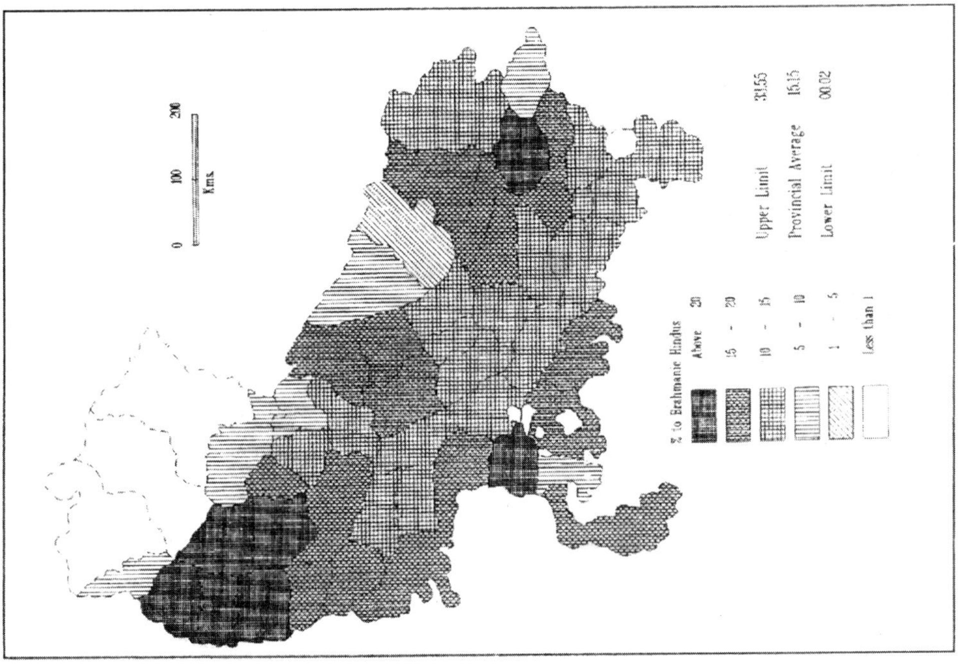

Figure 5.6 : United Provinces of Agrah and Oudh: Chamars as percentage of Brahmanic Hindu Population, 1931

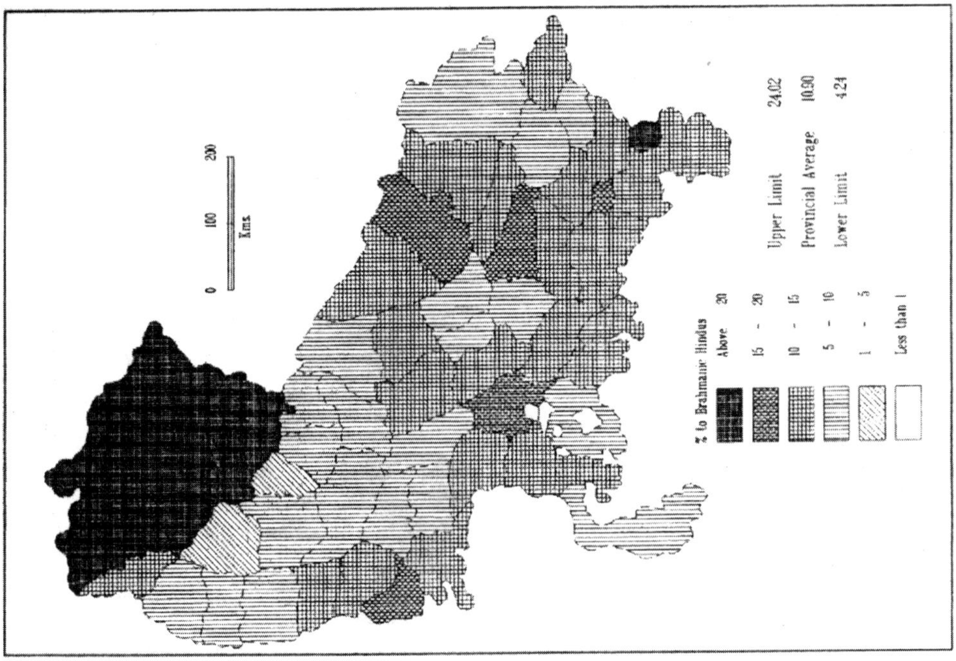

Figure 5.7 : United Provinces of Agrah and Oudh: Brahmans as percentage of Brahmanic Hindu Population, 1931

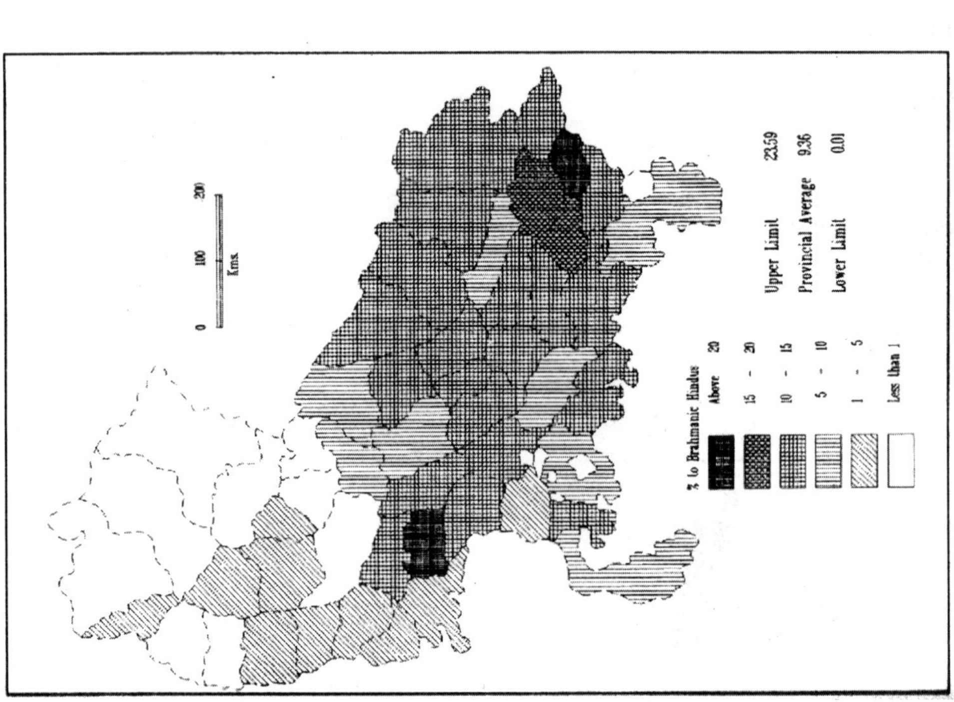

Figure 5.8 : United Provinces of Agrah and Oudh: Ahirs as percentage of Brahmanic Hindu Population, 1931

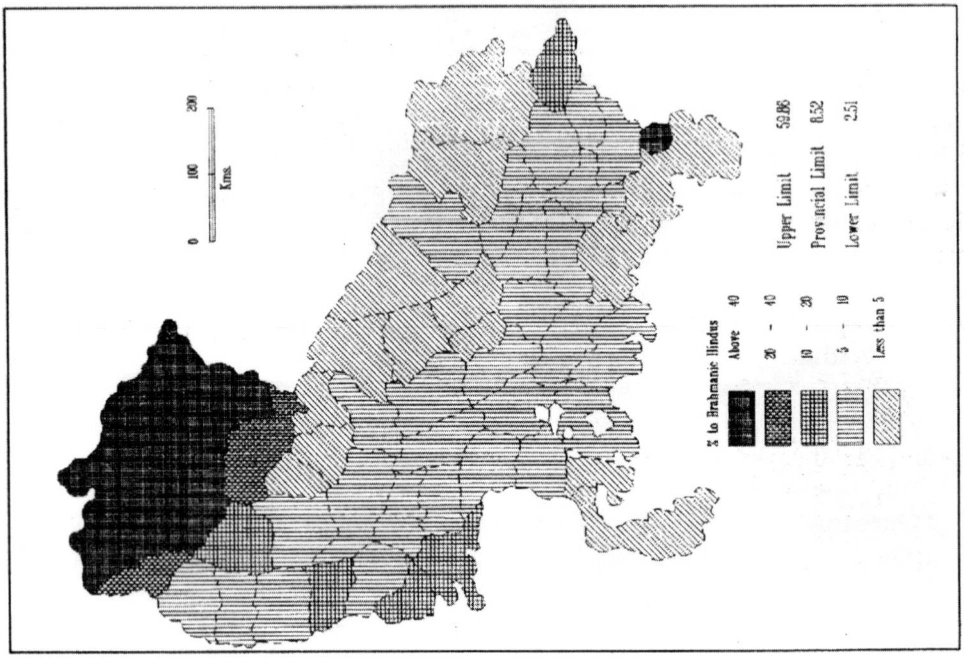

Figure 5.9 : United Provinces of Agrah and Oudh: Rajputs as percentage of Brahmanic Hindu Population, 1931

These were: Bijnor in the west and Balia in the east, the respective percentages being 13.5 and 15.7.

Vaishya: Vaishyas have always been an important component of population. Being the trading community they handled almost exclusively all exchange of goods and offered credit facilities to the people. But their proportionate share was always low (Fig. 5.10). At the 1931 census the provincial average of Vaishyas was just 2.8 per cent. There were not many districts in which the percentage of Vaishyas marked any significant departure from this average. Reference may, however, be made to the western districts of Muzaffarnagar, Meerut, Agrah and Muttra where their proportionate share in population was nearly 5 to 6 per cent. The reasons for this relatively high proportionate share may be historical.

Kurmi: With a provincial average of 4.2 per cent Kurmis were not widely distributed (Fig. 5.11). Their percentages were very high in Bareilly (14.5), Barabanki (14.2) and Pilibhit (12.1). The Kurmis constituted a large proportion of population in Benares and Partabgarh (10.6 per cent each), as well as Basti (8.7 per cent) and Mirzapur (8.5 per cent). Their percentages were also generally high in the districts of Faizabad division. The case of Barabanki has already been referred to.

Pasi: As a caste Pasis constituted an insignificant proportion of the Brahamanic Hindu population of the United Provinces (Fig. 5.12). The provincial average was as low as 3.5 per cent. They were fairly preponderant in the districts of Lucknow division with the percentages ranging between 11 and 17. Their proportionate share was also high in Barabanki. In Allahabad the proportionate share of Pasis was around 10 per cent. It was about 9 per cent in Partabgarh.

Clustering and Concentration of Caste-Groups[23]

It may be observed from Tables 5.4 to 5.8 that certain caste-groups show a strong tendency of clustering and concentration in a few pockets. In order to examine this question an index of concentration was computed for several castes, particularly, Jats, Gujars, Pasis, Doms and Lodhs.

Among the castes mentioned above Jats display the highest degree of concentration (Fig. 5.13). This is evident from the fact that about one-fourth of the total Jat population of the United Provinces was concentrated in just one district of Meerut. In a cluster of districts in the upper and central *doab* including Muzaffarnagar, Meerut, Bulandshahr, Aligarh, Muttra and Agrah some 83 per cent of the Jat population was concentrated. There were two districts east of the Ganga—Bijnor and Moradabad—in which Jat concentration was quite high. Together these eight districts shared among themselves about 96 per cent of the Jat population of the United Provinces. It may, however, be recalled that this belt of Jat concentration was a continuation of the neighbouring Punjab (now Haryana) where Jats were heavily concentrated (Table 5.4).[24]

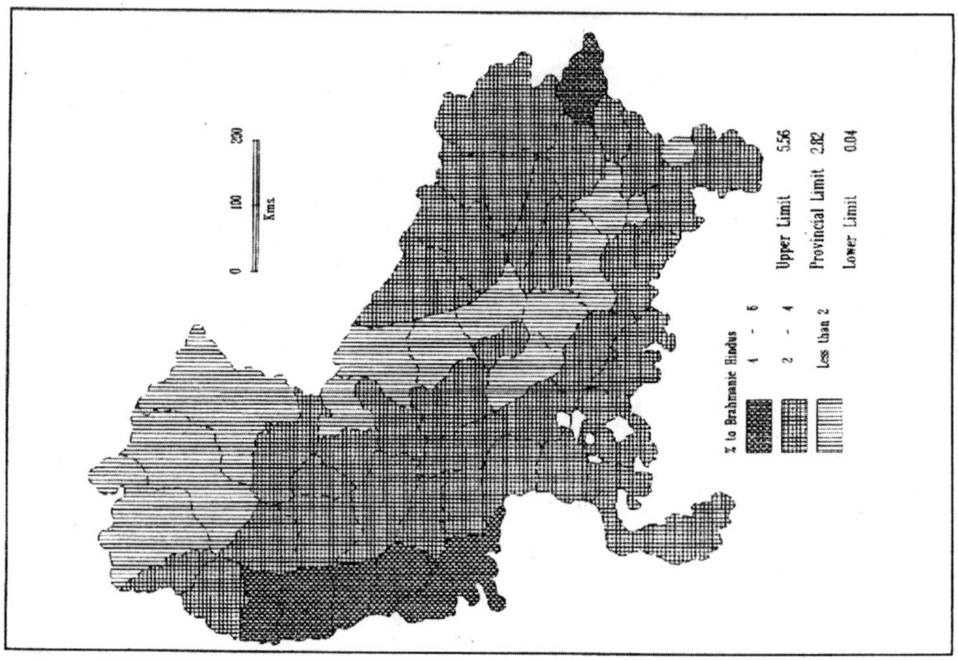

Figure 5.10 : United Provinces of Agrah and Oudh: Vaishyas as percentage of Brahmanic Hindu Population, 1931

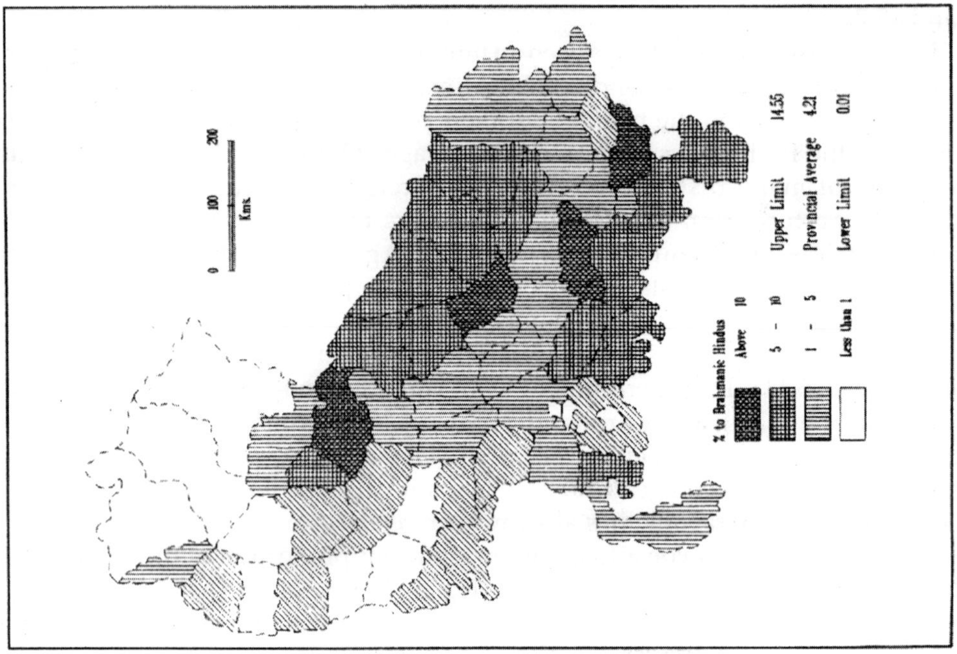

Figure 5.11 : United Provinces of Agrah and Oudh: Kurmis as percentage of Brahmanic Hindu Population, 1931

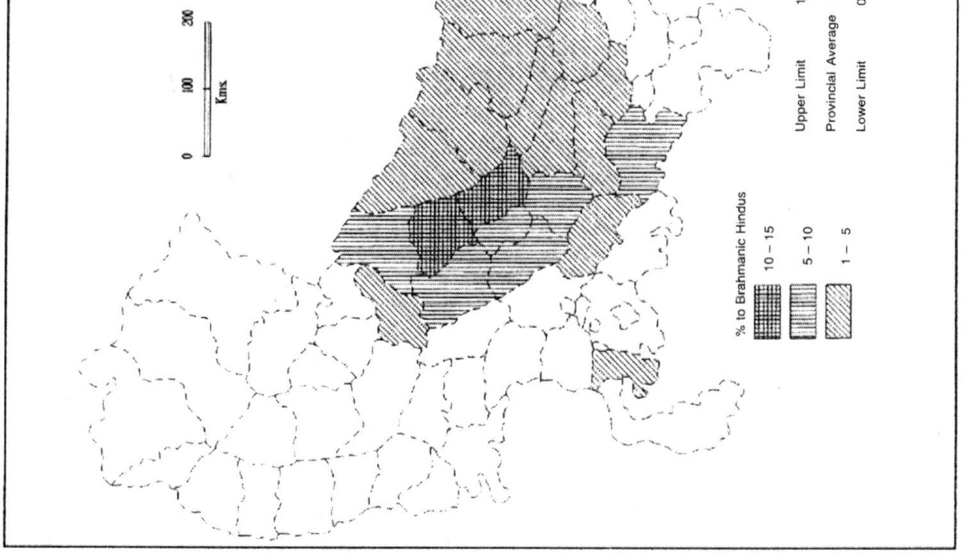

Figure 5.12 : United Provinces of Agrah and Oudh: Pasis as percentage of Brahmanic Hindu Population, 1931

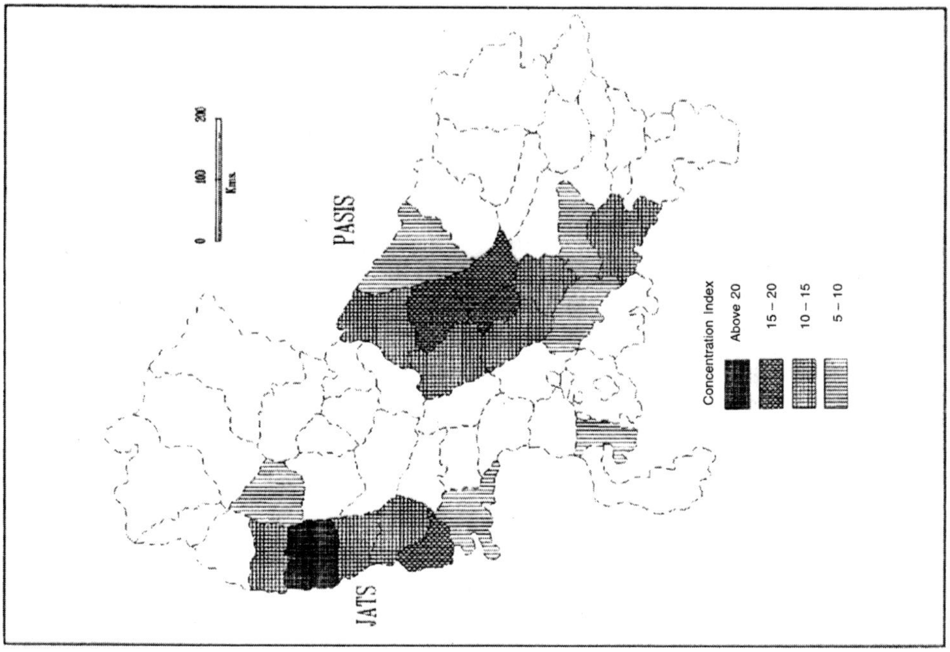

Figure 5.13 : United Provinces of Agrah and Oudh: Concentration of Jats and Pasis, 1931

Table 5.4 : Concentration of the Jats

Districts	*Index of Concentration (%)*	*Districts*	*Index of Concentration (%)*
Meerut	23.78	Agrah	7.50
Muttra	17.43	Bijnor	7.41
Aligarh	12.97	Moradabad	4.24
Bulandshahr	11.56		
Muzaffarnagar	10.59	*Cumulative Percentage*	95.48

Like the Jats, Gujars also reveal a tendency of concentration in some districts of the Ganga-Yamuna *doab* and the neighbouring Rohilkhand division. In fact, Jats and Gujars are concentrated largely in the same districts. Three-fourths of the Gujar population of the United Provinces was concentrated in just four districts of Saharanpur, Muzaffarnagar, Meerut and Bulandshahr. About 84 per cent of the Gujar population was concentrated in a belt encompassing Saharanpur, Muzaffarnagar, Meerut, Bulandshahr, Muttra and Agrah districts. If Bijnor, Moradabad and Bareilly are added to this list the index of concentration goes up to 93.5 per cent (Table 5.5).

Table 5.5 : Concentration of the Gujars

Districts	*Index of Concentration (%)*	*Districts*	*Index of Concentration (%)*
Meerut	27.69	Agrah	4.10
Bulandshahr	20.55	Muttra	2.98
Saharanpur	18.33	Bareilly	2.66
Muzaffarnagar	10.44	Bijnor	1.99
Moradabad	4.73	*Cumulative Percentage*	93.47

Pasis and *Doms* also have their enclaves of concentration, although their tendency of clustering is not as striking as in the case of Jats and Gujars. Pasis were heavily concentrated in the Lucknow, Faizabad and Allahabad divisions (Fig. 5.13). In fact, one-third of the Pasi population was living in the three districts of Sitapur, Barabanki and Rai Bareilly. Similarly, about 75 per cent of the Pasi population was found in a cluster of districts incorporating Lucknow, Unao, Rai Bareilly, Sitapur, Hardoi, Kheri, Faizabad, Gonda, Bahraich, Partabgarh, Sultanpur and Barabanki (Table 5.6).

Table 5.6 : Concentration of the Pasis

Districts	*Index of Concentration (%)*	*Districts*	*Index of Concentration (%)*
Sitapur	10.55	Gorakhpur	4.36
Barabanki	10.23	Bahraich	3.57
Rai Bareilly	8.89	Faizabad	2.94
Allahabad	8.88	Gonda	2.92
Hardoi	7.69	Sultanpur	2.92
Lucknow	6.91	Fatehpur	2.57
Unao	6.76	Jaunpur	2.03
Kheri	5.96		
Partabgarh	4.98	*Cumulative Percentage*	92.16

Doms were mainly concentrated in the central and eastern parts of the United Provinces as well as the Bundelkhand division.[25] Notable concentrations were found in Hamirpur, Jhansi and Gorakhpur districts. These three districts together accounted for more than one-third of the Dom population of the United Provinces. About three-fifths of their population was found in just seven districts, namely, Hamirpur, Jhansi, Gorakhpur, Jalaun, Mirzapur, Barabanki and Banda (Table 5.7).

Table 5.7 : Concentration of the Doms

Districts	*Index of Concentration (%)*	*Districts*	*Index of Concentration (%)*
Hamirpur	13.23	Jaunpur	3.25
Jhansi	10.54	Benares	2.68
Gorakhpur	10.29	Gonda	2.22
Jalaun	6.17	Bahraich	2.21
Mirzapur	6.13	Lucknow	2.13
Barabanki	5.73	Faizabad	1.99
Banda	5.62	Ballia	1.91
Azamgarh	4.06	Ghazipur	1.88
Basti	4.05		
Allahabad	3.82	*Cumulative Percentage*	87.91

One may also cite the case of *Lodhs* who also displayed a strong tendency of concentration in a few districts, particularly in the Meerut, Agrah, Jhansi, Allahabad, Faizabad and Lucknow divisions. Striking concentrations were found in Bulandshahr, Etah, Mainpuri, Rai Bareli, Unao, Hamirpur and Jhansi districts (Table 5.8).

Table 5.8 : Concentration of the Lodhs

Districts	*Index of Concentration (%)*	*Districts*	*Index of Concentration (%)*
Etah	8.82	Bahraich	3.78
Unao	7.07	Farrukhabad	3.66
Bulandshahr	6.76	Fatehpur	3.32
Rai Bareilly	5.66	Cawnpore	3.14
Mainpuri	5.13	Basti	3.06
Hamirpur	4.87	Kheri	3.02
Jhansi	4.82	Barabanki	2.89
Aligarh	4.58	Rampur	2.87
Lucknow	4.26	Pilibhit	2.77
Etawah	3.89	Agrah	2.12
Sitapur	3.82	*Cumulative Percentage*	90.31

It has already been noted that the *Ahirs* were fairly widely distributed. However, there were several districts in eastern United Provinces (Basti, Gorakhpur, Azamgarh and Jaunpur) with strong Ahir concentrations. *Mallahs* also displayed a tendency of concentration. In fact, more than 83 per cent of their population was found in Gorakhpur, Benares, Allahabad and Agrah divisions.

Patterns of Caste Combination

The way caste-groups combine in space also reveals striking spatial patterns. In order to explore this question five districts, *viz.*, Almora, Muzaffarnagar, Bijnor, Sitapur and Allahabad were randomly chosen (Fig. 5.14).

This study of the 17 castes of the United Provinces gives an idea of the way caste-groups are distributed in space or clustered and concentrated in a few enclaves. More field-based studies can unravel the historical processes of peopling and colonisation of the plains of the Ganga by the pioneering caste-groups. Little work has been done to explore this part of the social history. While caste is a social reality of great contemporary relevance, historical geographies of caste remain a forbidden area.[26]

The caste combination patterns reveal a logic and a history. There is a guiding principle of mutual interdependence.

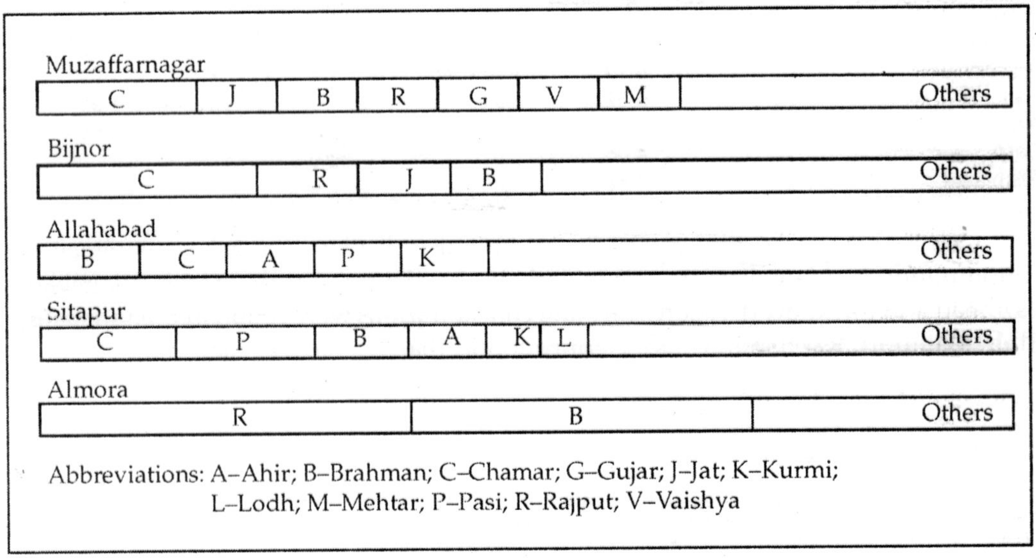

Figure 5.14 : Patterns of Caste Composition in the selected Districts of the United Provinces, 1931

Madras Presidency

The preceding study of the caste-groups of the United Provinces displays the geographic patterning of castes in Northern India. However, caste is a regional phenomenon, and it may be necessary to look into the database on caste for other ethno-lingual regions of the country. One such region selected for this study is the Madras Presidency. A pick of the 1931 census data on the caste-groups of Madras Presidency may throw some light on the geography of caste in southern India. As is generally known, the British Presidency of Madras incorporated parts of Karnataka, Kerala, Tamil Nadu, Andhra Pradesh and Orissa. Thus, a study of the Madras Presidency really means encompassing all the four southern states.

The 1931 census published several tables on religion, race, tribe or caste.[27] The census Table XVII (*Race, Tribe or Caste*) was published in two parts. In Part I, castes and tribal groups were arranged in an alphabetical order and classified as Primitive Tribes (PT), Depressed Classes (DC) and other castes. In all 155 communities, both caste and tribe were listed along with their population with a male-female break-up. The chief habitat of each of these communities was also indicated. In Part II of Table XVII those communities were listed whose numerical strength was at least one per thousand (0.1 per cent) of the population of the Presidency. Part II of the Table also indicated the geographical distribution of caste by districts and princely states. However, only those districts were mentioned in which a particular community, caste or tribe, contributed to more than one per thousand of the population. Subsumed in the population of the Presidency were 7.3 million depressed classes and 1.3 million Primitive Tribes. These figures were, however, confusing since some communities were counted twice as they were designated as primitive tribes as well as depressed classes. The multiplicity of the caste-groups is due to the fact that there were several regional names for the same caste-group, more particularly castes, such as barbers, washermen and oilmen. So far as the barbers were concerned, 15 variants were listed. Likewise, there were six variants in the case of washermen and eight variants in the case of oilmen (Appendix V.1).

This study of the Madras Presidency is restricted to the 40 selected castes. Appendix V.2 shows their population arranged in descending order. The caste-groups include Brahmans (Tamil, Telugu, Kanarese and Oriya as well as Visvabrahmans—Tamil and Telugu). The sample also includes depressed classes, such as Adi-Andhra, Adi-Dravida, Paraiyan, Mala, Holeya and Valluvan. Nayars and Yadavas are also included in the sample.

Numerical Strength

Many of the 155 caste-groups of the Madras Presidency had a population of less than 500 persons. In fact, there were five caste-groups with a population of less than 100 persons. On the other hand, there were only three caste-groups with a population of one million or more. Arranged in a descending order these groups were Vanniyan (2.9 million), Adi-Dravida (1.6 million) and Paraiyan (1.1 million). The different sects of Brahmans, such as Tamil, Telugu and the Kanarese Brahmans were less numerous. The first two had a population of less than half a million each. While the Kanarese Brahmans and the Oriya Brahmans had a numerical strength of about one to one-and-a-half lakh each, the Tamil Visvabrahmans numbered a little over half a million. Among the minor caste-groups were included Pano, Valluvan and Holeya with a population of 50—70,000. The selected castes listed in Appendix V.3 had a cumulative population of 18.94 million. Together they accounted for 45 per cent of the total Hindu population of the Presidency. Barring Vanniyan, Adi-Dravida, Paraiyan and Yadava, none of these castes constituted more than 2 per cent of the Presidency's Hindu population. Of the four castes mentioned above, Vanniyan accounted for about 7 per cent of the Hindu population and the Adi-Dravida constituted about 4 per cent of the Hindu population. Yadavas were only 2 per cent of the Hindu population. As many as 21 caste-groups had a proportionate share of less than one per cent each.

Spatial Distribution

In all, 13 caste-groups have been randomly selected to analyse the patterns of spatial distribution (Appendix V.3). As the name implies, several of these caste-groups are specific to the Andhra region (*e.g.*, Adi-Andhra, Telugu Brahman and Telugu Visvabrahman) or the Tamil region (*e.g.*, Adi-Dravida, Tamil Brahman and Tamil Visvabrahman). Similarly, Madigas were specific to the Andhra region. Cheruman and Nayar were living in the coastal districts of Karnataka only. Yadavas, on the other hand, were found over the entire Presidency area, even though their proportionate share was generally small.

At the Presidency level, Vanniyan accounted for 6.9 per cent of the Hindu population. However, there were vast inter-district variations in their distribution (Table 5.9). Their proportions were very high in South and North Arcot districts as well as in Salem and Chingleput—the respective percentages being 35.1, 28.81, 25.45 and 21.95. The proportionate share of Vanniyans was also high in Madras, Tanjore and Trichinopoly (Fig. 5.15).

Table 5.9 : Madras Presidency: Distribution of the Vanniyans, 1931

*Districts**	*Percentage*
Presidency Average	6.99
Madras	13.39
Chingleput	21.95
North Arcot	28.81
Salem	25.45
South Arcot	35.09
Tanjore	8.85
Trichinopoly	9.81

Note: * Districts with exceptionally high percentage.

With a Presidency-level average of 3.85 per cent Adi-Dravidas were more numerous in North and South Arcot, Nilgiris, Chingleput and Madras districts, accounting for 10 to 21 per cent of the Hindu population in these districts (Fig. 5.16; Table 5.10).

Table 5.10 : Madras Presidency: Distribution of the Adi-Dravidas, 1931

*Districts**	*Percentage*
Presidency Average	3.85
Madras	12.19
Chingleput	17.88
North Arcot	15.51
South Arcot	20.74
Nilgiris	10.39

Note: * Districts with exceptionally high percentage.

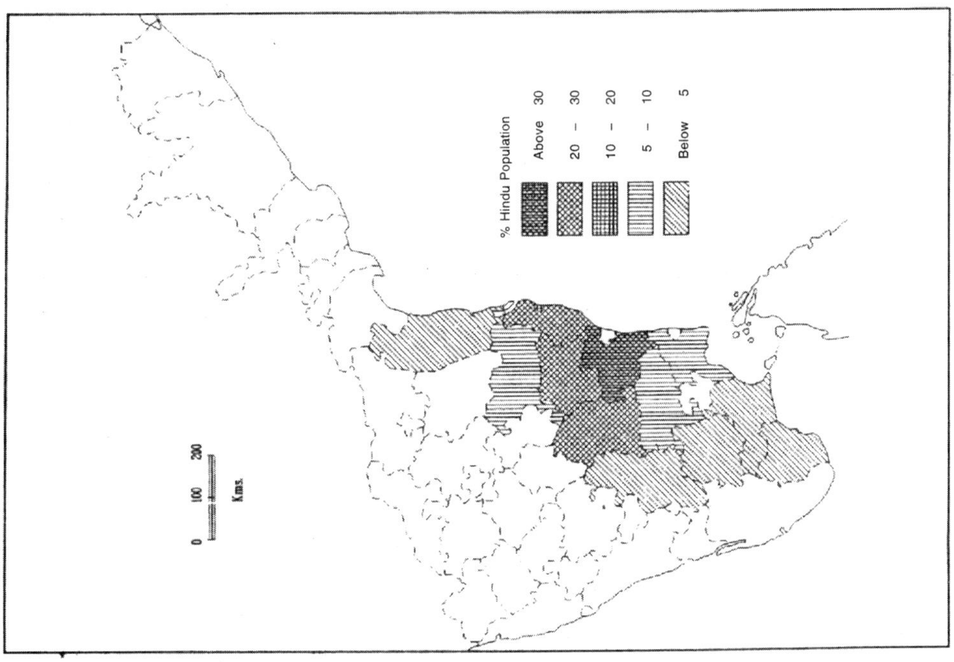

Figure 5.15 : Vanniyans as percentage of Hindu Population, 1931

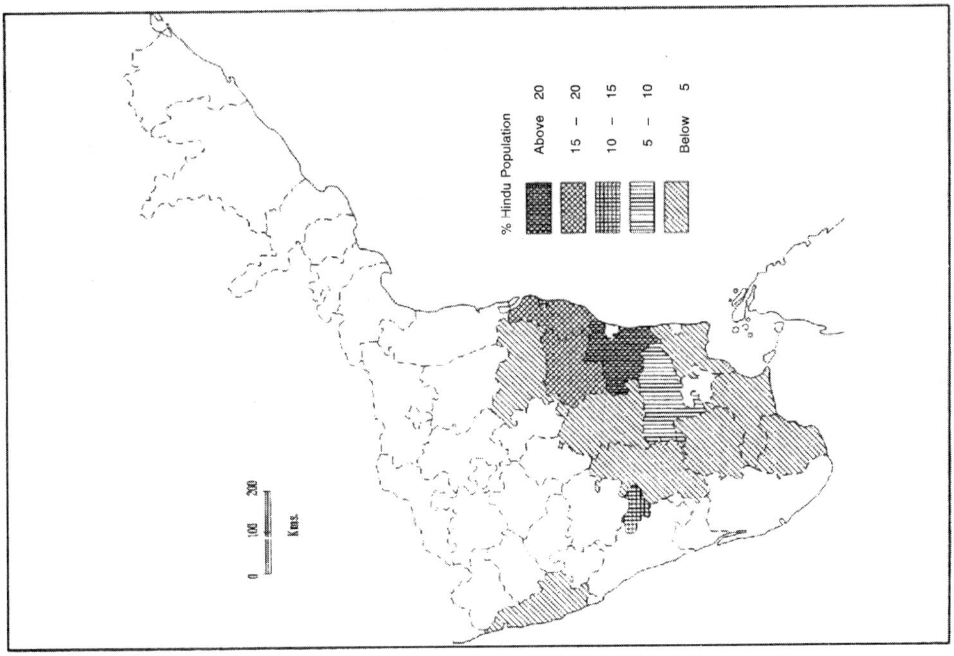

Figure 5.16 : Adi-Dravidas as percentage of Hindu Population, 1931

The Paraiyans accounted for less than 3 per cent of the Hindu population in general. However, there were three districts, *viz.*, Tanjore, Chingleput and Nilgiris in which they had an exceptionally high proportionate share (Table 5.11). Yadavas had a generally low share in population, even though their percentages were exceptionally high in Pudukkottai, Tinnevelly and Chingleput districts (Table 5.12). Although Adi-Andhras were widely distributed, their percentages were strikingly high in East and West Godavari districts, Kistna and Anantapur (Fig. 5.17; Table 5.13).

Table 5.11 : Madras Presidency: Distribution of the Paraiyans, 1931

*Districts**	*Percentage*
Presidency Average	2.65
Chingleput	9.82
South Arcot	5.88
Tanjore	12.77
Nilgiris	8.31

Note: * Districts with exceptionally high percentage.

Table 5.12 : Madras Presidency: Distribution of the Yadavas, 1931

*Districts**	*Percentage*
Presidency Average	2.15
Chingleput	5.21
North Arcot	5.86
Ramnad	7.72
Tinnevelly	6.31
Pudukkottai	6.87

Note: * Districts with exceptionally high percentage.

Table 5.13 : Madras Presidency: Distribution of the Adi-Andhras, 1931

*Districts**	*Percentage*
Presidency Average	1.59
East Godavari	12.75
West Godavari	6.94
Kistna	5.24
Anantapur	5.37

Note: * Districts with exceptionally high percentage.

With a Presidency-level average of 1.18 per cent, Tamil Brahmans displayed a higher proportionate share in Madras and Tanjore districts (Fig. 5.18; Table 5.14).

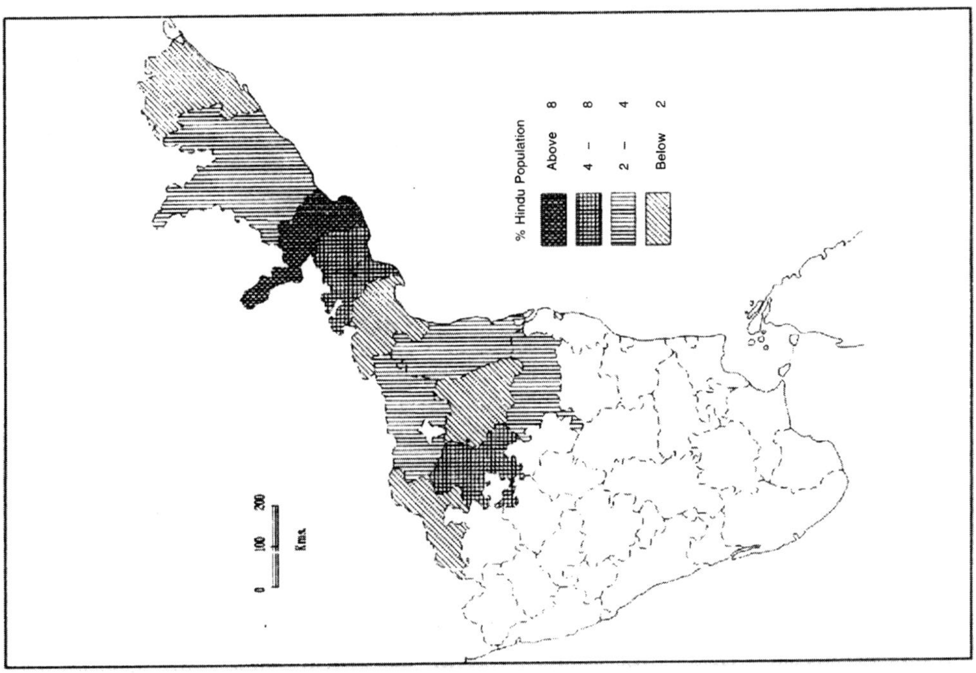

Figure 5.17 : Adi-Andhras as percentage of Hindu Population, 1931

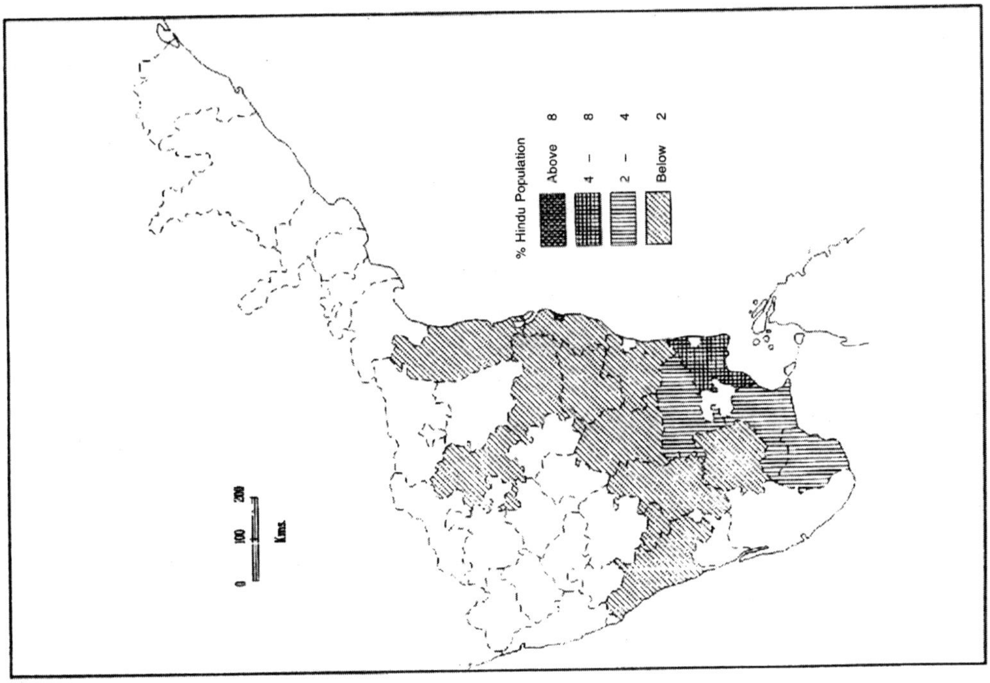

Figure 5.18 : Tamil Brahmans as percentage of Hindu Population, 1931

Table 5.14 : Madras Presidency: Distribution of the Tamil Brahmans, 1931

*Districts**	*Percentage*
Presidency Average	1.18
Madras	8.02
Tanjore	5.59

Note: * Districts with exceptionally high percentage.

Similarly, Telugu Brahmans were more numerous in East and West Godavari districts, Kistna and Guntur (Table 5.15). In general, Madigas constituted only 1.45 per cent of the population. However, their proportionate share was strikingly high in a number of Andhra districts (Fig. 5.19; Table 5.16).

Table 5.15 : Madras Presidency: Distribution of the Telugu Brahmans, 1931

*Districts**	*Percentage*
Presidency Average	1.12
East Godavari	4.20
West Godavari	4.18
Kistna	5.22
Guntur	5.01

Note: * Districts with exceptionally high percentage.

Table 5.16 : Madras Presidency: Distribution of the Madigas, 1931

*Districts**	*Percentage*
Presidency Average	1.45
West Godavari	5.11
Kistna	5.77
Nellore	5.27
Cuddapah	6.53
Kurnool	6.55
Bellary	7.80
Anantapur	7.47

Note: * Districts with exceptionally high percentage.

Clustering and Concentration of Caste-Groups

Among the castes of the Madras Presidency, Cherumans and Nayars displayed the highest degree of concentration—more than 97 per cent of the Cherumans and 92 per cent of Nayars were living in just one district of Malabar (Fig. 5.20; 5.21). Likewise, two-thirds of all Adi-Dravidas were confined to Chingleput and North and South Arcot districts (Table 5.17; Fig. 5.20). Even though Tamil Brahmans were fairly widely distributed, there were several districts to the south of Madras in which they were heavily concentrated (Table 5.18). Tanjore alone accounted for almost one-fourth of

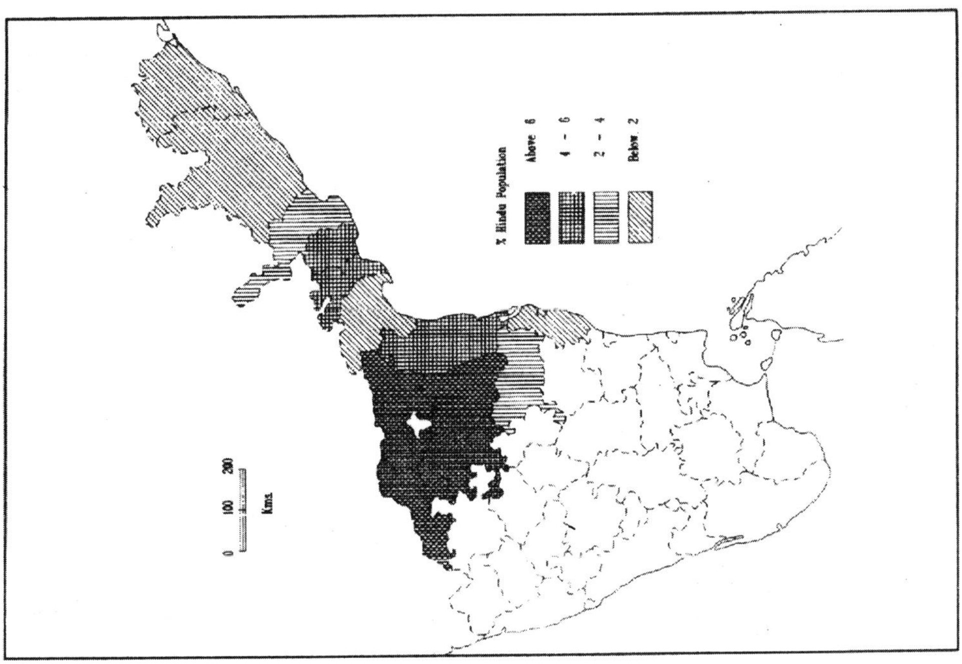

Figure 5.19 : Madras Presidency: Madigas as percentage of the Hindu Population, 1931

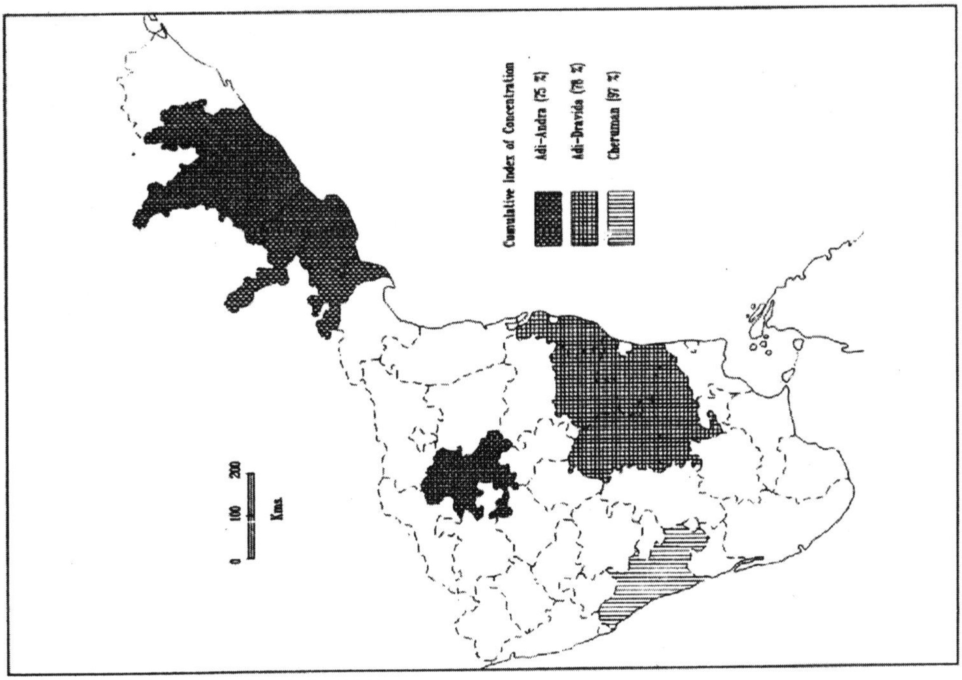

Figure 5.20 : Madras Presidency: Concentration of the Adi-Andhras, Adi-Dravidas and the Cherumans, 1931

the total Presidency population of Tamil Brahmans. The neighbouring districts of Trichinopoly, Madura, Ramnad and Tinnevelly together had about one-third share of all Tamil Brahmans. These five districts together accounted for almost three-fifths of their population. The concentration indices were also high for Chingleput, Coimbatore and North and South Arcot districts (Fig. 5.21).

Table 5.17 : Madras Presidency: Concentration of selected Caste Groups, Adi-Dravida, 1931

Districts	*Index of Concentration (%)*
Chingleput	17.40
North Arcot	19.91
Salem	5.83
South Arcot	29.48
Trichinopoly	5.44
Total	78.06

Table 5.18 : Madras Presidency: Concentration of selected Caste Groups, Tamil Brahman, 1931

Districts	*Index of Concentration (%)*
Madras	8.43
Tanjore	24.26
Trichinopoly	8.79
Ramnad	6.65
Tinnevelly	9.22
Malabar	7.34
Total	64.69

About three-fourths of the population of Adi-Andhras was concentrated in five districts (Table 5.19; Fig. 5.20). Four of these districts formed a compact block in coastal Andhra. The domain of the Telugu Brahmans by and large overlapped with that of the Adi-Andhras (Table 5.20). They formed a compact block in coastal Andhra with three-fourths of their population concentrated in these six coastal districts (Fig. 5.21).

Table 5.19 : Madras Presidency: Concentration of selected Caste-Groups, Adi-Andhra, 1931

Districts	*Index of Concentration (%)*
Vizagapatnam	10.97
East Godavari	35.60
West Godavari	11.85
Kistna	8.39
Anantapur	7.62
Total	74.43

Table 5.20 : Madras Presidency: Concentration of selected Caste-Groups, Telugu Brahman, 1931

Districts	*Index of Concentration (%)*
Vizagapatnam	11.22
East Godavari	16.53
West Godavari	10.05
Kistna	12.05
Guntur	17.40
Nellore	6.92
Total	74.17

The Kanarese Brahmans, on the other hand, were dispersed in three enclaves in the interior part of the peninsula as well as coastal Karnataka (Table 5.21). The four districts (Bellary, Anantapur, Coimbatore and South Kanara) together accommodated two-thirds of their population (Fig. 5.21). Vanniyans formed a compact block in North and South Arcot, Salem, Chingleput, Tanjore and Trichinopoly districts (Table 5.22; Fig. 5.23). Over 92 per cent of their population was clustered here.

Table 5.21 : Madras Presidency: Concentration of selected Caste-Groups, Kanarese Brahman, 1931

Districts	*Index of Concentration (%)*
Bellary	12.18
Anantapur	6.47
Coimbatore	7.84
South Kanara	38.78
Total	65.27

Table 5.22 : Madras Presidency: Concentration of selected Caste-Groups, Vanniyan, 1931

Districts	*Index of Concentration (%)*
Chingleput	11.75
North Arcot	20.34
Salem	20.30
South Arcot	27.43
Tanjore	6.46
Trichinopoly	5.79
Total	92.07

The domains of Paraiyans and Madigas were mutually exclusive. The former were heavily concentrated in the coastal districts of the Tamil region (Table 5.23), while the latter were clustered in the coastal and interior districts of the Andhra region (Table 5.24; Fig. 5.22).

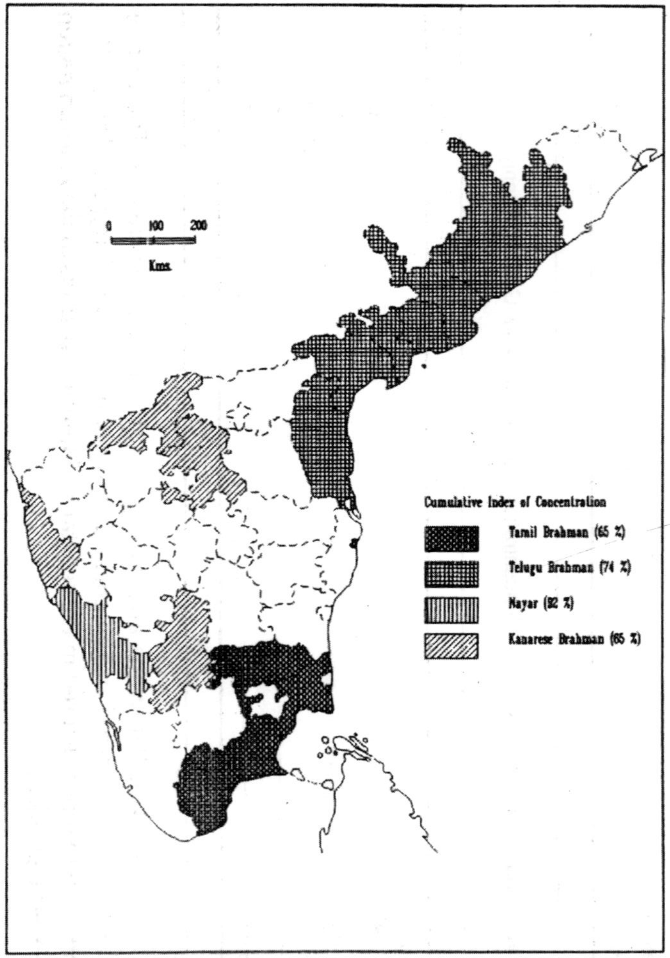

Figure 5.21 : Madras Presidency: Concentration of the Brahmans and the Nayars, 1931

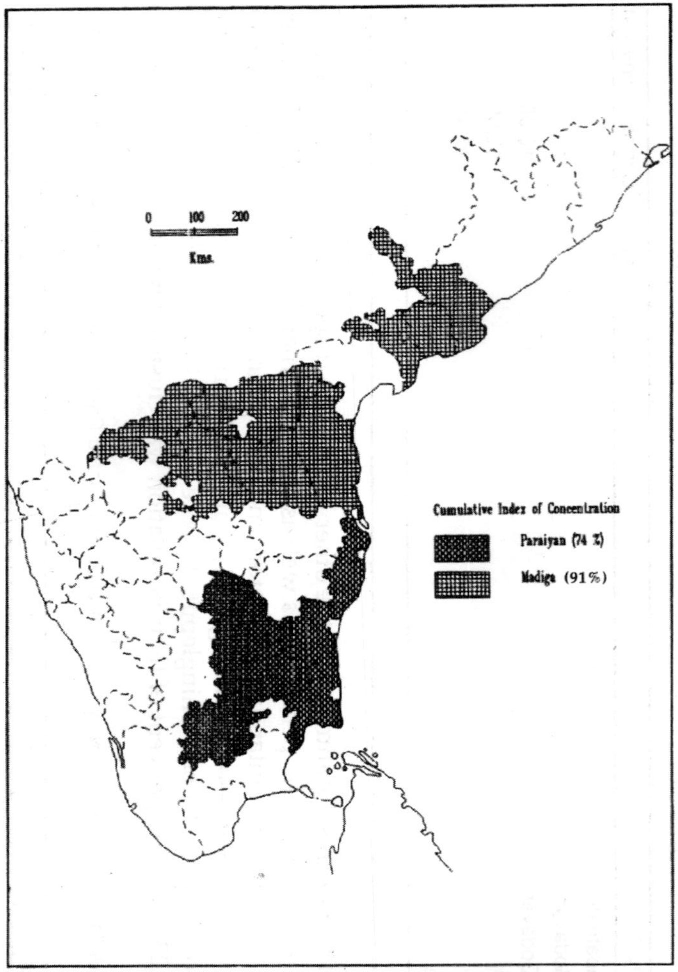

Figure 5.22 : Madras Presidency: Concentration of the Paraiyans and the Madigas, 1931

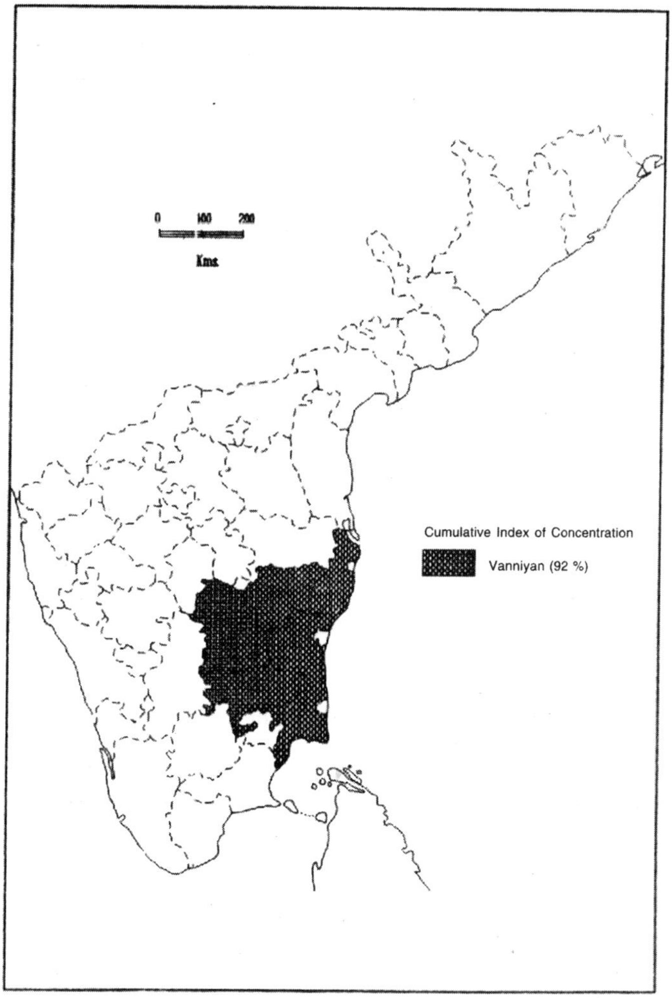

Figure 5.23 : Madras Presidency: Concentration of selected Castes, Vanniyans, 1931

Table 5.23 : Madras Presidency: Concentration of selected Caste-Groups, Paraiyan, 1931

Districts	*Index of Concentration (%)*
Chingleput	13.86
Salem	8.91
South Arcot	12.11
Tanjore	24.56
Trichinopoly	7.09
Madurai	7.47
Total	74.00

It may be safely assumed that insofar as the patterns of clustering and concentration of caste-groups are concerned, 1931 position may still hold good.

Table 5.24 : Madras Presidency: Concentration of selected Caste-Groups, Madiga, 1931

Districts	*Index of Concentration (%)*
Vizagapatnam	5.75
East Godavari	7.28
West Godavari	9.47
Kistna	10.26
Nellore	11.34
Cuddapah	8.40
Kurnool	8.61
Bellary	10.92
Anantapur	11.50
Chittoor	7.20
Total	90.73

Patterns of Caste Combination

Caste-groups do not live in isolation. In fact, they form specific patterns of combination and spatial association at all levels of reference from the village to the district. This phenomenon can be illustrated by citing the example of a number of districts of the Madras Presidency. The districts chosen for this study include East Godavari, South Arcot, Malabar and Tanjore. The following patterns of caste combination may be observed (Table 5.25).

Table 5.25 : Madras Presidency: Patterns of Caste Combination, 1931

Districts	*Castes*	*Per cent of all Hindus*
East Godavari	Adi-Andhra	10.75
	Telugu Brahman	4.20
	Madiga	2.40
	Telugu Visvabrahman	1.95
	Yadava	0.52
	Others	80.18
South Arcot	Vanniyan	35.09
	Adi-Dravida	20.74
	Paraiyan	5.88
	Yadava	3.92
	Tamil Visvabrahman	1.97
	Tamil Brahman	1.23
	Others	31.17
Malabar	Nayar	21.48
	Cheruman	9.02
	Tamil Brahman	1.58
	Paraiyan	0.21
	Others	67.71
Tanjore	Paraiyan	12.77
	Vanniyan	8.85
	Tamil Brahman	5.59
	Adi-Dravida	3.64
	Yadava	3.23
	Tamil Visvabrahman	2.79
	Others	63.13

This study is, however, generalised. A clearer picture may emerge if all Hindu castes are taken into account and the unit of reference is lower than the district.

Assam

Caste-groups within the tribal fastness of north-eastern India present yet another scenario. With an aggregative population of 5.2 million, the Hindus in the British Province of Assam were classified as Brahmo, Arya and others at the 1931 census. Brahmo and Arya Hindus were a minuscule, numbering 448 and 12 respectively. They were mostly categorised as other Hindus. The Hindus accounted for 56.28 per cent of the population of Assam. Muslims constituted a little over 30 per cent of the population. Besides, there were about a million people constituting 10.73 per cent of the population who professed tribal religion. As is generally known, Assam in 1931 incorporated whole of the Northeast, excluding Tripura which was a part of the Bengal Presidency. Barring Manipur and Khasi States, the whole region was a British territory. Sylhet was also a part of Assam.

In order to understand the structure of the caste society of Assam, several tables were generated from the data published by the 1931 census. The selection of the castes enumerated by this census also left much to be desired.[28] Several ethnic groups such as Manipuri and Nepali were also listed as caste groups, although both of them subsumed various castes. Sometimes the caste names were also confusing.[29]

Listed in Table 5.26 are 13 caste groups with their population arranged in a descending order. These included Brahmans (other than Manipuri Brahmans), Ahoms, Kayasthas, Ahirs, Kurmis and Rajputs. There are several occupational castes (*viz.*, Nai, Teli, Dhobi and Mali).

Table 5.26 : Assam: Selected Hindu Castes, 1931 (arranged in descending order)

Caste	*Population*	*Percentage*
Manipuri	324,432	6.23
Ahom	249,434	4.79
Brahman*	159,116	3.06
Kayastha	135,590	2.61
Nepali	120,239	2.31
Ahir	56,398	1.08
Nai	33,434	0.64
Kurmi	26,327	0.51
Tilli	23,386	0.45
Teli	17,278	0.33
Dhobi	8,398	0.16
Mali	6,996	0.13
Rajput	4,094	0.08
Total of 13 Castes	1,165,122	22.39
Hindu Exterior Castes	596,918	11.47
All Hindus	5,204,190	

Source: Census of India, 1931, Vol. III, Assam, Part II, Table XVI, *Religion*, pp. 255-57; Table XVII, *Caste, Tribe and Race*, pp. 259-66.

Note: *Other than Manipuri Brahmans.

Manipuris were the most numerous, accounting for over 6 per cent of Assam's Hindu population. Ahoms with about 5 per cent of the population followed. 'Hindu exterior castes', numbering more than half a million consisted of 14 different caste groups (Table 5.27). Among them, Namasudra and Kaibartta (Nadiyal) were the most numerous; they together accounted for more than 50 per cent of the population of the so-called exterior castes. Certain castes were also classified as 'tea-garden coolie castes'. They numbered more than 1.23 million and together with Hindu exterior castes, constituted more than 35 per cent of the Hindu population of Assam (see also Appendix V.4).

Table 5.27 : Assam: Hindu Exterior Castes, 1931

Caste	*Population*	*Percentage of HEC**
Namasudra	170,469	28.56
Kaibartta (Nadiyal)	149,074	24.97
Patni	51,408	8.61
Yogi	44,422	7.44
Mali	38,635	6.47
Dhupi (Dhobi)	22,521	3.77
Hira	16,628	2.79
Bania (Brittial)	14,348	2.40
Sutradhar	12,575	2.11
Jhalo and Malo	10,826	1.81
Dugla (Dholi)	9,523	1.60
Muchi	7,312	1.22
Mahara	5,424	0.91
Sweeper	2,364	0.40
Total Population of HEC	596,918	

Note: *Hindu Exterior Castes.

Patterns of Spatial Distribution and Concentration

The geographic patterns of distribution of selected caste groups are evident from Appendix V.5. Ahoms, who constituted 4.8 per cent of the Hindu population at the provincial level, were found mainly in Darrang, Nowgong, Sibsagar and Lakhimpur districts as well as the Sadiya Frontier Tract. They were most numerous in Sibsagar and Lakhimpur. In fact, Ahoms constituted two-fifths of the Hindu population in Sibsagar and as much as one-third in Lakhimpur. Accounting for more than 3 per cent of the Hindu population on an average, Brahmans were more widely distributed. The districts, which were above the provincial average, included, Kamrup (5.33 per cent), Darrang (4.51 per cent) and Sylhet (3.95 per cent). Exceptions apart, Ahirs and Kayasthas generally constituted less than 2 per cent of the Hindu population (Figs. 5.24 and 5.25).

The Hindu castes of Assam displayed a strong tendency of concentration in a few districts (Table 5.28). Thus, 80 per cent of Ahirs were found in Sylhet, Sibsagar, Lakhimpur and Cachar; while 94 per cent of the Ahoms were confined to Sibsagar and Lakhimpur, the former district having the highest index of concentration. Brahmans, however, were more ubiquitous, although they were heavily concentrated in Sylhet, Kamrup, Sibsagar and Darrang. The four districts together accounted for 80 per cent of the Brahman population. Concentration indices of Kurmis were also high for Sibsagar and Lakhimpur districts. About 63 per cent of their population was concentrated in Sylhet only. Kayasthas were generally thinly distributed (Figs. 5.26 to 5.29).

It may be noted that the geographic patterning of the caste-groups discussed above is of a historic value, as things have changed a lot since 1931 and particularly after the partition of India in 1947. Nonetheless, 1931 data on caste remains an important benchmark, indispensable in any socio-geographical interpretation of the caste phenomenon.

Castes of the Scheduled Category

Caste acquired a new meaning in India after independence. With the introduction of reservation policy in 1950, caste became a powerful instrument of political mobilisation. A large number of caste groups were assigned the status of the Scheduled Castes. This was done on the basis of a scheduling policy which has been evolving since 1950. In fact, there were overriding political compulsions under which certain groups were brought under the schedule. Meandering as this policy has been, it resulted in additions to the list of the Scheduled Castes time and again. The scheduling policy varied from state to state.

Table 5.28 : Assam: Concentration of the selected Hindu Castes, 1931

S. No.	*District/ Territory*	*Ahir*	*Ahom*	*Brah-man*	*Kayastha*	*Kurmi*	*Hindu Exterior Castes*
	Assam						
	Assam Valley Division						
1	Goalpara			3.93	3.53		2.61
2	Kamrup			23.77	5.17		7.24
3	Darrang	8.28	1.67	12.93	2.86	13.74	2.62
4	Nowgong	4.46	1.69	5.94	3.87		7.83
5	Sibsagar	16.83	61.48	14.96	5.86	27.03	6.14
6	Lakhimpur	16.13	32.66	5.72	5.36	21.53	4.05
7	Garo Hills						
	Surma Valley and Hill Division						
8	Cachar	13.25		3.32	8.24	12.17	8.22
9	Sylhet	33.71		28.12	62.87	15.28	60.82
10	Khasi and Jaintia Hills						
11	Naga Hills						
12	Lushai Hills						
	Sadiya Frontier Tract	2.00					
	Balipara Frontier Tract						
	Elsewhere	7.47	0.50	1.31	2.25	12.94	0.47

Source: Census of India, 1931, Vol. III, Assam, Part II, Table XVI, *Religion*, pp. 255-57; Table XVII, *Caste, Tribe and Race*, pp. 259-66.

Note: All figures in percentages.

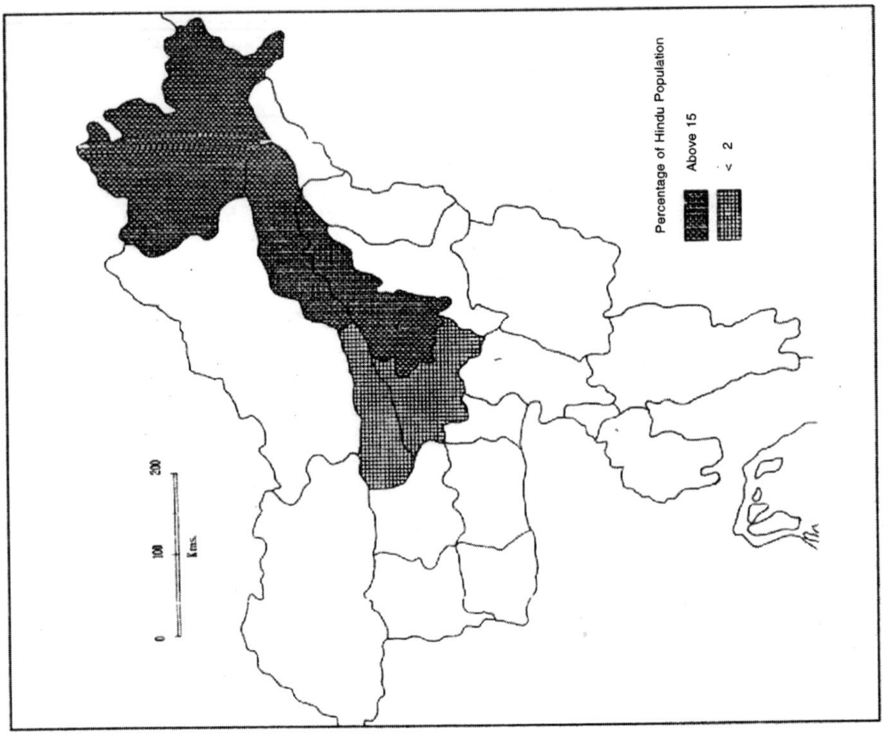

Figure 5.24 : Ahoms as percentage of the Hindu Population, 1931

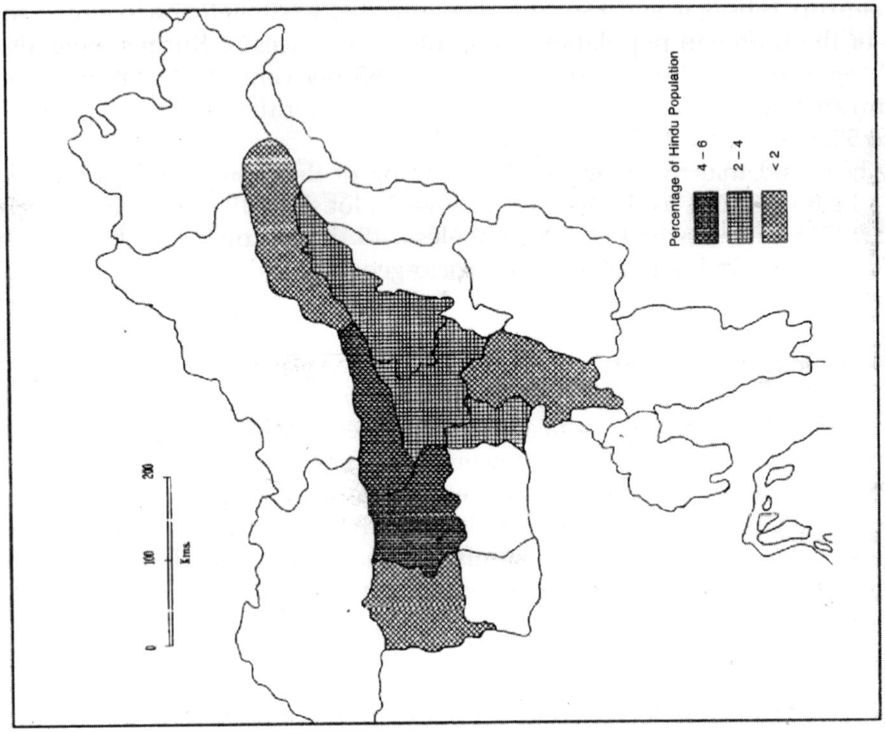

Figure 5.25 : Brahmans as percentage of the Hindu Population, 1931

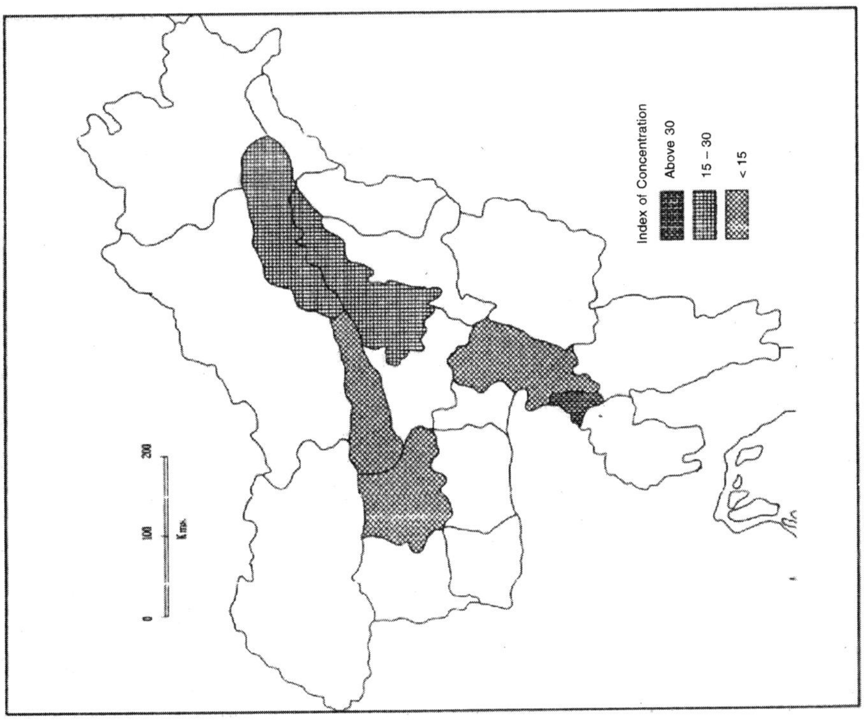

Figure 5.26 : Assam: Concentration of the Ahirs, 1931

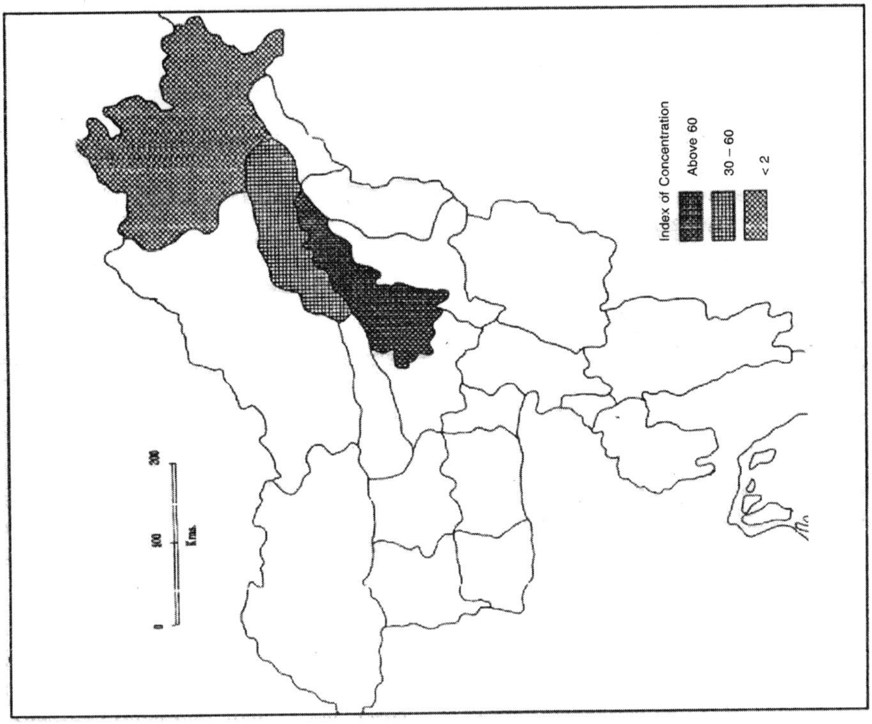

Figure 5.27 : Assam: Concentration of the Ahoms, 1931

Moreover, there were specific regions within the same state, or extending over several states, in which a particular caste enjoyed the scheduled status.[30] The major groups among the castes of the scheduled category display a peculiar geographic pattern of distribution. Many of them are ubiquitous; some of them are distributed across the states. But the majority of these castes are specific to a given state, or even to a cluster of districts in a state.

As already noted, these castes are an integral part of the social structure of the regions of their habitation. In their economic life, as well as in other spheres of life, they are dependent on the higher castes. This dependence has not decreased with time. With the advent of the agrarian mode of production these caste groups got associated with agriculture. In fact, they were the main suppliers of labour. This explained their heavy concentration in the states of the North Indian Plain as well as over the coastal plains of the peninsular states. These caste-groups were, however, conspicuous by their absence in the hilly and the forested tracts, which were predominantly inhabited by the tribal communities. The tribal society was by and large egalitarian. There was, therefore, little chance of the emergence of a stratified social order. Moreover, a clear-cut division of labour, which could lead to the emergence of an occupational specialisation, was alien to the tribal social order. This is the reason why backward castes, low castes or the untouchable castes, remained a phenomenon of the peasant society. It may also be observed that the Scheduled Castes were mostly a rural phenomenon. However, with growing industrialisation they were drawn into a variety of industries, particularly cotton textiles and leather. This led to their agglomeration in the cities associated with these industries. The caste-based discrimination, however, continued. The urban industrial sector offered employment to these castes in departments of work, which were generally treated as unclean or 'polluted'.

The main demographic features of the Scheduled Castes may be recapitulated here briefly. The 1991 census enumerated 138.22 million persons in the category of the Scheduled Castes. These castes thus accounted for 16.48 per cent of population at the all-India level (Table 5.29a; see also Table 5.29b). However, there are striking differences in the distribution of scheduled castes in the different regions/states of the country. A notable feature is that these castes are associated with agriculture. This explains their agglomeration in the alluvial plains with a high potential for agriculture. Away from the alluvial plains of the north and the coastal plains of the south, one observes a sudden decrease in the proportion of these castes in population. This is particularly true for the hilly and the forested tracts, which happen to be the abode of tribal communities. It is thus obvious that aspects of spatial distribution cannot be meaningfully discussed without correlating them to the economic parameters. Another striking fact is that an overwhelming proportion of the scheduled castes (about 90 per cent) is confined to rural areas. It explains their overwhelming dependence on agriculture. Despite their basic dependence on agriculture they have very little access to land. A very small fraction of their population consists of small landholders. In fact, they mostly work as landless agricultural labourers, or as artisans. They also provide a variety of services to the land-owning castes generally considered as polluting and unclean services.

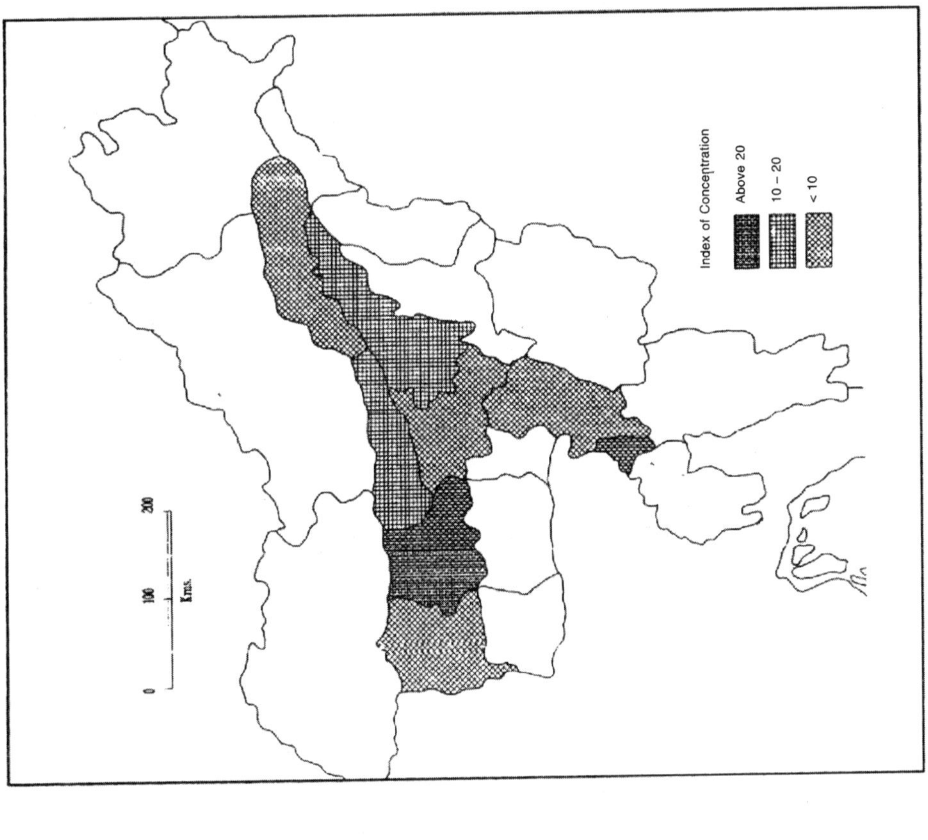

Figure 5.28 : Assam: Concentration of the Brahmans, 1931

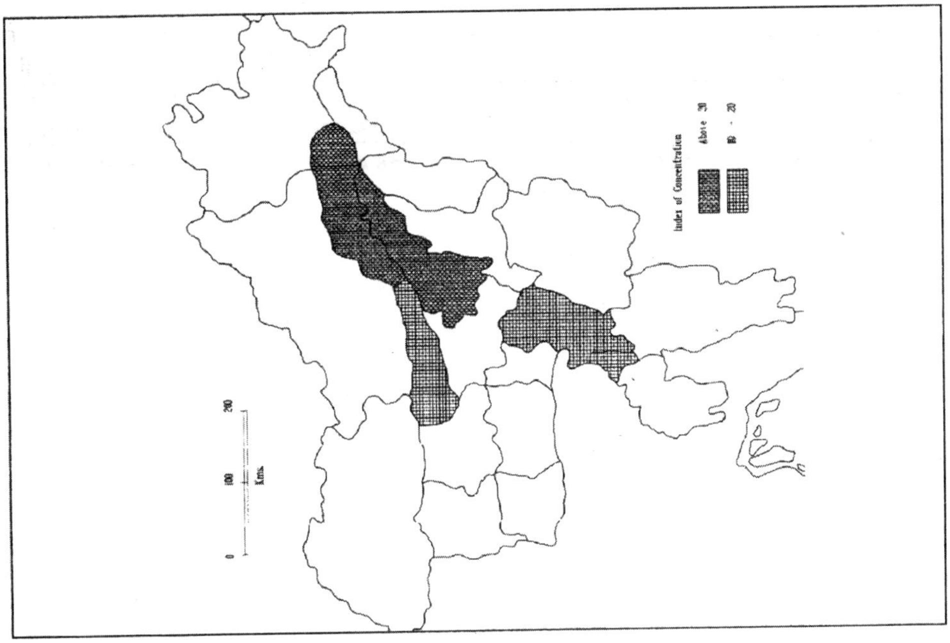

Figure 5.29 : Assam: Concentration of the Kurmis, 1931

Table 5.29a : Population of the Scheduled Castes by States/Union Territories, 1991

Regions/States	*SC Population*	*Per cent of Total Population*	*Per cent of Hindu Population*
India*	**138,223,277**	**16.48**	**20.10**
Northwest			
Jammu and Kashmir**	497,363	8.31	
Himachal Pradesh	1,310,296	25.34	26.42
Punjab	5,742,528	28.31	82.16
Haryana	3,250,933	19.75	22.14
Chandigarh	105,977	16.51	21.77
North			
Rajasthan	7,607,820	17.29	19.41
Madhya Pradesh	9,626,679	14.54	15.68
Uttar Pradesh	29,276,455	21.04	25.75
Delhi	1,794,836	19.05	22.77
East			
Bihar	12,571,700	14.56	17.66
West Bengal	16,080,611	23.62	31.61
Orissa	5,129,314	16.20	17.11
Sikkim	24,084	5.93	8.67
North-East			
Assam	1,659,412	7.40	11.03
Arunachal Pradesh	4,052	0.47	1.27
Nagaland	—	0.00	0.00
Manipur	37,105	2.02	3.50
Mizoram	691	0.10	1.99
Tripura	451,116	16.36	18.92
Meghalaya	9,072	0.51	3.49
West			
Gujarat	3,060,358	7.41	8.28
Maharashtra	8,757,842	11.10	13.68
Goa	24,364	2.08	3.22
Daman and Diu	3,891	3.83	4.36
Dadra and Nagar Haveli	2,730	1.97	2.06
South			
Andhra Pradesh	10,592,066	15.93	17.87
Karnataka	7,369,279	16.38	19.17
Tamil Nadu	10,712,266	19.18	21.63
Pondicherry	131,278	16.25	18.86
Kerala	2,886,522	9.92	17.32

Source: (i) Census of India, 1991, Series-1, India, Part II-B (i), Vol. II, *Primary Census Abstract, General Population.*
(ii) Table C-9, *Religion*, 1991.

Notes: * Excluding Jammu and Kashmir.
** Population according to 1981 census.

Table 5.29b : Population of the Scheduled Castes by States/Union Territories, 2001

State/Union Territory	*Caste Population*	*Proportion of SC Population (%)*
India	**166,635,700**	**16.2**
States		
Andhra Pradesh	12,339,496	16.2
Arunachal Pradesh	6,188	0.6
Assam	1,825,949	6.9
Bihar	13,048,608	15.7
Chhattisgarh	2,418,722	11.6
Goa	23,791	1.8
Gujarat	3,592,715	7.1
Haryana	4,091,110	19.3
Himachal Pradesh	1,502,170	24.7
Jammu and Kashmir	770,155	7.6
Jharkhand	3,189,320	11.8
Karnataka	8,563,930	16.2
Kerala	3,123,941	9.8
Madhya Pradesh	9,155,177	15.2
Maharashtra	9,881,656	10.2
Manipur	60,037	2.8
Meghalaya	11,139	0.5
Mizoram	272	0.0
Nagaland	—	—
Orissa	6,082,063	16.5
Punjab	7,028,723	28.9
Rajasthan	9,694,462	17.2
Sikkim	27,165	5.0
Tamil Nadu	11,857,504	19.0
Tripura	555,724	17.0
Uttaranchal	1,517,186	17.9
Uttar Pradesh	35,148,377	21.1
West Bengal	18,452,555	23.0
Union Territories		
Andaman and Nicobar Islands	—	—
Chandigarh	157,597	17.5
Dadra and Nagar Haveli	4,104	1.9
Daman and Diu	4,838	3.1
Delhi	2,343,255	16.9
Lakshadweep	—	—
Pondicherry	157,771	16.2

Source: Census of India, 2001, Series-1, *Primary Census Abstract, Total Population*, Table A-5.

Nomenclature

It is generally known that caste names vary from region to region. This is mainly due to the variations in language and dialect. As already pointed out, caste is a regional phenomenon. It is, therefore, understandable that the same castes would be known by different names in different language regions. Even the common castes of barber, washerman, oilman, gardener, potter and boatman have hundreds of regional variants in the country. This adds immensely to the lists of Scheduled Castes in different states of India (Table 5.30). The number of castes is as small as 4 in Sikkim, 7 in Manipur, 13 in Jammu and Kashmir and 16 in several other north-eastern states. On the other hand, the number is very large in southern and eastern states, such as Karnataka (101), Orissa (93), Tamil Nadu (76) and Kerala (68). The number is also generally large in the northern states of Uttar Pradesh, Rajasthan and Madhya Pradesh.

Table 5.30 : Number of Castes listed under the Scheduled Category, 1991 Census

S. No.	*Region/State*	*Number of Castes*	*S. No.*	*Region/State*	*Number of Castes*
Northwest			17	Manipur	07
1	Jammu and Kashmir	13	18	Mizoram	16
2	Himachal Pradesh	56	19	Tripura	32
3	Punjab	37	20	Meghalaya	16
4	Haryana	37	*West*		
5	Chandigarh	36	21	Gujarat	30
North			22	Maharashtra	59
6	Rajasthan	59	23	Goa	05
7	Madhya Pradesh	47	24	Daman and Diu	05
8	Uttar Pradesh	66	25	Dadra and Nagar Haveli	04
9	Delhi	36	*South*		
East			26	Andhra Pradesh	59
10	Bihar	23	27	Karnataka	101
11	West Bengal	59	28	Tamil Nadu	76
12	Orissa	93	29	Pondicherry	15
13	Sikkim	04	30	Kerala	68
Northeast			*Islands*		
14	Assam	16	31	Lakshadweep	00
15	Arunachal Pradesh	16	32	Andaman and Nicobar Islands	00
16	Nagaland	00			

Source: Census of India, 1991, Series-1, Part II-B (i), Vol. II, *Primary Census Abstract, General Population.*

A second series of problems arise from the official scheduling policy. A perusal of the lists of Scheduled Castes (Appendix V.6) shows that sometimes tribes are also recognised as castes and are mentioned in the list of Scheduled Castes. For example, Bhumij, which is a Scheduled Tribe in the Chhotanagpur division and the Santal Parganas district of Bihar, is treated as a Scheduled Caste in certain parts of the same state. Similarly, Thoti is a Scheduled Tribe in some districts of Andhra Pradesh. However, the group is treated as a Scheduled Caste in Karnataka, Tamil Nadu, Pondicherry and Kerala. Several tribal groups, such as Chero, Gond, Kharwar and Sahariya, are treated as Scheduled Castes in Uttar Pradesh. These are serious anomalies indeed. Various castes are also known by alternative names. Some examples may be cited here just for an illustration:

> Chamar or Ramdasia (J and K); Chamar, Jatia Chamar, Rehgar, Raigar, Ramdasi, Ravidasi (Punjab); Chamar, Bhambhi, Banbhi, Bhamabi, Jatia, Jatav, Jatava, Mochi, Raidas, Rohidas, Regar, Raigar, Ramdasia, Asadaru, Asodi, Chamadia, Chambhar, Changar, Haralayya, Harali, Khalpa, Machigar, Mochigar, Madar, Madig, Telugu Mochi, Kamati Mochi, Ranigar, Rohit, Samgar (Rajasthan);

Chamar, Dhusia, Jhusia, Jatava (Uttar Pradesh); Chamar, Chamari, Bairwa, Bhambi, Jatav, Mochi, Regar, Nona, Rohidas, Ramnami, Satnami, Surjyabanshi, Surjyaramnami, Ahirwar, Chamar Mangan, Raidas (Madhya Pradesh).

Regional Combinations

A perusal of the list of major groups among the Scheduled Castes (Appendix V.7 and V.8) shows that the way the castes are distributed reveals an intrinsic pattern in their regional combinations. This exercise has been attempted for all the macro regions of India, such as the north-west, north, east, west and the south. The states falling within each of these macro regions have been grouped together and the six first ranking castes of each state have been listed. Evidently, the first ranking castes vary from state to state (*e.g.*, Kori or Koli in Himachal Pradesh, Mazhabi in Punjab and Chamar in Haryana). The first ranking castes are Dusadh in Bihar, Pan or Pano in Orissa and Rajbanshi in West Bengal. Thus, there is a certain combination of castes, which is specific to each region. This reveals the historical processes through which these caste-groups came together.

Numerical Strength

The Scheduled Castes present a highly diverse picture in terms of their population size. At the 1981 census, for example, there were 28 caste groups with a population of one million or more. The Chamars with a population of 25.8 million were, by far, the most numerous. Adi-Dravidas who were second in rank were a poor match to the numerical strength of the Chamars. The population of caste-groups, such as the Pasi, Madiga, Mehtar, Mala, Dusadh and Mahar, varied between 2 and 4 million. There were 22 caste groups with a population ranging between one lakh and ten lakhs (1, 00,000 to 1 million). There were seven other caste groups with populations ranging between 20,000 and 94,000.

Distribution

A perusal of Table 5.29a and 5.29b shows that the Scheduled Castes are highly unevenly distributed among the states and the union territories. Uttar Pradesh has by far the largest share, with 21.2 per cent of all Scheduled Castes concentrated in that state. The northern and the eastern regions together have almost 60 per cent of the Scheduled Caste population. Almost three-fourths of the population of the Scheduled Castes is found in the seven major states *viz.*, Uttar Pradesh, West Bengal, Bihar, Tamil Nadu, Andhra Pradesh, Rajasthan and Maharashtra.

In terms of percentage of population, these castes were quite preponderant in Punjab, Himachal Pradesh, Haryana, Uttar Pradesh and West Bengal. The highest proportion is seen in the north-western states of Punjab and Himachal Pradesh, as well as the northern states of Uttar Pradesh and West Bengal. The proportions are also quite high in Tamil Nadu, Karnataka, Delhi, Chandigarh and Orissa. Another striking feature of the distribution is that the proportion of Scheduled Caste population is generally low in states in which the Scheduled Tribes are heavily concentrated.

What proportion of the Hindu population is constituted by the Scheduled Castes? Table 5.29a and 5.29b throws some light on this question. One-fifth of the Hindu population consists of Scheduled Castes at the all-India level; however, the departure from this all-India average is quite striking. The proportionate share of Scheduled Castes among the Hindus generally remains between 17 and 31 per cent in as many as 17 states and union territories. Leading among the states and union territories are Punjab, West Bengal, Himachal Pradesh, Haryana, Uttar Pradesh and Tamil Nadu. Punjab, where 82 per cent of the Hindu population is comprised by the Scheduled Castes, stands out as a case in itself, indeed a fit case for further research. The proportion of Scheduled Castes is also quite high among the Hindu population of West Bengal (31.6 per cent) and Uttar Pradesh (25.75 per cent).

District-level Patterns

A study of the percentage distribution of the scheduled castes by districts reveals that in as many as 211 districts, out of a total of 440, the proportionate share of the scheduled castes is generally moderate, ranging between 10 and 20 per cent. There are fewer districts on either side of this category. The proportions range between 20 and 30 per cent in 94 districts. These districts form contiguous pockets in parts of the Gangetic and plateau regions of West Bengal, central Bihar, central, eastern and southern Uttar Pradesh, eastern and northern Rajasthan, parts of Haryana and Punjab. Coastal districts of Andhra Pradesh and Tamil Nadu also fall in the same category (Fig. 5.30). There are 13 districts in which the Scheduled Caste proportions are on a higher side, *i.e.*, between 30 and 42 per cent. Districts falling in this category constitute five major clusters in north-western, northern, eastern and southern regions of India. Notable among these districts are Jalandhar, Faridkot and Hoshiarpur (Punjab), Sirmaur and Solan (Himachal Pradesh), Sitapur, Hardoi and Unnao (Uttar Pradesh), Sonbhadra (Bihar), Jalpaiguri, Bankura, Birbhum and South 24 Parganas (West Bengal) and Nilgiris (Tamil Nadu). In 61 districts, castes of the scheduled category account for 5-10 per cent of the district populations (Table 5.31a and 5.31b).[31]

Table 5.31a : Percentage Distribution of Scheduled Castes by Districts, 1991

Percentage Category	*Number of Districts*	*Percentage of Districts in each Category*
Above 50	1	0.23
20-50	108	24.55
10-20	211	47.95
5-10	61	13.86
1-5	30	6.82
Below 1	22	5.00
Nil	7	1.59
Total	440	100.00

Source: Census of India, 1991, Series-1, Part II-B (i), Vol. II, *Primary Census Abstract, General Population.*

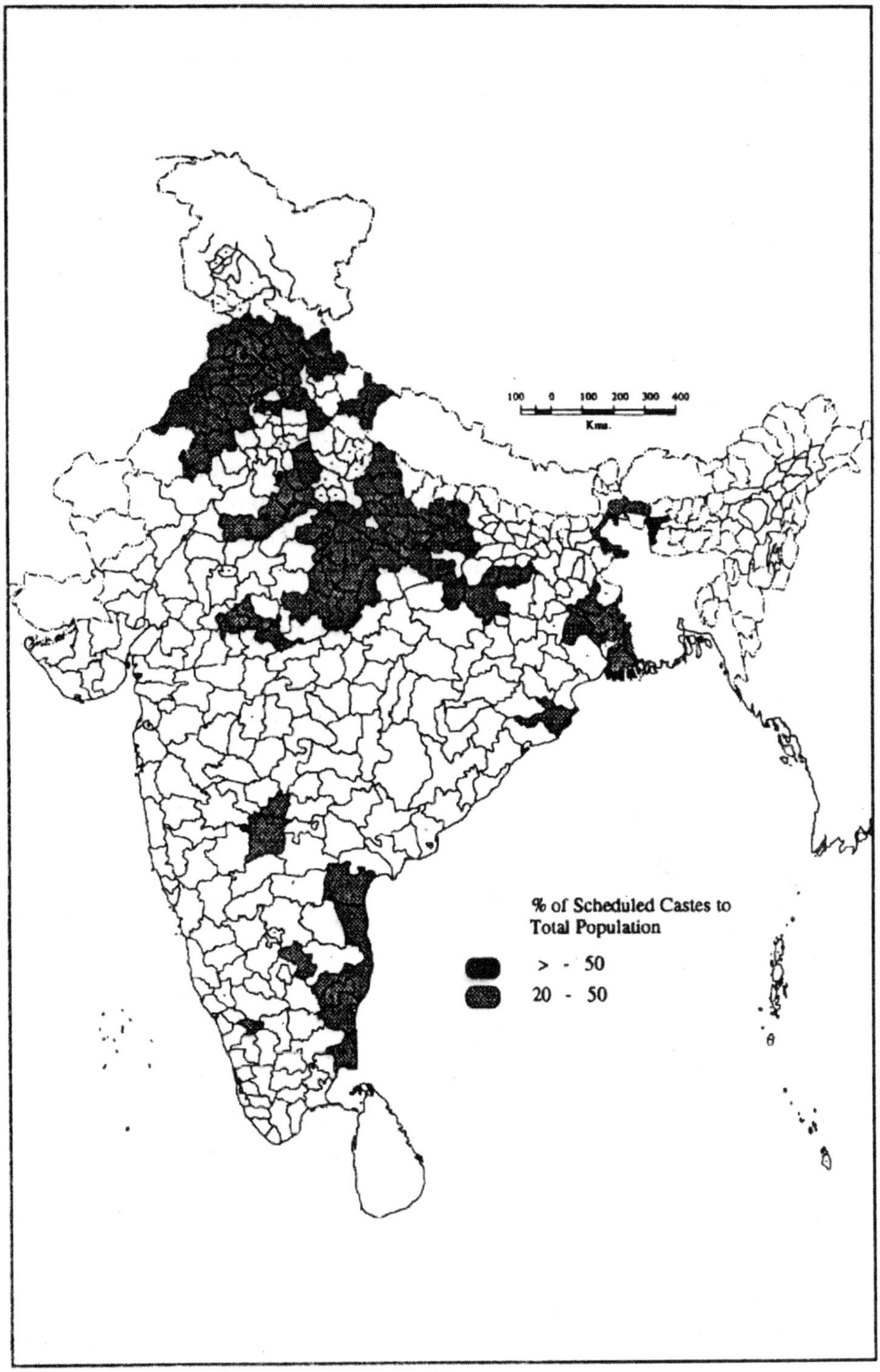

Figure 5.30 : India: Percentage of Scheduled Castes in Total Population, 1991

Table 5.31b : Districts Classified by proportion of Scheduled Caste Population, 2001

Percentage Category	*Number of Districts*
25.01 and Above	61
20.01-25.00	87
15.01-20.00	165
10.01-15.00	107
10.00 and Below	160
No Scheduled Castes	13
Total	593

Source: Census of India, 2001, Series-1, *Primary Census Abstract, Total Population*, Table A-5.
Note: Classification of data for all 593 districts of India.

As already pointed out, the Scheduled Castes display a strong tendency of clustering in the alluvial plains of the north. This fact is corroborated by an analysis of the distribution of their population at the district level. There are two pockets in which the Scheduled Castes have predominance. They are: (a) The north Indian plain from Punjab to West Bengal; and (b) The districts of the coastal plains from Orissa in the east to Gujarat in the west.

On the periphery of these regions there is a thinning out of the Scheduled Caste population implying a transition towards the more rugged and less fertile tracts. Then there are regions such as Central Vindhyan Complex encompassing parts of Rajasthan, Gujarat, Maharashtra and Madhya Pradesh, Chhotanagpur Plateau, Orissa highlands, hilly tracts of Uttar Pradesh, sub-Himalayan Himachal Pradesh and the districts in the north-east where they have a low concentration. These spatial variations in the relative concentration of the Scheduled Castes is directly related to the presence or otherwise of the tribes. Ecologically while tribal economies are related to the hilly and the forested tracts the Scheduled Castes are an integral part of the agrarian economy. This explains the phenomenon of mutual exclusivity of the castes and the tribes (Fig. 5.31).

Mapping the aggregative population of the Scheduled Castes has its own significance. However, it may be even more important to examine the spatial patterns in the distribution of specific communities among the Scheduled Castes. This will indeed be a colossal exercise, as their number is too large to be covered in a single exercise of this scale. A selection of the first ranking scheduled castes of Rajasthan, Bihar, Gujarat and Maharashtra has been randomly made in order to illustrate the broad geographical patterns. The first ranking castes chosen for this exercise include Chamars (Rajasthan), Dusadh (Bihar), Mahiyavansi (Gujarat) and Mahars (Maharashtra). A series of three maps has been generated for each of these castes showing their percentage strength in the overall Scheduled Caste population at the district level. More research on these lines may perhaps unravel the historical processes through which these castes have managed to carve out their niches in the Indian social space.

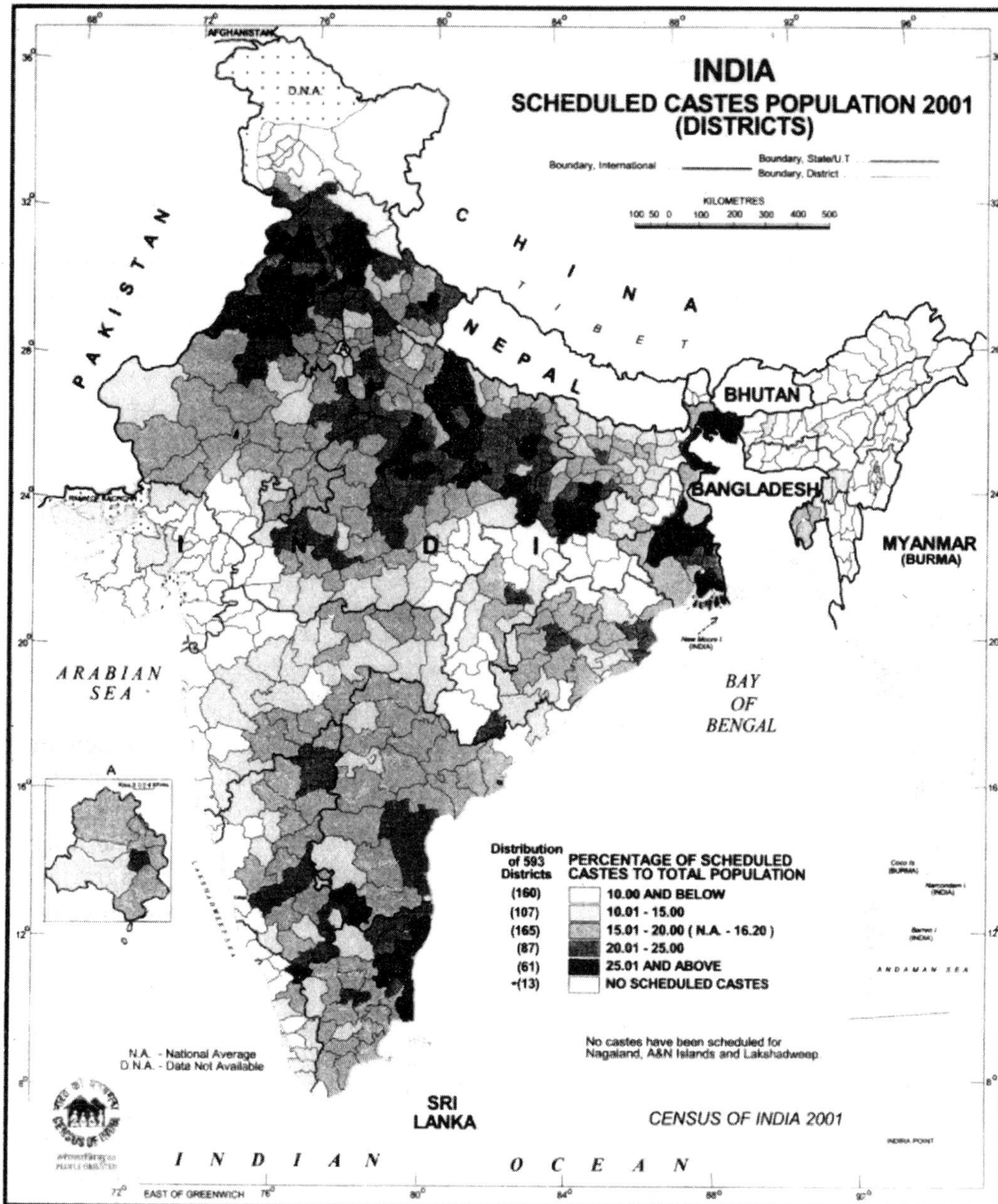

Based upon Survey of India map with the permission of the Surveyor General of India. The territorial waters of India extend into the sea to a distance of twelve nautical miles measured from the appropriate base line.

The interstate boundaries between Arunachal Pradesh, Assam and Meghalaya shown on this is as interpreted from the North-Eastern Areas (Reorganisation) Act 1971, but has yet to be verified.

Figure 5.31 : India: Percentage of Scheduled Castes in Total Population, 2001

NOTES AND REFERENCES

1. Scholars such as Kroeber and Risley point out that caste-like features are found in other countries as well. The examples of Egypt, United States of America and medieval Europe are cited (*cit*. Ram Ahuja, *Indian Social System*, 1994, p. 229).
   This is, however, a far-fetched comparison. Caste happens to be a unique feature of Indian society and there is no parallel in the world.
2. This is known on the authority of the skeletal remains dug out from the Indus valley site.
3. Notable contributions on caste came from H.H. Risley, *The People of India*, 1915; G.S. Ghurye, *Caste and Race in India*, 1932; *ibid*, *Caste and Class in India*, 1957; J. H. Hutton, *Caste in India, Its Nature, Function and Origin*, 1961; F.G. Bailey, *Caste and Economic Frontier*, 1957; M.N. Srinivas, *Caste in Modern India and Other Essays*, 1962; Irawati Karve, *Hindu Society—An Interpretation*, 1968; David G. Mandelbaum, *Society in India*, Volume I: *Continuity and Change*; Volume II: *Change and Continuity*, 1970; Louis Dumont, *Homo Hierarchichus: The Caste System and its Implications*, 1970; M. Marriott, *Caste Ranking and Community Structure in Five Regions of India and Pakistan*, 1960.
4. O.H.K. Spate and A.T.A. Learmonth, *India and Pakistan*, 1972, p. 199.
5. A sample survey of Aminbhavi was conducted by C.D. Deshpande on the request of O.H.K. Spate. Later, L.S. Bhat furnished some useful information on the recent changes at Aminbhavi as quoted below:
   'The village is now a real satellite of Dharwar, separated by only four miles from the nearest suburb and marginal village lands are cultivated by Dharwar residents'. Despite the growing interaction with the city and the changes in land use and social attitudes, 'Aminbhavi is still a microcosm of rural India', Spate, *op.cit*., pp. 221-22.
6. Figures in parenthesis show the percentage to the village population.
7. Spate and Learmonth, *op.cit*, p. 203.
8. K.D. Sharma, 'Social Morphology of Ḥimalayan Towns', in Aijazuddin Ahmad (ed.), *Social Structure and Regional Development*, 1993, pp. 129-49.
9. *ibid*, pp. 141-45.
10. K.N. Singh, 'Caste and Clan in the Indian Rural Settlement System', in Aijazuddin Ahmad (ed.), *op. cit*., p.11.
11. K.N. Singh, 'The Territorial Basis of Medieval Town and Village Settlement in Eastern Uttar Pradesh', *Annals of the Associations of American Geographers*, Vol. LVIII, 1965, pp. 203-20; *ibid*, 1993, *op.cit*.; Richard Fox, 'Rajput Clans and Rural Settlements in Northern India', in Richard Fox (ed.), *Urban India: Society, Space and Image*, 1970.
12. No research findings are available to verify the authenticity of these popular beliefs.
13. Andre Beteille, *Caste, Class and Power: Changing Patterns of Stratification in a Tanjore Village*, 1965.
14. K.N. Singh, in Aijazuddin Ahmad (ed.), *op. cit*., p. 58.
15. 'in pre-British India, in many parts of the country, the lower castes were serfs or slaves, either attached to the land and liable to be transferred along with it, or attached to the landowner and liable to be sold by him.... But even now the agricultural hierarchy is mixed up in different ways and degrees with the caste hierarchy in several parts of India'. M.N. Srinivas, *India: Social Structure*, 1986, pp. 15-16.
    The word 'pre-British' needs attention. In fact, enslavements of the low castes emerged as a phenomenon during the British period. In the period after independence the problem of bonded labourers continued unabated and remains largely unresolved.
16. 'The great bulk of our town dwellers are poor - terribly, terribly poor. They live huddled together in dismal, dark and smelly *chawls* or slums, sleeping four or five or even ten in a small, dark, smoky room, eating of the barest....' Minoo Masani, *Our India*, 1940, p. 27.

Those urban dwellers were pushed out of the villages and mostly drawn from among the ranks of the landless castes.

R. Palme Dutt noted that the transformation of the land systems and the creation of landlordism contributed immensely to the Indian poverty. The Permanent Land Settlement of Lord Cornwallis in 1793 for Bengal, Bihar and Orissa imposed terms and conditions 'which were very onerous for the *zamindars* and the cultivators and very profitable for the Government'. This is evident from an extract of the Report of the Collector of Midnapore in 1802 quoted below:

'The system of sale and attachment has in the course of a very few years reduced most of the great *zamindars* in Bengal to distress and beggary, and produced a greater change in the landed property of Bengal than has, perhaps, ever happened in the same space of time in any age or country by the mere effect of internal regulation' (R. Palme Dutt, *India Today*, 1940, pp. 227-31; 237-57).

'On the lowest rung of the economic ladder of India stand those permanent agricultural labourers who rarely received cash and whose conditions vary from absolute to mitigated slavery. Such is the custom of the country in many parts of India that the zamindar, malguzar or ordinary cultivator nearly always contrives to get his servant into his debt, thus obtaining the hold over him which extends even to his posterity. In the Bombay Presidency, there are Dublas and Kolis, who to a greater or lesser (extent) are bond slaves. Most of their families have been serving for several generations practically as slaves to their master's households.... In the south-west of Madras (Presidency) there are the Izhavas, Cherumas (Cherumans), Puleyas and Holeyas, all virtually slaves' (R. Mukherjee, *Land Problems of India*, pp. 225-29, *cit.*, R.P. Dutt, *op.cit.*, pp. 240-41).

17. For example, Report of the Agrarian Reforms Committee of 1949, Indian National Congress also the Communist Party of India slogans *Land to the Tiller*. Vinoba Bhave's *Sarvodya Movement and its components of Bhudan-Gramdan Movement*. See also Government of U.P., *Report of the United Provinces Zamindari Abolition Committee*, Vols. I and II, Allahabad, 1948; K.V. Tripathi, *'Zamindari Abolition and Post-Abolition Land Reforms in Uttar Pradesh', A.I.C.C. Economic Review*, Vol. V, No. 24, April 15, 1954. *See* also, P.C. Joshi, *Land Reforms in India*, 1975.
18. An outstanding example is F.G. Bailey, *Caste and the Economic Frontier*, ELBS Edition, 1972.
19. Collection of data on the ownership of land is not an easy exercise since people do not declare facts. The land, although owned by a family, is sometimes not shown in official records. Mandavdhare's work was naturally beset with difficulties.
20. 'The *jajmani* system bound together the different castes living in a village or a group of neighbouring villages. The caste-wise division of labour and the consequent linking up of different castes in enduring and pervasive relationships provided a pattern of alliances which cut across the ties of caste'. See M.N. Srinivas, *op.cit*, p. 14. The system was in practise all over India in one form or the other. It was known as *bara balute* in Maharashtra, *Mirasi* in Madras and *adade* in Mysore.
21. See also A.R. Desai, *Rural Sociology in India*, Section VIII, Agrarian Unrest, 1969, pp. 389-423. Also see A.R. Desai, *Peasant Struggles in India*, 1981; Kathleen Gough, 'Indian Peasant Uprisings' in A.R. Desai, 1981, *ibid*, pp. 85-126.
22. Satish Deshpande, 'Counting on Caste for Social Justice', *The Times of India*, New Delhi, August 18, 1998. Deshpande's remark 'social scientists opposing the collection of 'divine' caste statistics must open their eyes (and minds) to caste as a form of inequality' did not find much favour in the social science circles.
23. Clustering implies agglomeration in space, while concentration implies a high proportion in population in a given unit of reference.
24. Joseph E. Schwartzberg, 'The Distribution of Selected Castes in the North Indian Plain', *The Geographical Review*, Vol. LV, 1965, p. 484.

25. There are numerous villages and towns which carry the word Dom as a suffix or prefix to their name, *e.g.*, Domariyaganj in eastern parts of Uttar Pradesh.
26. The distribution of castes in space attracted the attention of several American social geographers. Of particular interest was the study of caste-groups by Joseph E. Schwartzberg. He studied the geographical distribution of selected caste-groups of the North Indian Plain. His basic objective was to understand the spatial patterns of caste association in the Indian rural space and to highlight the social implications of such a pattern of distribution. His project of mapping caste distribution, to which he attached great importance in view of the complex role that caste played in the day-to-day functioning of the Indian rural society, was completed in two phases of field work in 1958-59 and 1962-63. Primarily, his basic caste data were derived from the 1931 census—the last census of British India which collected and compiled data for individual castes at the district level. He supplemented his study of the census data with field research during which data were generated for 10 selected castes at the household level from 212 villages distributed over the North Indian Plain from Rajasthan to West Bengal. His household-level study covered castes which were high as well as middle ranking and low in ritual hierarchy. Schwartzberg's samples included castes, such as Brahman and Rajput (high ranking), Jat, Kurmi, Lodh and Ahir (middle ranking) and Chamar, Pasi and Nai (low ranking). The sample also included Sheikh, a Muslim caste. Schwartzberg's pioneering study revealed how certain castes are specific to certain regions, while others were ubiquitous. Those which were represented in most of the villages were Brahmans, Chamars and the Nais. This is understandable in view of the fact that specific services were provided by the Brahmans (rituals and ceremonies), Nais (barber and messenger in marriage ceremonies) and Chamars (agricultural labourers, handling dead bodies of animals and removing their skins, leather workers). On the other hand, there were cultivating castes, such as Rajput, Jat, Kurmi, Lodh and Ahir who displayed a strong tendency of clustering in certain districts. Their mutually exclusive domains possess clues to the origins of the process of settling down on land and the eventual emergence of the clan territories (Joseph E. Schwartzberg, 'The Distribution of Selected Castes in the North Indian Plain', *The Geographical Review*, Vol. LV, 1965, pp. 477-495).
27. See, for example, Census of India, 1931, Vol. XVIII, United Provinces of Agrah and Oudh, Part II, *Imperial and Provincial Tables*, Table XVII, *'Race, Tribe or Caste'*, Allahabad, 1933, pp. 499-519.
28. See, for example, the following comment:
'in the interest of economy the only caste and tribe sorted for at this census were those for which the figures are likely to be necessary for administrative purposes' (Census of India, Vol. III, Assam, Part II, Tables XVII, *'Caste, Tribe or Race'*, Shillong, 1932, p. 259).
29. '...certain castes which are indigenous to Assam have the same name as caste for other provinces which appear to have nothing in common with them. Thus the upcountry Mali is quite a different caste from the indigenous Mali (Bhuinmali) of Sylhet ', *ibid*, p. 259.
30. The statutory list of Scheduled Castes is notified in pursuance of Article 341 of the Constitution of India. The Article as amended is quoted below:
'(1) The President may with respect to any state or union territory, and where it is a state, after consultation with the Governor thereof, by public notification, specify the caste, races or tribe or parts of or groups within castes, races or tribes which shall for the purpose of this constitution be deemed to Scheduled Castes in relation to that State or Union Territory, as the case may be.
(2) Parliament may by law includes in or excludes from the list of Scheduled Castes specified in a notification issued under clause (1) any caste, race or tribe or part of or group within any caste, race or tribe, but save as aforesaid a notification issued under the said clause shall not be varied by any subsequent notification'.

31. Reference may be made to the classical study of the distribution of Scheduled Castes attempted by G.S. Gosal and A. B. Mukerji, 'Distribution and Relative Concentration of Scheduled Caste Population in India', Census of India, 1971, *Economic and Socio-cultural Dimensions of Regionalisation,* Census Centenary Monograph No. 7, New Delhi, pp. 473-82.

SUGGESTIONS FOR FURTHER READING

Gosal, G.S. and A.B. Mukerji (1971): 'Distribution and Relative Concentration of Scheduled Caste Population in India', in Chandra Sekhar (ed.), *Economic and Socio-Cultural Dimensions of Regionalisation*, pp. 473-482.

Hutton, J.H. (1961): *Caste in India: Its Nature, Function and Origin,* Bombay: Oxford University Press.

Schwartzberg, J.E. (1965): 'The Distribution of Selected Castes in the North Indian Plain', *The Geographical Review,* Vol. LV, No. 4, pp. 477-495.

Singh, K.N. (1993): 'Caste and Clan in the Indian Rural Settlement System' in Aijazuddin Ahmad (ed.), *Social Structure and Regional Development,* Jaipur: Rawat Publications, pp. 51-75.

Srinivas, M.N. (1962): *Caste in Modern India and Other Essays,* Bombay: Asia Publishing House.

6

Speech Communities

Language: A Bridge, not a Cleavage

India is the home of a very large number of languages. In fact, so many languages and dialects are spoken in India that it is often described as a 'museum of languages'. The language diversity is by all means baffling. In popular parlance it is often described as 'linguistic pluralism'. But this may not be a correct description. The prevailing situation in the country is not pluralistic, but that of a continuum. One dialect merges into the other almost imperceptibly; one language replaces the other gradually. Moreover, along the line of contact between two languages, there is a zone of transition in which people are bilingual. Thus languages do not exist in watertight compartments. While linguistic pluralism is a state of mutual existence of several languages in a contiguous space, it does not preclude the possibility of inter-connections between one language and the other. In fact, these links have grown over millennia of shared history. While linguistic pluralism continues to be a distinctive feature of the modern Indian state, it will be wrong to assume that there has been no interaction between the different groups. On the contrary, the give-and-take between the language groups has been very common, often resulting in systematic borrowings from one language to the other. The cases of assimilation of one language into the other are also not uncommon.

Let us look at the nature of linguistic diversity observed in India today. According to the Linguistic Survey of India conducted by Sir George Abraham Grierson towards the end of the nineteenth century, there were 179 languages and as many as 544 dialects in the country.[1] However, this number has to be taken with caution. It may even be misleading in the sense that dialects and languages were enumerated separately, although they were taxonomically part of the same language. Of the 179 languages, as many as 116, were speech-forms of the Sino-Tibetan family, spoken by small tribal communities in the remote Himalayan and the north-eastern parts of the country. Even the 1961 census recorded 187 languages. This was despite the fact that the census investigation was far more systematic and the classification was based on modern linguistic criteria. Much of this diversity may be understood properly in the light of some more statistics. For example, 94 out of the 187 languages were spoken by small populations of 10,000 persons or less. In the final analysis, about 97 per cent of the country's population was found affiliated with just 23 languages.

The diversity of languages and dialects is a reality and it is not the numerical strength of the speakers of a language, which is important. The important fact is that there are people who claim a certain language as their mother-tongue even though the linguists do not recognise them.

Another related development, which contributed to the linguistic diversity, was the development of the script. Different Indian languages were written in different scripts. This made learning of different languages a difficult exercise. However, with the growth of scripts, written languages have been successful in maintaining their record with the consequence that several literary traditions have evolved. With the development of a script, oral communication is supplemented by a more powerful form of written communication. In the course of time some of the minor dialect and language groups have lost their identity as they have been assimilated into developed languages. It is a known fact that most of the languages still serve the purpose of oral communication only, as speakers of these languages are still illiterate or preliterate.

It may be assumed that in the beginning various speech communities were confined to their own enclaves, more or less unaware of the existence of other language/dialect groups in the neighbourhood. Sometimes, the boundary between two dialects, or two languages, was knife-edged, as it was described by a hill-line or a river or an expanse of the sea. Within the enclaves, these groups have been communicating through a common language, or a dialect, for centuries. This became the basis of their identity. This traditional association with a language gave them a sense of belonging and thus inculcated in them a feeling of unity with the larger speech community. It may, however, be noted that inter-communication through a language or dialect is, always limited in space. Individuals in their daily course of life have a limited reach. In situations where the communication is largely oral the sphere of communication is even smaller. Thus, with the passage of time, each speech community gets differentiated from other communities in the neighbourhood. This process leads to splitting of the spoken language into diverse dialects. The dialect formation is, however, within the same speech area. With the expansion of the speech territory more dialect groups emerge and the distance between them increases. Sometimes the outlying dialects are so isolated from the parent language that they acquire linguistic nuances of their own, sufficient enough to be recognised as an independent branch. A study of historical linguistics reveals that India has gone through all these phases of language development. The present linguistic map of India is naturally a product of these developments.

Language and Dialect

The faculty of speech is by far the most distinctive human trait. Human beings use a system of language for communication which distinguishes them from the rest of the animal kingdom. It was through language that communication between the different members of a human group started in the early stages of social evolution. Language thus facilitated multiple forms of human cooperation. Eventually, a division of labour emerged, a prototype of which is unimaginable in the animal world. However, there is no gainsaying the fact that animals also communicate with one another. They also produce vocal sounds although their sounds are simple. One can differentiate between warning calls, mating calls and those expressing anger or affection. This system of communication is simple as it lacks structure. A structured language was the invention of the human mind, and the most effective tool of communication. In this language, words could be replaced easily to change the content of meaning.

In its basic characteristics a human language is essentially a signalling system in which a variety of vocal sounds are employed. These vocal sounds are produced by the peculiar constitution of the human speech organs. There is a combination of the different speech organs—the tongue, glottis, vocal chords and the palate—in producing vocal sounds, which are essential elements in human articulation of language. It appears that in the beginning speakers of a language restricted their communication to relatively small number of vocal sounds out of the many sounds which human beings were capable of making. However, the number of vocal sounds varied from language to language which indicated variations in social evolution and the material conditions of existence. Most languages are satisfied with the use of twenty or thirty such sounds. But there are other languages, which have, as many as sixty sounds, or even more. There are others, which have less than twenty sounds. These sounds constitute the system of a language. As we know the purpose of a language is communication and a language sooner or later tends to become symbolic, more complex and expressive of abstract ideas. The beginnings of all languages were, however, simple.

There are very specific purposes, for which the language is used. The main purpose is, of course, to express oneself, to convey ones feelings, sometimes to express a desire or a prayer for help. The human beings also communicate their ideas through body language either alone or in combination with vocal sounds or words. Even today, the body language continues to be a powerful means of expression. The exchange of ideas, feelings and calls for pray or help continue in the daily course of life of a human being. Thus, an intricate pattern of human cooperation and a feeling of togetherness is evolved. It is obvious that a language needs a group of people among whom communication continues through this language. This group of people who communicate in a certain language may be described as the 'speech community'. In the course of time, several speech communities are formed, each occupying a chunk of a geographically contiguous space (Fig. 6.1).

Each language eventually expands over a territory, homogenous in terms of its language structure—vocal sounds, words, sentences and conventionalised symbols. When a language is written in a script it tends to stabilise its distinguishing features and promotes communication over long distances between the people.

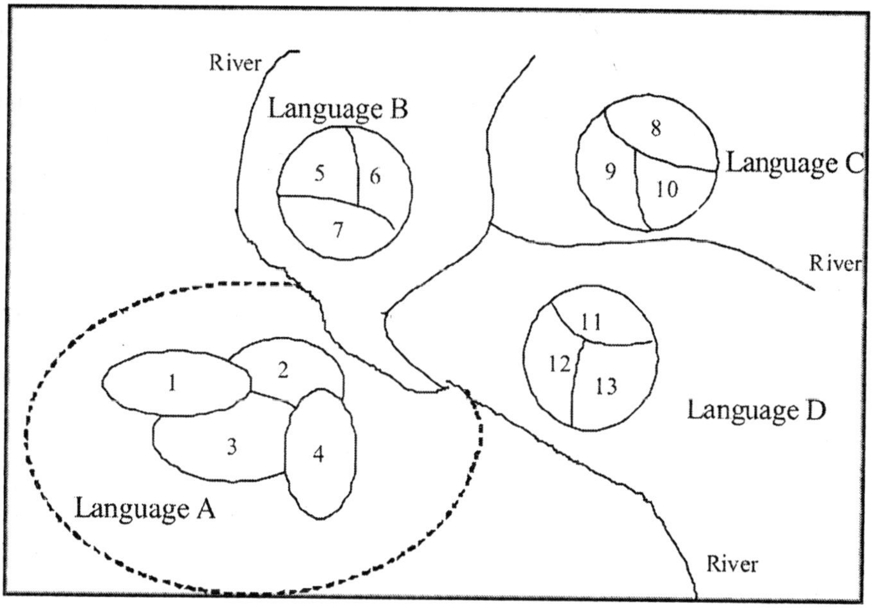

Figure 6.1 : Language Divergence in Space

Notes: (i) Language territory shown as A, B, C, and D.
(ii) Dialect area shown as 1, 2, 3...13.

Origins of Language

Origins of language are shrouded in mystery. However, it is possible to reconstruct the bits of this history. It is generally agreed that in the history of social evolution language must have arisen with the discovery of the art of tool-making.[2] Understandably, the early tool-making communities must have depended on cooperation between different members of the group on a highly organised basis. This would have been possible through the use of a certain language. Thus evolution of languages must have progressed hand in hand with the evolution of material cultures. As the history of material cultures shows the change in techniques of tool-making was initially slow, but later on it picked up. Language also evolved with the same pace. Expressions became more and more complex with the passage of time. In fact, at every stage of evolution there was a direct relationship between material culture and the language in use. Evidently progress in material cultures shows that the functions of brain were becoming more and more complex and with these changes language also became complex. The way languages evolved from vocal sounds to words and sentences revealed how they became symbolic as humans tended to express abstract rather than concrete ideas.

It is obvious that in the course of evolution many languages were invented independently at different points of time in different regions of the world. They became further ramified as the social space within which intercommunication continued was always limited (Box 6.1). As a result, new groups were formed and new speech communities came into being. This is how the 'families of languages' developed. It is also understandable that the early languages were oral and writing became possible much later. In the beginning there was no need for maintaining a written record. When such a need arose writing was initially mostly pictorial. The discovery of the script in the history of development of languages must have taken a painstakingly long time during which picture/signs became conventionalised. Our knowledge of the early scripts is still incomplete. For example, the script of the Indus Valley (Harappan) Civilisation continues to pose difficulties. We have not been able to decipher it simply because we are not familiar with the system of language in which communication was conducted by the Harappan people.

Box 6.1 : Language Families

The process of change in a language often leads to divergent development. Imagine a language which is spoken only by the population of two small adjacent villages. In each village, the language will slowly change, but the changes will not be identical in both villages.... If communications between the two villages are bad, and members of one village seldom meet anybody from the other, then the rate of divergence may well be high. When a language is diverged into two forms like this, we say that it has two *dialects*.... Suppose now that the inhabitants of one of the villages pack up their belonging and migrate *en* masse. They go off to a distant country and under conditions quite different from their own home.... After a few hundred years the two dialects may have got so different that they are no longer mutually intelligible. We should now say that they were two different languages.... When two languages have evolved in this way from some single earlier language, we say that they are related (it is how the families of languages are formed).

—Charles Barber, *The Story of Language*, 1964: 70-71.

India as a Linguistic Area

Despite the widely perceived linguistic diversity, India's unity as a socio-linguistic area is quite impressive. Several linguists have analysed the basic elements of India as a socio-linguistic area. Describing language as an 'autonomous system', Lachman M. Khubchandani recognised the major characteristics of the speech forms of modern India.[3] Each region of the country is characterised by the plurality of cultures and languages 'with a unique mosaic of verbal experience'. In Khubchandani's view, modern languages of India represent a striking example of the process of diffusion, grammatical as well as phonetic, over many contiguous areas. However, he considers linguistic plurality only as a superficial trait. 'Indian masses through sustained interaction and common legacies have developed a common way to interpret, to share experiences, to think'. What has emerged is a kind of organic plurality, although the geographical distribution of speech-communities suggests a kind of linguistic heterogeneity. Some of the basic elements of India's linguistic unity may be seen in the fuzzy nature of language boundaries, fluidity in language identity and complementarity of inter-group and intra-group communication. Khubchandani also emphasised the need of linking languages with the ecology of cultural regions described by him as *Kshetras*. As a language area India is being put to mutually contradictory linguistic interpretations, which confuse the issue. Perhaps a better understanding of the linguistic scene can be developed if the static account of the multiplicity of languages is replaced by recognition of the elements of cultural regionalism. Similarly, the issue of linguistic homogeneity, which has been argued by several linguists, is fraught with complexities. In this context, one can cite the example of the states of the Indian Union carved out on the principle of linguistic homogeneity. The reality is that these states are not necessarily homogeneous in their language composition and cultural attributes.[4]

In an earlier study, Khubchandani examined the evidence on plural languages and plural cultures of India. He dwelt upon the question of language in a plural society. The processes of language modernisation and language promotion were also analysed on the basis of a review of the language policies and planning in India. In this work, Khubchandani noted that people in certain regions of India displayed a certain degree of fluidity in their declaration of mother-tongue. On this basis, he recognised two zones in which the country could be divided: a *fluid* zone and a *stable* zone. The fluid zone extended over the north-central region where Hindi, Urdu, Punjabi, Kashmiri and Dogri are spoken. The stable zone, on the other hand, incorporates western, southern and eastern regions. People in these regions did not reveal any fluidity in their mother-tongue declaration.[5]

Reference may also be made to the seminal work of Murray B. Emeneau who analysed the characteristics of India as a language area. Tracing the history of development of the Indo-Aryan and the Dravidian languages he evaluated the shared experiences of the different speech communities. Emeneau defined linguistic area as 'an area, which includes languages belonging to more than one family but sharing traits in common which are found not to belong to other members of (at least) one of the families'.[6]

Geographical Patterning

The geographic patterning of languages in the South-Asian subcontinent can perhaps be understood in the context of the space relations the region had with other parts of Asia. As already pointed out, the Sub-continent marks a southward projection of the Asian landmass into the Indian Ocean. The overland connections with West and Central Asia, Tibet, China and other regions of Southeast Asia helped the process of infiltration of linguistic influences into the South Asian Region. This is evident from the fact that the languages spoken in the peripheral regions of South Asia, such as Baluchistan, Pak-Afghan borderlands, Kashmir, Gilgit, Hunza, Baltistan and Ladakh as well as the hilly parts of Himachal Pradesh and the regions in the Northeast have strong affinity with the languages spoken in the regions beyond the Hindu-Koh Himalayas. The remote Himalayan areas became the abode of Tibeto-Chinese languages. Similarly, the north-eastern region continued to receive influences from the neighbouring parts of Myanmar, Thailand and Indo-China. These regions are now the domain of the Tibeto-Chinese (Sino-Tibetan) or Tibeto-Burman languages. The people in the Plains of North India from Sind to Assam acquired different branches of the Indo-European family of languages. The peninsular region continued to retain the Dravidian speech-forms even though the north was completely swayed over by the Indo-European languages. Between the Indo-European and the Dravidian one finds the Austric-speaking tribes nestled in the hills of the mid-Indian region.

The linguistic heterogeneity of India can perhaps be brought to some order when one realises that these speeches really belong to four language families: Sino-Tibetan (Tibeto-Burman), Austro-Asiatic, Dravidian and the Indo-European. In the course of usage over millennia of years, these language families have found for themselves niches in the Indian social space in different parts of the subcontinent. Their geographical patterning throws some light on the routes through which these language families reached India. In fact, despite the vast heterogeneity, Indian languages experienced parallel trends in linguistic and literary development during the long phases of shared history. This has made India 'a composite region' in terms of linguistic attributes (Table 6.1).[7]

Table 6.1 : Broad Classification of Modern Indian Languages

Family	*Sub-family*	*Branch/ Group*	*Speech Area*
Austric *(Nishada)*	Austro-Asiatic	Mon-Khmer	Meghalaya, Nicobar Islands
		Munda	West Bengal, Bihar, Orissa, Assam, Madhya Pradesh, Maharashtra
	Austro-nesian		Outside India
Dravidian (Dravida)		South Dravidian	Tamil Nadu, Karnataka, Kerala
		Central Dravidian	Andhra Pradesh, Madhya Pradesh, Orissa, Maharashtra
		North Dravidian	Bihar, Orissa, West Bengal, Madhya Pradesh
Sino-Tibetan *(Kirata)*	Tibeto-Myanmari	Tibeto-Himalayan	Jammu and Kashmir, Himachal Pradesh, Sikkim
		North Assam	Arunachal Pradesh
		Assam-Myanmar	Assam, Nagaland, Manipur, Mizoram, Tripura, Meghalaya
	Siamese-Chinese		Outside India
Indo-European (Arya)	Indo-Aryan	Iranian	Outside India
		Dardic	Jammu and Kashmir
		Indo-Aryan	Jammu and Kashmir, Punjab, Himachal Pradesh, Uttar Pradesh, Uttrakhand, Rajasthan, Haryana, Madhya Pradesh, Bihar, Orissa, West Bengal, Assam, Gujarat, Maharashtra, Goa

Historical Process of Language Diffusion

The history of Indian languages is not easy to reconstruct. As an overview of the processes of peopling of India shows, Negroids were the first people to arrive. However, we do not exactly know about their language affiliation. The subsequent waves of migration were so strong that the Negroids lost their identity completely, leaving behind little traces of either their racial or linguistic past.

The story of the four families of languages may be briefly recapitulated here, although it is not easy to establish the chronological sequence in which the speakers of the Austric, Sino-Tibetan and the Dravidian languages came to India. It is almost certain that these families were already there at the time of the advent of the Indo-Aryan. This is, however, an established fact that the Sino-Tibetan speech communities were Mongoloids racially. The original Sino-Tibetan, the parent of the early Chinese, is supposed to have developed somewhere in western China around 400 B. C. It is also believed that the diffusion of this language eventually affected the regions lying to the south and southwest of China—Tibet, Ladakh, northeastern India, Myanmar and Thailand. Perhaps the Vedic Aryans were familiar with this group. They described the Tibeto-Burman-speaking Mongoloids of the Brahmaputra valley and the adjoining regions as *Kirata*.

The speakers of the Kirata family of languages are distributed all along the Himalayan axis from Baltistan and Ladakh to Arunachal Pradesh. They occupy the regions surrounding the Brahmaputra valley in the northeast from Nagaland to Tripura and Meghalaya. There are striking differences between the languages of the Kirata family distributed over such a vast geographical area. The speakers of the Tibeto-Himalayan branch of the Kirata languages occupy the Himalayan regions from Baltistan to Sikkim and beyond to Arunachal Pradesh. The Bhotia group consists of the Balti, Ladakhi, Lahauli, Sherpa and the Sikkim Bhotia dialects. Linguists also recognise a Himalayan group consisting of Lahuli of Chamba, Kanauri and Lepcha, which is distinguishable on the basis of certain linguistic traits. In the east, there is a north-Assam branch including the dialects of Arunachal Pradesh, such as Miri and Mishing. In other parts of the northeast, the languages belong to the Assam-Burmese branch and are divided into Bodo, Naga, Kachin and Kuki-Chin groups. The speakers of the Kirata languages came to India in different streams at different points of time. Understandably, the groups in the northwest were unrelated to the groups in the northeast. Similarly, the Kachin and the Kuki-Chin groups followed separate routes of migration. This is why there is a vast variety of dialects within the Kirata family and the roots of linguistic heterogeneity go far beyond the Indian borders into the neighbouring parts of Tibet, Myanmar and Indo-China.

Anthropologists as well as linguists believe that the Austric-speaking groups came earlier than the Dravidian speaking communities. The Austric speech communities were already there in the mid-Indian region before the advent of the Dravidian. The present geography of the Austric dialect groups holds some clues to the historical processes of their diffusion into India. Generally, the Austric family of languages is recognised as consisting of a Mon-Khmer and a Munda branch. The Mon-Khmer speakers belong to two separate groups, *viz.*, Khasi and the Nicobarese, both separated by a distance of more than 1,500 kilometres, which spans over an expanse of the Bay of Bengal. There is no clarity among the scholars about the routes taken by the speakers of the Mon-Khmer dialects. The Khasi speakers themselves are surrounded by other Kirata and Arya dialects in the Meghalayan plateau.

The advent of the Dravidian in India is generally associated with a branch of the Mediterranean racial stock which was already there in India before the rise of the Indus valley civilisation. In fact, archaeologists believe that they were the builders of the Harappan civilisation along with the Proto-Austroloids.

The Dravidian speech communities were found over most of the northern and the northwestern region of India before the advent of the Indo-Aryan. However, following the rise of the Indo-Aryan in northwestern India, a linguistic change came, and the Dravidian-speaking area shrank in its geographical extent. The present distribution of the Dravidian dialects in different parts of north India, such as Baluchistan, Chhotanagpur Plateau and eastern Madhya Pradesh, where Baruhi, Kurukh-Oraon and the Gondi are spoken respectively, suggest the earlier stage of distribution of this family of languages. In fact, Gondi is spoken in many parts of Central India from Madhya Pradesh and Maharashtra to Orissa and Andhra Pradesh. While Dravidian speech forms were in use for many centuries in the pre-Christian era, the literary development in the Dravidian speech community could take place only in the first few centuries after Christ. It is believed that the old Tamil, old Kannada and the old Telugu had already come into being by 1000 A.C. Malayalam acquired its form a little later.

With the Vedic Sanskrit, a branch of the Indo-European, the Indo-Aryan established itself in northwestern India. It had definite relations with the different Indo-European languages, such as the Persian, Armenian, Greek, French, Spanish, German and the English. An early form of Indo-European seems to have genetic relations with the Hittite speech of Asia minor. The linguists have recognised a primitive form of Indo-European in its earlier stage of development. They called it Indo-Hittite. A branch of the Indo-European, which had already established itself in Mesopotamia, came to be described by the linguists as Indo-Iranian. It is this Indo-Iranian branch which spread over Iran and the northwestern regions of India by the middle of the second millennium B.C.

Among the different families of languages spoken in India, the Indo-European seems to be the last to arrive. The advent of Indo-European in the South Asian Sub-continent brought about a major change in the linguistic affinity of the people of northern India. The form of Indo-European, which was spoken in India, came to be known as Indo-Iranian or Indo-Aryan. Its advent in India is seen with the rise of the Vedic Sanskrit. However, the old Sanskrit changed into Prakrit and several speech-forms developed in different parts of northern and western India. The region lying between the Saraswati and Ganga, encompassing the Upper Ganga-Yamuna *doab* and adjoining parts of Haryana, to the west of the Yamuna, became the stage for the transformation of classical Sanskrit into a Prakrit form. From this early stage of development of Prakrit came the different Indo-Aryan vernaculars, which are now spoken in north-western, north-central, central and eastern parts of India. The Suraseni emerged in the core region of the midland (Madhyadesa of the *Puranas*) as the popular language. Its core area extended over western Uttar Pradesh and the adjoining parts of Haryana. A developed form of this parent language is described by the linguists as Western Hindi (Fig. 6.2). Around the core region of Suraseni, other speech-forms developed on the west, south and east. These languages formed an Outer Band around the core language. On the west and the northwest lay the Punjabi and the Pahari dialects. Rajasthani and Gujarati emerged on the southwest. On the east, a form of language, now known as Eastern Hindi, emerged in Kosali (Awadhi). Linguists believe that these outer dialects were all more closely related to each other than any one of them was to the language of the midland.

> 'In fact, at an early period of the linguistic history of India, there must have been two sets of Indo-Aryan dialects—one the language of the midland and the other the group of dialects forming the Outer Band.'[8]

This first stage was followed by a subsequent phase of expansion. As the population of the midland region increased, expansion became a necessity. Thus, on the periphery of the languages of the outer band developed new speech forms which were by and large not related to the language of the midland. For example, while Punjabi was closely related to the language of the upper *doab* it got transformed into Lahnda in southwestern Punjab. This language had little relationship with the language of the midland. With increasing distance, changes became quite pronounced.

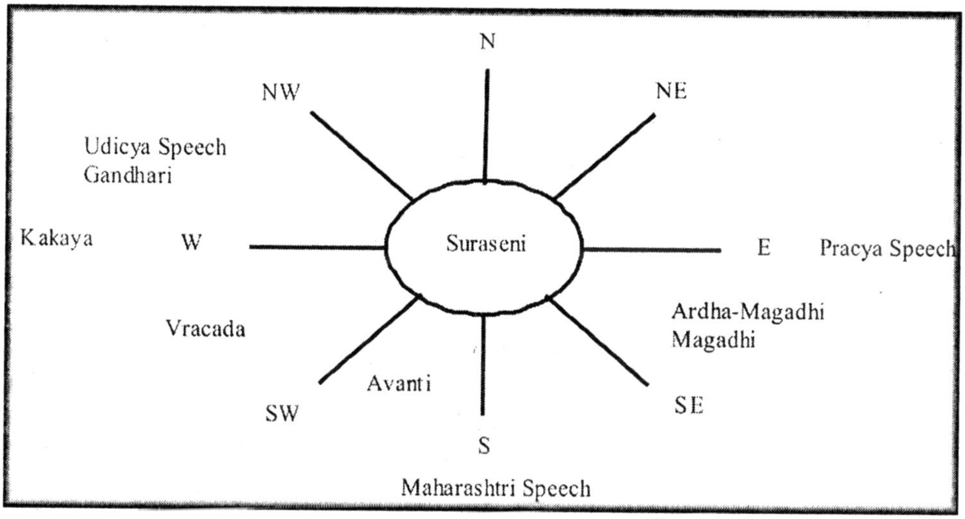

Figure 6.2 : Evolution of the Indo-Aryan Languages: Geographical Patterning (First Stage)

The geographical distribution of the Indo-Aryan languages may be briefly summarised here as follows: The midland language occupies the Ganga-Yamuna *doab* and the regions to its north and south. This core region is encircled by different speech forms in eastern Punjab, Rajasthan and Gujarat. Further beyond in the west and the northwest, there is a band of outer languages—Kashmiri, Sindhi, Lahnda and Kohistani. The languages of this band may be described as constituting the northwestern group of the outer languages. On the southern periphery lies the Marathi. In the intermediate band are situated languages, such as Awadhi, Bagheli and

Chhattisgarhi. On the eastern periphery lie the three dialects of Bihari, *viz.*, Bhojpuri, Maithili, and Maghadi. The Bihari, is surrounded by Oriya in the southeast and Bengali in the east. The languages of the eastern branch of the Indo-Aryan extend further in the east where Assamese occupies the Brahmaputra valley (Fig. 6.3).

Linguists believe that the development of the Indo-Aryan languages completed itself through several phases. The *Prakrits* developed into two stages: Primary Prakrits and Secondary Prakrits. The *Primary Prakrits,* which were the first to evolve out of the classical Sanskrit, were synthetic languages with a complicated grammar. In the course of time, they 'decayed' into *Secondary Prakrits.*

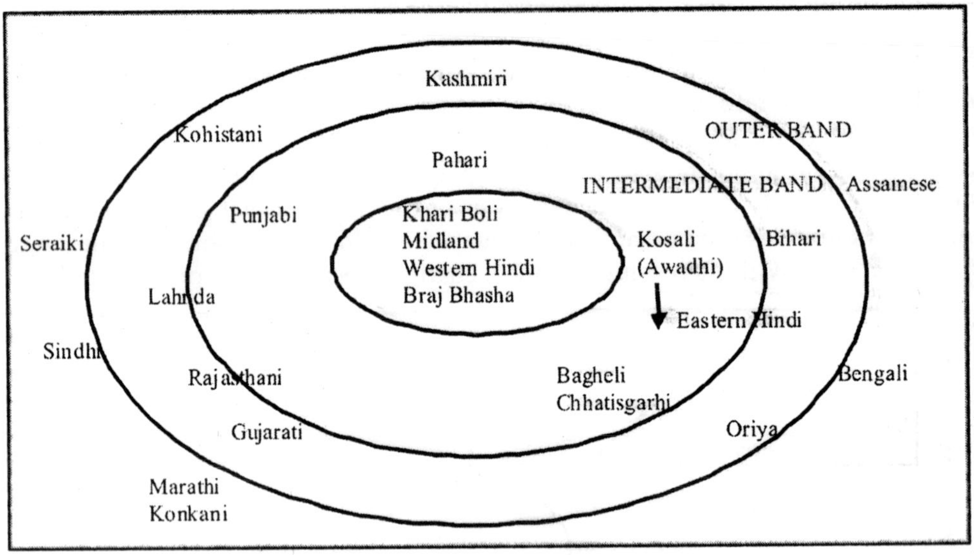

Figure 6.3 : Evolution of the Indo-Aryan Languages: Geographical Patterning (Second Stage)

> 'Here we find the languages still synthetic, but diphthongs and harsh combinations are eschewed, till in the latest developments we find a condition of almost absolute fluidity, each language becoming an emasculated collection of vowels hanging for support on an occasional consonant. This weakness brought its own nemesis and from, say 1000 A.C., we find in existence the series of modern Indo-Aryan vernaculars, or, as they may be called *Tertiary Prakrits*'.[9]

The last stage of development of the Prakrits is known as literary *Apabrahmsa.* It is supposed that the modern vernaculars are the direct children of these Apabrahmsas. The sequence of change was like this. The Suraseni Apabrahmsa was the parent of Western Hindi and Punjabi. Closely connected with it were Avanti, the parent of Rajasthani, and Gaurjari, the parent of Gujarati. The other intermediate language—Kosali (Eastern Hindi)—sprang from Ardha-Magadhi Apabrahmsa. The chronological sequence may be roughly reconstructed here (Table 6.2). The different stages through which the Indo-Aryan languages passed can be depicted as on Fig. 6.4.

Table 6.2 : Stages in the Development of Indo-Aryan Languages

Period	*Language*	*Prakrits*
1500-600 B.C.	Vedic Sanskrit	
600-200 B.C.	Asokan Prakrits	Pali, Eastern/Western
200 B.C.-200 A.C.	Transitional Middle Indo-Aryan	
200-600 A.C.	Middle Indo-Aryan	Primary/Secondary Prakrits
600-1000 A.C.	Late Middle Indo-Aryan	Apabrahmsas
Beyond 1000 A.C.	New Indo-Aryan	

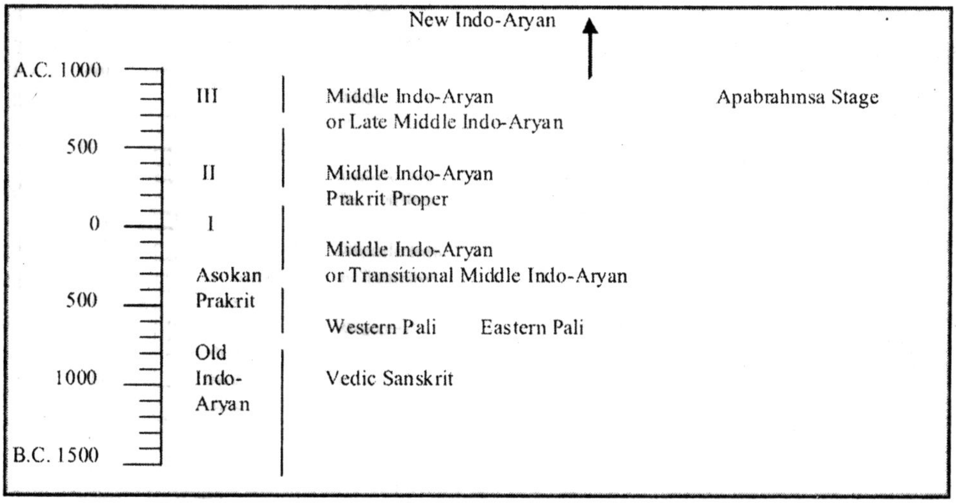

Figure 6.4 : Time-Scale of the Indo-Aryan Languages (Tentative)

Classification

In a country where so many languages/dialects are spoken, and many of them are used for oral communication only, linguistic classification may not be an easy exercise. The scientific study of Indian languages, their grammar, phonetics and vocabulary which goes back to the nineteenth century is still ridden with problems. For one thing, linguists are still unsure of genetic relationships between one language group and the other. Their knowledge of some of the minor languages is pathetically inadequate. This leaves the problem of classification always open to revision. A second set of problems arises from the recognition of the major languages and their specification in the Eighth Schedule of the Indian Constitution. There were political compulsions under which some languages were given this special status. The Eighth Schedule mentions eighteen languages; twelve of them have their own territory where they receive maximum state patronage and seem to have great potential for development. The Eighth Schedule also includes languages, such as the Sanskrit, Sindhi, Nepali, and the Urdu. The first three do not have a speech territory as such. The speakers of the Urdu, Sindhi and the Nepali are distributed across several states. Minor speech communities, such as the Manipuri (with a population of 1.27 million) and Konkani (with a population of 1.72 million) have also been given the status of scheduled languages. The anomaly in this approach is that while some of the minority speech groups have found a place in the Eighth Schedule, major Austric languages, such as Santali (speakers 5.22 million), Bhili (speakers 5.57 million) or Gondi (speakers 2.12 million) have been completely ignored. The official language policy leaves the issue amenable to political manipulation. Like the Austric languages, all small Tibeto-Burman languages have also been excluded from the Eighth Schedule. Hindi, which has the largest number of speakers, is an aggregate of at least fifty different dialect groups. There are at least seven states, which recognise Hindi as their official language.

Of the four language families (Tibeto-Burman, Austro-Asiatic, Dravidian and the Indo-Aryan branch of the Indo-European), the most diverse is the Tibeto-Burman as their speakers communicate in 70-80 different languages. Next is the Indo-Aryan with 19 languages grouped under it. The Dravidian family incorporates 17 different speech communities; while the Austro-Asiatic has 14 languages. However, this analysis is incomplete because of the fact that the 1991 census used an eligibility condition for recognising a language as a mother tongue if it had more than 10,000 speakers at the all-India level. This resulted in the exclusion of 0.56 million speakers of different minor languages from finding a reference in the census records. There is, therefore, no recognition of these small speech communities. Due to operational difficulties, the 1991 census could not be conducted in the state of Jammu and Kashmir. This resulted in the exclusion of the Dard Group of languages (Dardi Shina, Kohistani and Kashmiri) from the census count. The compilation of data for the 18 scheduled languages also contributed to the multiple problems of classification. For example, minor speech communities, such as Chakma and Hajong, were clubbed together with Bengali. Secondly, Yerava and Yerukala were amalgamated with Malayalam and Tamil respectively. Such examples are many. It is obvious that the census preferred to ignore the minor dialect groups.

The story of Hindi is equally interesting. For example, 50 dialect groups have been grouped under Hindi with the result that there is no scope for an analytical study of the geographical spread of these dialect groups. In the course of time, many speakers of these dialects have tended to declare Hindi as their mother-tongue without making reference to the dialect they use. This is evident from the fact that some 233 million speakers declared Hindi as their mother tongue. Gradually, that stage is not far when many of the distinguished dialect groups, such as Braj Bhasha, Awadhi, Bhojpuri, Magadhi, Maithili and Marwari will lose their identity at least in the census records. This withdrawal of patronage by the speakers of these dialects is a symptom of their eventual decline, if not death.

A broad classification scheme of the four language families is given in Table 6.1 (for detailed classificatory schemes, see Appendix VI.1, VI.2, VI.3, and VI.4.

Numerical Strength

Of the four language families, Indo-European has by far the largest strength of speakers. In fact, three-fourths of the country's population claimed one or the other language of the Indo-European family as their mother tongue. The Dravidian Family comes next with 22.5 per cent of the total population of the country claiming affinity to it. The speakers of the other two families—Austro-Asiatic and the Tibeto-Burman—consist of small groups. Their overall proportionate share is low—1.13 and 0.97 per cent respectively. As already indicated, Austro-Asiatic languages are spoken by a host of tribal groups. This is also true for most of the Tibeto-Burman languages.

Among the languages of the Austro-Asiatic family, Santali is the most outstanding speech community, the numerical strength of its speakers being as high as 5.2 million. Other languages of the Munda branch, such as Ho, or of the Mon Khmer branch, such as Khasi, have a numerical strength of less than one million speakers each. Santali speakers account for 55 per cent of the entire strength of the Austro-Asiatic family. Speakers of the Ho, Khasi and Mundari languages account for 10, 9.6 and 9.1 per cent respectively of all Austric speakers. There are many language groups within the Austro-Asiatic family whose numerical strength is insignificant. Reference may be made to Bhumij, Nicobarese, Gadaba and Juang. However, their declining numerical strength shows that conditions are not favourable for their growth. As indicated earlier, the 1991 census adopted a policy of excluding all languages from the census count whose speakers numbered less than 10,000 persons at the all-India level at the time of census enumeration. This policy was by and large negative to the interests of the tribal languages.

As is evident from Appendix VI.1, VI.2, VI.3, and VI.4, there are striking differences in the numerical strength of the languages of the Tibeto-Burman family. The major speech communities include Manipuri/Meithei (1.27 million), Bodo (1.22 million), Tripuri (0.69 million), Garo (0.67 million), Lushai (0.54 million) and Miri/Mishing (0.39 million). The Manipuri and Bodo groups together account for one-third of the total strength of Tibeto-Burman speakers.

As is generally known, the major Dravidian speech communities consist of Telugu, Tamil, Kannada and Malayalam. They have been ranked here in descending order of the strength of their speakers. The Dravidian family also includes minor groups, such as Gondi (2.12 million), Tulu (1.55 million), Kurukh-Oraon (1.42 million), Kui (0.64 million), Koya (0.27 million) and Khond (0.22 million). Many of them are tribal dialects and have an imminent risk of extinction. Gondi, for example, presents a case of language loss, as its speakers are getting assimilated into the regional languages of the state of their habitation. The same is true for other tribal dialects, unless otherwise they have come under the cover of state protection.

In terms of numerical strength of speakers, Hindi is the foremost among the Indo-European languages. With 337.27 million speakers who claimed Hindi, or its different dialects, as their mother-tongue, Hindi has no comparison with other languages of the family. Bengali, Marathi and Urdu, which follow in the same order, have a numerical strength ranging between 43 and 69 million. Bengali and Marathi account for about 10 per cent each of the total strength of speakers of the Indo-European family. Among the dialects of Hindi, Bhojpuri was claimed by 23.1 million speakers. One can compare Bhojpuri with Assamese (total speakers: 12.96 million) and Punjabi (total speakers: 23.08 million). The other dialects of Hindi, such as Maithili, Magadhi, Awadhi, Braj Bhasha, Marwari or Chhattisgarhi figure poorly. In fact, the dialect speakers tend to declare Hindi as their mother tongue. The strength of those who declared these dialects as their mother tongue seems to be diminishing with successive censuses. The progress of the languages of the Dard Group, namely Shina, Kohistani, and Kashmiri, cannot be monitored since 1991 census was not conducted in Jammu and Kashmir.

As many as 13 of the Indo-European languages have been listed in the Eighth Schedule of the Indian Constitution. They are: Kashmiri (Dard Group), Sindhi (northwestern group), Hindi, Urdu, Punjabi, Nepali, Gujarati (eastern, east-central, central and northern groups), Bengali, Assamese and Oriya (eastern group) and Marathi and Konkani (southern group). While Konkani with a total strength of 1.76 million speakers, is mentioned in the Eighth Schedule, Santali finds no place, although its speakers numbered at 5.22 million at the 1991 census (AppendixVI.5; see also Appendix VI.6).

Language Domains

A generalised study of the domains of various languages spoken in India may be helpful in understanding the historical processes leading to their geographical spread and concentration. It may also be helpful in identifying the basic elements of India's linguistic geography. It may be worthwhile to recapitulate the historical processes that led to the evolution of language regions in India (Box 6.2). It is understood that the Indo-Aryan was the last to arrive. It was preceded by the Dravidian, Sino-Tibetan and the Austric. However, there is no clarity about the chronological sequence in which the different families came to affect the situation in India. This question has been partly answered by the linguists. Which came first, the Austro-Asiatic, Sino-Tibetan or the Dravidian? The Vedic Aryans had the knowledge of the Tibeto-Burman speaking Mongoloids whom they described as the *Kiratas*. *Yajurveda* and the *Atharvaveda* as well as Mahabharata and Manu Samhita also mentioned the *Kiratas*.

Box 6.2 : Evolution of Languages

Among the four language-groups, which were established in India in very early times, the Aryan speech family was the last to come. It was preceded by the Dravidian, Sino-Tibetan and the Austric. In the evolution of Indian people and Indian culture, there has been an intermixture of races, languages and the cultural *milieus*. Although the Austric and Sino-Tibetan languages are now confined to small populations, they have had their share in developing and modifying the other languages. The Dravidian and the Aryan speeches have, of course, been the most important of all; after the Aryan, the Dravidian was the first to develop literature. The other groups had no written literature until long after. There has been a good measure of interaction among these languages. The Aryan has been profoundly modified by the Dravidian, and *vice versa*; and that applies to other languages as well. This kind of linguistic interaction has given rise, after 3000 years of free play, to a Common Indian Type for the modern languages of all the four families of speech, through the evolution of a certain amount of similarity in phonetic structure, morphology, and above all, syntax and vocabulary... Indian languages show... important resemblances. That is because they share in a common or pan-Indian character evolved through the racial and linguistic intermixture, which has been at work since the beginning of history.

—S.K. Chatterji and S.M. Katre, *The Gazetteer of India*, Vol. I, 1975: 373-374.

Austro-Asiatic

The domain of the Austro-Asiatic languages lies in the mid-Indian region and extends from Maharashtra to West Bengal. The two outliers of this domain—Khasi and Nicobarese—have their enclaves in Meghalaya and Nicobar Islands respectively. The two pockets are separated by a vast expanse of the sea. Santali is the foremost among the Munda languages. The Santali speakers are mainly concentrated in Bihar, West Bengal and Orissa. About one-half of them live in Bihar, 35 per cent in West Bengal and 13 per cent in Orissa. The Santals living in Assam, numbering 1,35,000, also declared Santali as their mother tongue at the 1991 census. Another significant language of the Munda branch is Munda/Mundari. Of the 1.27 million speakers of Mundari, 54 per cent live in Bihar, 31 per cent in Orissa and only 6 per cent in West Bengal. The domain of the Ho language lies in Bihar and Orissa. Two-thirds of all Ho speakers are confined to Bihar and the remaining one-third to Orissa. The territories of the Kharia, Korku and Savara languages extend over Bihar, Orissa and Madhya Pradesh. However, the Savara speakers are mostly confined to Orissa.

Tibeto-Burman

The territory of the Tibeto-Burman languages is by and large conterminous with the Himalayas and extends from Baltistan and Ladakh in Jammu and Kashmir to Arunachal Pradesh. It extends further to encompass other northeastern states. The Bhotia and the Himalayan groups of the Tibeto-Burman family are confined to Jammu and Kashmir, Himachal Pradesh, hilly Uttar Pradesh and Sikkim. The Tibetan speakers, however, have a wider spread as they are distributed over many states in India. The Tibetans are of course in exile in India and live in camps and colonies especially created for them in several states. Notable among the languages of the North Assam Branch of the Tibeto-Burman family are Miri/Mishing and Adi. More than 97 per cent of the Adi speakers are confined to Arunachal Pradesh. The Miri/Mishing speakers, on the other hand, are confined to Assam. Of the languages of the Bodo group, Bodo is largely specific to Assam, where 97 per cent of its speakers live. The domains of the Garo and Tripuri lie in Meghalaya and Tripura respectively. About 80 per cent of the Garo speakers are confined to Meghalaya whereas 17 per cent of them are based in Assam. About 93 per cent of the Tripuri speakers are confined to Tripura, although in recent years a section of their population has also moved out to Mizoram and Assam. The Bodo group also includes Karabi/Mikir and Rabha dialects. Their speakers are mostly concentrated in Assam and Meghalaya. However, a small proportion of Rabha speakers is also found in the northern districts of West Bengal. Likewise, the Koch is confined to Meghalaya and Assam, Dimasa to Assam and Nagaland, and Lalung is specific to Assam alone.

Most of the speech territory of the Naga group of languages is shared between Nagaland and Manipur. While Ao, Angami, Lotha, Pochury, Phom, Yimchingure and Khiemnungan are exclusive to Nagaland, Kabui and Tangkhul are specific to Manipur. On the other hand, Khezha and Mao are spoken both in Manipur and Nagaland.

However, a small proportion of their speakers is also located in Assam. The Kuki-Chin languages are confined to the states of Manipur and Mizoram. Manipuri (including Meitei) has its domain in the central valley of Manipur where 87 per cent of its speakers live. A section of the Manipuri population (about 10 per cent) has also moved out to Assam. Manipuri speakers were also enumerated in Tripura, Nagaland and other parts of the northeast, although in small numbers. Lushai is confined to Mizoram. Manipur presents a case of linguistic plurality. In fact, the state is the home of many speech communities belonging to both the Naga and Kuki-Chin groups. Notable among these dialects are Thado, Paite, Halam, Hmar, Kabui, Tangkhul, Gangte, Khezha, Kom, Kuki, Liangmei, Lushai, Mao, Maram, Maring, Vaiphei, Zeliang, Zemi and Zau. Lakher has its domain in Mizoram only. Migration in recent years has taken the Kuki speakers to other parts of the northeast, such as Assam, Nagaland and Tripura.

Manipur may be chosen as an example to illustrate the territoriality of minor language groups in contiguous geographical space. The people of Manipur exhibit a complex pattern of ethnic diversity, where each ethnic or dialect group tends to concentrate in a monolithic world of its own. Broadly speaking, the population of Manipur consists of two different groups: (a) Palaeo-Mongoloids consisting of (i) the Meiteis, and (ii) the hill tribes; and (b) immigrants mostly consisting of Palae-Mediterraneans further sub-divided into (i) the Pangals (Muslim settlers), and (ii) the Mayangs or Kols. Each of these groups can be further sub-divided on the basis of language/dialect and racial attributes. While the Meiteis, Pangals and Mayangs are plain-dwellers, the tribes, such as Kuki-Chins and Nagas are hill-dwellers. The ethno-lingual situation in Manipur suggests that geographical factors have promoted the emergence of homogenous dialect territories. Each dialect is confined to a pocket where people communicate in a given dialect. These monolithic dialect territories are contiguous. This linguistic plurality has survived the onslaught of time.

The presence of as many as 29 major speech communities in Manipur has contributed to a type of ethno-centrism for the survival of speeches or *Patois* coupled with other socio-cultural differences. Ethnic groups have often indulged in competition resulting in inter-ethnic conflicts. In any case ethnic groups strive for the preservation of their dialects even if it results in diminishing interaction between different dialect groups. Over time linguistic plurality has resulted in bilingualism or multi-lingualism. Many tribes have adopted elements of Meitei-Lon for mutual inter-communication.

Dravidian

As is generally known, the four southern states of Andhra Pradesh, Karnataka, Tamil Nadu and Kerala are the home of the major Dravidian languages, *viz.*, Telugu, Kannada, Tamil and the Malayalam. The speakers of these languages have also moved out to other states, particularly the neighbouring states of the south in the recent past. The geographical spread of these languages is evident from Table 6.3.

Table 6.3 : Distribution of Major Dravidian Languages by States, 1991

Language	*States*
Telugu	Andhra Pradesh (83.40), Tamil Nadu (6.02), Karnataka (5.04)
Kannada	Karnataka (90.94), Tamil Nadu (3.69), Maharashtra (3.24), Andhra Pradesh (1.59)
Tamil	Tamil Nadu (91.38), Karnataka (3.26), Andhra Pradesh (1.42), Pondicherry (1.36)
Malayalam	Kerala (91.79), Karnataka (2.65),Tamil Nadu (2.29), Maharashtra (1.33)

Source: Table compiled by the author.
Note: Figures in parentheses shows the proportion of speakers of respective languages.

Evidently, these languages display a high degree of concentration in their home states. The highest degree of concentration is seen in the case of Malayalam followed by Tamil. On the other hand, the lowest degree of concentration is revealed in the case of Telugu.

There are several minor speech-communities within the Dravadian family. Notable among them are: Yurukala, Yerava, Tulu, Coorgi, Gondi, Malto and Kurukh-Oraon. The Kurukh-Oraon and Malto are confined to Bihar. They belong to the northern branch of the Dravidian family. Gondi, which is classified as a language of the central Dravidian branch, is the traditional dialect of the Gonds. However, recent census data show a steep decline in the numerical strength of the Gondi speakers. At the 1991 census, the Gondi-speaking population numbered just 2.12 million. This is an indication of the loss of language due to assimilation into the dominant regional languages. More than 90 per cent of the Gondi (mother-tongue) speakers live in Madhya Pradesh (70 per cent) and Maharashtra (21 per cent). The remaining population is found in Andhra Pradesh and Orissa. In other states, their number is too small.

Indo-European

Both in terms of numerical strength and the territorial extent the Indo-European languages surpass all other language families in India. The speech territory extends from Rajasthan in the west to Assam in the east and from Jammu and Kashmir in the north to Goa in the south. In fact, the domain of the Indo-European family extends beyond the borders of Rajasthan on the west and continues over adjoining Pakistan. Notable among the languages of this family are Hindi, Bengali, Marathi, Urdu, Gujarati, Oriya, Punjabi and Assamese. Keeping in view their importance, as many as 13 of the Indo-European languages have been included in the Eighth Schedule of the Indian Constitution. While Hindi and Urdu are spoken across many states, including southern states, other languages, such as Bengali, Marathi, Gujarati, Oriya, Punjabi and Assamese are specific to their own states. For example, while Bengali is specific to West Bengal, Marathi and Gujarati have their domain in Maharashtra and Gujarat respectively. The dominance of Hindi is evident from the fact that there were 337 million speakers who claimed it as their mother tongue in the 1991 census. About 81 per cent of the total population of Bihar, 91 per cent of Haryana and 89 per cent of Himachal Pradesh claimed affinity to Hindi. The respective percentages for Rajasthan and Madhya

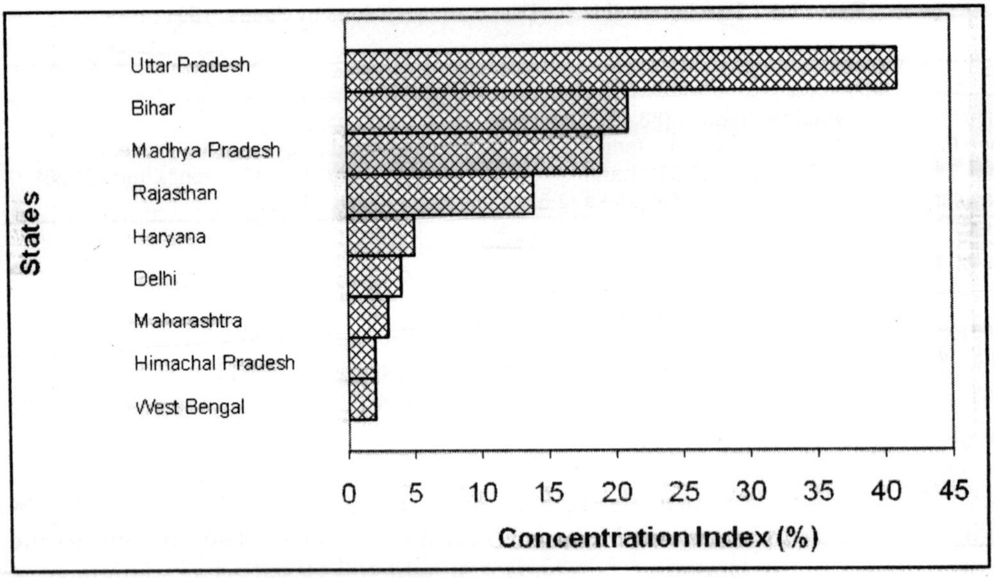

Figure 6.5: Distribution of Hindi Speakers, 1991

Pradesh were 89 and 90. The story of the Hindi-speaking population is rather complicated. There are no less than 50 dialects, which are grouped under Hindi. The speakers of these dialects declared them as their mother tongue in the same way as millions of others accepted Hindi as their mother tongue without making any reference to the dialect used by them. These dialects are actually regional variants of a spoken language of which the standardised form written in the Devnagri script is the official Hindi (Appendix VI.7). Three-fifths of all Hindi speakers are concentrated in the two northern states of Uttar Pradesh and Bihar. Of the remaining, about 17 per cent live in Madhya Pradesh and 12 per cent in Rajasthan. The rest of the Hindi-speaking population is found in Haryana, Delhi, Himachal Pradesh, Maharashtra and West Bengal (Fig. 6.5). In terms of numerical strength Bengali comes next to Hindi. While its speakers are heavily concentrated in West Bengal, a sizeable proportion of Bengali speakers is also found in the neighbouring states of Assam, Bihar and Tripura. Marathi is next to Bengali. About 93 per cent of its speakers live in Maharashtra alone. However, Marathi is also spoken by a section of population in Karnataka as well as Madhya Pradesh. Urdu holds the fourth rank among the Indo-Aryan languages. Its core region overlaps with that of the Hindi. Its territorial extent is as vast as that of Hindi, although there is no state, barring Jammu and Kashmir, where it enjoys the status of the official language. About one-half of all Urdu speakers are concentrated in the states of Uttar Pradesh and Bihar. But the strength of Urdu speakers is also sizeable in Maharashtra, Andhra Pradesh and Karnataka. A section of population in Tamil Nadu also claims Urdu as its mother tongue (Fig. 6.6). Gujarati has its domain in Gujarat, although other dialects, such as Gujrao/Gujrau and Saurashtri are also claimed as mother tongues by a sizeable section of the population of Gujarat. Migration and settlement in neighbouring Maharashtra have resulted in the emergence of Gujarati speakers in that state. About 93 per cent of Oriya speakers live in Orissa alone, although the

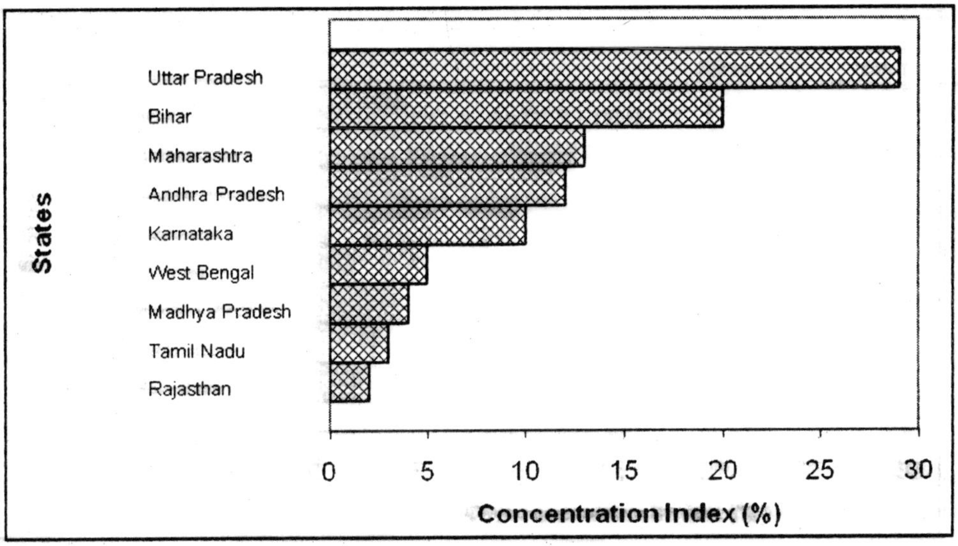

Figure 6.6 : Distribution of Urdu Speakers, 1991

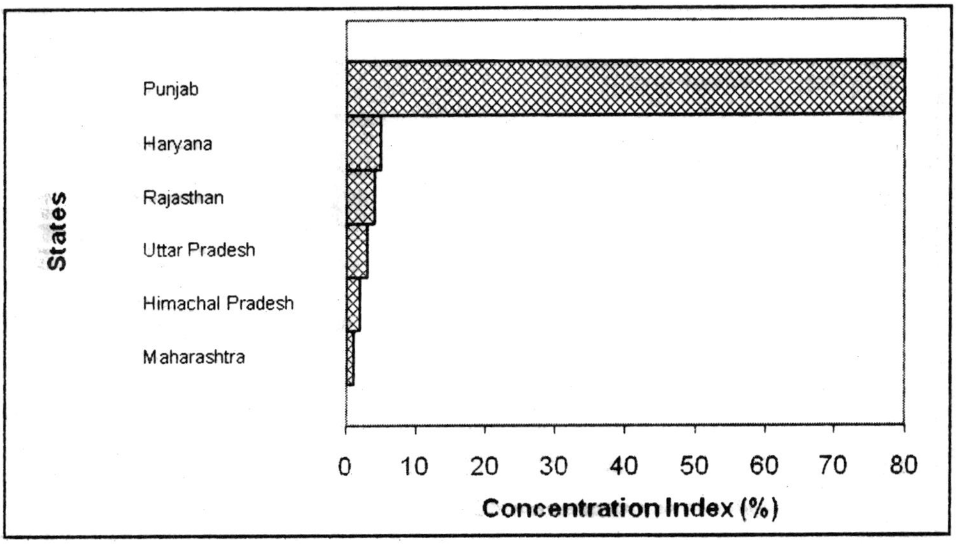

Figure 6.7 : Distribution of Punjabi Speakers, 1991

language is also spoken in the neighbouring parts of Madhya Pradesh and Bihar as well as Andhra Pradesh, West Bengal and Assam. While the domain of Punjabi lies in Punjab, it is widely spoken over the entire north-western region, particularly Haryana, Himachal Pradesh, Jammu and Kashmir and northern Rajasthan. Its territorial extent is wider as Punjabi is spoken in the neighbouring Punjab and Pakistan. Within India, migration processes have taken Punjabi speaking population to different parts of the country (Fig. 6.7). In the east, almost 99 per cent of the Assamese speakers are confined to Assam. The domain of the Assamese is surrounded on the north, east, southeast and south by Tibeto-Burman and Austric languages. There is a slight spill-over of the

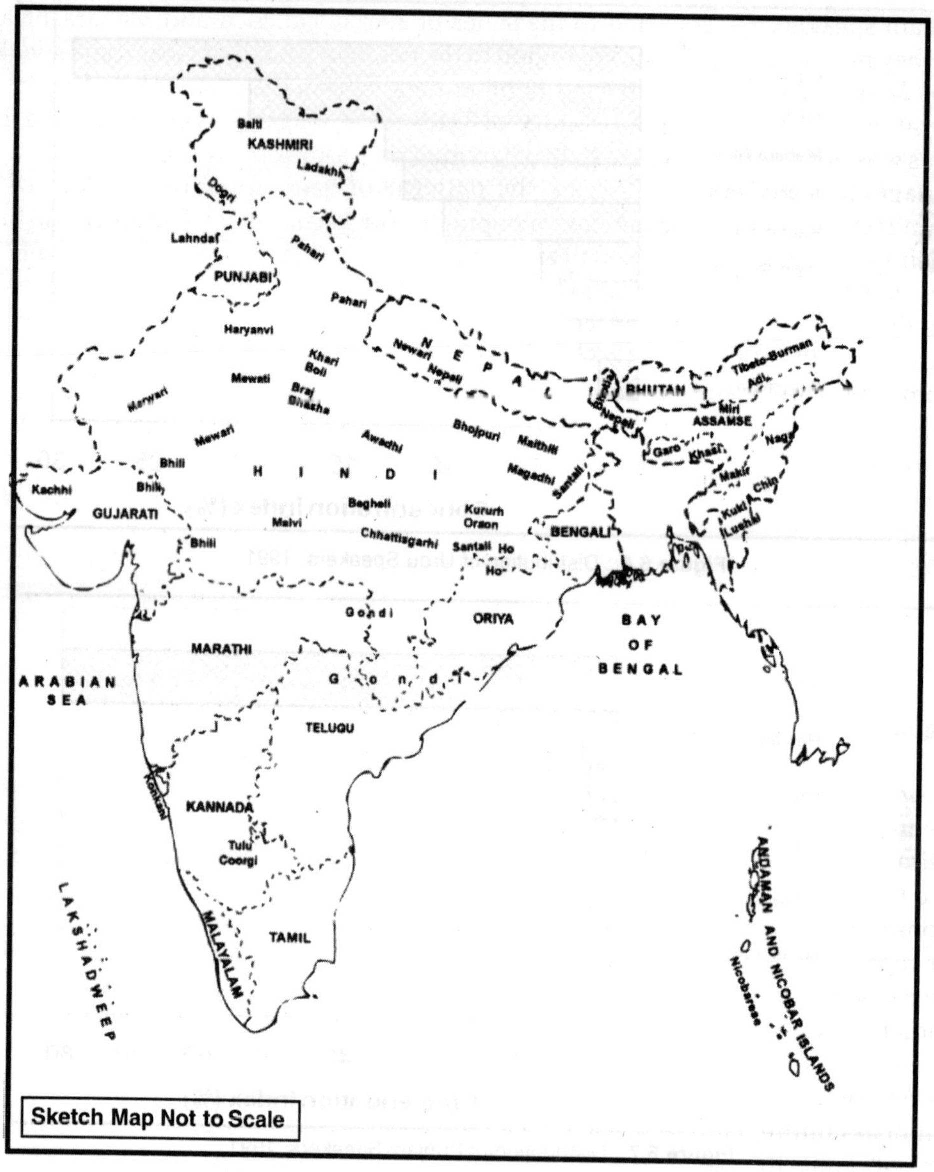

Figure 6.8 : Major Languages of Modern India

Assamese population into the neighbouring states of Arunachal Pradesh and Meghalaya (Fig. 6.8).

There are other Indo-European languages, such as Bhili/Bhilodi, Konkani, Kashmiri, Nepali and Sindhi, which have their own specific pockets in northern and western India. An overwhelming majority of the Bhili/Bhilodi speakers is concentrated in Rajasthan and Madhya Pradesh. Together these states share more than 80 per cent of the total strength of its speakers. Of the remaining, 17 per cent live in Maharashtra and 1 per cent in Dadra and Nagar Haveli. The domain of the Konkani lies on the Konkan coast from Maharashtra to northern Kerala. More than 90 per cent of the

Konkani speakers are confined to the states of Karnataka, Goa and Maharashtra. In fact, they mainly live in the littoral region in the neighbourhood of Goa. Some speakers of the Konkani have also dispersed to other neighbouring states, such as Kerala and Gujarat as well as the union territory of Dadra and Nagar Haveli. Since, the 1991 census was not conducted in the state of Jammu and Kashmir, the home of the Kashmiri language, it is difficult to describe the patterns of geographic distribution of the Kashmiri speakers. Outside the state, a population of 56,000 persons returned Kashmiri as their mother tongue. The Nepali speaking population is distributed in a number of states, mostly in the neighbourhood of Nepal. Of the 2.07 million Nepali speakers, more than 40 per cent are concentrated in West Bengal and another 21 per cent in Assam. A small proportion (12.35 per cent) of the Nepali speakers, are also found in Sikkim. They are scattered all over the northeast although in small numbers. The domain of Sindhi lies in the Sind province of the neighbouring state of Pakistan. The present Sindhi speaking population in India, however, consists of population displaced in the wake of partition in 1947. Initially, the Sindhis came to the neighbouring regions of Rajasthan and Gujarat. Later, they dispersed to other western and northern states. At the 1991 census, about two-thirds of all Sindhi speakers in India were enumerated in Gujarat and Maharashtra. Of the remaining one-third, the two states of Rajasthan and Madhya Pradesh shared together 15 per cent each. A small proportion of Sindhi speakers is also found in Delhi and Uttar Pradesh.

Language Scene in Tribal Areas

The language scene in tribal areas of India deserves a mention. During the 50 years since independence, the tribes have been exposed to diverse influences—economic, political and socio-cultural. The scene in northeastern India is somewhat different. There the tribes have been empowered to manage their own political affairs. In other regions of India, a certain number of seats have been reserved for the tribes to ensure their representation in the state and the national legislative bodies. These measures have paved the way for their rehabilitation in the national polity. However, a majority of Indian tribes live in the mid-Indian region where their participation in the political processes is nominal. Their traditional habitats lie divided between several states. They do not have much of a say in policy formulation. This has left an imprint on their traditional culture, language and social structure. Language seems to have suffered the most. First, the developmental processes initiated since independence seem to have contributed towards the disintegration of tribal economies, and their communitarian way of life. The tribes have lost their hold on the forest resources and have been forced to depend on the market forces. In fact, the free market economy has encircled completely the petty tribal commodity trade. Secondly, expansion of primary education has brought tribal children face to face to a new cultural situation. In the course of schooling they have been exposed to the regional languages of the states of their habitation. This has paved the way for their becoming bilingual. The ultimate effect is on their traditional dialects, which are on the way to decline and eventual death.

It has been noted that the Indian tribes display a very high degree of diversity in their language affinity. Despite the relative isolation of the tribal communities, there have been contact areas in which give-and-take between the tribal and non-tribal languages has continued throughout history. The geographic patterning of tribal languages suggests that along the zone of contact between them and the non-tribes, progressive interaction has resulted in the fusion of linguistic element on either side. This is evident from the fact that while the tribes communicate mainly in the Nishada, Kirata and Dravadian languages, they have also adopted several speech-forms of the Indo-Aryan family. The incidence of bilingualism and multi-lingualism among the tribes has increased phenomenally.

One may develop an understanding of the linguistic plurality observed in tribal areas by selecting the case of Austric-speaking tribes. In India, the Austric-speaking tribes are grouped into Mon-Khmer and Munda branches of languages. We have already seen that the Munda-speaking zone extends over a vast area from the Aravallis in the west to the Raj Mahal Hills in the east.

Language Shift

A striking feature of the language scene in tribal areas is the growing shift in language affinity of the tribal communities. This fluid situation in which the tribes are losing their linguistic identity and are being identified with languages spoken by other tribes or the dominant regional languages of the states in which they have been living is observed in many parts of India. An evaluation of the census data reveals gaps between the numerical strength of the ethnic tribals, say the Mundas, Santals and the Gonds and those sections of the Munda, the Santal and the Gond population who declared their own dialects as their mother tongue, say at the 1961 census. This lack of conformity between ethnic identity and language affinity reveals the process of language shift in a significant way. There can be several plausible explanations for this phenomenon. It may be assumed that by 1961 a major shift in the linguistic/dialectal affinity of the Indian tribes had already taken place in certain regions of the country. The 1961 census may, however, be taken as a benchmark.

It may be assumed that as tribal/non-tribal interaction was growing, a section of the tribal population shifted to other dialects/languages with which it has no traditional affinity. This shift to the dominant languages of the regions of their habitation indicated a process of language shift and assimilation into the regional languages.

The language shift was, however, not necessarily from a tribal to a non-tribal dialect. In fact, several tribal groups shifted over to the other tribal dialects as contacts between them were growing fast. As a result they lost their own traditional dialects.[10] The 1961 census data on linguistic affinity of the tribal communities as revealed in their declaration of a particular language as their mother tongue makes it possible to analyse the following dimensions of language shift among the tribes:

(a) Tribes speaking a dialect with which they are traditionally identified. For example, Santals, declaring Santali as their mother tongue or Gonds declaring Gondi as their mother tongue. This reveals that the tribes in certain regions of the country display continuity in their language affinity. We may call it a case of language retention;

(b) Tribes declaring a regional language as their mother tongue. For example, Santals declaring Bengali as their mother tongue in West Bengal, or Gonds declaring Oriya as their mother tongue in Orissa. This shows the on-going process of language shift indicating that the tribal communities are getting assimilated into the dominant regional languages. Tribal regions where the process of regional development has brought tribes face to face to non-tribes have witnessed this phenomenon more significantly;

(c) Tribes on the periphery of their traditional areas have a tendency to declare as their mother tongue a language which is spoken by a dominant tribal group or the official language of a neighbouring state. This process indicates that the tribes are getting exposed to other tribal/regional languages. As a result they are getting assimilated into these languages (Table 6.4).

Table 6.4 : Language Shift

Tribes as % of District Population	*Radical*	*Important*	*Significant*	*Marginal*	*Insignificant*
80-100	The Dangs		Kohima Mokokchung	Jhabua	United Khasi and Jaintia Hills, Tuensang
50-80	Mandla	Lahul and Spiti, Dhar, Surguja, Sundergarh	Mayurbhanj, Koraput	Ranchi, Bastar	Mikir Hills, Kinnaur, Dungarpur, Banswara
20-50	Panch-Mahals, Vadodara, Bharauch, Surat, Shahdol, Sidhi, Nashik, Thane, Sambal-pur, Sirohi	Khargone, Chindwara, Seoni, Kalahandi, Udaipur	Raigarh, Keonjhar	Betul, Dhule, Baudh-Khondmals	Santal Parganas, Singhbhum, Chamba, Sawai Madhopur, Jalpaiguri
10-20	Visakhapatnam, Sabar Kantha, Panna, Satna, Rewa, Raisen, Bilaspur, Durg, Dhenkanal, Bolangir, Chittorgarh	Khammam, Kamrup, Darrang, Palamau, Raipur, Yeotmal	Adilabad, Lakhimpur, Hazaribagh, Ratlam, Chandrapur, Purulia	Goalpara, Dhanbad, Bundi, Jhalawar, Darjeeling, West Dinajpur, Bankura	Jaipur, Kota
5-10	Nellore, Nowgong, Banaskantha, Shivpuri, Guna, Hoshangabad, Kolaba, Ahmad-nagar	Srikakulam, Sibsagar, Dewas, Jalgaon, Balasore	Khandwa, Coorg		Amravati, Ganjam, Alwar

Note: The language shift is described here as *radical* if 80-100 per cent of the tribal population have declared a regional language as their mother-tongue. The shift is *important* if the proportion of tribes declaring a regional language as their mother tongue is 50 to 80 per cent. It is *significant* if the proportion is between 20 and 50 per cent. The shift is *marginal* if the tribes claiming a regional language as their mother-tongue have a proportionate share between 5 and 20 per cent. The shift is *insignificant* if their proportion is less than 5 per cent.

Language Retention

While collection of data on mother tongues may be replete with problems, the position as recorded by the 1961 census was that one-half of the tribal population of India retained their own dialects as their mother tongues. This was an evidence of language retention. The situation, however, varied from tribe to tribe and from region to region. The geographic patterning of the tribes still claiming affinity to their own tribal dialects revealed three major formations:

(a) Areas of tribal fastness in which tribes were by and large living in a state of exclusivity. For example, in Mizoram, Manipur, Meghalaya, Tripura, Nagaland, Arunachal Pradesh, West Bengal, Rajasthan, and Himachal Pradesh, 70-100 per cent of tribes retained their own traditional dialects as their mother tongue;

(b) Areas of tribal-non-tribal inter-mingling, where tribes were living in a state of varied degrees of exposure to non-tribal economic and cultural influences. One can cite the case of Assam, Orissa, Andhra Pradesh, Madhya Pradesh, Maharashtra and Mysore (now Karnataka) where 25-60 per cent of tribes retained their own language; and

(c) Areas where tribes have been assimilated into dominant cultures of the regions of their habitation. In these areas less than 10 per cent of the tribal population claimed affinity with their own traditional tribal dialect (Table 6.5).

A number of doctoral theses, written under the direction of this writer at the Centre for the Study of Regional Development of the Jawaharlal Nehru University, explored these questions at length. In two of these theses the question of language shift and retention as registered among the Austric-speaking tribes of the mid-Indian region was examined. These studies revealed that the Santals and Korkus by and large preferred to retain their traditional dialects. On the other hand, there were other Austric-speaking tribes who displayed a tendency of shift to the regional languages. The language shift was the highest among the Savaras. The Kharias, the Mundas and the Hos followed. Studies also revealed that the Bhils of Rajasthan, Gujarat and Madhya Pradesh preferred to claim regional language as their mother-tongue. A study of the household-level data generated through fieldwork from Wanera Para, Umedgarhi, Nai Abadi and Regania villages of Bagidora tehsil of Banswara district, as well as from Banswara town, revealed that the Bhils by and large maintained Bhili as their mother tongue. On the other hand, the Korkus of Punasa, Richhi and Udaipur villages of Khandwa district tended to switch over to the regional languages. In fact, they declared Nimadi as their mother tongue. However, no generalisations can be made about Korkus on this basis as in other villages they continue to retain their own dialect and declare it as their mother tongue at the successive censuses.

Table 6.5 : Geographical Patterns in Language Retention

Proportion	*Areas*	*Tribal Communities*
90-100	United Mikir and Kachar Hills	Garo, Khasi, Jaintia, Kachari, Mizo, Mikir, Hmar
	United Khasi and Jaintia Hills	Garos, Khasis, Jaintia
	Tuensang	Naga
	Alwar, Bharatpur,	Mina
	Sawai Madhopur, Jaipur, Tonk	Bhil
	Kota, Dungarpur, Banswara	
	Amravati, Betul	Gonds, Pardhan, Kamar, Halba, Sahariya
	Santal Parganas,Singhbhum,	Santal, Oraon, Munda
	West Dinajpur, Malda,	Mahli, Kora, Mal-Paharia,
	Birbhum	Lohara, Kharwar
	Ganjam, Nilgiris	Savara, Khond, Lodha Kurumba, Palliyan, Pariyan, Kadar, Kammayakan
70-90	Hazaribagh, Ranchi, Dhanbad	Santal, Oraon, Munda, Lohara, Kharwar, Bedia
	Barddhaman, Bankura, Medinipur	Santal, Oraon, Munda, Kora, Bhumij, Mahli
	Jhabua, Khandwa, Bastar	Bhil, Gond, Halba, Bhattra, Sahariya, Boro, Kachari,
	Goalpara, Cachar	Miri, Rabha, Barman
	Baudh-Khondmals,	Konda-Dhora, Gond, Gadaba, Bhuiya, Kolha,
	Mayurbhanj	Bhumij, Santal, Ho
	Bundi, Jhalawar	Mina, Bhil, Varli, Pardhi
	Dhule, Chandrapur	Bhil, Naikdu, Dhanka, Gamit
50-70	Mikir Hills	Mikir, Dimasa (Kachari), Kuki, Hmar, Hajong
	Ratlam	Bhil
	Kohima, Mokokchung	Naga, Dimasa, Kuki
	Keonjhar, Koraput	Gond, Koya, Savara, Konda-Dhora, Gadaba, Parja, Khond, Jatapu, Lodha, Gond, Munda, Bhuiya, Kolha, Bhumij, Santal, Ho, Kol, Saunti, Kissan, Mundari, Bathudi, Jwang
	Purulia	Santal, Oraon, Munda, Bhumij, Mahli, Kora, Malpaharia, Lohara, Korwa,Savara

Another finding of this research is that tribes living in rural areas have a greater affinity with their traditional dialects as compared to the tribes in urban areas. In regions of tribal concentration, for example, tribes enjoyed a certain degree of isolation which helped them retain their language and culture. Their stay in cities and towns, on the other hand, diluted their cultural identity and their language was the first casualty. Investigations at the household level confirmed the language shift among the Mundas of Ranchi town and the Korkus of Khandwa tahsil, East Nimar district. On the contrary, the Bhils of Banswara district, Santals of Santal Parganas, Korkus of Khalwa tahsil (East Nimar district) and the Mundas of the rural parts of Ranchi district have continued to retain their language. The study noted a strong correlation between language shift and a number of associated factors, such as urbanisation, proportion of Hinduised tribes, and the proportion of non-primary tribal workers. Literacy also revealed a high positive correlation with language shift. In fact, the school-going tribal children were receiving education through the medium of regional languages. Obviously, schooling became a powerful instrument of bilingualism and/or language shift. In terms of exposure of the mid-Indian tribes to regional languages, Bhils stand first, followed by Mundas, Korkus and Santals. In any case, loss of language is symptomatic of the loss of cultural identity. While the incidence of bilingualism, among the Indian tribes, is very high. It does not mean that they have always retained their traditional languages. This is understandable in view of the fact that most of the tribes are getting exposed to external influences, particularly at the schools and the market places. Interaction at these places is possible through a common language, generally a regional language or a pidgin, such as the Sadan/Sadari in Ranchi, which is adopted by the tribes for day-to-day communication. Back at their homes, their own dialect reigns supreme. This may not be true for the displaced tribals whose number is increasing day by day.

NOTES AND REFERENCES

1. Grierson, George A., 1903-1928, *Linguistic Survey of India*, 12 Volumes, Calcutta, Government of India. A reprint was published by Motilal Banarasidas in 1967.
2. C.L. Barber, *The Story of Language*, The English Language Book Society and Pan Books Ltd., London, 1965, p. 27.
3. Lachman M. Khubchandani, 'India as a Socio-linguistic Area', in Aijazuddin Ahmad (ed.), *Social Structure and Regional Development*, 1993, pp. 101-13; also see, 'India as a Socio-linguistic Area', in N.H. Itagi (ed.), *Spatial Aspects of Language*, 1994, pp. 33-43.
4. *ibid.*, *Social Structure and Regional Development*, p. 108.
5. *ibid.*, *Plural Languages, Plural Cultures: Communication, Identity and Socio-political Change in Contemporary India*, Hawaii, 1983; also see Lachman M. Khubchandani, 'Mother Tongue in Multi-lingual Societies' in Chandra Sekhar (ed.) *Economic and Socio-cultural Dimensions of Regionalisation*, Census of India, 1971, Census Centenary Monograph, No. 7, pp. 427-50.
6. Murray B. Emeneau, 'India as a Linguistic Area', *Language*, Vol. XXXII, No. 1, 1956, pp. 3-16.
7. Lachman M. Khubchandani, 'India as a Socio-linguistic Area', *op.cit.*, p. 104.
8. *The Imperial Gazetteer of India*, The Indian Empire, Vol. I, Descriptive, Chapter on Language, p. 358.
9. *ibid.*, p. 360.
10. Moonis Raza and Aijazuddin Ahmad, *An Atlas of Tribal India*, 1990, pp. 226-42. Also see Aijazuddin Ahmad, 'An Overview of the Tribal Atlas of India', in Ashish Bose, *et al.* (ed.), *Demography of Tribal Development*, Delhi, 1990, pp. 69-73.

SUGGESTIONS FOR FURTHER READING

Bennett, Charles J. (1980): 'The Morphology of Language Boundaries: Indo-Aryan and Dravidian in Peninsular India', in David E. Sopher (ed.), *An Exploration of India: Geographical Perspectives on Society and Culture*, Longman Group Limited, London, pp. 234-51.

Itagi, N.H. (ed., 1994): *Spatial Aspects of Language*, Central Institute of Indian Languages, Mysore.

Lachman M. Khubchandani (1983): *Plural Languages, Plural Cultures: Communication, Identity and Socio-political Change in Contemporary India*, East-West Centre, Hawaii.

Mazumdar, S.M. (1970): *Marxism and the Language Problem in India*, People's Publishing House, New Delhi.

Sakharov, I.V. (1974): 'Ethno-linguistic Geography of India—Facts and Problems', in A. Chandra Sekhar (ed.), *Economic and Socio-cultural Dimensions of Regionalisation*, Census of India, 1971, Centenary Monograph, No. 7, Government of India, Ministry of Home Affairs, New Delhi, pp. 387-426.

7

Communities of Faith

Cast in a Regional Mould

India presents a baffling diversity in religious persuasions and faiths. Although the traditional religion of the land is Hinduism, many other faiths and belief systems, from tribal forms of religion to Buddhism, Christianity and Islam have coexisted for centuries. They have created for themselves cultural niches within a shared social space. These faiths are indigenous (Indic) as well as introduced from outside (extra-Indic). The Indic religions have all evolved from early Hinduism which has been undergoing changes in content and ritual practices in response to the prevailing cultural, ethno-lingual and ecological diversities in different regions of the country. Within Hinduism a number of sects, such as Vaisnavism and Sivaism, emerged on the scene adding further diversity to the cultural mosaic. These sects have a specific geographic patterning of their own in the country. This shows how ideological differences and philosophical interpretations lead to diverse socio-cultural practices and the associated rituals based on religious faiths. Thus, it is evident that the differences in religious ideologies may lead to sect formation even within the same religion. These differences have led to the emergence of regional nuances in religious practices. In the same way, protest movements within Hinduism eventually led to the emergence of new faiths, such as Buddhism and Jainism. These protest movements also led to reform within Hinduism. Another Indic religion—Sikhism—was genetically linked to these changes. In its original form it was a fine blend of the basic elements of Hinduism and Islam.

Religious faiths, which originated in West Asia, *e.g.*, Christianity, Zoroastrianism and Islam, also found their followers in India in large numbers. Initially following a sea route to India, both Christianity and Islam had their early base in the littoral regions of South India, particularly the western coastal region, from where they spread into the interior parts. Later missionary activity systematically organised by the Christian missions during the subsequent centuries, particularly the eighteenth and the nineteenth centuries found many responsive groups among the tribes and the Hindu depressed castes. The spread of Islam in northern and western India was a later phenomenon. In fact, it followed the sequence of developments leading to the Muslim conquest of the northern parts of the country in the medieval period. Unlike the Christian missionary activity, Islamic enterprise was never systematically organised.[1]

However, the emergence of Muslim seats of power in different regions of the country provided an added incentive to conversion. Evidently, coexistence of multiple faiths and a pervasive spirit of tolerance have been a distinguishing feature of the Indian society through the ages.

Social Expression of Religious Identity

Although religion is a matter of personal faith, religious identity of an individual in India is often expressed at the social plane. Unlike the western world where mass celebration of the religious occasions is infrequent, more so the public display of festivities is rare, religious celebrations in the oriental societies is a sociological phenomenon. The Indian society conforms to this norm. Mass festivals are common and the year is dotted with religious events, major as well as minor, which have far-reaching social implications. In fact, in some religious groups there are several occasions during the year when people publicly display their adherence to a certain form of religious ritual. For example, large processions are taken out with great zeal. Likewise, people offer mass prayers in Mosques and Churches on certain festivals. Mass prayers are also held in Mosques on every Friday. The celebration of festivals acquires dimensions, which transcends the limits of the private sphere of life. They become occasions of public expression of religious identity. These practices have continued and co-existed giving strength to the pluralistic nature of India's religio-cultural ethos.

Elements of Religious Identity

The issue of religion, or religion-based identity, may be approached in several ways. First, religion is a matter of faith, a personal affair and a philosophy of life of an individual or a group of individuals. Secondly, and flowing from the first, followers of a certain religion by virtue of their adherence to a common faith may develop a community feeling. This leads to conscious or unconscious expression of solidarity with the followers of that religious faith. This community feeling characterises all religious group formations. Thirdly, a common code of social conduct based on a religious faith may lead to public expressions of a particular religious identity, *e.g.*, dressing in a particular way, avoidance of certain items of food, and mass assemblies and public demonstrations on religious occasions. These divergent codes of conduct and socio-cultural practices eventually lead to a consciousness of religious and cultural differences. Followers of other religions are often ranked on a scale constructed in the light of a particular religious ideology and are then rated as superior, inferior or even untouchable. If religion is a matter of personal faith, and there is little adherence to a publicly manifested code of conduct, it does not affect anybody. But if there is a public assertion of one's religious identity expressed pronouncedly in dress-ways, food-ways, avoidance of or preference for certain items of food, cooking habits, eating habits, inhibitions in inter-dining and so on, a religious group acquires an identity of its own and gets differentiated from other religious groups on a social basis. Other forms of discriminatory social behaviour follow. This promotes, on the one hand, an internal feeling of solidarity and, on the other, a feeling of division. Such divisive tendencies may acquire acute forms and may result in a variety of social conflicts. When groups are formed and perceived on religious basis, social authority is often likely to be wielded by a priestly class (the authority of the Church as in Roman Catholics or the authority of the *Ulema* as in Islam, although the two are not comparable in orientation and rigour). This sooner or later acquires political nuances. When such a stage is reached, religion is likely to become the basis of social mobilisation, which eventually may lead to a social discord. The highest stage in this regimentation is reached when a state identifies itself with a particular religion and subjects the followers of other religions, or religious minorities, if any, to a discriminatory treatment. Theocratic states based on dissimilar religious formations may eventually confront each other in situations of war in an attempt to subjugate each other. Crusades were the best example of such conflicts when the contesting parties were fighting in the name of religion.

The above discussion shows that religion in the world societies has not always been purely a matter of simple faith. Actions of individuals or groups often transcend the limits of personal space. Then religion becomes a manifested basis of social differentiation. In that role, it has far-reaching operational implications, which do not always seem to hint at harmony or cohesion. At the same time, there is no gainsaying the fact that in the world society, religion as a moral philosophy has played a role of promoting harmony, peace and commitment to civilized public behaviour. The values inculcated by religious teachings are universal and reveal the essential unity of all religions. Religion has acted as a civilizing force promoting humanism, respect for other forms of identity and a spirit of sacrifice in an endeavour to achieve higher goals for human coexistence. Religion has induced individuals to subordinate themselves to the higher ideals of humanism and sacrifice their own comforts for the collective good of the humankind. However, human history is also full of instances when religion-based spirit of harmony and compassion has been largely ignored in order to establish the supremacy of a given religious formation. The same factors, which are cohesive in a given formation, become the basis of rivalry and competition between the different religious groups. While it is true that religion promotes spiritualism, spiritual values have often been superseded by the human lust for secular authority and material well-being. Despite the religious teachings for good moral behaviour, conflict between good and evil has continued through history.

Religion in Indian Society: A Historical Perspective

Let us now examine the place of religion in the Indian society in its historical context. Religion is a form of social organisation. While it is personalised, social expression of one's religious identity leads to significant behavioural patterns. The attitudes adopted by different religious groups reveal that ideology is a determining force in social behaviour. People chalk out their social interaction modes in the light of the religious faith they profess. The ramifications of a differential pattern of social behaviour are seen in patterns of social interaction, celebration of festivals, organisation of cultural activities, management of social space and personal manners. Western education has brought about a certain degree of social transformation; nonetheless the hold of religious ideologies is too strong. At the same time, it is true that an enlightened class of Indians is thoroughly secular and capable of rising above the religious identities in all situations of crisis.

While Hinduism is the religion of the land, there is no one pan-Indian form of religion. In fact, Hinduism has been evolving through the ages. Moreover, it has interesting regional forms and each cultural region has its own distinguishing traits expressed in rituals, customs, ceremonies, festivals and social practices. An early form of Hinduism, based on the worship of mother goddess gradually changed into a religious form commonly referred to as Vedic Hinduism (Box 7.1). The advent of Vedic religion led to drastic modification of the ancient faith around the middle of the second millennium B.C. While Vedic religion remained as a superstructure, regional forms of faith based on a blending of local varieties with the newly introduced elements continued as a substratum.

Box 7.1 : Mother Earth

That the worship of chthonic deities such as 'Mother Earth' generally presupposes a relative importance of agriculture is fairly obvious, but such parallelism is not always direct. Nor can it be maintained that the heavenly gods, as representative of a hero's paradise beyond the earth, have everywhere been noble gods rather than chthonic deities of the peasantry. Even less can it be maintained that the development of 'Mother Earth' as a goddess parallels the development of matriarchal clan organisation. Nevertheless, the chthonic deities who controlled the harvest have customarily borne a more local and popular character than the other gods. In any case, the inferiority of earth divinities to Celestial personal gods who reside in the clouds or on the mountains is frequently determined by the development of a feudal culture, and there is a tendency to permit originally tellurian deities to take their place among the gods who are resident in the skies. Conversely, the chthonic deities frequently combine two functions in primarily agrarian cultures: they control the harvest, thus granting wealth, and they are also the masters of the dead who have been laid to rest in the earth. This explains why frequently ... these two most important practical interests, namely earthly riches and fate in the hereafter, depend upon them. On the other hand, the heavenly gods are the lords of the stars.... The classic paradigm of this fairly abstract form of deity-formation is the highest conception of the ancient Hindu pantheon, Brahma, as the Lord of Prayer. Just as the Brahmin priests monopolise the power of effective prayer.

—Max Weber, *The Sociology of Religion*, 1971:13-14.

It is commonly known that the transformation of early Hinduism into Vedic form of religion started with the advent of the Indo-Aryan language, particularly Sanskrit, which became the vehicle for this change. The Vedic theology according to one interpretation 'begins with the worship of the things of heaven, and ends with the worship of the things of earth'.[2] The Gods of Heaven included Surya, Savitar and Bhaga, which really implies the worship of sun in different forms. Then was the worship of the gods of the intermediate sky, Indra, and earth-born gods, Agni, Soma, etc. Gradually, the concept of *Sraddha*, or periodical feast of the dead, led to the emergence of the cult of sacrifice. The Rigveda recorded the practices and the rituals associated with the different forms of worship as the Vedic religion spread to other regions of India from its homeland in the Sapta-Sindhava region. It acquired distinct regional forms. The Hindu pantheon recognised a Super Being, an *Atman* or *Parmatman* which permeated all beings, including the gods they worshipped. The Vedic theology was not a fixed set of ideas. In fact, it continued to evolve from the period of the *Vedas* to that of the *Brahmanas* and the *Upanishads.* During these evolutionary stages, significant changes were registered in the Hindu philosophy and the very concept of gods underwent a change.[3]

As Brahmanism became rigid, protest movements against the ascetic fraternity of the Brahmans were launched. These protest movements eventually led to the emergence of new faiths, such as Buddhism and Jainism. Buddhism was a heretical movement. Basically it was a reformation movement and a protest against the ascendency of the priestly class. Buddhism in its original form was not a religion as such. It was simply a monastic organisation. It insisted on a non-Brahmanic order. In its historical context, it appears that it was a culmination of the on-going conflict between the Brahman and the Kshatriya. In the background of Magadh, one can understand that the Kshatriya was in a dominating position. The fact that these protest movements originated in Magadha explains the nature of the caste conflict so peculiar to the region. Early Buddhism tried to disentangle people from the Brahmanical cult. Among the basic elements of Buddhism were the sanctity of animal life (*Ahimsa*) and the craving for salvation (*Nirvana*). However, the early Buddhist gospels were a continuation of the old Hindu beliefs and ethics. Buddha laid an extraordinary stress on the issue of *Nirvana.* It is a remarkable feature of India's religious tolerance that inspite of its opposition to Brahmanical supremacy, Buddhism co-existed with Brahmanism for more than a millennium. In its early days Buddhism benefited from its practice of holding *Sangha* (congregation of monks or monastic order) in the propagation and consolidation of Buddhist faith. Through these congregations, Buddhists preachers redefined their position *vis-a-vis* the basic philosophical issues. It is also believed that Buddhism also benefited when the state adopted it, perhaps as a state religion under Asoka. Asoka's role in the propagation of Buddhism to other parts of the world, such as Sri Lanka, Central and Eastern Asia, is too well known. With the passage of time Buddhism got divided into two schools of thought—Hinayana and Mahayana. The Mahayana School of Buddhism, which developed under Kanishka, promised salvation to the entire Universe as against the Hinayana concept of salvation of the few. It is a known history that Buddhism started declining in its homeland, while it flourished abroad. Hsuan Tsang' s visit to India during 629-45 A.C. confirmed its general state of decay. It is understood that the main cause of this decline was Brahmanical revivalism attended by a reformation movement within Brahamanism. The rise of Brahamanism is attributed to the efforts of Kumarila Bhatta, a Brahman preacher of Bihar and his disciple, Sankaracharya. There were other factors too. For example, the Buddhist creed was based on a high standard of morality, much higher than the level of common people. Moreover, rejection of the sacrificial cult and abstraction of the concept of god acted as distracting factors, hastening the decay of Buddhism. The common Hindu was more interested in gods, which were concrete objects of worships, such as Siva and Krishna. Thus the decline of Buddhism may be an outcome of the resurgence of Brahamanism as well as the natural decay of the Buddhist faith among the masses.

The ascetic fraternity of the Brahmans led to another protest movement, which came to be known as Jainism. The movement emerged in the lifetime of Buddha himself. Like Buddha, its leader Vardhamana, popularly known as Mahavira Jina, also came from Magadha. The Brahman authority was so strong that these protest movements gained popularity. Jainism also aimed at *nirvana*, although the Jain concept of *nirvana* was a little different than in Buddhism. Within Jainism, a division between Svetambara and Digambara took place at an early stage. Svetambara originated in the northern and western region of the country while Digambara had its base in the south. The Digambaras followed the principle of nudity. A third sect which consisted of Dhondias also emerged. Jainism received state patronage under the Chalukyas of Gujarat and Marwar. With this began the process of construction of famous Jain temples in different regions of the country. Unlike Buddhism, Jainism did not suffer a setback. The Jain order survived without much of a conflict, external or internal. Today, the main Jain sanctuaries are situated in the isolated hills, such as Parasnath in Bengal, Palitana in Kathiawar and Mount Abu in Rajasthan. The census records show a successive decline in the numerical strength of Jain population. It may also be noted that the home of Jainism today lies in Gujarat and adjoining Marwar region of Rajasthan, where the followers have been drawn mostly from among the trading communities and not in Bengal, Magadh or Orissa where the Jain faith originated.

Reform movements initiated by Gautam Buddha and Mahavira, resulted in new formulations of ritual as well as social customs. There was a phase, although short-lived, in Indian history when the tide of Buddhism seemed to submerge the Hindu faith. Buddhism had its sway over a vast region from Bengal to Kashmir and from the Himalayas to the Kaveri till a new Brahmanical upsurge brought an equally spectacular change.

The protest movements represented by Buddhism and Jainism also led to reformation within Brahmanism. These reform movements eventually resulted in the emergence of a new form of Hinduism, which is currently in practice in all parts of India. Its basic elements consist of use of one sacred language (Sanskrit), through which the ritual is practised, pilgrimage to holy places and the rule of a priestly class, which determines the life of the ordinary Hindu men and women. The religion of the peasant, although simpler in its theological content, is equally controlled by the Brahamanical authority.

In the course of time, two sects, *viz.*, Vaisnavism and Sivaism emerged among the Hindus. While the former focuses on the worship of Visnu, the latter focuses on the worship of Siva.[4] Each sect has its own order of rituals performed on specific occasions. However, both the gods are worshipped by the common Hindu folk throughout the country. Both Siva and Visnu are mentioned in the *Mahabharata* as two separate gods, and at the same time each represented by the other. The Hindu trinity of gods consists of both of them as well as a third god, Brahma, who was treated as the chief of the gods in the epic period. The modern belief is that while Brahma occupies a central position, he is represented by both Visnu and Siva and in their worship Brahma is also worshipped indirectly.

As pointed out earlier, a remarkable feature of Hindu society is a spirit of tolerance and of accommodation of multiple forms of faith.[5] It was because of this spirit of tolerance that other faiths which came from outside flourished. Christianity and Islam came from outside and the people embraced these faiths without much of a social conflict. This has been a historic tradition that successive penetration by non-Indic religions was not resisted. Political conflicts were there between the local kingdoms and the invaders, but they did not result in religious conflicts. Gradually these religious faiths created for themselves niches in the Indian social space. As indicated earlier, among the Semitic religions, the earliest to make an impact in India was Christianity. Syrian Christians appeared on the west coast of India in the very first century of the Christian era. Later in the seventh century A.C., Arab traders brought the message of Islam to the people living on the west coast of India. This happened much before the Muslim (political) conquest of northern India.

It is thus obvious that the religious composition of the Indian population has been changing with conversions from one faith to other. The spatial patterns of distribution of different religious groups were also greatly modified by large scale migration following the Partition of India in 1947. Partition brought about a significant change in the distribution and relative strength of different religious faiths in north-western, northern and north-eastern India.

Spatial Distribution of Religious Groups

The different religious communities of India include major groups, such as the Hindus, Muslims, Christians, Sikhs, Buddhists and the Jains, as well as minor religious faiths, such as Jews and Zoroastrians. Moreover, several tribal communities continue to retain faith in tribal religions based on totemism and animism. Hindus account for 82 per cent of the total population and are the largest religious group in the country. However, in some districts Muslims, Christians, Sikhs or Buddhists are more numerous than the Hindus. The Muslims are the largest minority group and account for 12.12 per cent of the total population. Christians constitute 2.3 per cent of the population and the Sikhs 1.94 per cent. Buddhists and Jains are numerically insignificant accounting for 0.7 and 0.5 per cent of population respectively. It may be noted that while Hindus are generally found everywhere, other religious groups are concentrated in a few pockets only (Table 7.1).

Table 7.1 : Religious Composition of Population, 1991

Religious Groups	*Population*	*Percentage of Total Population*
Hindus	687,646,721	82.00
Muslims	101,596,057	12.12
Christians	19,640,284	2.34
Sikhs	16,259,744	1.94
Buddhists	6,387,500	0.76
Jains	3,352,706	0.40
Others*	3,269,355	0.39
No Religion**	415,569	0.05
All India Population	838,567,936	100.00

Source: Census of India, 1991, Table C-9, *Religion*.
Notes: * Other religious persuasions.
** Religion not stated.

It may be useful to identify the main patterns in the spatial distribution of the major religious groups in order to understand the role of religion in defining the parameters of Indian social space and the socio-cultural regionalism based on it.

The Hindus

Hindus are numerically predominant everywhere. However, they are not merely a demographic phenomenon. They have exercised an abiding influence on the sociology and the cultural ecology of all other religious groups, which have been derived from Hinduism at different stages of their evolutionary history. The intertwined way of give-and-take between Hinduism and other faiths, such as Christianity and Islam, has given Indian culture a uniqueness of its own. The common features of culture and tradition are shared by all religious groups.

Numerical Strength

With a total population of 687.6 million, Hindus constitute the largest religious community. The Hindu population registered a net increase of 122 million during the 1981-91 decade. There are no specific spatial patterns, which can be highlighted in the distribution of Hindu population. In fact, the way the Hindu population is distributed is not different from that of the total population. Two-fifths of the Hindu population lives in the Hindi-speaking northern states (*viz*., Haryana, Delhi, Uttar Pradesh, Bihar, Rajasthan and Madhya Pradesh). The two States of Uttar Pradesh and Bihar alone account for more than 27 per cent of the country's Hindu population. Likewise, the four southern states accommodate one-fourth of the country's Hindu population. In contrast, the northwestern States of Jammu and Kashmir, Himachal Pradesh, Punjab and Haryana have less than 4 per cent of the country's Hindu population. Similarly, Hindus in the north-eastern states of Assam, Arunachal Pradesh, Nagaland, Manipur, Mizoram, Tripura and Meghalaya constitute less than 3 per cent of the country's aggregative Hindu population (Appendix VII.1).

Spatial Distribution

A demography of religions may be helpful in understanding the dynamics of population of different religious groups. It may also be useful to evaluate the spatial patterns in the distribution of religious groups. As noted above, in terms of numerical strength the followers of Hindu religion enjoy a dominating position. At the all-India level they constitute as much as 82 per cent of the total population of the country. Seen in this context, the followers of all other religious persuasions put together have a relatively insignificant share in overall population—just 18 per cent. Despite this insignificant position, the question of religious minorities continues to be a vexed problem in India. The minority-majority relations have often resulted in social and political problems with far reaching implications for the civil administration. The Hindu proportion is higher in the rural segment of population—the national average being 84 per cent—thus revealing the predominantly rural character of the Hindu population. As against this, the proportion of Hindus in the urban population is around 76 per cent. Barring the peripheral areas of the country and a few pockets in the interior, Hindus remain a dominant religious group everywhere in the country. However, in the peripheral areas Hindus are outnumbered by the Muslims (*e.g.*, Jammu and Kashmir), Sikhs (*e.g.*, Punjab), Christians (*e.g.*, Mizoram, Nagaland) and Buddhists (*e.g.*, Arunachal Pradesh). In some regions of the country, such as parts of Orissa, Madhya Pradesh and Andhra Pradesh, Hindus account for more than 97 per cent of the total population. The proportion of Hindu population is equally high—above 95 per cent—in the sub-Himalayan districts of Uttar Pradesh and Himachal Pradesh. The proportion of Hindus in population remains well above 90 per cent in eastern Madhya Pradesh, eastern Gujarat, southern Karnataka, Tamil Nadu and coastal Andhra Pradesh. On the other hand, in some districts along the west coast Hindu percentages are low—below 70 per cent. Similarly, in the tribal areas of the northeast, such as Meghalaya, Nagaland and Mizoram their proportion is less than 20 per cent and in some cases even less than 5 per cent. Hindus are also a small minority in the Kashmir valley, so much so that in some districts their proportion is less than 2 per cent. In several districts of the northern States of Uttar Pradesh, Haryana and Bihar which happen to be the areas of Muslim concentration, the Hindu proportion goes down to less than 60 per cent. In some districts their share in population may be less than 50 per cent.

The regions in which Hindus are overwhelmingly dominant may be grouped into the following categories:

(a) Regions of tribal concentration and those in the interior of the Peninsula where the tribes have been largely Hinduised. These regions are situated away from the entry points through which Christians or Islamic influences percolated (*e.g.*, Orissa Highlands, adjacent parts of Andhra Pradesh and the Vindhyan complex in mid-India) thus leaving the original Hindu population unaffected by these developments.

(b) Regions in the sub-Himalayan parts of the North and the Northwest (*e.g.*, Himachal Pradesh and Uttaranchal Hills) where Muslim influences were feeble.

(c) Regions in the Aravallis and the Indo-Gangetic Divide comprising parts of the undivided Punjab. These regions had a high proportion of Hindus in the residual population after the exodus of Muslims in the wake of Partition.

(d) Regions in the Chambal badlands as well as in the former princely states of central India.

(e) Regions, such as the former Rajput princely states of Sirohi, Dungarpur and Banswara (Table 7.2).

Table 7.2 : India: Districts with the Hindu proportion remaining over 94 per cent, 1991

Type of Region	*Hindu Proportion*	
	Above 98 per cent	*94-98 per cent*
(a) Regions of tribal dominance or those lying away from the north-western entry points	Srikakulam, Vizianagaram, Bastar, Bolangir, Dhenkanal, Kalahandi	Visakhapatnam, East Godavari, Panch Mahals, Jhabua, Betul, Narsimhapur, Mandla, Bilaspur, Rajnandgaon, Durg, Raipur, Sambalpur, Keonjhar, Baleswar, Cuttack, Koraput, Ganjam, Puri, Salem, Periyar, Dharmapuri, Dadra and Nagar Haveli, Yanam
(b) Isolated Sub-Himalayan Hills	Hamirpur, Mandi, Uttar Kashi, Chamoli, Tehri-Garhwal, Pithoragarh, Almora	Kangra, Bilaspur, Kullu, Shimla, Solan, Garhwal
(c) Indo-Gangetic Divide Region of the old Punjab with residual population after Muslim exodus to Pakistan	Rohtak, Rewari, Mahindergarh, Bhiwani	Sonipat, Jind
(d) Peninsular Interior		Mandya, Morena, Tikamgarh, Chhatarpur, Panna, Satna, Rewa, Shahdol, Sidhi, Sonbhadra
(e) Former Rajput Princely States		Sirohi, Dungarpur, Banswara

Source: Based on Census of India, 1991, Table C-9, *Religion*.
Note: Table prepared by the author.

Similarly areas in which Hindus have been reduced to a minority may be categorised as follows:

(a) Regions of tribal dominance in the Northeast where the tribes have been Christianised.
(b) Regions on the Northwestern periphery, such as Jammu and Kashmir and Punjab where either Muslims or Sikhs are concentrated.
(c) Regions of sizeable Muslim population, such as Rohilkhand and the Upper Ganga-Yamuna *doab,* or parts of West Bengal and Assam which have been traditional nodes of Muslim convergence (Table 7.3; Fig. 7.1).

Table 7.3 : India: Districts with the Hindu proportion below 21 per cent, 1991

15-21 per cent	*10-15 per cent*	*5-10 per cent*	*Below 5 per cent*
Tawang, East Kameng, Senapati, East Khasi Hills, West Garo Hills, Amritsar, Sangrur, Faridkot	Upper Subansiri, Chandal	West Siang, Churachandpur, Ukhrul, East Garo Hills, Phek, Mokokchung, Mon	Tamenglong, Jaintia Hills, West Khasi Hills, Aizawl, Lungloi, Chhimtuipui, Zunheboto, Wokha, Tuensang, Lakshadweep

Source: Based on Census of India, 1991, Table C-9, *Religion*.

The Buddhists

At the 1991 census, a total of 6.38 million Buddhists were enumerated. They constituted 0.76 per cent of the country's population. The pockets of traditional Buddhism are located in Ladakh, Himachal Pradesh, Sikkim, Mizoram and Tripura. Buddhism which was once holding sway over many regions of the country gradually declined in following. Some Buddhist following continued in the peripheral regions of the country. The bulk of the Buddhist population today lives in Maharashtra (as much as 79 per cent). These neo-Buddhists are converts from Hindu low castes. They were initiated into Buddhism by Baba Saheb Ambedkar in protest against the high caste domination.

In many districts of Maharashtra, these neo-Buddhists account for 5-17 per cent of the population. The Buddhist proportion is significantly high—more than 12 per cent—in Akola, Nagpur, Wardha, Buldana, Amravati, Chandrapur, Parbhani, Bhandara and Gadchiroli. From 5 to 10 per cent of the population consist of Buddhists in Nanded, Yavatmal, Jalna, Aurangabad, Ratnagiri, Greater Bombay and Satara. The Buddhist proportion is very high (above 60 per cent) in the North Sikkim district and significantly high in East, South and West Sikkim. More than one-tenth of the population in South Tripura and Darjeeling consists of Buddhists. There are two main pockets of Buddhist concentration in Mizoram. They are situated in Chhimtuipui and Lunglei districts. In the former, more than 28 per cent of the district population consists of Buddhists. In the latter, their share is about 16 per cent. Another pocket of Buddhist concentration is found in Arunachal Pradesh where Buddhists constitute around 80 per cent of population in Tawang. About one-half of the population in West Kameng district is Buddhist in its religious persuasion. The Buddhists' presence is also quite significant in Changlang district. About three-fifths of the population of Lahaul and Spiti in Himachal Pradesh consists of Buddhists. Kinnaur also has a significant proportion of Buddhists in its population (Table 7.4; Fig. 7.2).

Table 7.4 : Frequency Distribution of Districts with sizeable Buddhist Population, 1991

Percentage Categories	*No. of Districts*	*Names of Districts*
Above 60	2	Tawang, North Sikkim
40-60	2	Lahaul and Spiti, West Kameng
20-40	6	Changlang, Kinnaur, Chhimtuipui, East Sikkim, South Sikkim, West Sikkim
10-20	14	Lohit, Parbhani, Nanded, Buldana, Akola, Amravati, Wardha, Nagpur, Bhandara, Chandrapur, Gadchiroli, Lunglei, South Tripura, Darjeeling
Below 10	8	Dibang Valley, North Tripura, Greater Bombay, Ratnagiri, Satara, Aurangabad, Jalna, Yavatmal

Source: Based on Census of India, 1991, Table C-9, *Religion*.
Note: Districts in which the Buddhist proportion in population is less than 5 per cent have been ignored.

The Jains

About 60 per cent of the country's 3.35 million Jains live in the three states of Rajasthan, Gujarat and Maharashtra. The Jain population is largely concentrated in the urban

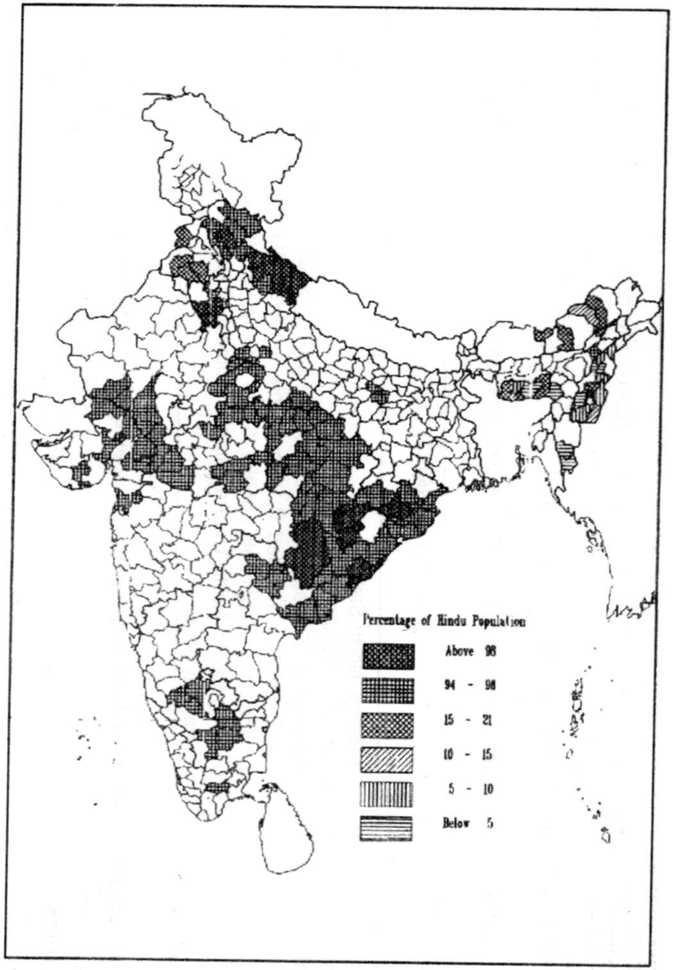

Figure 7.1 : India: Hindu Population, 1991

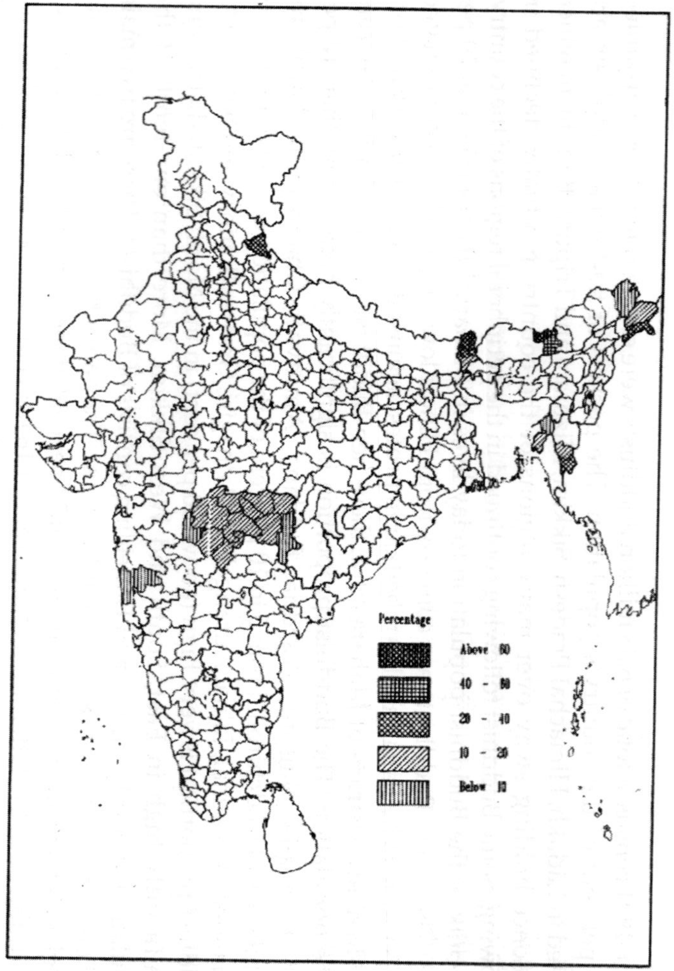

Figure 7.2 : India: The Buddhist Population, 1991

centres of these three states as well as in the neighbouring states of Madhya Pradesh and Uttar Pradesh.

Their preference for urban areas is, however, understandable in view of the fact that the Jains are mainly a trading community. Even in small towns they control petty business. The proportion of the Jains in the population of these states is, however, insignificant. For example, the Jains account for just 1.28 per cent of the total population in Rajasthan, 1.22 per cent in Maharashtra and 1.19 per cent in Gujarat. As against this, their proportion in the urban population of these states is high—3.4 per cent in Rajasthan, 3.5 per cent in Maharashtra and 2.6 per cent in Gujarat. A perusal of Table 7.5 reveals that the Jains have favoured their concentration in the dry regions of Rajasthan and Gujarat. The two districts in which their share is the highest in urban population are Barmer (13.4 per cent) and Jalor (10.5 per cent). These two districts apart Jains generally constitute from 2-10 per cent of the urban segment of the population in a cluster of districts in Rajasthan, Gujarat, Madhya Pradesh and Maharashtra. In another cluster of adjacent districts their proportion varies between 5 and 10 per cent. These districts lie in the western and northern parts of Madhya Pradesh, Bundelkhand region of Uttar Pradesh and southern and eastern parts of Rajasthan. In no less than 30 districts distributed over Rajasthan, Gujarat, Madhya Pradesh, Maharashtra and western Uttar Pradesh, Jains account for 2-5 per cent of the urban population. Elsewhere in India they are conspicuous by their absence (Table 7.5).

Table 7.5 : Frequency Distribution of Districts according to the proportion of Jains in Urban Population, 1991

Percentage Categories	*No. of Districts*	*Names of Districts*
Above 10	2	Barmer, Jalor (Rajasthan)
5-10	15	Lalitpur (U.P.), Udaipur, Banswara, Dungarpur, Chittoorgarh, Tonk, Sirohi (Rajasthan), Surendarnagar (Gujarat), Guna, Sagar, Damoh, Mandsaur, Ratlam, Jhabua, Vidisha (Madhya Pradesh)
2-5	30	Bhavnagar, Kachch, Banas Kantha, Sabar Kantha (Gujarat), Bikaner, Bhilwara, Bundi, Jhalawar (Rajasthan), Firozabad, Mainpuri (Uttar Pradesh), Shivpuri, Tikamgarh, Panna, Ujjain, Shajapur, Dhar, Indore, Sehore, Raisen, Jabalpur, Narsimhapur, Seoni, Balaghat, Rajnandgaon (Madhya Pradesh), Greater Bombay, Ahmadnagar, Pune, Satara, Sangli, Kolhapur (Maharashtra)

Source: Based on Census of India, 1991, Table C-9, *Religion*.
Note: Table prepared by the author.

The Christians

Christians are among the major religious minorities in India today. They may perhaps be treated as a unique religious group on several grounds. First, like the Muslims, they are widely distributed in the country forming a sizeable proportion of population in many states and union territories. Secondly, Christianity was introduced by European missionaries from the very early stages. It, therefore, became a powerful vehicle of social and cultural change in the country. It brought in its wake a series of changes popularly expressed by the term 'Europeanisation'. Thirdly, since the missionaries generally worked among the poor and the most deprived sections of the Indian population, Christianity indirectly contributed towards the alleviation of poverty and the upliftment of the down-trodden masses. Fourthly, Christian Missionaries had a wide sweep and were in a position to reach the most isolated and the backward parts of the country. As a result, Christian converts were drawn from diverse ethno-lingual groups. Christianity thus acted as a bridge between diverse elements within India's tribal and caste-based social order. Lastly, the European connection was important. It was through this channel that financial resources could flow into India for social work of great local relevance. In fact, the pioneering work that the Christian missions initiated in the field of education, health and social rehabilitation remains a landmark. It has no parallels in Indian history.

Advent of Christianity in India

Christianity spread in India in several phases. The beginnings are traceable in the establishment of the Syrian Church in Malabar, supposed to have been founded by St. Thomas, one of the 12 Apostles of Jesus. The common belief is that he preached in India and was martyred here. The belief, however, remains unsubstantiated. Another development which took place in 345 A.C. was the arrival of a Christian Missionary, Bishop of Edessa, also named as Thomas. He came from Iran and started preaching in south India. The Syrian Church was already active in India at the beginning of the 6th century A.C. It formed a branch of the Nestorian Order. Christian presence in India was also noted by Marco Polo, who visited south India in the thirteenth century A.C. Christianity received an added impetus with the arrival of the Portuguese in the fifteenth century. Soon the Franciscan Missionaries started their work in India with Goa being recognised as Bishopric in 1534. Eight years later St. Francis Xavier reached Goa. As in the case of the earlier missionaries, his work remained confined to the Malabar coast and the southern districts of what is now known as Tamil Nadu. So far converts to Christianity were Europeanised so much that there was a total break from the Indian cultural tradition. This, however, proved to be a setback. This *modus operandi*, however, changed with Robert de Nobili (died 1605) who settled in Madurai and allowed the Christian converts to retain their cultural practices even after conversion. His method of work was so appealing that even the high caste Hindus converted to Christianity.

The French who came by and large the same time as the Portuguese, helped propagate Catholic faith. While the Portuguese were having their sway on the West Coast, the French founded their early settlements on the East Coast, operating mainly in the region lying to the south of Madras (now Chennai) particularly from their enclave in Pondicherry. The net result was that the efforts of the Portuguese and the French helped in the propagation of Christianity. The Catholic Church could strike its roots in the southern region from coast to coast as the land was dotted with Churches, schools and hospitals. The missionaries picked up the local languages and this added to their effectiveness in the missionary work. The Catholic population multiplied with multi-pronged social welfare activity serving mostly the deprived and the down-trodden sections of Indian population.

The first Protestant Mission was established in 1705 by the Danish Lutherans. A Baptist Mission was established at Serampore in 1792. While the East India Company was not directly involved in missionary work, there were Anglican Chaplains who were employed as Company's functionaries. They took interest in the promotion of Christianity. By 1813, the Company finally granted permission to Anglican bodies for missionary work. As a result the first Anglican Bishopric was established at Madras. The East India Company also agreed to the foundation of the Episcopal See at Calcutta. Both Catholic and Protestant Missions continued their work during the nineteenth century. However, the Catholics were largely confined to the southern region of India. The missionary work was also carried out by the American Board of Foreign Missions in the early decades of the nineteenth century. Their efforts were mainly focused on the United Provinces of Agrah and Oudh as well as Punjab. Field stations were established at important towns in these provinces during the period 1834-55. The Telugu Mission and Assam Mission, launched in 1840-41 proved to be highly successful (Box 7.2).

The fact that the Roman Catholics constitute a major chunk of the Indian Christian community is also evident from the number of Catholic institutions, such as Churches, schools, colleges and hospitals. The Church plays an important role in the social integration of the community. The distribution of Catholic Church in India, related as it is with the concentration of Catholic population, appears to be an outcome of the long history of diffusion of Christianity.

Box 7.2 : The Ecclesiastical Organisation

The Catholic Church has 15 Metropolitan areas, each presided over by an Archbishop with several suffragan Bishops in the area. These Metropolitan Sees include three of the Syrian Rite, those of Ernakulam, Changanacherry and Trivandrum. The number of Bishoprics is over 60. The former Anglican Church is now known as the Church of India, Pakistan, Burma and Ceylon. The Metropolitan resides in Calcutta and there are 13 Episcopal Sees under him. The Methodist Episcopalians have four residing Bishops in India. The Metropolitan, or Catholics, of the Jacobite Syrian Church resides in Kottayam and has nine Bishops under him. There are four other independent Bishops of the Syrian Rite in Kerala.

—*The Gazetteer of India*, Indian Union, Country and People, Vol. I, 1965: 497.

The emergence of Catholics in the north was rather delayed. The progress of Christianity in the north may be related with the British ascendency. However, the British were mostly Protestants. Most of the Catholic Churches in North India are, therefore, mostly recent, even as recent as independence. The spread of Catholic faith in the northern region, initially subdued, left the Protestants behind. The major concentration, however, remains in the south, west and the northeast. The distribution of the Catholic Churches follows the same pattern.

As noted earlier, the spread of Christianity owes much to the dedicated social work of missionaries in the area of education and health. The Christian colleges in

Indian cities were by far the best institutions of higher learning. The Christian missions established no less than a hundred first-grade colleges, hundreds of high schools and middle schools and thousands of primary and elementary schools in different parts of the country. Their main focus was on women's education which was grossly neglected in India. As part of their social work, the missionaries also established orphanages, homes for the aged and the handicapped, hospitals, dispensaries and leprosy and tuberculosis sanatoria (Box 7.3).

> **Box 7.3 :** Christianity at the Beginning of the Twentieth Century
>
> The Christian community now numbers only three millions, of whom more than two-and-a-half million are native converts, and the remainder Europeans or Urasians. Of the native Christians, about two-fifths are Roman Catholics, and one-eighth Romo-Syrian; one-ninth belong to the Anglican body, one-eleventh are Jacobite Syrians, one-twelfth Baptist... Nearly two-thirds of the total Christian population are found in Madras, including the native states of Cochin and Travancore. In these states, where the Syrian Church is strongest, nearly a quarter of the entire native population profess Christianity. In British territory, it is in the eight southern districts, the scene of the labours of St. Francis Xavier and Swartz, that Christians are most numerous. Then come the district of the Telugu country—Kistna where they are mainly Baptist and Lutherans; Nellore, nearly all Baptists; and Kurnool, Baptist with a respectable minority of Anglicans.
>
> —*The Imperial Gazetteer of India*, The Indian Empire, Vol. I, 1908: 443.

Numerical Strength

The 1991 census enumerated 19.64 million Christians in India. The Christian population increased from 10.53 million to 19.64 million in 1991, registering an average annual growth rate of 2.88 per cent. The Christian population reveals a strong tendency of concentration in the southern states of Kerala, Tamil Nadu, Andhra Pradesh and Karnataka. This is, however, in conformity to or with the historical processes through which Christianity spread in the country. About 56 per cent of the total Christian population of the country lives in the four southern states alone. Kerala alone has almost one-third of the country's Christian population, while Tamil Nadu takes care of about one-sixth of the national total. A second major concentration of Christians is seen in the northeastern states which together share 22 per cent of the total Christian population of the country (Appendix VII.2). As noted earlier, the Christian population consists of Catholics as well as Protestants. Subsumed in the Christian population are more than half a million orthodox Syrian Christians and more than a lakh Anglo-Indians consisting of Protestants as well as Catholics. At the 1901 census, nearly 3 million Christians were enumerated. Of these, 2.5 million were native converts and the remainder Europeans or Eurasians.

Spatial Distribution

A perusal of district-level data shows pockets of Christian concentration in the southern state of Kerala where as many as seven districts have Christian proportion ranging between 20 and 50 per cent. The Christian proportion is particularly high in Kottayam

(45.83 per cent), Idukki (42.23 per cent) and Ernakulam (73.83 per cent). In all these districts, Christians have a sizeable population in both the rural and urban segments of population. Gumla in the Chhotanagpur region of Bihar, North and South Goa districts and Kanyakumari also fall in the same category. On the periphery of these pockets of high concentration in Kerala and Tamil Nadu, the Christian population thins out although their share remains between 10 and 20 per cent.

The proportion of Christians in population remains above 50 per cent in as many as 20 districts situated mostly in the north-eastern states of Manipur, Meghalaya, Mizoram and Nagaland. However, while their share in population is high—in some districts above 90 per cent—their numerical strength is evidently low. In Mizoram, for example, their share in the total population is 83.8 per cent, followed by Nagaland with 80.2 per cent of its population consisting of Christians. The Christian proportion also remains high in Meghalaya and Manipur. Goa has a sizeable Christian population with at least one-third of its population being Christian. Outside these pockets of high concentration, one notices small Christian population in a number of districts in Uttar Pradesh and Punjab. Gurdaspur in Punjab is a notable example (Table 7.6; Fig. 7.3; *see* also Appendix VII.3).

Table 7.6 : Frequency Distribution of Districts according to the percentage of Christians in Total Population, 1991

Percentage Category	*Number of Districts*
Above 90	11
80-90	3
50-80	6
20-50	13
10-20	10
5-10	27
2-5	46
1-2	31
Below 1	296

Source: Based on Census of India, 1991, Table C-9, *Religion*.
Note: Table prepared by the author.

The Muslims

Like the Christians, Muslims are an important web in the social fabric of India. While India is the original home of Hinduism which constitutes the system of beliefs and rituals for the great majority of our people, Indian ethos has liberally accommodated Islamic elements of religion, philosophy and culture, which penetrated the subcontinent at different points of time in history. There is evidence to show that this give-and-take continued for centuries, and contributed to the distinguishing traits of India's composite culture.

The Muslims of India are integrated with other sections of the Indian population—Hindus, Buddhists, Sikhs and Christians—at different levels of regional hierarchy.

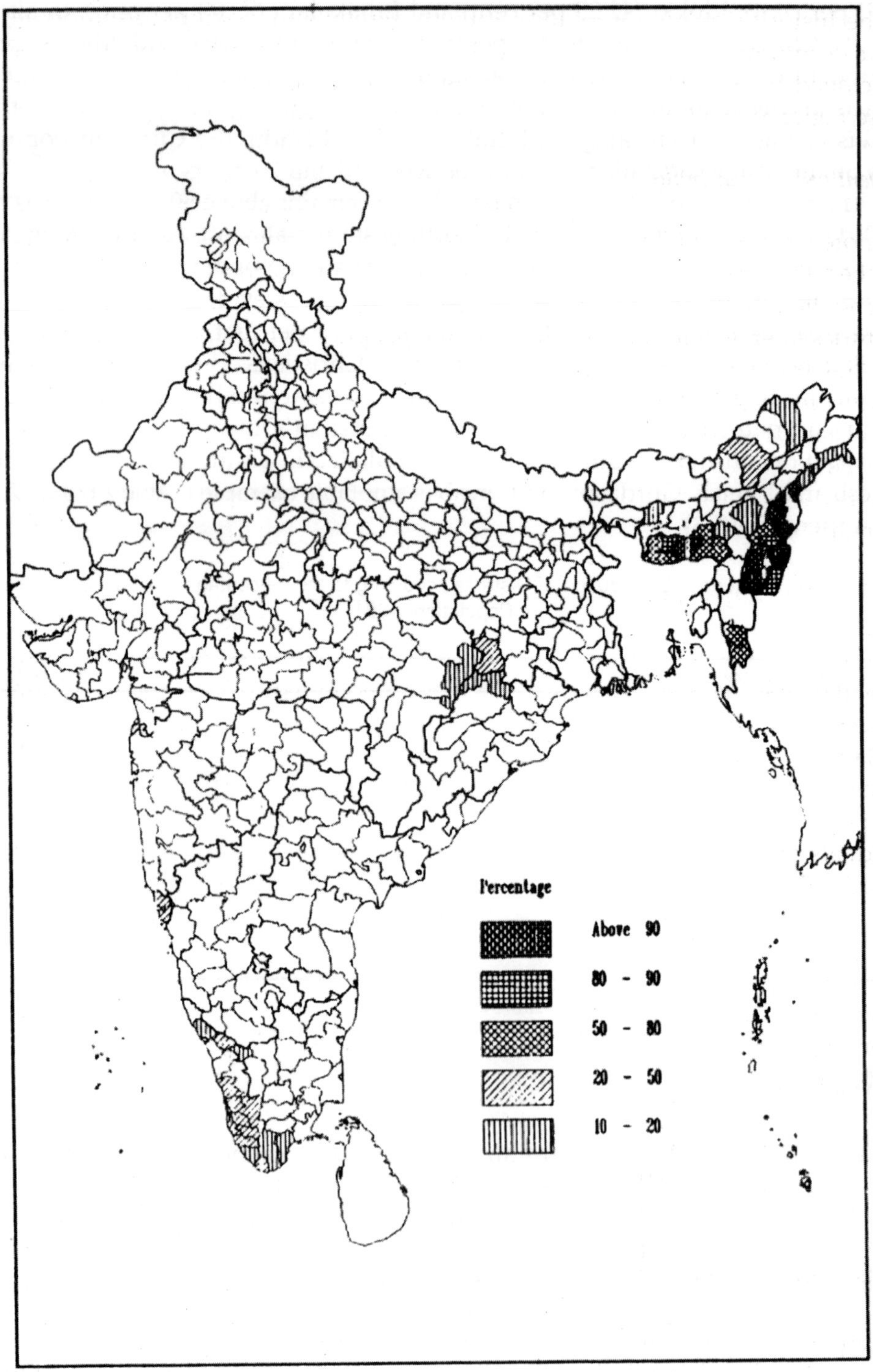

Figure 7.3 : India: The Christian Population, 1991

Responding to distinctly different environmental conditions, assimilating diverse ideas in the historical process of cultural intermingling and reaching disparate levels of socio-economic development, Muslims of India, like other communities, have developed their cultural traits under distinct regional moulds. It is in the context of these regional facets that the basic parameters of their identity can be defined.

Advent of Islam in India

As noted earlier, Indian ethos has accommodated elements of other faiths which reached the Indian subcontinent at different points of time in history. The earliest among these faiths to make an impact on the Indian people was Christianity.[6] Several centuries later, Islam was introduced to the people living on the west coast of India by the Arab traders and this happened much before the Arab conquest of Sind. The origins of Muslim society in India may be traced in the chequered history of India's contact with Islam. The following major phases may be identified:

First, Arab trading settlements which already existed on the west coast of India emerged as centres of dissemination of information about the Muslim faith, a few years after the Prophet's proclamation of his mission in the seventh century A.C. Secondly, Arab sea-farers who had trade contacts with the people in the coastal regions of Gujarat and Baluchistan, either single-handedly or in cooperation with Persians, also became carriers of the message of Islam by around the same time. Thirdly, Arab conquest of Sind in the early years of the eighth century set the stage for the political ascendancy of Islam in the lands lying to the west of Indus. The process culminated in the establishment of Delhi Sultanate in 1192. Fourthly, northern and central parts of India from Kabul to Bengal and from Kashmir to Tapti (now Tapi) were annexed by successive empires under the Tughlaqs, Khiljis, Lodhis and the Mughals. Fifthly, while the powerful Mughal Empire crumbled after the death of the last emperor in 1707, residuals of the Mughal dynastic rule survived in many parts of India, particularly Awadh, Bihar, Bengal and central India. Sixthly, many of these centres of local power were recognised as princely states by the British who helped them survive as islands of Muslim feudal order till independence in 1947. Lastly, while the political fortunes of the ruling elites—Turks, Afghans, Mughals—fluctuated, Sufis established their *silsilahs* in different parts of India as a parallel development. This continued as a phenomenon throughout the medieval period. The Sufi *khanqahs* often became centres of dissent against the despotic Muslim rulers. The Sufi message of love, compassion, peace and universal brotherhood appealed to the masses cutting across the barriers of religion, caste and creed. This paved the way for a better understanding of the Islamic faith, eventually leading to conversion to Islam.

Keeping in view the nature of influences exercised from different directions at different points of time as outlined above, it is possible to identify the following ethnic roots of the Muslim community of India:

(a) Malabar and adjoining parts of the Deccan, such as the dominions of the erstwhile Nawab of Hyderabad, were exposed to the Arab ethnic influences;

(b) Hyderabad became a centre of intermingling of Telugu culture with the North Indian culture. The latter had already found a base in the Deccan environment;
(c) Gujarat, Makran sea-coast and parts of coastal Maharashtra came under the influence of Arabs as well as Persians;
(d) Sind, Punjab and other parts of northern India received layers after layers of Arab, Afghan, Turkman (Turkic), Uzbek and Persian influences leaving behind their traces in the ethnic composition of the Muslim community living in northern, northwestern and central parts of India; and
(e) These exogenetic influences imply only the nature of initial contacts. The factual position is that the Muslim masses were largely derived from the local ethnic groups, both Hindu and Buddhist, and carried with them across the religious boundaries their distinctive ethnic and cultural characteristics even after conversion. This largely explains the ethnic and cultural diversity of the contemporary Muslim society not only in India but also in the neighbouring countries of Pakistan and Bangladesh. Their social structure appears to be the end-product of this long process of miscegenation.

It is generally known that trade relations between the Arabs and the Indians existed much before historical records were maintained.[7] Much before the advent of Islam in Arabia, Arabs had settlements on the west coast of India. Obviously Islam was introduced to the coastal region of South India within a few years of its rise in Arabia. Most probably the trading settlements started disseminating information about the Islamic faith.[8] Inter-marriages between Arabs and the local people resulted in the emergence of the well-known Muslim community of Malabar, called the *Moplahs*.[9] These stray references apart, there is no record of any systematic Muslim missionary effort in South India in the early centuries of Islam. Evidently, South India was introduced to Islam much earlier than North India. So far as North India is concerned, the Arab conquest of Sind by the young Muslim general, Mohammed Bin Qasim, in 711 A.C., was an isolated affair and affected only the situation in the trans-Indus region. Northern India, however, felt shock waves of Turk and Afghan invasions, finally resulting in the establishment of the Sultanate in Delhi in 1192. From 1192 to 1707 different dynasties ruled over India, particularly over the northern region of the country from Kabul to Bengal and from Kashmir to Khandesh.

It may be recalled that the role of the Sufis in the spread of Islam was far more important than the role of the state. Arab chronicles speak of Multan and Uch as centres of missionary activity in the early years of Arab conquest of Sind. Lahore became another centre of Sufi activity by the beginning of the tenth century A.C. A sufi saint Sheikh Ismail who came to Lahore in the wake of invasions of Mahmud of Ghazni established himself as a successful missionary much before a Muslim governor was appointed by Mahmud of Ghazni.[10] It appears that Gujarat also came under the influence of Arabs and Persians at around the same time as South India. It was mainly because the region had a tradition of maritime trade with the Persians and the Arabs. The role of sufis became obvious in the propagation of Islam with Khwaja Moinuddin

Chishti coming to Ajmer while the city was the seat of Hindu power. As founder of the Chishtiyah *silsilah* of sufis, he played an important role as a missionary.[11]

Numerical Strength

With a total population of 101.6 million, Muslims constitute a little over 12 per cent of the country's population. This figure, however, excludes the Muslims of Jammu and Kashmir where due to operational difficulties, the 1991 census count was not made. At the earlier census of 1981, the total Muslim population was 75.5 million. At the 1981 census, Assam was excluded from census operations for the same reason. The two figures are, therefore, not comparable. The data can be made comparable only by excluding the two states of Jammu and Kashmir and Assam from this analysis. After this adjustment, the size of the Muslim population comes to 71.4 million in 1981 and 95.2 million in 1991. The Muslim population, thus, registered a net increase of 23.8 million during the 1981-91 decade, recording a decadal growth rate of 32.7 per cent or an average annual exponential growth rate of 2.83. This was by far the highest growth rate registered by any religious community during the decade. Such a high growth rate of the Muslim population was found to be alarming by many and naturally it evoked wide ranging reactions from different sections of the Indian society.

About one-fourth of the 101.6 million Muslims enumerated at the 1991 census were found in Uttar Pradesh, about one-sixth in West Bengal and about one-eighth in Bihar. The three states together shared amongst themselves more than one-half of the total Muslim population. If Assam is added to this list, the four states together make up for three-fifths of the national total. This high concentration of Muslims is in conformity with the general pattern of population density in the country. It is also in conformity with the historical processes which contributed to the spread of Islam in this country. The Muslim population is also sizeable in the states of Maharashtra, Andhra Pradesh, Karnataka and Kerala. These four states together share one-fourth of the country's Muslim population. Thus, more than 84 per cent of the Muslim population is concentrated in the eight states of the Indian Union. These patterns of distribution indicate that there are two major clusters: (i) North-Indian cluster, encompassing Uttar Pradesh, Bihar, West Bengal and Assam; and (ii) South-Indian cluster, consisting of Andhra Pradesh, Karnataka and Kerala. Maharashtra appears to be transitional to the southern cluster (Appendix VII.4).

Spatial Distribution

The distribution of Muslim population in India today is the result of a process extending over almost a millennium. While it is not intended here to analyse this process in depth, it is necessary to indicate the factors, which have played a role in determining the current distribution patterns.[12] These factors are enumerated below:

(i) The place of origin of Muslims outside the subcontinent and the routes taken by them—both land and sea—have greatly influenced the density of Muslim population as witnessed in India today. It is evident that the farther we go from the entry points and the routes of migration, the proportion of the Muslims in the total population decreases. This broadly explains the thinning out of the Muslim population as one moves from west to east or north to south in the undivided India. The concentration of Muslims in regions, such as Bengal, may, however, be explained by relating it to the process of mass conversion rather than to the routes of migration;

(ii) The existing distribution pattern is also the result of the process of mass conversions from Buddhism and Hinduism to Islam that took place on the eastern and northern peripheries of the subcontinent in Kashmir and Bengal. A part of Bengal in which the Muslims were in majority was later separated from India to constitute an eastern wing of Pakistan in 1947. After the war of liberation in 1971, the territory was renamed as Bangladesh. Another pocket of Muslim dominance lies in Kashmir. The origins of Muslim society in Kashmir may also be related to the process of mass conversion facilitated by the Sufi *silsilahs;*

(iii) The centres of political authority in the principalities, states and kingdoms, where political power was in the hands of the ruling Muslim elites acted as centres of attraction for the Muslim masses in the surrounding regions. As a consequence, a peculiar pattern of concentration of Muslim population emerged. Best examples of this phenomenon may be seen in the erstwhile princely States of Hyderabad, Bhopal, Tonk, Junagadh and Rampur.

(iv) The agglomeration of Muslims in urban centres, it appears, has been greatly influenced by the migration of Muslim artisans from villages and small towns to large industrial centres. This happened particularly in industries which were connected with traditional Muslim crafts. Today a large concentration of Muslim population is seen in the metropolitan areas of Calcutta, Mumbai (formerly Bombay), Ahmedabad, Kanpur and so on. In each of these centres, Muslim artisans and industrial workers are generally attached to certain industries, such as textiles and leather goods;

(v) One can also identify a process of spillover of the Muslim masses from the rural areas with a pressure on agricultural land to pioneer fringes in their neighbourhood. This led to the redistribution of rural population. This may be illustrated by citing the example of East Bengal from where a spillover of Muslim population to the neighbouring districts of Assam continued throughout the early part of the nineteenth century.

(vi) The mass exodus of Muslims from India in the wake of partition of the country in 1947 greatly modified the demographic picture as it had evolved through centuries. Muslim exodus from northern India was counter-balanced by an influx of Hindus and Sikhs from the newly-created territory of Pakistan.

(vii) The demographic picture has been further modified since partition. This redistribution of population caused either by the developmental processes, or communal disharmony, is changing gradually the religious composition of population in many large cities of India. This has often led to the formation of Muslim enclaves within the major cities, such as Kanpur, Ahmadabad, Moradabad, Firozabad and Aligarh.

The distribution of Muslim population in India today reveals strong tendencies of clustering and concentration in certain parts of the country, such as Jammu and Kashmir, Uttar Pradesh, Bihar, West Bengal, Haryana, Rajasthan and Kerala. The following pockets of Muslim concentration may be identified:

(a) Parts of Jammu and Kashmir, such as the Upper Jhelum Valley, the Upper Chenab Valley (*e.g.*, Kishtwar) and the adjoining areas: In these pockets, Muslims constitute more than 90 per cent of the population. Outside the Valley of Kashmir, there is a general thinning out of Muslim population. However, Muslims constitute two-thirds of the population of Doda and Punch and a little over one-third of the population of Ladakh and Udhampur. In Jammu and Kathua, the Muslim proportion sharply declines, although it remains around 10 per cent; and

(b) Delhi-Mewat and the Ganga Valley: In this cluster the Muslim proportion remains significant all over the region from the National Capital Territory of Delhi to Murshidabad and Maldah districts of West Bengal. The following patterns of the second order may be noted:

   (i) Murshidabad and Maldah with the Muslim proportions ranging between 46 and 56 per cent;

   (ii) The Muslim proportions are quite significant in Rampur (Uttar Pradesh), West Dinajpur (West Bengal), Purnia (Bihar), Moradabad and Bijnor (Uttar Pradesh); and

   (iii) These districts of high agglomeration are skirted by districts in which the Muslim proportion generally remains between one-third and one-fifth. The districts in this category include Saharanpur, Bareilly, Muzaffarnagar, Bahraich, Pilibhit, Meerut and Gonda (Uttar Pradesh), Birbhum, Nadia and Twenty-Four Parganas (West Bengal).

(c) Brahmaputra and the Barak Valleys of Assam, particularly Goalpara, Nowgaon, Kamrup and Darrang districts of Assam where the Muslim proportion ranges between 20 and 40 per cent;

(d) Dry regions of Rajasthan and Gujarat, particularly the bordering districts of Jaisalmer, Barmer and Kachch with Muslim proportion ranging between 10 and 20 per cent;

(e) The peninsular interior including Malwa, Khandesh, Marathwara and other parts of the old princely states of Hyderabad and Mysore: While the Muslims account for one-fourth of the population of Hyderabad, in other districts of the peninsular interior, their proportion ranges between 10 and 25 per cent. Districts, such as Ujjain, Indore, East Nimar, Sehore (Madhya Pradesh), Aurangabad, Parbhani, Nanded, Osmanabad and Akola (Maharashtra), Bellary, Bijapur, Dharwar, Gulbarga, Bidar and Raichur (Karnataka), Cuddapah, Anantapur, Kurnool, Medak and Nizamabad (Andhra Pradesh) may be cited as examples; and

(f) Malabar, particularly the coastal districts of Kerala, such as Kozhikode, Cannanore and Palghat, Ernakulam, Trichur, Quilon and Trivandrum (Kerala).

Evidently, the pockets of Muslim concentration conform to the geographic patterns in the density of general population in India (Box 7.4).

Box 7.4 : Density of Muslim Population

Even more interesting is the correspondence between the zones of high Muslim concentration and the high population density regions of the country. Muslims have the highest numerical strength in the high density zones of West Bengal, in the adjoining districts of Bihar and in Kerala—24-Parganas, Murshidabad, Purnia and Kozhikode holding the four leading positions. The fertile, alluvial plains of the Ganga and the Brahmaputra Valley and the Malabar Coast, being the most densely peopled parts of the country, also have the highest Muslim concentrations. However, if the Muslims are conspicuous by their absence in some areas of high density, such as the Punjab plains, the explanation lies in the distorting effects of the political processes, which were generated in the recent past. In consonance with the general distributional pattern, the density of Muslim population also declines towards the arid/semi-arid west, the Malwa/Central Indian uplands, the peninsular interior and the Ghats.

—Moonis Raza, Aijazuddin Ahmad and Nafis Ahmad Siddiqui in Zafar Imam (ed.), *Muslims in India*, 1975: 119.

The district-level patterns lead to several conclusions. First, the concentration of Muslims in the Kashmir Valley is significant in several ways. In the valley districts, Muslim proportion generally remains above 90 per cent. Similarly, in the districts surrounding these pockets of high concentration, Muslims remain significant in terms of their numerical strength. To the east of the Kashmir valley lies Doda district where the Muslim proportion is quite high. Secondly, Muslims are also predominant in a large number of districts in the North Indian plain from Uttar Pradesh to West Bengal, where their proportion ranges between 20 and 60 per cent. Included in this category are the districts of Murshidabad (61.4 per cent), Rampur (47.95 per cent), Moradabad (42.7 per cent), Bijnor (40.35 per cent), Bareilly (32.79 per cent), Pilibhit (23.12 per cent), Saharanpur (36.12 per cent), Muzaffarnagar (34.52 per cent), Meerut (27.49 per cent) and Ghaziabad (21.16 per cent). Thirdly, the share of Muslims in the district population is fairly significant in several other regions, such as Haryana (Gurgaon), Rajasthan, Gujarat, Madhya Pradesh, Andhra Pradesh and Kerala.

While Muslims are a phenomenon in themselves in several parts of India, there are hundreds of other districts in which they are not so numerous. They have been living for ages as an inseparable part of the rural and urban milieu and bound together by age-old ties in economy, artisan industry, arts, crafts, folk cultures and social customs (Table 7.7; Figs. 7.4-7.7; Appendix VII.5 and VII.6).

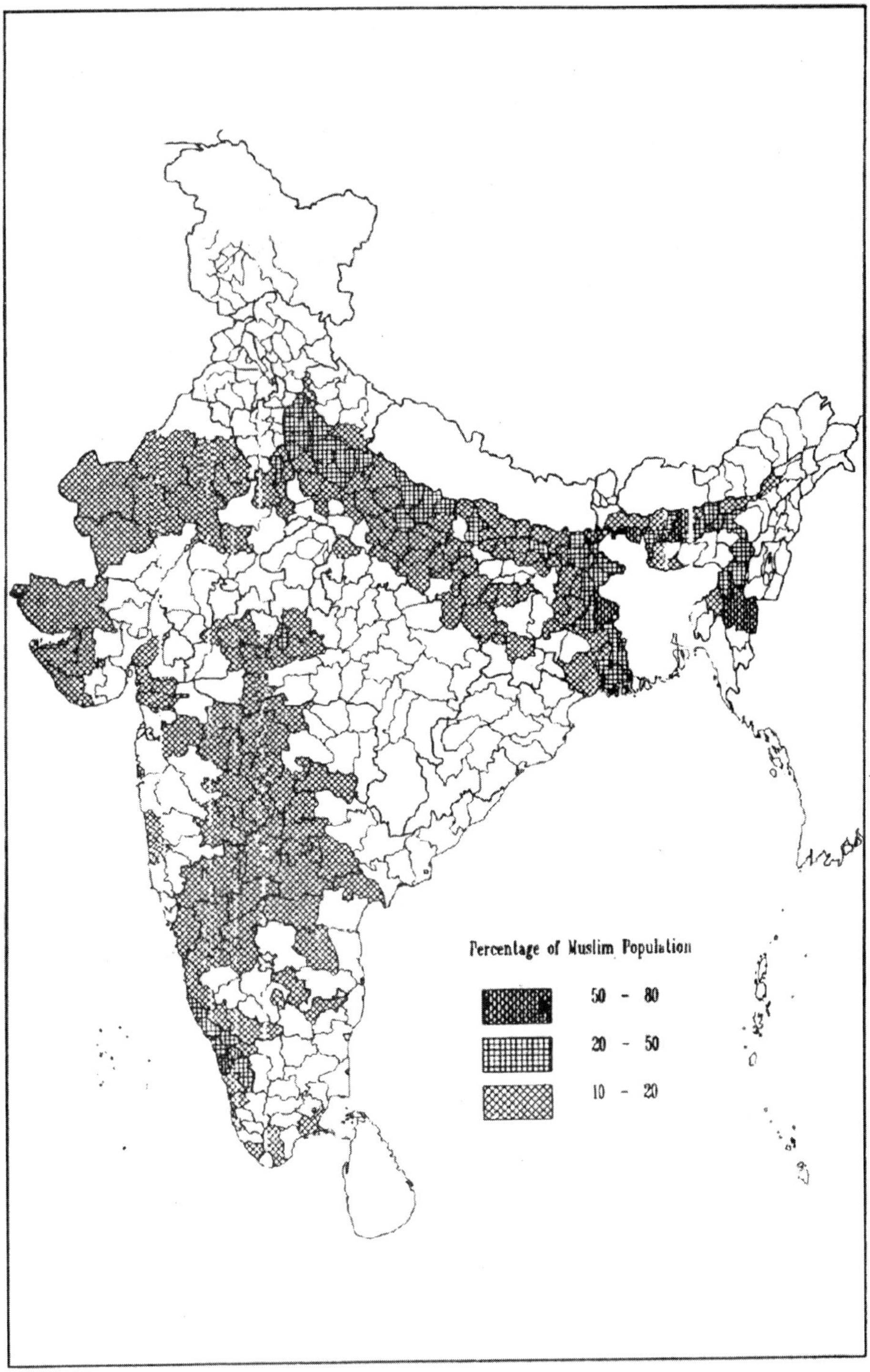

Figure 7.4 : India: Muslim Population, 1991

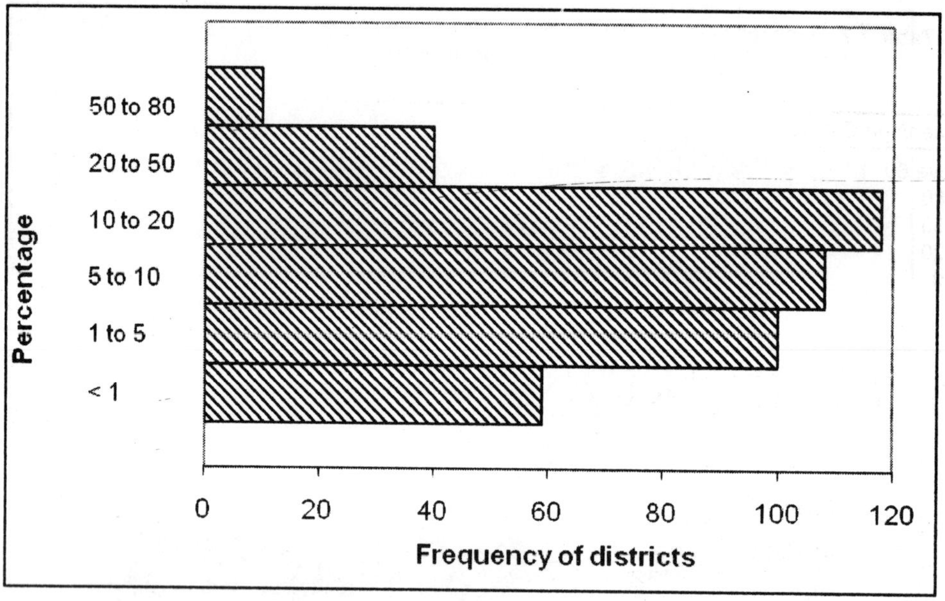

Figure 7.5 : Frequency Distribution of Districts according to the percentage of Muslims in the Total Population of the District

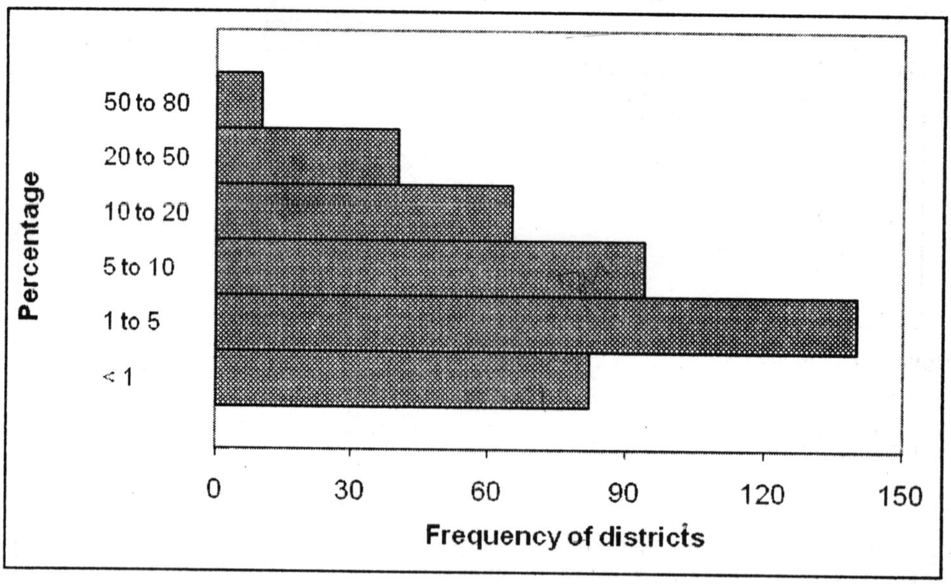

Figure 7.6: Frequency Distribution of Districts according to the percentage of Muslims in the Rural Population of the District

Table 7.7 : Frequency Distribution of Districts according to the percentage of Muslims in Total Population, 1991*

Percentage Categories	*Number of Districts*
Above 80	Nil
50-80	10
20-50	43
10-20	117
5-10	108
1-5	100
Below 1	59

Source: Based on Census of India, 1991, Table C-9, *Religion.*
Note: * Excludes Jammu and Kashmir.

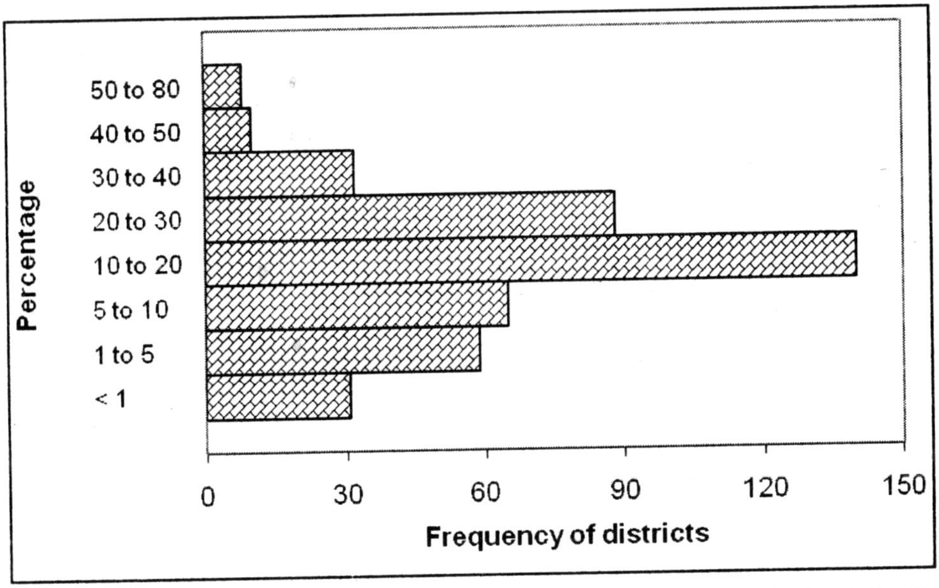

Figure 7.7 : Frequency Distribution of Districts according to the percentage of Muslims in the Urban Population of the District

Muslims in the Urban Social Space

The above description is restricted to the proportion of Muslims in the overall population. While Muslims are generally a phenomenon in the rural areas, there are certain districts in the north, northwest and the interior of the peninsula where they constitute a substantive proportion of urban population. Their degree of urbanisation is much higher in these regions. In a nutshell, there were more than 36 million Muslims living in the cities and towns of different sizes at the 1991 census: the urban percentage being as high as 35 as against the national average of 26. At the national level, Muslims constitute about 16 per cent of the urban population of the country. The degree of urbanisation among the Muslims is obviously high. There are several reasons for this high level of urbanisation. These reasons are historical as well as those related to the partition of the country. The traditional association of Muslims with certain branches of industry, including artisan industry, also led to their agglomeration in selected cities and towns. In the course of time, the capital cities of princely states, some of whom were residuals of Mughal power (*e.g.*, Shahjahanabad, Lucknow, Agra, Murshidabad, Bhopal, Hyderabad, Aurangabad, Junagadh and Rampur) acquired a typical Muslim character. Many of these cities are still prominent as centres of Muslim culture. Because of their traditional association with certain arts and crafts, Muslims were attracted to many other cities, such as Varanasi, which has a predominantly Hindu character.

There are several clusters in which the Muslims are an important component in the urban population. First, the dominance of Muslims in the valley of Kashmir and in Kishtwar and Punch may be noted. It has resulted in their agglomeration in urban areas as well. In all the districts of Kashmir valley as well as in Ladakh, Kathua and Doda districts, Muslims constitute an overwhelming proportion of urban population. Secondly, in western Uttar Pradesh there are several cities and towns (*e.g.*, Amroha, Sambhal and Rampur) in Rampur and Moradabad districts of Uttar Pradesh where the Muslim proportion is around 70 per cent. The Muslim proportion is also very high in Malegaon in Maharashtra (67.4 per cent) and the Garden Reach area of Twenty-Four Parganas district in West Bengal. Thirdly, Muslim percentages remain significantly high (40-55 per cent) in several towns and cities of Cuddapah, East Nimar, Thane, Sikar, Meerut, Moradabad and Shahjahanpur districts. Reference may be made to places, such as Bhiwandi, Burhanpur, Cuddapah and Sikar, where 40-55 per cent of the population is Muslim. Lastly, from one-fifth to two-fifths of the urban population consists of Muslims in as many as 83 towns/cities spread over the states of Uttar Pradesh, Bihar, West Bengal, Madhya Pradesh, Gujarat, Maharashtra, Andhra Pradesh, Karnataka, Tamil Nadu and Kerala. Notable among the urban centres in this category are Hyderabad, Nizamabad, Aurangabad, Purnea, Bhagalpur, Gulbarga, Raichur, Bijapur, Bellary, Hospet, Cannanore, Calicut, Nanded, Bharuch, Saharanpur, Muzaffarnagar, Meerut, Bulandshahr, Aligarh, Firozabad, Etawah, Bareilly, Jaunpur and Bhagalpur. Muslims have a traditional association with these cities and are intrinsically linked to the social and economic life of these urban places. The Muslim population is also sizeable in many other cities and towns of India (Appendix VII.7).

Cultural Topography

As in other regions of the world, the Muslim population of India is divided into two sects, *viz.*, *Shia* and *Sunni*. The *Sunnis* are, however, in majority. In fact, the *Shia* population may not be constituting more than 10 per cent of the Muslim population. Moreover, the *Shias* are mostly concentrated in a few pockets, such as Lucknow, Amroha, Allahabad, Kashmiri Gate area of Delhi, Rampur, and Hyderabad and in the Kargil district of Jammu and Kashmir. But they are also found, although in small numbers, in almost every town and city of India. In such situations they generally prefer to live in a cluster. They are generally a well-knit community and their social and cultural activities are intrinsically linked to an *Imambarah*, which acts as the religio-cultural hub of the community. In areas of their sizeable population, they generally have separate mosques. Elsewhere, they offer prayers in the common mosques. They, however, follow a separate schedule of time for offering daily prayers. The *Shias* follow a separate theological tradition. In fact, there are striking differences between the *Sunnis* and the *Shias* insofar as the interpretation of certain aspects of the Islamic law is concerned. They are the followers of a lineage of *Imams* and *Mujtahids* descending down from Hazrat Ali and his two sons, Imam Hassan and Imam Husain. These practices put them in a separate category both in terms of the interpretation of *Shariat* and the Quranic law as well as the Islamic customs.

The *Sunnis*, who constitute an overwhelming majority of the Muslim population of India, follow several schools of theological thought, notable among them being *Hanafi, Hambali, Shaafai* and *Maliki*. The *Hanafis* are, however, predominant. There are shades of differences among these schools in the interpretation of Islamic law as well as in Islamic practices. The founders of these schools—Imam Abu Hanifa, Imam Hanbal, Imam Shaafay and Imam Malik—held divergent views on many issues basic to Islamic theology. The interpretation of Islamic law (*Shariat*) has given rise to several traditions of Islamic jurisprudence. Another peculiarity of Indian Islam is the rise of the two indigenous schools of theological thought, which emerged at Deoband (in Saharanpur district of Uttar Pradesh) and at Bareilly. These schools wield great influence on the Muslim masses who have been virtually divided into the Deobandis and the Barelwis. The *Dar-ul-Uloom* at Deoband, an internationally known Institution of Islamic learning, often issues *fatwas* (religious decrees) on religious, legalistic, social, cultural, and even political matters of general public concern. The divergent views held by these schools have created a wedge within the *Sunni* community. The Barelwi School which is more liberal admits Sufi tradition as the necessary ingredient of Islamic faith. The Deobandi School, on the other hand, is highly critical of any form of *mazar* worship.

Several groups, such as the Ismailis (followers of the Agha Khan), Bohras and Khojas, mainly found in the states of Gujarat and Maharashtra, are a category in themselves. The leaders of these religious sects, who wield great power, determine the course of life of their followers. Their say is supreme even in secular matters.

Pilgrimage Centres

The *dargahs* of the sufis have emerged as places of pilgrimage par excellence. While there are several sufi *silsilahs* in India, such as Chishtiya, Suharwardiya or Naqshbandiya, this description is restricted to the *dargahs* of the Chishtiya *silsilah* only. These *dargahs* have a hierarchy determined by their local, regional or national significance. Ajmer is at the apex of this hierarchy because the founder of the *silsilah* Khwaja Moinuddin Chishti, is buried there. His *urs* (ceremonies related to the death anniversary) is of great national and international importance. Pilgrims assemble at his tomb for the annual *urs* ceremonies. In some years, the congregation may be as large as 5 lakh persons or even more. The pilgrims, however, continue to pour in throughout the year. They come from all over the country as well as the neighbouring countries of Bangladesh, Pakistan, Maldives and Mauritius. The British Governor-General, Lord Curzon once remarked, 'there is a grave at Ajmer which rules over Asia'. In hierarchical order, Ajmer is followed by the *dargah* of Bakhtiyar Kaki at Mehrauli in Delhi. The *dargah* of Sheikh Nizamuddin Awliya in Delhi is the next in hierarchy which is followed by the *dargah* of Amir Khusrau also in Delhi. These *dargahs* have an all-India importance. Then there are other *dargahs* which have regional importance. Notable among them are those at Gulbarga (Karnataka), Kaliar Sharif (Uttar Pradesh), Kachhauchha Sharif (Uttar Pradesh), Nagaur (Rajasthan), Behsauri Sharif (Uttar Pradesh), Gorakhpur (Uttar Pradesh) and Charar-e-Sharif (Jammu and Kashmir).

It is interesting to note that while the Muslim *ulemas*, particularly of the Deoband School, have been opposed to the sufi practices, the Muslim masses are deeply involved in these practices. The *Urs* ceremonies continue to be a distinguished feature of popular Islam. This is despite the fact that the *ulemas* consider the *Urs* ceremonies as a heresy. This is one example where *ulemas'* advice is not heeded to by the Muslim masses. However, in many other matters, such as interpretation of marriage, and divorce laws and the laws of inheritence, the *ulema* continue to hold their sway. They are recognised as interpreters of the *Shariat*.

The Sikhs

The Sikhs originated in the Punjab, but they are found in all parts of India. They may be seen even in the far-off regions of the country, carrying with them the vital elements of the Punjabi culture. The contribution of the Sikhs to the Indian economy, particularly agriculture, transport and industry is far more impressive than their numerical strength. They are an important component in armed forces and in the services sector.

Rise of Sikhism

Sikhism developed as a result of the teachings of Guru Nanak (1469-1539) who was a great believer in the unity of God and the universal brotherhood of humankind. He was a great reformer and had insights into the essential philosophy of both Hinduism and Islam. In its original form, Sikhism emerged as a religious reform movement and attracted the attention of masses. Initially, the Sikh converts came mostly from among the ranks of the Hindu agricultural castes, particularly the Jats.[13] The initial concepts of the Sikh faith were developed as a result of the interpretation of the teachings of Guru Nanak and a line of Gurus who succeeded him. A Sikh believes in the teachings of the ten Gurus and the *Guru Granth Sahib*, the holy book. Some of the salient features of Sikh faith are belief in one God (monotheism), rejection of idolatory and of discrimination based on caste and social hierarchy. The Sikhs also insist on the futility of ritual and form. The Gurudwara occupies the central place in the Sikh cultural and religious practice. With the passage of time, Sikhism acquired a new form under Guru Govind Singh (1675-1708) who insisted on separate Sikh identity and prescribed for the Sikhs five marks of distinction.[14] These were supposed to be necessary elements of difference from the other communities. In the face of the political threats from the contemporary rulers, it became necessary to give Sikhs a distinctive individuality of their own. Guru Govind Singh thus laid down the foundation of the *Khalsa Panth* on the *Baisakhi* day in 1699.[15] The *Guru Granth Sahib,* the holy book of the Sikhs, contains a summary of the teachings of the early Sikh Gurus as well as the teachings of other saints who popularised the idea of unity of human kind and love for all.

Numerical Strength

The last census, conducted in 1991, enumerated 16.26 million Sikhs in the country. Of this 12.76 million or 78.5 per cent were found living in the state of Punjab alone, thus indicating the traditional association of the Sikhs with the land of the five rivers. Besides Punjab, the neighbouring state of Haryana accommodates about 6 per cent of the total population of the Sikhs. This segment of the Sikh population owes its origin to the process of spill-over from the densely populated parts of the Punjab to the relatively open tracts of land in the newly created state of Haryana. Thus, the concentration of Sikhs in the States of Punjab and Haryana (both parts of the undivided Punjab) should be seen in the context of Sikh history. Sikhism originated in Punjab and the Sikhs remained confined to this region. However, the partition created conditions for almost a complete exodus of Sikhs from west Punjab and their resettlement in the irrigated agricultural lands on this side of the border. The redistribution of Sikh population in the wake of partition introduced Sikh elements in the neighbouring Haryana and Rajasthan where the irrigated colonies, such as in Ganganagar and Kurukshetra districts, emerged as the new foci of Sikh resettlement. Sikhs also settled down in the *terai* region of Uttar Pradesh, transforming this once malaria-infested wetland into a granary of northern India. This transformation came due to the sturdy Sikh farmer, an alien to the region and yet tied to the soil.

The post-Partition migration of the Sikhs to the regions lying to the east of the Ravi and the Satluj rivers was a second major migration in Sikh history. The first major redistribution had taken place during the colonial period when they migrated to the new canal colonies to the north and west of Lahore. In fact, the Sikh Jats became a symbol of irrigation agriculture and perhaps the most active agent of agrarian revolution that followed the construction of canals in Punjab. During the phase of planned economic development since 1950, the Sikhs have been on the move showing a strong tendency of outmigration from Punjab to the other states of the Indian Union. They have also migrated out of the country in considerable numbers.

Today the three states of Punjab, Haryana and Rajasthan accommodate around 90 per cent of the country's Sikh population (Appendix VII.8).

Spatial Distribution

As noted above, the Sikhs are mostly found between the Ghagghar and the Ravi rivers. This concentration is, however, understandable in the context of the country's Partition in 1947 and the reorganisation of Punjab afterwards. Today the major concentration of the Sikhs is seen in nine districts of Punjab where they constitute an overwhelming proportion of population. Included in this category is Faridkot where more than 80 per cent of population consists of Sikhs. In Amritsar, Firozepur, Ludhiana, Kapurthala, Rupnagar, Patiala, Sangrur and Bhatinda, they constitute from 50 to 80 per cent of the district population. They are also an important component of population (20-50 per cent) in Jalandhar, Hoshiarpur, Gurdaspur and Sirsa. They have a sizeable population (10-20 per cent) in Ganganagar, Kurukshetra and Ambala (Table 7.8). In all the districts of high dominance the Sikhs are mostly a rural phenomenon. For example, in five districts (*viz.*, Amritsar, Ludhiana, Faridkot, Sangrur and Bhatinda) Sikhs constitute more than 80 per cent of the rural population. In the six adjoining districts (Table 7.9) they account for 50-80 per cent of the rural population. This reveals the traditional dependence of the Sikhs on agriculture and allied activities. However, a section of the community is also engaged in trade and commerce activities based largely in urban centres. The Sikhs constitute around 40-50 per cent of urban population in Amritsar, Faridkot, Rupnagar, Patiala and Bhatinda (Table 7.10). From one-fifth to two-fifths of the urban population is comprised by Sikhs in the remaining districts of Punjab. Moreover, their presence is significant in major Haryana towns, particularly in Ambala, Sirsa and Yamunanagar districts.

Table 7.8 : Frequency Distribution of Districts according to the percentage of Sikhs in Total Population, 1991

Percentage Categories	*No. of Districts*	*Names of Districts*
Above 80	1	Faridkot
50-80	8	Amritsar, Firozepur, Ludhiana, Kapurthala, Rupnagar, Patiala, Sangrur, Bhatinda
20-50	4	Jalandhar, Hoshiarpur, Gurdaspur, Sirsa
10-20	3	Ganganagar, Kurukshetra, Ambala

Source: Based on Census of India, 1991, Table C-9, *Religion.*
Note: Table prepared by the author.

Table 7.9 : Frequency Distribution of Districts according to the percentage of Sikhs in Rural Population, 1991

Percentage Categories	*No. of Districts*	*Names of Districts*
Above 80	5	Amritsar, Ludhiana, Faridkot, Sangrur, Bhatinda
50-80	6	Gurdaspur, Firozepur, Jalandhar, Kapurthala, Rupnagar, Patiala
20-50	3	Kurukshetra, Sirsa, Ganganagar
10-20	2	Ambala, Kaithal

Source: Based on Census of India, 1991, Table C-9, *Religion.*
Note: Table prepared by the author.

Table 7.10 : Frequency Distribution of Districts according to the percentage of Sikhs in Urban Population, 1991

Percentage Categories	*No. of Districts*	*Names of Districts*
Above 40	5	Amritsar, Faridkot, Rupnagar, Patiala, Bhatinda
20-40	7	Sangrur, Kapurthala, Ludhiana, Hoshiarpur, Jalandhar, Firozepur, Gurdaspur
10-20	3	Ambala, Sirsa, Yamunanagar
5-10	2	Kurukshetra, Ganganagar

Source: Based on Census of India, 1991, Table C-9, *Religion*.
Note: Table prepared by the author.

Cultural Topography

As stated earlier, the Gurudwara is the religio-cultural hub of the community. Sikhs visit the Gurudwaras as a matter of routine and particularly on occasions, which are important in the life of an individual, or the community as a whole. One such occasion is the *Baisakhi* day, which marks the birth of the Khalsa Panth and the two Gur Purbs (birthdays of Guru Nanak and Guru Govind Singh) as well as the occasion of the martyrdom of Guru Arjan Dev and Guru Tegh Bahadur. On such occasions, the *Guru Granth Sahib* is taken in procession through the streets. Sikhs also celebrate Holi and Diwali. Some of these celebrations are held inside the Gurudwaras.

There are several Gurudwaras, which have an all-India importance. Harmandir Sahib at Amritsar is the foremost among them. Other important Gurudwaras are at Patna Sahib, Nanded Sahib, Anandpur Sahib and Damdama Sahib. These Gurudwaras attract large crowds on special occasions.

The Sikh community consists of several sects, such as the Nihangs, Namdharis and Udasis. However, over the last three centuries several sects emerged and gradually lost their importance. Reference may be made to Nirankaris, Nanak Panthis, Niranjanis, Sutra-Shahis, Sanwal-Shahis, Dhirmalids, Sevapanthis, Sat-Kartaris, Nirmalas, as so on. The Nihangs are easily distinguished by their dark blue dress. The Namdharis or Kukas are distinguished by their headgear and white dress. Udasis who are ascetics are themselves divided into four orders.

The rise of the Akalis is a recent phenomenon and may be traced to the early part of the twentieth century. It was as a result of the Akali efforts that the Gurudwara Act of 1925 was passed. The affairs of the Gurudwaras are now controlled by the Shiromani Gurudwara Prabandhak Committee, which is an all-India body.

Some Preliminary Conclusions

This study of the religious groups should be seen in the context of the regional synthesis of identities, including the religious identities in India today. The regions present an example of remarkable cultural synthesis where the people belonging to different religious faiths, castes, language groups and ethnic formations have been united together by a common cultural tradition specific to the region. It is this cultural tradition which places a distinctive stamp on their identity. Hindus, Muslims, Christians and

Sikhs have all been cast in regional moulds. It is in the personality of the region that their roots lie and of which they are an inseparable part. To visualise them simply as elements of demographic composition will be a distortion of the social reality.

The religious communities, nestled as they are in regional rubrics, are distributed in a way so as to form a peculiar pattern of combination in space. While Hindus constitute the base everywhere, there are regions which stand out strikingly as nodes of Hindu dominance—sub-Himalayan northwest, peninsular interior, particularly eastern Madhya Pradesh and Orissa. On the other extreme are the regions along the Himalayan axis in the extreme northwest and the northeast in which Hindus are outnumbered by either the Muslims, Sikhs, Christians, or the Buddhists. The facts that these regions lie on the periphery of the country lends them a spatial geo-political connotation. These regional combinations give a diversity of meaning to the patterns of inter-community relations. For example, there is a characteristic blending of the Sikhs and the Hindus in Punjab. The North Indian Plain from Delhi to Bengal presents shades of Hindu-Muslim combination. There are ways in which these spatial patterns of combinations express themselves in cultural practices and social and economic intercourse. The Brahmaputra and the Barak valleys in the northeast display a combination of Hindus, Muslims and Christians, the latter acquiring dominance in the hills surrounding the Assam valley. Hindus, Christians and Muslims again emerged in a combination in Malabar where they together constitute the Malayali cultural realm. The regional fabric of culture, tradition and social practices, have been woven by these diverse threads.

It may be noted that the Indian tradition is multi-religious and not pluralistic. It is not an accident of history that different religious groups have come together to live in a shared social space. These religious formations are, in fact, products of an evolutionary history, which has contributed to the emergence of inter-twined identities with common roots in the indigenous tradition. The impact of Hindu philosophy is indeed over-arching. Take for example, the status of priesthood and the intellectual supremacy of the priestly class (Box 7.5). Even Islam, which does not recognise the class of clergy, appears to have succumbed to the local tradition in yielding to the authority of the class of *ulema*. The religious synthesis is thus expressed not only in the regional frame but also in the philosophical content.

Box 7.5 : Intellectualism and Religion

The destiny of religions has been influenced in a most comprehensive way by intellectualism and its various relationships to the priesthood and political authorities. These relationships were in turn influenced by the provenience of the class which happened to be the most important carrier of the particular intellectualism ... the development of intellectualism by the priesthood was true to the highest degree in India, in Egypt, in Babylonia, in Zoroastrianism, in Islam, and in ancient and medieval Christianity. So far as theology is concerned the development of intellectualism by the priesthood has also taken place in modern Christianity. In the religions of Egypt, in Zoroastrianism, in some phases of ancient Christianity, and in Brahmanism during the age of Vedas (*i.e.*, before the rise of lay asceticism and the philosophy of the *Upanishads*) the priesthood succeeded in largely monopolising the development of religious metaphysics and ethics. Such a priestly monopoly was also present in Judaism and in Islam. But in Judaism it was strongly reduced by the strong impact of lay prophecy, and in Islam the very impressive power of the priesthood was limited by the challenge of Sufi speculation.

—Max Weber, *The Sociology of Religion*, 1971: 118-19.

NOTES AND REFERENCES

1. '.... the position of the early Mohammadan dynasties was too precarious to admit any general propaganda. Even in the time of the early Mughals, the emperors were too indifferent towards spiritual affairs, too much engrossed in schemes of conquest and administration, to undertake the task of conversion in earnest', *The Imperial Gazetteer of India: The Indian Empire,* Vol. I, Descriptive, p. 434.
2. *ibid,* p. 403.
3. '.... Indian Philosophic Thought developed in several stages.... The four Vedas, the Brahamanas, Arayankas and Upanishads are creations of early stages. The *Upanishads....* recognised intuition rather than reason as a path to ultimate truth. They also represent a strong reaction against the merely ritual and sacrificial duties on which stress have been laid earlier', *The Gazetteer of India, Country and People,* Vol. I, p. 419.
4. The main tenets of the Vaisnava beliefs have been stated in the *Visnu Purana.* However, Vaisnavism owed its origin to the work of Ramanuja, a Brahaman from the south. A succession of preachers, which included Ramanand, carried forward his line of thought. Kabir was a later-day disciple of the same line.
5. 'Receptivity and all-Comprehensiveness ... are the main characteristics of Hinduism. Since it has had no difficulty in bringing diverse faiths within its ever-widening fold, it has something to offer to almost all minds', M. Monier-Williams, *Brahamanism and Hinduism or Religious Thought and Life in India,* London, 1887, *cit, The Gazetteer of India,* Vol. I, *op. cit.,* p. 413.
6. O.H.K. Spate, *India and Pakistan,* 1967, pp. 161-62.
7. Saiyid Sulaiman Nadwi, 1935, *Arabon ki Jahazrani,* cit. I.H. Qureshi, *The Muslim Community of the Indo-Pakistan Subcontinent,* 1962.
8. I.H. Qureshi, p. 11.
9. *ibid,* p.14; 'their Imam known as Thangal was permitted to ride in a palanquin alongside with the ruler, the *Zamorin',* Tara Chand, p. 35.
10. Abd-ur-Rahman, *Bazm-e-Sufia,* 1949, pp. 394 - 440.
11. Khwaja Sahib passed away in 1236 A.C. His two main disciples were Khwaja Qutubuddin Bakhtiar Kaki, buried in Delhi, and Sheikh Hamiduddin of Nagaur. Khwaja Bakhtiar Kaki's disciple was Baba Farid, while Baba Farid's disciple was an enthusiast of the fame of Sheikh Nizamuddin Awliya. Another disciple of Baba Farid was Sheikh Ali Sabir, buried at Kaliar Sharif near Roorkee. These *silsilahs* of the *sufis* helped in the propagation of the universal values of Islam—equality, brotherhood, tolerance of other faiths, love of humanity and the service of human kind irrespective of differences in colour, creed, caste or custom. It is due to the services of the *sufis* that the masses were drawn towards Islam. Even those who did not embrace Islam continued to remain followers of the *sufis.* Even today the shrines of these *sufis* are visited by the people of all faiths and religions.
12. *cit.* Aijazuddin Ahmad, *Muslims in India,* Vol. 1, Bihar, pp. 14-15; also see Moonis Raza, Aijazuddin Ahmad and Nafis Ahmad Siddiqui, 'Muslims of India: Some Aspects of Regional Demography' in Zafar Imam (ed.) *Muslims in India,* New Delhi: Orient Longman, 1975, pp. 113-32.
13. G.S. Gosal and A.B. Mukerji, 'The Religious Composition of India's Population', *Tijdschrift voor Econ en Soc., Geografie,* 1970, p. 97.
14. These marks of distinction were *kes* (long hair), *kachcha* (a pair of shorts), *kara* (iron bangle), *kangha* (comb), and *khanda* or *kirpan* (sword).
15. *Khalsa* means pure. It has remained the principal Sikh order ever since its inception, *The New Encyclopaedia Britannica,* Vol. X, 1987, p. 800.

SUGGESTIONS FOR FURTHER READING

Gosal, G.S. and A.B. Mukherji (1970): 'The Religious Composition of India's Population', *Tijdschrift voor Econ en Soc., Geografie,* Vol. LXI, No. 2, pp. 91-101.

8

The Social Fabric–An Overview

Some Preliminary Conclusions

The separate chapters on tribe, caste, language and faith may give the impression that India is a sum of castes, tribes, and communities of speech and of faith. In fact, such an impression is farthest from the truth. The approach in these chapters was essentially analytical and not synthetic. It would be difficult to agree to the view that the population of the subcontinent or for that matter of India is a summation of social identities. It is not a cumulative or additive formation. It is a social fabric. The weft and the web is made up of a conglomeratic formation. Like a mosaic floor every grain is made up of a different rock and at the same time visible but is an integral part of the structure. Take for example, the caste groups like the Brahmans or the Sudras cannot be isolated from overall cultural realm in which they live. There are Bengali Brahmans, Tamil Brahmans, Kashmiri Brahmans, Pushkarnia Brahmans or the Surjupari Brahmans. This being a Brahman is an abstract expression. They are really a part of the social fabric of which the basic identity is expressed in their language, dialect and literature. Thus we notice that the caste hierarchy is meaningful only if we look at it as a part of the cultural realm in which they are living. Inter-regional and inter-ethnic comparisons would be misleading. Every realm is an expression of fusion and not fission. We have tried to develop some understanding of this blending of ethnic and linguistic traits as a collectivity as well as individuality of each individual who is recognised in the context of a distinctive culture-realm.

In this chapter an attempt has been made to place the elements of ethno-lingual structure in the context of historico-geographical framework. Let us find out the nature of the cultural realms as a collectivity in the context of the subcontinent. The Santals, for example, are a tribal group living in the eastern part of the country. They are an ethno-lingual group, a citizen of the Indian state, a Hindu or a low-caste group at the same time. Even though, they may be living away from their traditional homeland. A Santal is believed to be an ethnic group. In the post-independence period things have happened both in terms of economic functions and the spoken language. While Santali dialect is the hallmark of their identity, the development of primary education in the states in which they are living has contributed to a regular change in their linguistic affinity. The Santali language has been modified as their children are exposed to education in different regional languages: Bengali in the state of West Bengal and Oriya in the state of Orissa or the Assamese in Assam. A Santali boy or a girl learns Santali at home but he/she is exposed to the regional languages at the school. And that makes a difference. In a way the Santali population is getting subsumed in the regional languages. In many cases they become bi-lingual or multi-lingual.

The preceding chapters present aspects of the spatial organisation of Indian society in its ethnic, tribal, caste, linguistic and religious dimensions. While these elements define the parameters of socio-cultural diversity of our people, it will be wrong to assume that they express themselves in isolation. In fact, they are elements of a composite identity, inter-twined and inseparable from each other. It is also evident that the Indian social identity is not pluralistic. A Tamil, for example, is a member of a language group, which in itself is a culture world, perceived at the highest level of identity. The language binds a Tamil (or for that matter a Kannadiga, a Punjabi or a Kashmiri in similar culture realms) to a larger ethno-lingual formation. Subsumed in the Tamil language world may be other smaller worlds, such as the Yerukala or the Toda. These dialect groups living within the over-arching unity of the Tamil language have their own spheres of communication and community-based identity and social practice. These lower-level identities divide the larger Tamil identity into smaller sets. Besides, being the member of a language group a Tamil may also be a Hindu, a Muslim or a Christian. His Hindu identity is further split into caste or tribal configurations—Tamil Brahman, Tamil Visvabrahman, Arya Vaisya, Yadava or Ayyanavar, Chakkaliyan, Adi Dravida, Holeya and Pulayan or Kadar, Konaga, Malasar, Mannan and Toda. As *jatis* or *Janajatis*, each of these groups have their own social identity, defined by the caste-specific or tribe-specific religio-magical rituals, ceremonies, social practices and the communitarian modes. However, their affiliation to the Tamil language and culture is basic as it lies over and above the narrow differences based on caste and religion. These examples show the inter-twined nature of social identity, which expresses itself at different levels from the *up-jati,* to the *jati* and the *bhasha, boli* and the *dharma* formations. It is the *bhasha* which defines the outer limit of culture worlds and interaction.

The Tamil example is not unique in any way. The case is the same in all other cultural regions where the expressions of religious, ethnic or caste identities assume by and large the same form. It is thus evident that the best expression of the cultural identity is at the *bhasha,* or the ethno-lingual level, which defines the character of cultural regionalism.

The evolution of cultural regions may be seen as an on-going process. Modern means of transport and communications, democratic institutions and the national and trans-national market forces are making in-roads into these cultural realms promoting their integration with the Indian cultural ethos transcendental to the region. These processes are, however, operating at varying degrees of intensity leaving vast gaps in exposure and integration.

The origins of the socio-cultural diversity in India lie in the physico-geographical framework of the subcontinent. It is the physical framework of the Indian subcontinent which provided the base for diversity in landforms and the ecological differences based on them. At the first level of generalisation, the three physiographic divisions of India—the Himalayas, the North Indian Plain and the Peninsular Plateau—set the stage for differentiation in ecologies. Within each of these macro regions, variations exist in the physical as well as climatic characteristics which contribute to the second order differentiation in the habitat and ecology. A combination of physical factors, such as form and slope of land, soil cover and climatic factors, such as amount and intensity of rainfall, and temperature regime defining the length of the growing season, provided diversities in the natural potential. This allowed the survival and the continuity of a variety of cultures from food gathering, hunting and pastoral modes of economy to shifting and sedentary agriculture, each confined to a specific ecological niche. The long history of migration of different groups that managed to reach India from different parts of Asia at different points of time shows how different culture-groups came to India and distributed themselves in space depending on the ecological setting in conformity with their own primordial modes of economy. The alluvial plains were vastly accessible because of their open nature. The river valleys thus remained in perennial contact with the outside world through the medium of the incoming streams of people. On the periphery of these plains, the rim of hills and uplands allowed the primitive economic modes, such as food gathering and pastoralism, to survive, unaffected by the march of time. This contributed to the emergence of a cultural mosaic of great diversity. The settlers in the river valleys were, however, destabilised time and again by fresh incursions with the result that those ousted from the river valleys ultimately sought refuge in the surrounding rim of hills and uplands. The give-and-take between the diverse types of ecosystems continued, although the intensity of interaction varied depending on the nature of conditions.

The cultural history reveals that the diversities were rooted in the environmental setting of the subcontinent. It also shows that the people who came to settle in different regions also came with diverse cultural traditions. They did not take similar paths in the history of social evolution. The cultural differentiation was also an end-product of primary differences in human initiative and sharpness. These contrasts were further strengthened by the fact that the human decision-making which was directed from the nodes of power neglected the inter-fluvial tracts and the rimlands because of their perceived poor agricultural endowment.

The geographic patterning of the cultural regions possess clues to the long history of evolution through which these cultural identities have taken their form. Beyond the Pir Panjal in the northwest lies the Kashmiri culture-realm. On its outskirts lie the little culture-worlds of Gilgit, Hunza, Baltistan, Ladakh and Kishtwar. From Pir Panjal and the *Daman-e-Koh* of the north-western rim of the mountains to the Yamuna extends the Punjabi realm. On its outskirts lie the Lhenda, Dogri, Pahari and the Haryanvi culture-worlds, all marking a distinct transition towards other cultural regions. In the southwest lies the Sindhi cultural realm nestled between the Kirthar and the Thar on either bank of the Indus. To the south lies the Marwari world encompassing lower-level identities, such as expressed in Bikaner, Jaisalmer, Shekhawati and Sirohi. To the east lies the Braj Bhumi, crossing into the central *doab* and subsuming within it the folk regions defined by the Meo, Ahir, Gujar or the Jat identities. To the north, Braj

Bhasha gives way to the Khari Boli. To the east of the Ganga, Awadhi dominates till it is replaced by the Bhojpuri. The Bihari cultural realm is composed of distinctive identities. Subsumed under it are not only the Bhojpuri, Maghai and the Maithili cultures, but also the Chhotanagpur (Jharkhand) tribal worlds, variegated ethno-lingually and existing at disparate levels of social evolution. To its east lies Bengal, the transition between Bihar and Bengal taking place through the tribal fastness of the Chhotanagpur plateau. The Bengali cultural identity transcends the national boundaries and embraces Bangladesh (as well as Tripura) within its fold. In Tripura it again has an interface with tribes. The Assamese culture-realm, mostly confined to the Brahmaputra valley, is the eastern outpost of the Indo-Aryan identity.

In the west and the northwest one observes a cultural transition from Sindhi to Gujarati and eventually to Marathi. The transition between Sindhi and Gujarati takes place through Kachchi. Further north in Rajputana identities, such as expressed in Mewar and Amber, gradually merge into Malwa which bridges the cultural gap between Rajasthan and Madhya Bharat (more elaborately Madhya Pradesh). Madhya Pradesh embraces the Bhili, Bundeli, Chhattisgarhi and Gondi worlds, in a composite union. In the east the Oriya realm, is on the one hand, transitional to Bengal and, on the other, to Andhra. The Nizam's dominions once held together diverse regions of Khandesh, Marathwada, Telengana and Kannada (Bidar-Gulbarga segment). This political interlude left a typically Deccani imprint on the cultural ethos of the people. The Telugu unites the Telengana, Rayalseema and the Andhra sub-cultures into a larger ethno-lingual formation. On the west it gives way to the Kannada realm. The Tamil and the Malyali realms occupy the rest of the south having their foci in the south-eastern and the south-western extremity of the peninsula.

Each of these major culture-realms of the subcontinent embrace tiny little worlds of the smaller culture-groups, distinctly different from each other in social history and cultural tradition. The cultural regions are not monolithic. Any view of the Indian state as a monolithic formation is incongruous. It is against the dictum of geography and history. In the present context, the socio-psychological integration of diverse culture-groups within the Indian state is necessary. But it is possible only if diversities are preserved, widely respected and accommodated within the existing administrative and legal framework. India is not only a federation of ethno-lingual states, each state in itself is an ethno-lingual confederacy.

SUGGESTIONS FOR FURTHER READING

Ahmad, Aijazuddin (1997): Ecology, Regional Differentiation and Cultural Synthesis: Rethinking India's Cultural Pluralism, in Rasheeduddin Khan (ed.), *Rethinking Indian Federalism*, Shimla: Indian Institute of Advanced Study, pp. 56-72.

APPENDICES

APPENDIX-IV.1

List of Tribal Communities, their Population and State/UT of Enumeration[a]

S. No.	Name of Community/ Group and Sub-group	Population	State/UTs of Enumeration[b]
1.	Adiyan	7, 192	Kerala, Tamil Nadu, Mysore
2.	Adi Group	95,783	Arunachal Pradesh
	(i) Adi	5,520	Arunachal Pradesh
	(ii) Abor	4,733	Arunachal Pradesh
	(iii) Ashing	959	Arunachal Pradesh
	(iv) Bokar	2,724	Arunachal Pradesh
	(v) Bori	78	Arunachal Pradesh
	(vi) Gallong	39,022	Arunachal Pradesh
	(vii) Karka/Korku	2,118	Arunachal Pradesh
	(viii) Komkar	73	Arunachal Pradesh
	(ix) Libo	14	Arunachal Pradesh
	(x) Millang	2,595	Arunachal Pradesh
	(xi) Millang Abor	3	Arunachal Pradesh
	(xii) Miniyong/Miniyang	19,171	Arunachal Pradesh
	(xiii) Padam	10,958	Arunachal Pradesh
	(xiv) Pailibo	1,190	Arunachal Pradesh
	(xv) Pangi	593	Arunachal Pradesh
	(xvi) Pasi	2,153	Arunachal Pradesh
	(xvii) Ramo	655	Arunachal Pradesh
	(xviii) Simong/Shimong	3,140	Arunachal Pradesh
	(xix) Tangam/Tanggam	84	Arunachal Pradesh
3.	Agariya	17,548	Madhya Pradesh
4.	Aimol	836	Manipur
5.	Aka	2,345	Arunachal Pradesh
6.	Anal	6,670	Manipur
7.	Andamanese	24	Andaman and Nicobar Islands
8.	Andh	78,560	Maharashtra, Andhra Pradesh, Madhya Pradesh
9.	Apatani	12,888	Arunachal Pradesh
10.	Arandan/Aranadan	5	Tamil Nadu, Kerala
11.	Asur	7,637	Bihar, West Bengal
12.	Bagata	71,919	Andhra Pradesh, Orissa
13.	Bagi	2,063	Arunachal Pradesh
14.	Baiga	1,78,840	Madhya Pradesh, Bihar, Orissa, Maharashtra, West Bengal

S. No.	Name of Community/ Group and Sub-group	Population	State/UTs of Enumeration[b]
15.	Bangni Group	25, 132	Arunachal Pradesh
	(i) Bangni	21,785	Arunachal Pradesh
	(ii) Khrodong Bangni	1	Arunachal Pradesh
	(iii) Sulung Bangni[c]	38	Arunachal Pradesh
	(iv) Tagin Bangni[d]	1,730	Arunachal Pradesh
	(v) Yanoo Bangni	1,578	Arunachal Pradesh
16.	Bangro	1,085	Arunachal Pradesh
17.	Banjara/Banjari	6,413	Orissa, Bihar
18.	Barda	1,100	Mysore, Maharashtra, Gujarat
19.	Bathudi	1,31,672	Orissa, Bihar
20.	Bavacha/Bamcha	2,831	Gujarat, Mysore, Maharashtra
21.	Bedia	51,360	Bihar, West Bengal
22.	Bhaina	24,740	Madhya Pradesh
23.	Bharia-Bhumia	2,08,982	Madhya Pradesh, Maharashtra, Orissa
24.	Bhattra	71,149	Madhya Pradesh, Maharashtra
25.	Bhil	39,25,625	Madhya Pradesh, Gujarat, Maharashtra, Rajasthan, Andhra Pradesh, Mysore, Tripura
26.	Bhil Mina	16,461	Rajasthan, Madhya Pradesh
27.	Bhottada	1,94,842	Orissa
28.	Bhuiya/Bhuyan	1,88,212	Orissa
29.	Bhumij	4,41,322	West Bengal, Orissa, Bihar
30.	Bhunjia	14,245	Orissa, Madhya Pradesh, Maharashtra
31.	Bhutia/Bhotia	68,096	Uttar Pradesh, West Bengal, Tripura, Sikkim
32.	Biar/Biyar	3,859	Madhya Pradesh
33.	Binjhal	83,873	Orissa
34.	Binjhi/Binjhoa	15,865	Bihar, Orissa
35.	Binjhwar	57,152	Madhya Pradesh, Maharashtra
36.	Birhor/Birhul	4,300	Bihar, Madhya Pradesh, Orissa, Maharashtra, West Bengal
37.	Birjia	3,644	Bihar, West Bengal
38.	Bogum	473	Arunachal Pradesh
39.	Bomdo	294	Arunachal Pradesh
40.	Bondo Poraja	5,338	Orissa
41.	Boro-Borokachari Group	8,80,227	
	(i) Boro-Bora Kachar	6,10,459	Assam, Meghalaya
	(ii) Barman	13,210	Assam
	(iii) Boro	—	Assam
	(iv) Dimasa	40,178	Assam, Meghalaya, Mizoram
	(v) Hojai	—	
	(vi) Kachari/Sonowal	2,02,948	Assam, Nagaland
	(vii) Madahi	—	Assam
	(viii) Mech	13,432	West Bengal, Assam
42.	Buksa	23,317	Uttar Pradesh
43.	Chakma	54,387	Tripura, Assam, West Bengal, Meghalaya, Mizoram
44.	Charan	1,700	Gujarat
45.	Chaudhri/Chodhara	1,88,922	Gujarat, Maharashtra
46.	Chenchu/Chenchwar	24,415	Andhra Pradesh, Mysore, Orissa
47.	Chero/Chiro	41,701	Bihar, Manipur, West Bengal
48.	Chik-Baraik	35,094	Bihar, West Bengal
49.	Chote	1,905	Manipur

S. No.	Name of Community/ Group and Sub-group	Population	State/UTs of Enumeration[b]
50.	Dafla	5,926	Arunachal Pradesh
51.	Dal	12,185	Orissa
52.	Damor/Damaria	15,774	Rajasthan, Madhya Pradesh
53.	Deori	25,763	Assam, Arunachal Pradesh
54.	Desua Bhumij	376	Orissa
55.	Dhanka (including Tain, Tetava, Valri)	1,92,391	Gujarat, Maharashtra, Rajasthan
56.	Dhanwar	24,170	Madhya Pradesh, Maharashtra
57.	Dharua	8,791	Orissa
58.	Dhodia/Dhedi	3,79,895	Gujarat, Dadra and Nagar Haveli, Maharashtra, Goa, Daman and Diu
59.	Didaayi	2,164	Orissa
60.	Dubla (including Halavia or Halpati)	4,08,226	Gujarat, Maharashtra, Goa, Daman and Diu; Dadra and Nagar Haveli, Mysore
61.	Era Vallan	678	Kerala, Tamil Nadu
62.	Gadaba	71,702	Orissa, Andhra Pradesh, Madhya Pradesh
63.	Gaddi	50,685	Himachal Pradesh
64.	Gamit/Gamta	4,05,431	Gujarat, Maharashtra, Mysore
65.	Gandia	2,225	Orissa
66.	Gangte	6,307	Manipur
67.	Garabha/Gadha	3,728	Madhya Pradesh
68.	Garasia	49,753	Rajasthan
69.	Garo	3,42,474	Meghalaya, Assam, Tripura, West Bengal, Nagaland
70.	Ghara	548	Orissa
71.	Gond	48,09,164	Madhya Pradesh, Maharashtra, Orissa, Andhra Pradesh, Bihar, Gujarat, West Bengal, Mysore
72.	Gorait	3,720	Bihar, West Bengal
73.	Gowdalu	5,146	Mysore
74.	Gujjar	20,634	Himachal Pradesh
75.	Hajong	20,189	Meghalaya, Assam, West Bengal, Mizoram
76.	Hakkipikki	2,561	Mysore
77.	Halam	19,076	Tripura
78.	Halba/Halbi	1,86,307	Madhya Pradesh, Maharashtra, Orissa
79.	Hasalaru	11,213	Mysore
80.	Hill-Miri	8,174	Arunachal Pradesh
81.	Hill-Pulaya	1,152	Kerala
82.	Hill-Reddi	4,306	Andhra Pradesh
83.	Hmar	36,740	Manipur, Assam, Meghalaya, Mizoram
84.	Ho	5,38,124	Bihar, Orissa, West Bengal
85.	Hojai	2,298	Assam
86.	Ianbo	210	Arunachal Pradesh
87.	Irular	1,06,939	Tamil Nadu, Kerala, Mysore
88.	Jad/Lamba/Bodh/Bhot	18,198	Himachal Pradesh
89.	Jamatia	34,192	Tripura
90.	Jatapu	82,357	Andhra Pradesh, Orissa
91.	Jaunsari	56,699	Uttar Pradesh
92.	Juang	24,384	Orissa
93.	Kadar	1,926	Kerala, Tamil Nadu
94.	Kamali	94	West Bengal
95.	Kamar	19,758	Madhya Pradesh, Maharashtra

S. No.	Name of Community/ Group and Sub-group	Population	State/UTs of Enumeration[b]
96.	Kammara	36,182	Andhra Pradesh, Kerala, Mysore, Tamil Nadu
97.	Kanaura/Kinnar	35,120	Himachal Pradesh
98.	Kandha/Ganda	7,183	Orissa
99.	Kanikaran/Kanikkar	14,292	Kerala, Tamil Nadu
100.	Kaniyan/Kanyan	1,265	Mysore, Tamil Nadu
101.	Karka	2,118	Arunachal Pradesh
102.	Karmali	26, 908	Bihar, West Bengal
103.	Karnmara	194	Tamil Nadu
104.	Kathodi/Kathari	150, 303	Maharashtra, Gujarat, Dadra and Nagar Haveli, Mysore, Rajasthan
105.	Kattunayakan	11, 071	Kerala, Tamil Nadu, Andhra Pradesh
106.	Kawar/Kanwar	4,17,739	Madhya Pradesh, Orissa, Maharashtra
107.	Keer	6,099	Madhya Pradesh
108.	Khamba	848	Arunachal Pradesh
109.	Khamiyang	29	Arunachal Pradesh
110.	Khampti	4,078	Arunachal Pradesh
111.	Khan	16,903	Bihar
112.	Kharia	2,74,540	Bihar, Orissa, Madhya Pradesh, Maharashtra
113.	Kharwar/Khairwar	2,05,489	Bihar, Madhya Pradesh, Orissa, West Bengal
114.	Khasi[e] (including Jaintia)	4,63,869	Meghalaya, Assam, Tripura
115.	Khond	9,11,835	Orissa, Andhra Pradesh, Madhya Pradesh, Bihar, Maharashtra, West Bengal
116.	Khowa	703	Arunachal Pradesh
117.	Kisan	1,80,741	Orissa, West Bengal, Bihar
118.	Kochu-Velan	10	Kerala, Tamil Nadu
119.	Koirao	1,620	Manipur
120.	Koireng	458	Manipur
121.	Kohna/Kokni/kukni	4,20,883	Maharashtra, Gujarat, Dadra and Nagar Haveli, Mysore, Rajasthan
122.	Kol Group	8,00,603	
	(i) Kol	1,15,606	Madhya Pradesh, Orissa, Maharashtra
	(ii) Kol (Dahait)	3,63,215	Madhya Pradesh
	(iii) Kolah/Kol-Loharas	11,054	Orissa
	(iv) Kolha	3,10,728	Orissa
123.	Kolam (including Manneruarlu)	82,910	Maharashtra, Andhra Pradesh, Madhya Pradesh
124.	Koli Group	5,47,291	
	(i) Koli	30,361	Gujarat
	(ii) Koli Dhor	75,958	Maharashtra, Gujarat, Mysore, Dadra and Nagar Haveli, Rajasthan
	(iii) Koli Mahadev	3,39,855	Maharashtra
	(iv) Koli Malhar	1,01,117	Maharashtra, Orissa
125.	Konda Dora (h)	1,10,842	Andhra Pradesh, Orissa
126.	Konda Kapu	3,407	Andhra Pradesh, Tamil Nadu, Kerala, Mysore
127.	Konda Reddy	43,812	Andhra Pradesh, Tamil Nadu, Kerala
128.	Kongbo	375	Arunachal Pradesh
129.	Kora	1,18,351	West Bengal, Bihar, Orissa
130.	Koraga	8,517	Mysore, Kerala, Tamil Nadu
131.	Korama	483	Mysore
132.	Korku[f]	2,85,659	Madhya Pradesh, Maharashtra
133.	Kom	6,550	Manipur

S. No.	Name of Community/ Group and Sub-group	Population	State/UTs of Enumeration[b]
134.	Korua/Korwa	92,726	Madhya Pradesh, Bihar, Orissa, West Bengal
135.	Kota	1,291	Tamil Nadu, Mysore, Kerala
136.	Kotia/Kotia-Bentho-Oriya	28,938	Andhra Pradesh, Orissa
137.	Koya	3,44,467	
	(i) Koya	59,241	Orissa, Maharashtra, Mysore
	(ii) Koya or Gond	2,85,226	Andhra Pradesh
138.	Kudia/Melakudi	7,136	Mysore, Kerala, Tamil Nadu
139.	Kuki Group[g]	1,71,939	
	(i) Kuki	34,915	Assam, Tripura, Nagaland
	(ii) Riang	64,722	Tripura
	(iii) Thadou	59,955	Manipur
	(iv) Vaiphei	12,347	Manipur
140.	Kulia	188	Andhra Pradesh
141.	Kuli	1,893	Orissa
142.	Kunbi	34,643	Gujarat
143.	Kunnba	2,754	Tamil Nadu
144.	Kurichchan	16,869	Kerala, Tamil Nadu
145.	Kuruba Group	25,024	
	(i) Kuruba	8,857	Mysore
	(ii) Jenu Kuruba	6,656	Mysore
	(iii) Kadu Kuruba	8,192	Mysore
	(iv) Kurumba	1,319	Kerala, Tamil Nadu
146.	Kuruman	26,708	Kerala, Tamil Nadu, Mysore
147.	Lahaula	3,144	Himachal Pradesh
148.	Lalung	95,609	Assam, Meghalaya
149.	Lamgang	2,622	Manipur
150.	Lepcha	14,582	West Bengal, Tripura, Sikkim
151.	Lodha	49,797	West Bengal, Orissa
152.	Lohara/Lohra	1,19,216	Bihar, West Bengal
153.	Madia	905	Orissa
154.	Mag/Magh	16,530	Tripura, West Bengal
155.	Mahli/Mahali	1,32,314	Bihar, West Bengal, Orissa
156.	Majhi	4,138	Madhya Pradesh
157.	Majhwar	33,489	Madhya Pradesh
158.	Mal-Paharia	79,654	Bihar, West Bengal
159.	Malai Arayan	4,194	Kerala, Tamil Nadu
160.	Malai Pandaram	1,569	Kerala, Tamil Nadu
161.	Malaikudi/Malayekandi	708	Tamil Nadu, Mysore
162.	Malakuraoan	274	Kerala, Tamil Nadu
163.	Malasar/Maha Malasar	3,147	Tamil Nadu, Kerala, Mysore
164.	Malayan	3,616	Kerala
165.	Maleru	1,321	Mysore
166.	Mali	1,978	Andhra Pradesh
167.	Malla Malasar/Mahamalasar	38	Tamil Nadu, Mysore, Kerala
168.	Malyali	1,59,426	Tamil Nadu
169.	Malayaryar	13,813	Kerala
170.	Man	964	Assam, Meghalaya
171.	Mankidi	333	Orissa
172.	Mankirdia	876	Orissa
173.	Manna Dhora	9,372	Andhra Pradesh
174.	Mannan	4,270	Kerala, Tamil Nadu

S. No.	Name of Community/ Group and Sub-group	Population	State/UTs of Enumeration[b]
175.	Maratha/Marati	68,008	Mysore, Kerala
176.	Matya	8,648	Orissa
177.	Mawasi	8,808	Madhya Pradesh
178.	Meda	325	Mysore
179.	Meyor	100	Arunachal Pradesh
180.	Miji	3,549	Arunachal Pradesh
181.	Mikir	1,84,089	Assam, Meghalaya, Arunachal Pradesh, Nagaland, Mizoram
182.	Mina/Meena	15,38,324	Rajasthan, Madhya Pradesh
183.	Mirdha	28,447	Orissa
184.	Miri/Mishing	2,63,410	Assam, Arunachal Pradesh
185.	Mishmi Group	22,561	
	(i) Mishmi	808	Arunachal Pradesh
	(ii) Diagaru Taraon	5,384	Arunachal Pradesh
	(iii) Idu/Ghulikata	8,136	Arunachal Pradesh
	(iv) Kaman/Miju	8,233	Arunachal Pradesh
186.	Mizo (Lushai) Group	2,94,580	
	(i) Mizo	2,56,954	Assam, Manipur, Tripura, Meghalaya
	(ii) Lakher	12,871	Assam, Mizoram, Meghalaya
	(iii) Paite	24,755	Manipur
187.	Mogia	1,466	Madhya Pradesh
188.	Momba	2,486	Arunachal Pradesh
189.	Monpa Group	26,493	
	(i) Monpa	23,319	Arunachal Pradesh
	(ii) But-Monpa	555	Arunachal Pradesh
	(iii) Lish Monpa	1,046	Arunachal Pradesh
	(iv) Panchan Monpa	747	Arunachal Pradesh
	(v) Tawang Monpa	826	Arunachal Pradesh
190.	Monsang	930	Manipur
191.	Moyon	1,360	Manipur
192.	Mru	836	West Bengal
193.	Mukha Dora/Nooka Dhora	13,235	Andhra Pradesh
194.	Muktum	2	Arunachal Pradesh
195.	Munda/Mundari	11,81,151	Bihar, Orissa, West Bengal, Madhya Pradesh, Tripura
196.	Muthuvan/Mudugar	8,862	Kerala, Tamil Nadu
197.	Naga Group	6,13,571	
	(i) Naga	4,54,621	Nagaland, Assam, Meghalaya
	(ii) Angami	70	Manipur
	(iii) Kabui	40,257	Manipur
	(iv) Kacha	13,026	Manipur
	(v) Mao	33,379	Manipur
	(vi) Maram	4,539	Manipur
	(vii) Maring	9,825	Manipur
	(viii) Sema	3	Manipur
	(ix) Tangkhul	57,851	Manipur
198.	Nagesia/Nagasia	63,037	Madhya Pradesh, West Bengal, Maharashtra
199.	Naikada/Nayak	3,17,435	Gujarat, Mysore, Maharashtra, Andhra Pradesh, Goa, Daman and Diu; Dadra and Nagar Haveli, Rajasthan
200.	Nat/Navdigar/Sapera/Kubutar	7,492	Madhya Pradesh

S. No.	Name of Community/ Group and Sub-group	Population	State/UTs of Enumeration[b]
201.	Nihal/Nahal	8,686	Madhya Pradesh, Maharashtra
202.	Nishang	15,462	Arunachal Pradesh
203.	Nishi	33,805	Arunachal Pradesh
204.	Noatia	10,297	Tripura
205.	Nocte Group	24,327	
	(i) Nocte	23,165	Arunachal Pradesh
	(ii) Liju Nocte	4	Arunachal Pradesh
	(iii) Ponthai Nocte	247	Arunachal Pradesh
	(iv) Tutcha Nocte	911	Arunachal Pradesh
206.	Nonong	1	Arunachal Pradesh
207.	Omanatya	17,671	Orissa
208.	Onges	112	Andaman and Nicobar Islands
209.	Orang	3,428	Tripura
210.	Oraon	17,02,663	Bihar, Madhya Pradesh, West Bengal, Orissa, Maharashtra
211.	Padhar	4,758	Gujarat
212.	Palliyan/Palleyan	4,053	Tamil Nadu, Kerala, Mysore
213.	Pallirar	263	Kerala, Tamil Nadu
214.	Paniyan	51,660	Kerala, Tamil Nadu, Mysore
215.	Pangwal	9,291	Himachal Pradesh
216.	Panika	43,988	Madhya Pradesh
217.	Pao/Pawara	23,074	Madhya Pradesh
218.	Pardhan/Pathari/Saroti	5,31,950	Maharashtra, Andhra Pradesh, Madhya Pradesh
219.	Paradhi/Pardhi/Parcdhi/Bahelia	43,579	Maharashtra, Madhya Pradesh, Gujarat, Mysore
220.	Paroja/Parja/Porja (Parangiperja)	2,27,450	Orissa, Andhra Pradesh, Madhya Pradesh, Maharashtra
221.	Parenga	3,032	Orissa
222.	Parhaiya	14,759	Bihar, West Bengal
223.	Patelia	48,903	Gujarat, Maharashtra, Rajasthan, Mysore
224.	Pawi	20,669	Assam, Meghalaya, Mizoram
225.	Pentia	6,266	Orissa
226.	Pomla	914	Maharashtra, Gujarat
227.	Ponkong	5	Arunachal Pradesh
228.	Pulayan	89,406	Kerala, Tamil Nadu
229.	Raji	1,918	Uttar Pradesh
230.	Rabari	4,693	Gujarat
231.	Rabha	1,41,096	Assam, West Bengal, Meghalaya
232.	Rajaur	1,478	Orissa
233.	Ralte	154	Manipur
234.	Rathawa	1,92,820	Gujarat, Mysore, Maharashtra
235.	Reddi Dhoras	5,254	Andhra Pradesh
236.	Rona/Rena	12	Andhra Pradesh
237.	Saharia[h]	2,32,366	Madhya Pradesh, Rajasthan
238.	Suhte	3	Manipur
239.	Santal	36,33,459	Bihar, West Bengal, Orissa, Tripura
240.	Saonta/Saunta	9,709	Madhya Pradesh
241.	Saora/Savara Group	4,87,078	
	(i) Saora/Savar/Saura or Sahara	3,42,757	Orissa
	(ii) Savar	3,548	Bihar, West Bengal
	(iii) Sawar/Sawara	59,546	Madhya Pradesh, Maharashtra
	(iv) Savara/Kapu Savara/ Mauliya Savara/Khutto Savara	81,227	Andhra Pradesh

S. No.	Name of Community/ Group and Sub-group	Population	State/UTs of Enumeration[b]
242.	Saur	27,798	Madhya Pradesh
243.	Sauria Patharia	59,205	Bihar, West Bengal
244.	Shabar/or Lodha	240,344	Orissa
245.	Sherdukpen	1,630	Arunachal Pradesh
246.	Sholaga	10,949	Tamil Nadu, Mysore
247.	Shom Pens	92	Andaman and Nicobar Islands
248.	Siddi	4,532	Gujarat, Goa, Daman and Diu
249.	Simte	4,177	Manipur
250.	Singpho	1,567	Arunachal Pradesh
251.	Siram	8	Arunachal Pradesh
252.	Soligaru	10,983	Mysore
253.	Sonr	1,149	Madhya Pradesh
254.	Sounti	55,178	Orissa
255.	Sugali/Lambadi	132,464	Andhra Pradesh
256.	Sulung	4,250	Arunachal Pradesh
257.	Swangla	2,767	Himachal Pradesh
258.	Synteng	659	Assam, Meghalaya, Mizoram
259.	Tagin	20,377	Arunachal Pradesh
260.	Tangsa Group	13,546	
	(i) Tangsa	6,941	Arunachal Pradesh
	(ii) Bangai Tangsa	1	Arunachal Pradesh
	(iii) Bolok Tangsa	3	Arunachal Pradesh
	(iv) Darog Tangsa	5	Arunachal Pradesh
	(v) Haisa Tangsa	1	Arunachal Pradesh
	(vi) Havi Tangsa	699	Arunachal Pradesh
	(vii) Hotang Tangsa	1	Arunachal Pradesh
	(viii) Katin Tangsa	1	Arunachal Pradesh
	(ix) Kemsung Tangsa	391	Arunachal Pradesh
	(x) Khalim Tangsa	2	Arunachal Pradesh
	(xi) Korang Tangsa	1	Arunachal Pradesh
	(xii) Langkai Tangsa	11	Arunachal Pradesh
	(xiii) Lichi Tangsa	2	Arunachal Pradesh
	(xiv) Longchang Tangsa	21	Arunachal Pradesh
	(xv) Longin Tangsa	9	Arunachal Pradesh
	(xvi) Longphi Tangsa	156	Arunachal Pradesh
	(xvii) Longri Tangsa	133	Arunachal Pradesh
	(xviii) Longsang Tangsa	375	Arunachal Pradesh
	(xix) Lowang Tangsa	1	Arunachal Pradesh
	(xx) Moglum Tangsa	1,486	Arunachal Pradesh
	(xxi) Moshang Tangsa	123	Arunachal Pradesh
	(xxii) Moshang Tangsa	1,288	Arunachal Pradesh
	(xxiii) Namsang Tangsa	3	Arunachal Pradesh
	(xxiv) Ngimong Tangsa	4	Arunachal Pradesh
	(xxv) Phong Tangsa	1	Arunachal Pradesh
	(xxvi) Rongrang Tangsa	538	Arunachal Pradesh
	(xxvii) Sanke Tangsa	10	Arunachal Pradesh
	(xxviii) Simsa Tangsa	2	Arunachal Pradesh
	(xxix) Taisin Tangsa	4	Arunachal Pradesh
	(xxx) Tikhak Tangsa	1,169	Arunachal Pradesh
	(xxxi) Yongkur Tangsa	29	Arunachal Pradesh
	(xxxii) Yougli Tangsa	135	Arunachal Pradesh

S. No.	Name of Community/ Group and Sub-group	Population	State/UTs of Enumeration[b]
261.	Taram	3	Arunachal Pradesh
262.	Tharu	67,994	Uttar Pradesh
263.	Thai Kampti	8	Arunachal Pradesh
264.	Thakur/Thakore	178,805	Maharashtra
265.	Tharua	293	Orissa
266.	Thoti	2,087	Andhra Pradesh, Mysore, Maharashtra
267.	Toda	945	Tamil Nadu, Mysore
268.	Tripura/Tripuri/Trippera	250,545	Tripura
269.	Uchai	1,061	Tripura
270.	Ulladan	3,692	Kerala
271.	Uralay	2,685	Kerala, Tamil Nadu
272.	Vaghri/Wagri	4,637	Gujarat
273.	Valmiki	28,967	Andhra Pradesh
274.	Varli	4,61,562	Maharashtra, Gujarat, Dadra and Nagar Haveli, Goa, Daman and Diu, Mysore
275.	Vitolia/Vitola/Kotwalia/ Barodia	13,972	Gujarat, Maharashtra, Mysore
276.	Wancho	28,650	Arunachal Pradesh
277.	Ya Tong	158	Arunachal Pradesh
278.	Yenadi	2,39,403	Andhra Pradesh
279.	Yerava	13,743	Mysore
280.	Yerukala	1,62,560	Andhra Pradesh
281.	Yobin	929	Arunachal Pradesh
282.	Zakhring	23	Arunachal Pradesh
283.	Zou	10,060	Manipur
284.	Saur	27,798	Madhya Pradesh
285.	Sauria Patharia	59,205	Bihar, West Bengal

NOTES

a. Based on 1971 census.
b. States arranged in order of numerical strength of tribal communities.
c. See also Sulung.
d. See also Tagin.
e. Sub-tribes of the Khasi Group.
(i) Khasi; (ii) Jaintia; (iii) Synteng; (iv) Pnar; (v) War; (vi) Bhoi; (vii) Lyngagam.
f. Includes Karku enumerated in M.P.
g. Sub-tribes of the Kuki Group:
(i) Biate, Biete; (ii) Changsan; (iii) Chongloi; (iv) Doungel; (v) Gamallhou; (vi) Gangte; (vii) Guite; (viii) Hanneng; (ix) Haokip, Haupit; (x) Haolai; (xi) Hengna; (xii) Hongsungh; (xiii) Hrangkhwal, Rangkhol; (xiv) Jongbe; (xv) Khawchung; (xvi) Khawathlang, Khothalang; (xvii) Khelma; (xviii) Kholhou; (xix) Kipgen; (xx) Kuki; (xxi) Lengthang; (xxii) Lhangum; (xxiii) Lhoujem; (xxiv) Lhouvun; (xxv) Lupheng; (xxvi) Mangiel; (xxvii) Misao; (xxviii) Riang; (xxix) Sairhem; (xxx) Selnam; (xxxi) Singson; (xxxii) Sitlhou; (xxxiii) Sukte; (xxxiv) Thado; (xxxv) Thangngeu; (xxxvi) Uibuh; (xxxvii) Vaiphei.
h. Other variants are Sahariya, Sehria, Sosia, Sor (Seharia).

Scheduling Anomalies

Name	*Other Variants*	*Remarks*
Bhuiya	Bhuiyan	ST in Orissa (*1971 Census*). Not mentioned by K.S. Singh, 1992 (hereinafter KSS).
Chiru		ST in Maharashtra (KSS). Not mentioned in *1971 Census* Maharashtra List.
Didayi	Didoyi	ST in Orissa (*1971 Census*), non-ST Hindu in Andhra Pradesh (KSS).
Gujjar		Muslim ST in Himachal Pradesh and Jammu and Kashmir, non-ST in Punjab.
Gaddi		ST in Himachal Pradesh, non-ST in Punjab and Jammu and Kashmir.
Gamit	Gamta	ST in Gujarat, Maharashtra and Mysore *(1971 Census)*, non-ST in Rajasthan (KSS).
Gond		Listed as ST in Madhya Pradesh, Maharashtra, Andhra Pradesh and other states, as SC in U.P. and non-ST in Assam (KSS).
Irula	Irular	ST in Tamil Nadu, Kerala and Mysore (Karnataka). Listed as Hindu caste in Pondicherry.
Kamar		ST in Madhya Pradesh, Maharashtra. Listed as Hindu caste in West Bengal, Bihar and Orissa (KSS).
Katin Tangsa		While 15 sub-tribes are mentioned under the Tangsa group, Katin Tangsa is not mentioned by KSS.
Kawar		Listed as ST in Madhya Pradesh and Maharashtra, non-ST Hindu in West Bengal and OBC in Bihar.
Kharwar		Listed as ST in Bihar, Orissa and West Bengal but SC in U.P. and non-SC and non-ST in M.P. (KSS).
Khamyang	Khamiyang	Listed as ST in Arunachal Pradesh but non-ST Buddhist in Assam (KSS).
Khampti		Listed as ST in Arunachal Pradesh but non-ST Buddhist in Assam (KSS).
Kharia		Listed as ST in Bihar, Orissa, West Bengal, M.P. and Maharashtra, but non-ST in Assam and SC in Tripura.
Jaintia		Mentioned separately in KSS while *1971 Census* clubs it with Khasis.
Khond	Kondh	*1971 Census* enumerated them in Orissa, Andhra Pradesh, M.P. and Bihar (KSS). However, does not mention them in Bihar.
Khotia-Bentho-Oriya		Mentioned in KSS as sub-group of Kotia in Andhra Pradesh; there is a reference to Bentia-Odia as a Hindu caste in Orissa (KSS).
Kisan		*1971 Census* enumerated them in Orissa and West Bengal, KSS mentioned them in Bihar also.
Kol		Mentioned separately in M.P. and Orissa lists *(1971 Census)* but a sub-tribe such as Kol Dahait (M.P.) and Kolah/Kol-Lohara (Orissa) also mentioned separately *(1971 Census)*. This creates unnecessary confusion.
Kolam		Mentioned twice in Maharashtra as Kolam and then Kolam including Mannervallur *(1971 Census)*. The Andhra list shows the second variant only. According to *1971 Census* they are found in M.P., Maharashtra and Andhra Pradesh, KSS does not, however, mention them in M.P.
Kolha		Listed as ST in Orissa *(1971 Census)*. They are not mentioned by KSS; on the other hand, Kol-Lohars are mentioned as ST in Orissa (KSS).
Koli		Listed as ST in Gujarat, Dadra and Nagar Haveli, Rajasthan, Delhi, Haryana, Punjab and non-SC in Daman and Diu (KSS).

Name	Other Variants	Remarks
Chedia Koli		Mentioned as OBC in Gujarat (KSS).
Konda Kammara		Listed in KSS as ST in Andhra Pradesh; there is no reference to them in *1971 Census*.
Korama		Listed as ST in Mysore *(1971 Census)*, KSS mentions them as SC in Karnataka.
Koya		Mentioned as ST in M.P. (KSS); however, the *1971 Census* does not list them at all. They are non-ST Hindu in Assam (KSS).
Kudiya	Kudiya or Melakudi	Both sub-groups have been shown separately *(1971 Census)*, While the Kerala list shows Kudia or Melakudi, KSS mentions kudiya only.
Kunbi		Several sub-groups within the Kunbi group are mentioned as Hindu castes in Maharashtra (KSS). Kunbi are also mentioned as Hindu castes in Maharashtra (KSS). Kunbi are also mentioned as OBC in M.P., Goa and Karnataka. They are listed as ST in Gujarat.
Kunnbas		Listed as ST in Tamil Nadu, but they are not mentioned in KSS.
Kurichchan	Kurichain	Other sub-groups mentioned as Kurichian Pathiri (KSS).
Kuruba		KSS mentions as OBC in Karnataka and Tamil Nadu and Kuruba Christians in Karnataka, while Kurumba/Kuruba shown as ST in Tamil Nadu as well as Kerala.
Kuruman	Mulla Kuruman Urali Kuruman (Kerala)	Listed as ST in Tamil Nadu and Kerala (KSS). The *1971 Census* shows shows them in Tamil Nadu, Kerala and Mysore (Karnataka).
Lodha		Treated as ST in Orissa *(1971 Census)*; they are grouped as Lodha/Kheria/Kharia in West Bengal *(1971 Census)*.
Manna	Manne Dora	Listed as ST in Andhra Pradesh, but non-ST Hindu in Orissa.
Mikir		Listed as ST in Assam, Meghalaya, Arunachal Pradesh and Nagaland; interestingly KSS does not mention them at all.
Mina/Meena		Listed as ST in Rajasthan and M.P., Hindu OBC in Haryana and Delhi (KSS).
Miri		KSS does not mention Miri; on the other hand, Mishing have been mentioned in Assam and Arunachal Pradesh.
Naga		KSS also lists them as ST in Orissa; there is, however, no mention of Nagas in the Orissa list *(1971 Census)*.
Mundari		The Orissa list shows Munda as well as Mundari separately *(1971 Census)*.
Santal		Listed as ST in Bihar, West Bengal, Orissa as well as in Tripura. But they are non-ST in Assam.

Source: Table compiled by the author.

List of Scheduled Tribes for the States and Union Territories of India:

Published by the Union Primary Census Abstract of 1991 Census, Part II-B (i), Vol. 1, based on the following orders:

(i) The Scheduled Tribes/Scheduled Caste orders (Amendment) Act, 1976 (No. 108 of 1976, dated 18th September, 1976).
(ii) The Scheduled Tribes/Scheduled Caste Lists (Modification) Order, 1956.
(iii) The Constitution (Goa, Daman and Diu) Scheduled Tribes Order, 1968.
(iv) The Constitution (Jammu and Kashmir) Scheduled Tribes Order, 1989.
(v) The Constitution (Meghalaya) Scheduled Tribes Order (Amendment) Act, 1987.
(vi) Act 81 of 1971 (Mizoram).
(vii) The Constitution (Nagaland) Scheduled Tribes Order, 1970, C.O.88.
(viii) The Constitution (Sikkim) Scheduled Tribes Order, 1978.
(ix) The Constitution (Dadra and Nagar Haveli) Scheduled Tribes Order, 1962, C.O. 64.

There are, however, discrepancies between these lists and the tribal list given in (Appendix IV.1) based on 1971 census. The following discrepancies may be noted:

(i) Many Scheduled Tribes of Arunachal Pradesh have been omitted in the List published by the 1991 census, even though the list is based on 1956 order—special mention may be made to Adi Group, and the Tangsa Group which do not find any mention in the 1991 census.
(ii) Khan, with a total population of 19,903 in 1971 is missing in the 1991 census list.
(iii) According to the Scheduled Caste/Scheduled Tribe Orders (Amendment) Act, 1976, the following additions were made to the list of tribes:

Name of the Tribe	*State*
Bharwad	Gujarat
Malai Vedan	Tamil Nadu, Kerala
Purum	Manipur
Koch	Meghalaya
Chaimal	Tripura
Jarawas	Andaman and Nicobar Islands
Shentinelese	Andaman and Nicobar Islands

Appendix-IV.4

Districts where the Gonds were enumerated in 1981

Andhra Pradesh
Srikakulam
Vizianagaram
Vishakapatnam
East Godavari
West Godavari
Krishna
Guntur
Prakasam
Nellore
Chittor
Kurnool
Mahbubnagar
Rangareddi
Hyderabad
Medak
Nizamabad
Adilabad
Karimnagar
Warangal
Khammam
Nalgonda

Bihar
Patna
Gaya
Aurangabad
Rohtas
Bhojpur
Saran
Siwan
Gopalganj
Paschim Champaran
Purbe Champaran
Sitamarhi
Muzaffarpur
Vaishali
Begusarai
Samastipur
Darbhanga
Madhubani
Saharsa
Purnea
Katihar
Munger
Bhagalpur
Santhal Pargana
Dhanbad
Giridih
Hazaribagh
Palamau
Ranchi
Singhbhum

Madhya Pradesh
Morena
Bhind
Gawalior
Datia
Shivpuri
Guna
Tikamgarh
Chattarpur
Panna
Sagar
Damoh
Satna
Rewa
Shahdol
Sidhi
Mandsaur
Ratlam
Ujjain
Shajapur
Dewas
Jhabua
Dhar
Indore
West Nimar
East Nimar
Rajgarh
Vidisha
Bhopal
Sehore
Raisen
Betul
Hoshangabad
Jabalpur
Narsimhapur
Mandla
Chhindwara
Seoni
Balaghat
Surguja
Bilaspur
Raigarh
Durg
Raipur
Bastar

Maharashtra
Greater Bombay
Thane
Raigarh
Ratnagiri

Nashik
Dhule
Jalgaon
Ahmednagar
Pune
Satara
Sangli
Solapur
Kolhapur
Aurangabad
Parbhani
Bid
Nanded
Osmanabad
Buldana
Ankola
Amravati
Yavatmal
Wardha
Nagpur
Bhandara
Chandrapur

Gujarat

Surendranagar
Bhavnagar
Banaskantha
Sabarkantha
Mahesana
Ahmadabad
Panch Mahals
Vadodra
Bharuch
Surat
Valsad
The Dangs

Karnataka

Bangalore
Belgaum
Bellary
Bidar
Bijapur
Chikmagalur
Chitradurga
Dakshin Kannad
Dharwad
Gulbarga
Hassan
Kodagu
Kolar
Mandya
Mysore
Raichur
Shimoga
Tumkur
Uttar Kannad

Orissa

Sambalpur
Sundargarh
Keonjhar
Mayurbhanj
Balasore
Cuttack
Dhenkanal
Phulbani
Bolangir
Kalahandi
Koraput
Ganjam
Puri

West Bengal

Jalpaiguri
Darjeeling
West Dinajpur
Maldah
Murshidabad
Nadia
24-Parganas
Calcutta
Haora
Hugli
Medinipur
Bankura
Purulia
Bardhaman
Birbhum

Gonds: Selected Demographic Indicators

(in per cent)

State/District	*Population 1981*	*Concentration Index*	*Growth Rate 1961-81*	*Growth Rate Decennial*
Madhya Pradesh	**5,349,883**	**71.82**	**72.88**	**36.44**
Chhattarpur	6,176	0.08	116.85	58.42
Panna	42,863	0.57	118.92	59.46
Satna	33, 946	0.45	68.12	34.06
Rewa	9, 509	0.12	77.94	38.97
Shahdol	309,060	4.14	50.02	25.01
Sidhi	147,914	1.98	65.59	32.79
Dewas	20,267	0.27	54.47	27.23
East Nimar	21,744	0.29	142.27	71.08
Vidisha	4,878	0.06	85.48	42.74
Sehore*	28,248	0.29	121.46	60.73
Raisen	87,498	1.17	76.31	38.15
Hoshangabad	84,779	1.13	134.98	67.49
Betul	242,119	3.25	98.87	49.43
Jabalpur	193,037	2.59	199.97	99.98
Narsimhapur	74,877	1.00	69.93	34.96
Mandla	526,902	7.07	48.30	24.15
Chhindwara	331,760	4.45	45.58	22.79
Seoni	266,237	3.57	46.70	23.35
Balaghat	210,199	2.82	177.36	88.68
Surguja	348,356	4.67	46.44	23.22
Bilaspur	347,029	4.65	70.62	35.31
Raigarh	98,683	1.32	43.79	21.89
Durg*	330,658	1.78	175.70	87.85
Raipur	379,849	5.09	88.32	44.16
Bastar	1,050,632	2.28	45.31	22.65
Gwalior	1,409	0.01		
Guna	2,077	1.02		
Mandsaur	1,884	0.02		
Ratlam	1,064	0.01		
Ujjain	1,909	0.02		
Indore	1,366	0.01		
West Nimar	1,417	0.01		
Bhopal	6,189	0.08		
Rajnandgaon	197,720	2.65		
Maharashtra	**1,162,735**	**15.61**	**326.59**	**163.29**
Nanded	22,324	0.29	58.57	29.28
Amravati	71,386	0.95	1,523.14	761.57
Yavatmal	1,41,462	1.89	64.87	32.43
Chandrapur	438,191	5.89	163.55	81.77

State/District	*Population 1981*	*Concen-tration Index*	*Growth Rate 1961-81*	*Growth Rate Decennial*
Nashik	1,675	0.02		
Dhule	1,141	0.01		
Jalgaon	1,502	0.02		
Osmanabad	1,418	0.01		
Akola	10,272	0.13		
Wardha	95,386	1.28		
Nagpur	174,494	2.34		
Bhandara	190,726	2.56		
Andhra Pradesh	**170,477**	**2.28**	**18.65**	**9.32**
Adilabad	138,642	1.86	48.54	24.27
Karimnagar	15,412	0.20	30.42	15.21
Warangal	9,203	0.12	-59.35	-29.67
Khammam	3,391	0.04	-77.18	-38.59
Orissa	**602,749**	**8.09**	**35.23**	**17.61**
Kalahandi	151,581	2.03	45.19	22.59
Koraput	88,570	1.19	60.24	30.12
Sambalpur	117,648	1.57	25.32	12.66
Bolangir	83,523	1.12	15.54	7.77
Phulbani	13,159	0.17	62.72	31.36
Dhenkanal	25,658	0.34	25.90	12.95
Keonjhar	59,136	0.79	50.73	25.36
Mayurbhanj	21,757	0.29	30.60	15.30
Sundergarh	39,976	0.53	14.71	7.35

Source: Table generated by the author based on Census of India, 1981, Series 11, Madhya Pradesh, Part IX (VIII); Series 12, Maharashtra, Part IX (III); Series 16, Orissa, Part IX (III); Series 2, Andhra Pradesh, Part IX, *Special Tables for Scheduled Tribes*.

Note: * 1981 Population adjusted according to the districts as in 1961.

Appendix-IV.6

Districts where Bhils were Enumerated in 1981

Andhra Pradesh

Srikakulam
Vizianagaram
Vishakapatnam
East Godavari
West Godavari
Guntur
Prakasam
Chittor
Anantapur
Kurnool
Mahbubnagar
Rangareddi
Hyderabad
Medak
Nizamabad
Adilabad
Karimnagar
Warangal
Khammam

Karnataka

Bangalore
Belgaum
Bellary
Bijapur
Chikmagalur
Chitradurga
Dakshin Kannad
Dharwad
Gulbarga
Hassan
Kodagu
Mandya
Mysore
Raichur
Shimoga
Tikamgarh
Uttar Kannad

Gujarat

Jamnagar
Rajkot
Surendranagar
Bhavnagar
Amreli
Junagarh
Kachch
Banaskantha
Sabarkantha
Mahesana
Gandhinagar
Ahmedabad
Kheda
Panch Mahal
Vadodra
Bharuch
Surat
Valsad
The Dangs

Madhya Pradesh

Morena
Bhind
Gawalior
Datia
Shivpuri
Guna
Tikamgarh
Panna
Sagar
Damoh
Satna
Rewa
Shahdol
Sidhi
Mandsaur
Ratlam
Ujjain
Shajapur
Dewas
Jhabua
Dhar
Indore
West Nimar
East Nimar
Rajgarh
Vidisha
Bhopal
Sehore
Raisen
Betul
Hoshangabad
Jabalpur
Narsimhapur
Mandla
Chhindwara
Seoni
Balaghat
Sarguja
Bilaspur
Raigarh
Rajnandgaon
Durg
Raipur
Bastar

Maharashtra

Greater Bombay

Thane	Buldana	Sikar
Raigarh	Ankola	Ajmer
Ratnagiri	Amravati	Tonk
Nashik	Yavatmal	Jaisalmer
Dhule	Wardha	Jodhpur
Jalgaon	Nagpur	Nagaur
Ahmednagar	Bhandara	Pali
Pune	Chandrapur	Barmer
Satara	***Rajasthan***	Jalor
Sangli	Ganganagar	Sirohi
Solapur	Bikaner	Bhilwara
Kolhapur	Churu	Udaipur
Aurangabad	Jhunjhunu	Chhittaurgarh
Parbhani	Alwar	Dungarpur
Bid	Bharatpur	Banswara
Nanded	Sawai Madhopur	Bundi
Osmanabad	Jaipur	Kota

Bhils: Selected Demographic Indicators

(in per cent)

State/District	Population 1981	Concen-tration Index	Growth Rate 1961-81	Growth Rate Decennial
Rajasthan	**1,840,966**	**24.98**	**96.27**	**48.14**
Ajmer	17,610	0.23	30.20	15.10
Tonk	7,612	0.10	15.35	7.68
Jaisalmer	10,532	0.14	131.17	65.59
Jodhpur	37,559	0.50	154.62	77.31
Pali	15,069	0.20	101.65	50.83
Barmer	108,205	1.46	251.97	125.99
Jalor	57,111	0.77	97.50	48.75
Sirohi	51,420	0.69	69.17	34.59
Bhilwara	69,113	0.93	44.42	22.21
Udaipur	392,709	5.32	70.77	35.39
Chittorgarh	80,687	1.09	77.27	38.64
Dungarpur	331,877	4.50	83.58	41.79
Banswara	582,723	7.90	187.00	93.50
Bundi	23,760	0.32	138.15	69.08
Kota	49,950	0.67	130.85	65.43
Jhalawar	51,863		78.02	39.01
Gujarat	**2,030,438**	**27.55**	**80.73**	**40.37**
Banaskantha	109,662	1.48	109.40	54.70
Sabarkantha	251,127	3.40	104.07	52.04
Ahmedabad	20,467	0.27	138.29	69.15
Kheda	35,276	0.47	189.53	94.77
Panch Mahals	712,224	9.66	76.73	38.37
Vadodra	197,173	2.67	65.92	32.96
Bharuch	456,314	6.19	61.57	30.79
Surat	207,151	2.81	116.29	58.15
The Dangs	27,071	0.36	14.22	7.11
Madhya Pradesh	**2,500,530**	**33.93**	**104.70**	**52.35**
Ratlam	165,142	2.24	185.34	92.67
Jhabua	662,030	8.98	51.94	25.97
Dhar	546,764	7.42	66.26	33.13
West Nimar	685,006	9.29	71.63	35.82
Sehore*	23,539	0.27	1441.52	720.76
Maharashtra	**993,068**	**13.47**	**72.70**	**36.35**
Nashik	167,321	2.27	44.05	22.03
Dhule	531,138	7.20	76.99	38.50
Jalgaon	141,561	1.92	65.80	32.90
Ahmednagar	69,920	0.94	63.46	31.73
Pune	3,476	0.04	157.29	78.65
Aurangabad	36,835	0.49	52.23	26.12
Bid	3,840	0.05	72.66	36.33
Nanded	4,709	0.06	226.56	113.28

Source: Census of India, 1981, Series 5, Gujarat, Part IX; Series 11, Madhya Pradesh, Part IX (viii); Series 1, Maharashtra, Part IX (iii); Series 18, Rajasthan, Part IX, *Special Tables for Scheduled Tribes.*

Note: * 1981 Population has been adjusted to the 1961 districts.

Appendix-IV.8

Districts where Santals were Enumerated in 1981

Bihar

Patna
Nalanda
Nawada
Gaya
Aurangabad
Rohtas
Bhojpur
Saran
Siwan
Gopalganj
Paschim Champaran
Purbi Champaran
Sitamarhi
Muzaffarpur
Vaishali
Begusarai
Samastipur
Darbhanga
Madhubani
Saharsa
Purnia
Katihar
Munger
Bhagalpur
Santal Pargana
Dhanbad
Giridih
Hazaribagh
Palamau
Ranchi
Singhbhum

West Bengal

Koch Bihar
Jalpaiguri
Darjeeling
West Dinajpur
Maldah
Murshidabad
Nadia
Twenty-Four Parganas
Calcutta
Haora
Hugli
Medinipur
Bankura
Purulia
Barddhaman
Birbhum

Orissa

Sambalpur
Sundargarh
Keonjhar
Mayurbhanj
Balasore
Cuttack
Dhenkanal
Phulbani
Bolangir
Kalahandi
Koraput
Ganjam
Puri

Santals: Selected Demographic Indicators

(in per cent)

State/District	Population 1981	Concentration Index	Growth Rate 1961-81	Growth Rate Decennial
West Bengal	**1,666,610**	**39.11**	**38.88**	**19.44**
Darjeeling	11,214	0.26	53.45	26.73
Jalpaiguri	28,906	0.67	-25.04	-12.52
Coochbehar	1,103	0.02	-10.62	-5.31
West Dinajpur	186,282	4.37	52.33	26.17
Maldah	122,364	2.87	45.31	22.66
Murshidabad	30,737	0.72	40.35	20.18
Nadia	11,264	0.26	147.94	73.97
24-Parganas	14,781	0.34	-53.30	-26.65
Haora	2,816	0.06	21.80	10.90
Hugli	104,718	2.45	41.93	20.97
Medinipur	355,321	8.33	52.04	26.02
Barddhman	232,437	4.88	50.29	25.15
Birbhum	130,498	12.45	39.68	19.84
Bankura	208,296	4.88	36.81	18.41
Puruliya	224,096	5.25	26.68	13.34
Calcutta	1,778	0.04	49.04	24.52
Bihar	**2,060,730**	**48.36**	**33.70**	**16.85**
Munger*	48,732	1.14	25.59	12.80
Bhagalpur	58,793	1.37	37.05	18.53
Saharsa	7,312	0.12	37.68	18.84
Purnea*	129,692	1.87	70.55	35.28
Santal Parganas	1,103,511	25.89	25.76	12.88
Hazaribagh*	246,286	1.27	41.72	20.86
Dhanbad	153,848	3.61	42.13	21.07
Singhbhum	306,798	7.20	42.13	21.07
Katihar	49,881	1.17		
Giridih	192,030	4.50		
Orissa	**530,776**		**29.09**	**14.55**
Dhenkanal	5,474	0.12	207.01	103.51
Keonjhar	41,134	0.96	51.46	25.73
Cuttack	9,745	0.22	307.57	153.79
Mayurbhanj	403,423	9.46	18.54	9.27
Balasore	59,465	1.39	65.71	32.86
Sundargarh	7,282	0.17	221.93	110.97

Source: Table generated by the author based on Census of India, 1981, Series 4, Bihar, Part IX (iii); Series 16, Orissa, Part IX (iii); Series 23, West Bengal, Part IX (iii), *Special Tables for Scheduled Tribes.*

Note: *1981 Population has been adjusted to the 1961 districts.

Appendix-IV.10

Gonds: Change in Agrarian Structure, 1961-81*

(in per cent)

State/District	*Cultivators*			*Agricultural Labourers*		
	1961	*1981*	*Change, 1961-81*	*1961*	*1981*	*Change, 1961-81*
Madhya Pradesh		**66.59**			**27.98**	
Guna	56.15	52.22	-3.93	27.96	33.50	5.54
Chhatarpur	73.15	53.78	-19.37	17.96	17.43	-0.53
Panna	52.54	41.83	-10.71	25.89	46.58	20.69
Satna	75.10	59.51	-15.59	16.15	30.49	14.34
Rewa	78.63	51.92	-26.71	12.50	42.83	30.33
Shahdol	86.04	69.98	-16.06	11.19	22.71	11.52
Sidhi	77.29	75.22	-2.07	18.81	20.00	1.19
Dewas	45.33	34.79	-10.54	46.52	58.48	11.96
East Nimar	53.03	41.14	-11.89	39.96	47.49	7.53
Vidisha	26.23	22.66	-3.57	60.74	59.93	-0.81
Sehore	44.48	29.80	-14.68	46.76	62.57	15.81
Raisen	44.20	33.92	-10.28	33.56	62.41	28.85
Hoshangabad	46.45	30.61	-15.84	32.81	54.79	21.98
Betul	73.73	55.56	-18.17	19.19	37.55	18.36
Jabalpur	60.45	49.85	-10.60	27.90	39.83	11.93
Narsimhapur	49.24	32.51	-16.73	36.62	63.30	26.68
Mandla	83.06	77.98	-5.08	14.19	18.70	4.51
Chhindwara	73.94	58.56	-15.38	19.33	35.57	16.24
Seoni	74.29	58.51	-15.78	21.85	37.23	15.38
Balaghat	80.05	60.12	-19.93	16.54	30.75	14.21
Sarguja	83.78	79.24	-4.54	10.55	15.86	5.31
Bilaspur	75.56	64.62	-10.94	20.78	30.49	9.71
Raigarh	75.60	63.96	-11.64	17.99	31.82	13.83
Rajnandgaon		75.17	75.17		21.93	21.93
Durg	74.15	55.68	-18.47	21.15	37.05	15.90
Raipur	67.03	60.08	-6.95	29.22	35.06	5.84
Bastar	83.95	82.96	-0.99	12.28	14.54	2.26
Maharashtra	**54.66**	**40.80**	**-13.86**	**39.62**	**49.30**	**9.68**
Nanded	40.15	35.12	-5.03	56.54	58.17	1.63
Akola		16.25	16.25		74.48	74.48
Amrawati	48.80	17.71	-31.09	32.53	75.64	43.11
Yavatmal	25.14	24.46	-0.68	69.94	70.49	0.55
Wardha		19.91	19.91		73.87	73.87
Nagpur		27.15	27.15		57.77	57.77
Bhandara		45.76	45.76		38.46	38.46
Chanda	71.48	58.16	-13.32	22.57	33.42	10.85

State/District	Cultivators			Agricultural Labourers		
	1961	*1981*	*Change, 1961-81*	*1961*	*1981*	*Change, 1961-81*
Andhra Pradesh	**61.80**	**50.73**	**-10.87**	**31.13**	**45.07**	**13.94**
Adilabad	65.69	54.94	-10.75	28.43	41.27	12.84
Karimnagar	34.28	33.68	-0.60	51.81	60.77	8.96
Warangal	62.89	28.71	-34.18	27.90	65.68	37.78
Khammam	55.27	27.64	-27.63	37.44	67.57	30.13
Orissa	**68.65**	**61.05**	**-7.60**	**20.79**	**32.88**	**12.09**
Kalahandi	69.62	61.78	-7.84	21.35	34.15	12.80
Koraput	77.76	77.71	-0.05	17.19	20.91	3.72
Sambalpur	60.20	49.85	-10.35	24.91	40.88	15.97
Bolangir	66.45	57.94	-8.51	20.39	36.56	16.17
Phulbani		59.38	59.38		29.61	29.61
Boudh-Khondmals	72.05		-72.05	12.24		-12.24
Dhenkanal	72.99	61.35	-11.64	19.91	31.33	11.42
Keonjhar	77.01	66.94	-10.07	17.40	24.38	6.98
Mayurbhanj	82.43	62.02	-20.41	10.78	27.04	16.26
Bihar		**52.65**	**52.65**		**33.32**	**33.32**
Ranchi	89.17	76.13	-13.04	6.95	19.14	12.19
Singhbhum	57.74	56.25	-1.49	23.33	30.17	6.84

* Only the rural segment of population has been considered.

Appendix-IV.11

Bhils: Change in Agrarian Structure, 1961-81*

(in per cent)

State/District	*Cultivators*		*Change*	*Agricultural Labourers*		*Change*
	1961	*1981*	*1961-81*	*1961*	*1981*	*1961-81*
Rajasthan	**85.81**	**75.48**	**-10.33**	**4.90**	**13.57**	**8.67**
Ajmer	65.71	58.30	-7.41	17.00	28.05	11.05
Tonk	61.50	54.30	-7.41	17.00	28.05	11.05
Jaisalmer	37.28	68.64	31.36	0.77	7.98	7.21
Jodhpur	87.28	81.02	-6.26	5.51	11.93	6.42
Pali	61.35	49.93	-11.42	15.10	31.62	16.52
Barmer	93.17			4.67		
Jalor	72.18	59.21	-12.97	14.40	32.15	17.75
Sirohi	54.09	60.09	6.00	13.20	22.38	9.18
Bhilwara	79.57	68.24	-11.33	6.88	18.54	11.66
Udaipur	85.99	76.72	-9.27	2.76	11.93	9.17
Chittorgarh	74.73	68.26	-6.47	9.91	17.92	8.01
Dungarpur	95.23	80.35	-14.88	1.21	10.60	9.39
Banswara	94.47	87.64	-6.83	2.04	7.56	5.52
Bundi	67.08	73.07	5.99	16.00	9.60	-6.40
Kota	54.89	33.44	-21.45	17.90	25.98	8.08
Jhalawar	77.32	70.26	-7.06	14.60	18.48	3.88
Gujarat	**70.40**	**52.75**	**-17.65**	**25.50**	**40.47**	**14.97**
Banaskantha	76.64	63.06	-13.58	6.20	29.28	23.08
Sabarkantha	95.73	77.63	-18.10	2.34	14.97	12.08
Ahmedabad	8.81	4.25	-4.56	31.40	68.13	36.73
Kheda	6.43	1.75	-4.68	74.50	84.44	9.94
Panch Mahals	96.61	88.63	-7.98	1.65	8.27	6.62
Vadodra	36.58	23.15	-13.43	57.90	71.72	13.82
Bharuch	43.58	31.64	-11.94	52.10	60.30	8.20
Surat	41.66	27.06	-14.50	53.50	63.56	10.06
The Dangs	61.98	67.22	5.22	32.20	18.20	18.85
Madhya Pradesh	**86.08**	**72.40**	**-13.68**	**10.80**	**23.87**	**13.07**
Ratlam	96.13	69.76	-26.37	1.98	25.78	23.80
Jhabua	94.59	90.99	-3.60	2.54	6.87	4.33
Dhar	79.66	74.87	-4.79	17.40	23.05	5.65
West Nimar	80.63	70.57	-10.06	15.60	26.00	10.40
Sehore	70.47	57.69	-12.78	23.00	35.90	12.90
Maharashtra	**27.26**	**24.56**	**-2.70**	**63.90**	**69.40**	**5.50**
Nashik	20.13	13.64	-6.49	64.00	79.76	15.76
Dhule	37.24	34.17	-3.07	57.70	60.75	3.05
Jalgaon	15.86	13.21	-2.65	73.90	70.66	-3.24
Ahmednagar	11.64	8.04	-3.60	77.20	84.33	7.13
Pune	13.07	4.90	-8.17	50.20	66.62	16.42
Aurangabad	11.77	12.83	1.06	77.90	79.81	1.91
Bid	6.95	8.69	1.74	75.50	73.08	-2.42
Nanded	32.17	30.67	-1.50	64.10	66.26	2.16

* Only the rural segment of population has been considered.

Santals: Change in Agrarian Structure, 1961-81*

(*in per cent*)

State/District	*Cultivators*		*Change*	*Agricultural Labourers*		*Change*
	1961	*1981*	*1961-81*	*1961*	*1981*	*1961-81*
Bihar	**80.91**	**67.84**	**-13.07**	**9.19**	**24.18**	**14.99**
Munger	70.15	59.29	-10.86	9.75	32.12	22.37
Bhagalpur	61.93	44.90	-17.03	22.34	52.35	30.01
Saharsa	60.21	58.99	-1.22	34.27	44.16	9.89
Purnea	56.13	40.60	-15.53	29.73	57.47	27.74
Santal Parganas	87.83	76.84	-10.99	5.21	17.37	12.16
Hazaribagh	79.80	70.50	-9.30	8.28	19.03	10.75
Dhanbad	70.05	53.16	-16.89	7.54	19.51	11.97
Singhbhum	71.91	57.17	-14.74	-17.47	31.74	-14.27
West Bengal	**54.97**	**36.91**	**-18.06**	**34.11**	**57.03**	**22.92**
Darjeeling	80.45	50.05	-30.40	5.72	36.31	30.59
Jalpaiguri	53.76	40.36	-13.40	6.44	21.63	15.19
Coochbehar	54.51	50.82	-3.69	7.58	39.28	31.70
West Dinajpur	65.10	42.87	-22.23	32.43	55.17	22.74
Maldah	82.70	56.91	-25.79	15.23	41.24	26.01
Murshidabad	33.95	22.34	-11.61	55.72	73.67	17.95
Nadia	19.37	12.07	-7.30	44.59	64.98	20.39
24-Parganas	47.40	13.22	-34.18	40.30	48.98	8.68
Haora	14.92	2.29	-12.63	20.37	71.91	51.54
Hoogly	28.29	10.83	-17.46	64.86	86.17	21.31
Barddhaman	27.28	13.17	-14.11	45.69	77.15	31.46
Birbhum	42.84	31.95	-10.89	46.51	63.43	15.92
Bankura	66.48	51.23	-15.25	25.50	42.69	17.19
Medinipur	46.93	34.63	-12.30	43.98	61.35	17.37
Purulia	79.67	62.33	-17.30	13.83	30.19	16.36
Orissa	**61.13**	**53.95**	**-8.18**	**28.05**	**37.87**	**9.82**
Dhenkanal	48.76	40.10	-8.66	12.26	30.62	18.36
Keonjhar	76.48	63.27	-13.21	16.48	27.67	11.19
Cuttack	46.36	26.97	-19.39	13.67	43.14	29.47
Mayurbhanj	63.65	57.79	-5.86	27.50	34.90	7.40
Balasore	34.12	29.35	-4.77	45.28	64.74	19.46

*Only the rural segment of population has been considered.

Appendix-IV.13

Gonds: Change in Literacy Status, 1961-81*

(*in per cent*)

State/District	*Male Literacy Rate*		*Change*	*Female Literacy Rate*		*Change*
	1961	*1981*	*1961-81*	*1961*	*1981*	*1961-81*
Madhya Pradesh		**20.23**			**3.59**	
Guna	2.04	8.09	6.05		0.80	0.80
Chhatarpur	3.19	4.53	1.34	0.06	0.44	0.38
Panna	5.64	11.13	5.49	0.02	0.97	0.95
Satna	11.11	19.88	8.77	0.31		-0.31
Rewa	6.85	8.76	1.91	0.03	0.68	0.65
Shahdol	8.45	17.63	9.18	0.38	1.62	1.24
Sidhi	5.46	12.84	7.38	0.08	0.75	0.67
Dewas	4.86	13.42	8.56	0.03	0.63	0.60
East Nimar	7.67	19.50	11.83	0.47	3.00	2.53
Vidisha	2.87	10.51	7.64	0.39	1.18	0.79
Sehore	6.18	15.36	9.18	0.71	1.38	0.67
Raisen	4.12	9.92	5.80	0.24	1.10	0.86
Hoshangabad	9.79	17.37	7.58	0.22	2.69	2.47
Betul	7.48	12.68	5.20	0.62	1.88	1.26
Jabalpur	16.46	18.32	1.86	1.26	3.91	2.65
Narsimhapur	12.47	25.26	12.79	1.19	4.47	3.28
Mandla	13.69	16.96	3.27	1.37	2.77	1.40
Chhindwara	8.79	21.55	12.76	0.79	3.81	3.02
Seoni	13.44	32.77	19.33	1.34	8.66	7.32
Balaghat	18.82	16.10	-2.72	2.75	1.90	4.85
Sarguja	9.98	29.47	19.49	0.47	4.48	4.01
Bilaspur	16.00	28.14	12.14	1.48	5.25	3.77
Raigarh	17.36	28.26	10.90	1.62	5.56	3.94
Rajnandgaon		40.30	40.30		11.77	11.77
Durg	20.30	33.72	13.42	2.50	7.13	4.63
Raipur	21.13	10.67	-10.46	2.33	1.99	-0.34
Bastar	5.70	23.60	17.90	0.57	3.42	2.85
Maharashtra	**11.79**	**34.55**	**22.76**	**1.04**	**11.86**	**10.82**
Nanded	9.37	30.53	21.16	0.40	6.64	6.24
Akola		51.10	51.10		25.37	25.37
Amravati	14.47	32.93	18.46	1.39	15.65	14.26
Yevatmal	16.91	35.36	18.45	1.97	12.38	10.41
Wardha		39.52	39.52		18.17	18.17
Nagpur		36.27	36.27		14.01	14.01
Bhandara		42.97	42.97		13.13	13.13
Chanda	9.35	29.23	19.88	0.62	8.68	8.06
Andhra Pradesh	**4.81**	**10.99**	**6.18**	**0.24**	**1.03**	**0.79**
Adilabad	4.97	10.02	5.05	0.25	0.96	0.71
Karimnagar	2.65	7.22	4.57	0.20	0.68	0.48

State/District	Male Literacy Rate		Change	Female Literacy Rate		Change
	1961	*1981*	*1961-81*	*1961*	*1981*	*1961-81*
Warangal	6.08	12.65	6.57	0.23	2.14	1.91
Khammam	3.59	9.00	5.41	0.20	0.97	0.77
Orissa	**19.43**		**-19.43**	**2.16**		**-2.16**
Kalahandi	13.03	20.81	7.78	0.81	1.78	0.97
Koraput	6.92	12.45	5.53	0.12	0.87	0.75
Sambalpur	30.58	42.35	11.77	4.02	10.46	6.44
Bolangir	15.42	26.93	11.51	1.39	3.30	1.91
Phulbani		39.54	39.54		6.75	6.75
Boudh-Khondmals	27.96		-27.96	2.81		-2.81
Dhenkanal	29.30	44.70	15.40	5.29	10.55	5.26
Keonjhar	16.96	47.94	30.98	3.09	13.23	10.14
Mayurbhanj	30.97	47.56	16.59	3.26	12.25	8.99
Bihar		**30.63**	**30.63**		**5.55**	**5.55**
Ranchi	18.63	21.90	3.27	2.44	4.53	2.09
Singhbhum	29.16	40.06	10.90	1.54	6.71	5.17

* Only the rural segment of population has been considered.

Change in Literacy Rate of Rural Bhils, 1961-81

(in per cent)

State/District	*Rural Male Literacy Rate*		*Change*	*Rural Female Literacy Rate*		*Change*
	1961	*1981*	*1961-81*	*1961*	*1981*	*1961-81*
Rajasthan	**4.77**	**11.85**	**7.08**	**0.20**	**0.72**	**0.52**
Tonk	2.39	5.72	3.33	0.15	0.21	0.06
Jaisalmer	1.71	5.28	3.57	0.10	0.15	0.05
Jodhpur	2.59	5.60	3.01	0.08	0.21	0.13
Pali	3.47	5.63	2.16	0.11	0.21	0.10
Jalor	1.16	2.71	1.55	0.01	0.03	0.02
Bhilwara	2.09	3.78	1.69	0.08	0.08	0.00
Udaipur	3.03	8.78	5.75	0.16	0.40	0.24
Chittorgarh	2.05	4.08	2.03	0.02	0.14	0.12
Dungarpur	8.03	18.84	10.81	0.32	1.35	1.03
Banswara	6.31	13.94	7.63	0.23	0.99	0.76
Bundi	1.90	3.17	1.27	0.02	0.11	0.09
Kota	6.12	9.98	3.86	0.37	0.54	0.17
Jhalawar	6.10	13.65	7.55	0.17	0.54	0.37
Gujarat	**16.26**	**27.05**	**10.79**	**2.67**	**7.78**	**5.11**
Banaskantha	4.67	13.07	8.40	0.29	1.49	1.20
Sabarkantha	19.17	37.34	18.17	2.30	12.02	9.72
Ahmedabad	24.94	25.54	0.60	4.73	8.75	4.02
Kheda	16.56	17.37	0.81	3.56	5.23	1.67
Panch Mahals	11.40	21.80	10.40	1.05	4.09	3.04
Vadodra	23.53	32.02	3.49	5.88	9.54	3.60
Bharuch	22.61	33.51	10.90	4.57	11.90	7.33
Surat	14.95	24.24	9.29	2.40	8.18	5.78
Tha Dangs	5.54	44.95	39.41	0.86	12.80	11.94
Madhya Pradesh	**3.46**	**8.60**	**5.14**	**0.21**	**1.12**	**0.91**
Ratlam	2.52	7.77	5.25	0.11	0.61	0.50
Jhabua	2.11	5.95	3.84	0.18	0.95	0.77
Dhar	3.82	9.18	5.36	0.19	0.98	0.79
West Nimar	4.77	10.22	5.45	0.29	1.61	1.32
Maharashtra	**11.08**	**19.18**	**8.10**	**1.21**	**4.27**	**3.06**
Nashik	9.39	16.05	6.66	0.89	3.47	2.58
Dhule	10.72	18.15	7.43	1.06	3.96	2.90
Jalgaon	13.97	20.20	6.23	1.88	3.23	1.35
Ahmednagar	15.28	23.23	7.95	2.03	5.03	3.00
Pune	13.99	17.85	3.86	2.07	2.90	0.83
Aurangabad	6.35	18.74	12.39	0.75	2.25	1.50
Bid	5.49	13.10	7.61	0.95	2.74	1.79
Nanded	8.34	24.60	16.26	0.41	3.69	3.28

Change in Literacy Rate of Rural Santals, 1961-81

(*in per cent*)

State/District	*Rural Male Literacy Rate*		*Change*	*Rural Female Literacy Rate*		*Change*
	1961	*1981*	*1961-81*	*1961*	*1981*	*1961-81*
Bihar	**10.68**	**20.20**	**9.52**	**1.29**	**3.84**	**2.55**
Munger	11.73	17.89	6.16	1.38	1.69	0.31
Bhagalpur	10.19	13.33	3.14	3.53	3.35	-0.18
Saharsa	14.10	25.31	11.21	1.13	4.74	3.61
Purnea	10.44	12.84	2.40	0.83	1.35	0.52
Santal Parganas	10.63	20.38	9.75	1.51	4.75	3.24
Hazaribagh	6.03	10.35	4.32	0.39	1.14	0.75
Dhanbad	11.11	20.92	9.81	0.79	1.74	0.95
Singhbhum	14.41	28.05	13.64	0.99	4.79	3.80
West Bengal	**9.85**	**20.57**	**10.72**	**1.08**	**3.80**	**2.72**
Darjeeling	8.02	14.50	6.48	0.94	2.64	1.70
Jalpaiguri	6.72	17.37	10.65	2.13	6.63	4.50
West Dinajpur	8.97	15.44	6.47	0.84	3.07	2.23
Maldah	7.26	12.72	5.46	0.72	2.28	1.56
Murshidabad	4.09	11.17	7.08	0.18	3.40	3.22
Nadia	9.22	20.62	11.40	0.42	3.41	2.99
24-Parganas	14.73	21.25	6.52	1.61	4.86	3.25
Hoogly	7.51	19.57	12.06	0.83	3.47	2.64
Barddhaman	5.37	11.44	6.07	0.46	1.87	1.41
Birbhum	6.15	12.48	6.33	0.47	2.14	1.67
Bankura	14.25	29.57	15.32	0.94	5.86	4.92
Medinipur	11.29	26.80	15.51	1.69	5.54	3.85
Puruliya	13.75	26.60	12.91	0.89	3.18	2.29
Orissa	**11.37**	**23.31**	**11.94**	**1.28**	**3.97**	**2.69**
Dhenkanal	8.65	21.07	12.42	0.00	2.99	2.99
Keonjhar	5.47	19.03	13.56	2.51	2.29	-0.22
Cuttack	15.66	18.18	2.52	2.81	1.73	-1.08
Mayurbhanj	12.26	24.41	12.15	1.06	4.28	3.22
Balasore	7.06	25.69	18.63	2.47	2.41	-0.06

Regional Variants of Barber, Washerman and Oilman Castes in Madras Presidency, 1931

Castes	*Population*	*Castes*	*Population*
Barber	**360,280**	***Washerman***	**678,522**
Ambattan	10,242	Agasa	19,926
Barber	1,026	Chakali (Tsakala)	404,765
Bhondari	24,934	Dhobi	48,429
Kavuthiyan	3,968	Ekali	3,092
Mangala	174,974	Vannan	198,891
Maruthavan	152	Veluttedan	3,419
Nai	19,444	**Oilman**	**226,405**
Nai Brahman	413	Gandla	29,391
Nasuvan	404	Ganiga	22,292
Navithan	102,915	Telikuia	19,414
Navutiyan	1,013	Telli	50,315
Pandithan	3,914	Vaniga Vaisya	1,695
Pariyari	15,238	Vaniger	3,297
Valanchian	746	Vaniyan	99,942
Velakattalavan	897	Vettakkattan	59

Source: Census of India, 1931, Vol. XIV, Madras, Part II, *Imperial and Provincial Tables*, Table XVII, p. 305.

Appendix-V.2

Madras Presidency: Selected Castes as percentage to all-Hindu Population, 1931

(Figures in per cent)

S. No.	Province/District/State	Hindu Population	Adi-Andhra	Adi-Dravida	Brahman Kanarese	Brahman Tamil	Brahman Telugu	Cheruman	Madiga	Nayar	Paraiyan	Vanniyan	Visvabrahmin Tamil	Visvabrahmin Telugu	Yadava
	Madras Presidency	41,685,148													
	British Territory	41,277,370													
1.	Ganjam	2,201,700	0.70				0.69		0.51					1.35	0.23
2.	Vizagapatnam	3,400,922	2.14				1.56		1.03					3.13	0.28
3.	Godavari East	1,855,439	12.75				4.20		2.40					1.95	0.52
4.	Godavari West	1,134,560	6.94				4.18		5.11					2.16	0.52
5.	Kistna	1,089,523	5.24				5.22		5.77					1.97	3.28
6.	Guntur	1,639,834	1.87				5.01		1.45					1.90	2.03
7.	Nellore	1,317,420	2.70			0.22	2.48		5.27		0.26	0.48	0.12	1.32	1.52
8.	Cuddapah	788,192	1.81		0.14		1.19		6.53					0.91	1.10
9.	Kurnool	805,032	2.78		0.19		1.53		6.55					1.26	
10.	Bellary	857,425	1.75		1.51		0.28		7.80		0.12			0.34	
11.	Anantapur	943,768	5.37		0.73	0.14	1.07		7.47					0.88	
12.	Madras	520,161	0.37	12.19	0.61	8.02	1.32		0.49	0.87	1.89	13.39	2.49	0.49	3.27
13.	Chingleput	1,576,137		17.88		1.77	0.35		0.26		9.82	21.95	2.06	0.15	5.21
14.	Chittoor	1,356,384	2.28	3.33	0.16	0.38	0.89		3.25		1.69	5.00	0.48	1.16	1.08
15.	North Arcot	2,078,222		15.51		1.30	0.16				1.91	28.81	1.87	0.12	5.86
16.	Salem	2,348,325		4.02	0.26	0.74	0.27				4.24	25.45	1.35	0.40	0.75
17.	Coimbatore	2,341,667		1.89	0.36	1.02	0.23			0.18	1.29	2.73	1.48	0.68	0.59
18.	South Arcot	2,301,513		20.74	0.14	1.23	0.20				5.88	35.09	1.97		3.92
19.	Tanjore	2,148,018		3.64	0.14	5.59	0.25				12.77	8.85	2.79		3.23
20.	Trichinopoly	1,737,105		5.07	0.24	2.50	0.28				4.56	9.81	2.35	0.11	2.17
21.	Madurai	2,021,336		1.25	0.11	1.18	0.28				4.13	0.94	3.11	0.86	2.62
22.	Ramnad	1,619,743		1.17		2.03	0.25				3.18	0.19	3.65	0.27	7.72
23.	Tinnevelly	1,698,950		2.29		2.68	0.33				3.98	0.18	4.86	0.22	6.31
24.	Nilgiris	131,053		10.39	0.20	0.94		0.77		2.09	8.31		0.72		
25.	Malabar	2,303,754				1.58		9.02		21.48	0.51				
26.	South Kanara	1,061,187		1.56	3.90			0.56		2.17					
	Princely States	407,778													
27.	Pudukkottai	367,540				2.56	0.41				8.93	0.17	3.83		6.87
28.	Banganapalle	29,176					1.55		9.16					2.04	
29.	Sandur	11,062			2.81		0.33		7.90		1.69				

Source: Census of India, 1931, Vol. XIV, Madras, Part-II, *Imperial and Provincial Tables*, Table XVII, Parts I and II, pp. 305-310.

Madras Presidency: Selected Caste Groups, Population and Proportionate Share, 1931

Caste	*Population*	*Per cent of Total Hindu Population*
Vanniyan (Vanniyakula Kshatriya)	2,944,014	6.99
Adi-Dravida	1,619,227	3.85
Paraiyan	1,117,197	2.65
Yadava	904,695	2.15
Mala	837,718	1.99
Pallan	825,224	1.96
Golla	806,479	1.92
Telaga	699,089	1.66
Adi Andhra	664,844	1.58
Madiga	612,411	1.45
Chakkailiyan	606,775	1.44
Boya	545,066	1.29
Nayar	537,618	1.28
Visvabrahaman, Tamil	524,773	1.25
Kallan	509,859	1.21
Brahaman, Tamil	494,721	1.18
Brahaman, Telugu	472,002	1.12
Arya Vaishya (Komati)	428,803	1.02
Maravan	423,012	1.00
Sengunthar (Kalkolan)	414,731	0.99
Chakali (Tsakala)	404,765	0.96
Visvabrahman, Telugu	373,191	0.89
Labbal	351,893	0.84
Cheruman	214,878	0.51
Vannan	198,891	0.47
Mangala	174,974	0.42
Brahman, Oriya	151,127	0.36
Bant	147,405	0.35
Kalingi	129,344	0.31
Brahman, Kanarese	106,642	0.25
Navithan	102,915	0.24
Vaniyan	99,942	0.24
Dumbo	79,643	0.19
Panchama	75,574	0.18
Pano	70,527	0.17
Razu	69,979	0.17
Valluvan	59,202	0.14
Telli	50,315	0.12
Holeya	49,567	0.12
Dhobi	48,429	0.12
(a) Total of 40 castes	18,947,461	45.01
(b) Total Hindu Population	**42,092,926**	
(a) as percentage to (b)	45.01	

Source: Census of India, 1931, Vol. XIV, Madras, Part II, *Imperial and Provincial Tables*, Table XVII, Parts I and II, pp. 305-310.

Appendix-V.4

Assam: Distribution of Selected Hindu Castes, 1931

S. No.	District/Territory	Total Hindu Population	Ahir	Ahom	Brahman	Kayastha	Kurmi	Hindu Exterior Castes
	Assam	5,204,190	56,398	249,434	159,116	135,590	26,327	596,918
	Assam Valley Division	3,407,831						
1.	Goalpara	385,877			6,247	4,790		15,561
2.	Kamrup	709,960			37,828	7,008		43,227
3.	Darrang	455,623	4,667	4,175	20,571	3,877	3,617	15,621
4.	Nowgong	325,710	2,517	4,218	9,452	5,245		46,721
5.	Sibsagar	841,035	9,491	153,352	23,803	7,941	7,115	36,673
6.	Lakhimpur	661,680	9,098	81,453	9,106	7,262	5,669	24,181
7.	Garo Hills	27,946						
	Surma Valley and Hill Division	1,493,956						
8.	Cachar	359,251	7,472		5,278	11,173	3,203	49,093
9.	Sylhet	1,113,426						
10.	Khasi and Jaintia Hills	10,841						
11.	Naga Hills	6,448						
12.	Lushai Hills	3,990						
	Sadiya Frontier Tract	26,002		4,987				
	Balipara Frontier Tract	3,811						
	Elsewhere		4,211	1,249	2,985	3,047	3,406	2,821

Source: Census of India, 1931, Vol. III, Assam, Part II, Table XVI, *Religion*, pp. 255-57. Table XVII, *Caste, Tribe or Race*, pp. 259-66.

Appendix-V.5

Assam: Selected Castes as percentage of Hindu Population, 1931

S. No.	District/Territory	Total Hindu Population	Ahir	Ahom	Brahman	Kayastha	Kurmi	Hindu Exterior Castes
	Assam	5,204,190	56,398	249,434	159,116	135,590	26,327	596,918
	Assam Valley Division	3,407,831						
1.	Goalpara	385,877			1.62	1.24		4.03
2.	Kamrup	709,960			5.33	0.99		6.09
3.	Darrang	455,623	1.02	0.92	4.51	0.85	0.79	3.43
4.	Nowgong	325,710	0.77	1.30	2.90	1.61		14.34
5.	Sibsagar	841,035	1.13	18.23	2.83	0.94	0.85	4.36
6.	Lakhimpur	661,680	1.37	12.31	1.38	1.10	0.86	3.65
7.	Garo Hills	27,946						
	Surma Valley and Hill Division	1,493,956						
8.	Cachar	359,251	2.08		1.47	3.11	0.89	13.67
9.	Sylhet	1,113,426			3.95			
10.	Khasi and Jaintia Hills	10,841						
11.	Naga Hills	6,448						
12.	Lushai Hills	3990						
	Sadiya FrontierTract	26,002		19.18				
	Balipara Frontier Tract	3,811						

Source: Census of India, 1931, Vol. III, Assam, Part II, Table XVI, *Religion*, pp. 255-57. Table XVII, *Caste, Tribe or Race*, pp. 259-66.

List of the Scheduled Castes, 1991

NORTHWEST

Jammu and Kashmir[1]

Barwala
Basith
Batwal
Chamar or Ramdasia
Chura
Dhyar
Doom or Mahasha
Gardi
Jolaha
Megh or Kabirpanthi
Ratal
Saryara
Watal

Himachal Pradesh[2]

Ad Dharmi
Badhi, Nagalu
Balmiki, Bhangi, Chuhra, Chura, Chuhre
Bandhela
Bangali
Banjara
Bansi
Barad
Barar, Burar, Berar
Batwal
Bauria, Bawaria
Bazigar
Bhanjra, Bharlare
Chamar, Jatia Chamar, Rehgar, Raigar, Ramdasi Ravidasi, Ramdasia, Mochi
Chanal
Chhimbe, Dhobi
Dagi
Darain
Darai, Daryai
Daule, Daole
Dhaki, Toori
Dhanak
Dhaogri, Dhuai
Dhogri, Dhangri, Siggi
Doom, Doomna, Dumna, Dumne, Mahasha
Gagra
Gandhila, Gandil, Gondola
Hali
Hesi
Jogi
Julaha, Julahe, Kabirpanthi, Keer
Kamoh, Dagoli
Karoack
Khatik
Kori, Koli
Lohar
Marija, Marecha
Mazhabi
Megh
Nat
Od
Pasi
Perna
Phrera and Pherera
Rehar, Rehara
Sanhai
Sanhal
Sansi, Bhedkut, Manesh
Sansoi
Sapela
Sarde, Sarera, Sarare,Siryare, Sarehde
Sikligar
Sipi
Sirkiband
Teli
Thathiar, Thathera

Punjab[3]

Ad Dharmi
Balmiki, Chuhra, Bhangi
Bangali
Barar, Burar, Berar
Batwal
Bauria, Bawaria
Bazigar
Bhanjra
Chamar, Jatia Chamar, Rehgar, Raigar, Ramdasi, Ravidasi
Chanal
Dagi
Darain
Deha, Dhaya, Dhea

Dhanak
Dhogri, Dhangri, Siggi
Dumna, Mahasha, Doom
Gagra
Gandhila, Gandal, Gondola
Kabirpanthi, Julaha
Khatik
Kori,Koli
Marija, Marecha
Mazhabi
Megh
Nat
Od
Pasi
Perna
Phrera
Sanhai
Sanhal
Sansi, Bhedkut, Manesh
Sansoi
Sapela
Sarera
Sikligar
Sirkiband

Chandigarh[4]
Ad Dharmi
Bangali
Barar, Burar, Berar
Batwal
Bauria or Bawaria
Bazigar
Balmiki, Chura or Bhangi
Bhanjra
Chamar, Jatia Chamar, Rehgar, Raigar,
Ramdasi, Ravidasi
Chanal
Dagi
Darain
Dhanak
Dhogri, Dhangri, Siggi
Dumna, Mahasha, Doom
Gagra
Gandhila, Gandil, Gondola
Kabirpanthi, Julaha
Khatik
Kori,Koli
Marija, Marecha
Mazhabi
Megh
Nat
Od
Pasi
Perna
Phrera
Sanhai
Sanhal
Sansi, Bhedkut or Manesh
Sansoi
Sapela
Sarera
Sikligar
Sirkiband

Haryana[5]
Ad Dharmi
Balmiki, Chuhra, Bhangi
Bangali
Barar, Burar, Berar
Batwal
Bauria, Bawaria
Bazigar
Bhanjra
Chamar, Jatia Chamar, Rehgar, Raigar,
Ramdasi, Ravidasi
Chanal
Dagi
Darain
Deha, Dhaya, Dhea
Dhanak
Dhogri, Dhangri, Siggi
Dumna, Mahasha, Doom
Gagra
Gandhila, Gandil, Gondola
Kabirpanthi, Julaha
Khatik
Kori,Koli
Marija, Marecha
Mazhabi
Megh
Nat
Od
Pasi
Perna
Phrera
Sanhai
Sanhal
Sansi, Bhedkut, Manesh
Sansoi
Sapela
Sarera
Sikligar
Sirkiband

NORTH
Rajasthan[6]
Adi Dharmi
Aheri
Badia
Bagri, Bagdi

Bairwa, Berwa
Bajgar
Balai
Bansphor, Bansphod
Baori
Bargi, Vargi, Birgi
Bawaria
Bedia, beria
Bhand
Bhangi, Chura, Mehtar, Olgana, Rukhi, Malkana, Halalkhor, Lalbegi, Balmiki, Valmiki, Korar, Zadmalli
Bidakia
Bola
Chamar, Bhambhi, Bambhi, Bhambi, Jatia, Jatav, Jatava, Mochi, Raidas, Rohidas, Regar, Raigar, Ramdasia, Asadaru, Asodi, Chamadia, Chambhar, Chamgar, Haralayya, Harali, Khalpa, Machigar, Mochigar, Madar, Madig, Telegu Mochi, Kamati Mochi, Ranigar, Rohit, Samgar
Chandal
Dabgar
Dhanak, Dhanuk
Dhankia
Dhobi
Dholi
Dome, Dom
Gandia
Garancha, Gancha
Garo, Garura, Gurda, Garoda
Gavaria
Godhi
Jingar
Kalbelia, Sapera
Kamad, Kamadia
Kanjar, Kunjar
Kapadia Sansi
Khangar
Khatik
Kori, Koli
Kooch Band, Kuchband
Koria
Madari, Bazigar
Mahar, Taral, Dhegumegu
Mahyavanshi, Dhed, Dheda, Vankar
Maru Vankar
Majhabi
Mang, Matang, Minimadig
Mang Garodi, Mang Garudi
Megh, Meghval, Meghwal
Menghvar
Mehar
Nat, Nut
Pasi
Rawal
Salvi
Sansi
Santia, Satia
Sarbhangi
Sargara
Singiwala
Thori, Nayak
Tirgar, Tirbanda
Turi

Uttar Pradesh[7]

Agariya
Bhadik
Badi
Baheliya
Baiga
Baiswar
Bajaniya
Bajgi
Balahar
Balai
Balmiki
Bangali
Banmanus
Bansphor
Barwar
Basor
Bawariya
Beldar
Beriya
Bhantu
Bhuiya
Bhuiyar
Boria
Chamar, Dhusia, Jhusia, Jatava
Chero
Dabgar
Dhangar
Dhanuk
Dharkar
Dhobi
Dom
Domar
Dusadh
Gharami
Ghasia
Gond
Gual
Habura
Hari
Hela
Kalabaz

Kanjar
Kapariya
Karwal
Khairaha
Kharwar (excluding Benbansi)
Khatik
Khorot
Kol
Kori
Korwa
Lalabegi
Majhwar
Mazhabi
Musahar
Nat
Pankha
Parahiya
Pasi, Tarmali
Patari
Rawat
Saharya
Sanaurhiya
Sansiya
Shilpkar
Turaiha

Delhi[8]
Adi Dharmi
Agria
Aheria
Balai
Banjara
Bawaria
Bazigar
Bhangi
Bhil
Chamar, Chanwar Chamar, Jatya or Raidasi,Jatav Chamar, Mochi, Ramdasia, Ravidasi,
Raidasi, Rehgarh or Raigar
Chohra (Sweeper)
Chuhra (Balmiki)
Dhanak or Dhanuk
Dhobi
Dom
Gharrami
Julaha (Weaver)
Kabirpanthi
Kachhandha
Kanjar or Giarah
Khatik
Koli
Lalbegi
Madari
Mallah
Mazhabi
Meghwal
Naribut
Nat (Rana)
Pasi
Perna
Sansi or Bhedkut
Sapera
Sikligar
Singiwala or Kalbelia
Sirkiband

Madhya Pradesh[9]
Audhelia
Bagri, Bagdi
Bahna, Bahana
Balahi, Balai
Banchada
Barahar, Basod
Bargunda
Basor, Burud, Bansor, Bansodi, Bansphor
Basar
Bedia
Beldar, Sunkar
Bhangi, Mehtar, Balmik, Lalbegi, Dharkar
Bhanumati
Chadar
Chamar, Chamari, Bairwa, Bhambi, Jatav, Mochi, Regar, Nona, Rohidas, Ramnami, Satnami, Surjyabanshi, Surjyaramnami, Ahirwar, Chamar Mangan, Raidas
Chidar
Chikwa, Chikvi
Chitar
Dahait, Dahayat, Dahat
Dewar
Dhanuk
Dhed, Dher
Dhobi (in Bhopal, Raisen and Sehore districts)
Dohor
Dom, Dumar, Dome, Domar, Doris
Ganda, Gandi
Ghasi, Ghasia
Holiya
Kanjar
Katia, Patharia
Khatik
Koli, Kori
Kotwal (in Bhind, Dhar, Dewas, Guna, Gwalior, Indore, Jhabua, Khargone, Mandsaur, Morena, Rajgarh, Ratlam, Shajapur, Shivpuri, Ujjain and Vidisha districts)
Khangar, Kanera, Mirdha

Kuchbandhia
Kumhar (in Chhattarpur, Datia, Panna, Rewa, Satna, Shahdol, Sidhi, and Tikamgarh districts)
Mahar, Mehra, Mehar
Mang, Mang Garodi, Mang Garudi, Dankhni, Mang, Uang, Mahasi, Madari, Garudi, Radhe Mang
Meghwal
Moghia
Muskhan
Nat, Kalbelia, Sapera, Navdigar, Kubutar,
Pardhi (in Bhind, Dhar, Dewas, Guna, Gwalior, Indore, Jhabua, Khargone, Mandsaur, Morena, Rajgarh, Ratlam, Shajapur, Shivpuri, Ujjain and Vidisha Districts)
Pasi
Rujjhar
Sansi, Sansia
Silawat
Zamral

EAST

Bihar[10]

Bantar
Bauri
Bhogta
Bhuiya
Bhumij (excluding North Chhotanagpur and South Chhotanagpur divisions and Santal Parganas District)
Chamar, Mochi
Chaupal
Dabgar
Dhobi
Dom, Dhangad
Dusadh, Dhari, Dharhi
Ghasi
Halalkhor
Hari, Mehtar, Bhangi
Kanjar
Kurariar
Lalbegi
Musahar
Nat
Pan, Sawasi
Pasi
Raswar
Turi

Orissa[11]

Adi Andhra
Amant, Amat
Audhelia
Badaik
Bagheti, Baghuti
Bajikar
Bari
Bariki
Basor, Burud
Bauri
Bauti
Bavuri
Bedia, Bejia
Beldar
Bhata
Bhoi
Chachati
Chakali
Chamar, Mochi, Muchi, Satnami
Chandala
Chandhai Maru
Cherua, Chhelia
Dandasi
Dewar
Dhanwar
Dhoba, Dhobi
Dom, Dombo, Duria Dom
Dosadha
Ganda
Ghantarghada, Ghantra
Ghasi, Ghasia
Ghogia
Ghusuria
Godagali
Godari
Godra
Gokha
Gorait, Korait
Haddi, Hadi, Hari
Irika
Jaggali
Kandra, Kandara
Karua
Katia
Kela
Khadala
Kodalo, Khodalo
Kori
Kummari
Kurunga
Laban
Laheri
Madari
Madiga
Mahuria
Mala, Jhala, Malo, Zala
Mang

Mangan
Mehra, Mahar
Mehtar, Bhangi
Mewar
Mundapotta
Musahar
Nagarchi
Namasudra
Paidi
Painda
Pamidi
Pan, Pano
Panchama
Panika
Panka
Pantanti
Pap
Pasi
Patial, Patikar, Patratanti
Patua
Rajna
Relli
Sabakhia
Samasi
Sanei
Sapari
Sauntia, Santia
Sidhria
Sinduria
Siyal
Tamadia
Tamudia
Tanla
Tiar, Tior
Turi
Ujia
Valamiki, Valmiki

West Bengal[12]
Bagdi, Duley
Bahelia
Baiti
Bantar
Bauri
Beldar
Bhogta
Bhuimali
Bhuiya
Bind
Chamar, Charmakar, Mochi, Muchi, Rabidas, Ruidas, Rishi
Chaupal
Dabgar
Damai (Nepali)
Dhoba, Dhobi
Doai
Dom, Dhangad
Dosadh, Dusadh, Dhari, Dharhi
Ghasi
Gonrhi
Halalkhor
Hari, Mehtar, Mehtor, Bhangi
Jalia Kaibartta
Jhalo Malo, Malo
Kadar
Kami (Nepali)
Kandra
Kanjar
Kaora
Karenga, Koranga
Kaur
Keot, Keyot
Khaira
Khatik
Koch
Konai
Konwar
Kotal
Kurariar
Lalbegi
Lohar
Mahar
Mal
Mallah
Musahar
Namasudra
Nat
Nuniya
Paliya
Pan, Sawasi
Pasi
Patni
Pod, Poundra
Rajbanshi
Rajwar
Sarki (Nepali)
Sunri (excluding Saha)
Tiyar
Turi

Sikkim[13]
Damai (Nepali)
Kami (Nepali), Lohar (Nepali)
Majhi (Nepali)
Sarki (Nepali)

NORTHEAST
Assam[14]
Bansphor
Bhuinmali, Mali

Brittial Bania, Bania
Dhupi, Dhobi
Dugla, Dholi
Hira
Jalkeot
Jhalo, Malo, Jhalo-Malo
Kaibartta, Jaliya
Lalbegi
Mahara
Mehtar, Bhangi
Muchi, Rishi
Namasudra
Patni
Sutradhar

Arunachal Pradesh[15]
Bansphor
Bhuinmali or Mali
Brittial Bania, Bania
Dhupi, Dhobi
Dugla, Dholi
Hira
Jalkeot
Jhalo, Malo, Jhalo-Malo
Kaibartta or Jaliya
Lalbegi
Mahara
Mehtar or Bhangi
Muchi or Rishi
Namasudra
Patni
Sutradhar

Manipur[16]
Dhupi, Dhobi
Lois
Muchi, Ravidas
Namasudra
Patni
Sutradhar
Yaithibi

Mizoram[17]
Bansphor
Bhuinmali, Mali
Brittial Bania, Bania
Dhupi, Dhobi
Dugla, Dholi
Hira
Jalkeot
Jhalo, Malo, Jhalo-Malo
Kaibartta, Jalia
Lalbegi
Mahara
Mehtar, Bhangi
Muchi, Rishi
Namasudra
Patni
Sutradhar

Meghalaya[18]
Bansphor
Bhuinmali, Mali
Brittial Bania, Bania
Dhupi, Dhobi
Dugla, Dholi
Hira
Jalkeot
Jhalo, Malo, Jhalo-Malo
Kaibartta, Jalia
Lalbegi
Mahara
Mehtar, Bhangi
Muchi, Rishi
Namasudra
Patni
Sutradhar

Tripura[19]
Bagdi
Bhuimal
Bhunar
Chamar, Muchi
Dandasi
Dhenuav
Dhoba
Dum
Ghasi
Gour
Gur
Jalia Kaibartta
Kahar
Kalindi
Kan
Kanda
Kanugh
Keot
Khadit
Kharia
Koch
Koir
Kol
Kora
Kotal
Mahisyadas
Mali
Mehtor
Musahar

Namasudra
Patni
Sabar

WEST

Maharashtra[20]

Ager
Anamuk
Aray Mala
Arwa Mala
Bahna, Bahana
Bakad, Bant
Balahi, Balai
Basor, Burud, Bansor, Bansodi
Beda Jangam, Budga Jangam
Bedar
Bhambi, Bhambhi, Asadaru, Asodi, Chamadia, Chamar, Chamari, Chambhar, Chamgar, Haralayya, Harali, Khalpa Machigar, Mochigar, Madar, Madig, Mochi, Telegu Mochi, Kamati Mochi, Ranigar, Rohidas Nona, Ramnami, Rohit Samgar Samagara, Satnami, Surjyabanshi Surjyaramnami
Bhangi, Mehtar, Olgana, Rukhi, Malkana, Halalkhor, Lalbegi, Balmiki, Korar Zadmali
Bindla
Byagara
Chalvadi, Channayya
Chenna Dasar, Holaya Dasar, Holeya Dasari
Dakkal, Dokkalwar
Dhor, Kakkayya, Kankayya, Dohor
Dom, Dumar
Ellamalvar, Yellamma-Lawandlu
Ganda, Gandi
Garoda, Garo
Ghasi, Ghasia
Halleer
Halsar, Haslar, Hulasvar, Halasvar
Holar, Valhar
Holaya, Holer, Holeya, Holiya
Kaikadi (in Akola, Amravati, Bhandara, Buldana, Nagpur, Wardha and Yavatmal districts and Chandrapur district other than Rajura tahsil)
Katia, Patharia
Khangar, Kanera, Mirdha
Khatik, Chikwa, Chikvi
Kolupulvandlu
Kori
Lingader
Madgi
Madiga
Mahar, Mehra, Taral, Dhegu Megu
Mahyavanshi, Dhed, Vankar, Maru Vankar
Mala
Mala Dasari
Mala Hannai
Mala Jangam
Mala Masti
Mala Sale, Netkani
Mala Sanyasi
Mang, Matang, Minimadig, Dankhni Mang, Mang Mahashi, Madari, Garudi, Radhe Mang, Mang Garodi,Mang Garudi
Manne
Mashti
Meghval, Menghvar
Mitha, Ayyalvar
Mukri
Nadia, Hadi
Pasi
Sansi
Shenva, Chenva, Sedma, Ravat
Sindhollu Chindollu
Tirgar, Tirbanda
Turi

Gujarat'

Ager
Bakad, Bant
Bawa-Dedh, Dedh-Sadhu
Bhambi, Bhambhi, Asadaru, Asodi, Chamadia, Chamar, Chambhar, Chamgar, Haralayya, Harali, Khalpa, Machigar, Mochigar, Madar, Madig, Mochi, Nalia, Telegu Mochi, Kamati Mochi, Ranigar, Rohidas, Rohit, Samgar
Bhangi, Mehtar, Olgana, Rukhi, Malkana, Halalkhor, Lalbegi, Balmiki, Korar, Zadmalli
Chalvadi, Channayya
Chenna Dasar, Holaya Dasar
Dangashia
Dhor, Kakkayya, Kankayya
Garmatang
Garoda, Garo
Halleer
Halsar, Haslar, Hulasvar, Halasvar
Holar, Valhar
Holaya, Holer
Lingader
Mahar, Taral, Dhegu Megu
Mahyavansi, Dhed, Dhedh, Vankar, Maru Vankar, Antyaj
Mang, Matang, Minimadig
Mang-Garudi
Meghval, Meghwal, Menghvar

Mukri
Nadia, Hadi
Pasi
Senva, Shenva, Chenva, Sedma, Rawat
Shemalia
Thori
Tirgar, Tirbanda
Turi
Turi Barot, Dedh Barot

Goa[22]
Bhangi
Chambhar
Mahar
Mahyavanshi
Mang

Daman and Diu[23]
Synonm
Hadi
Vankar

Dadra and Nagar Haveli[24]
Bhangi
Chamar
Mahar
Mahyavanshi, Dhed

SOUTH
Andhra Pradesh[25]
Adi Andhra
Adi Dravida
Anamuk
Aray Mala
Arundhatiya
Arwa Mala
Bariki
Bavuri
Beda Jangam, Budga Jangam
Bindla
Byagara
Chachati
Chalavadi
Chamar, Mochi, Muchi
Chambhar
Chandala
Dakkal, Dokkalwar
Dandasi
Dhor
Dom, Dombara, Paidi, Pano
Ellamalawar, Yellammalawandlu
Ghasi, Haddi, Relli Chachandi
Godagali
Godari
Gosangi
Holeya
Holeya Dasari
Jaggali
Jambuvulu
Kolupulvandlu
Madasi Kuruva, Madari Kuruva
Madiga
Madiga Dasu, Mashteen
Mahar
Mala
Mala Dasari
Mala Dasu
Mala Hannai
Mala Jangam
Mala Masti
Mala Sale, Netkani
Mala Sanyasi
Mang
Mang Garodi
Manne
Mashti
Matangi
Mehtar
Mitha, Ayyalvar
Mundala
Paky, Moti, Thoti
Pambada, Pambanda
Pamidi
Panchama, Pariah
Relli
Samagara
Samban
Sapru
Sindhollu, Chindollu

Karnataka[26]
Adi Andhra
Adi Dravida
Adi Karnataka
Adiya (in Coorg district)
Ager
Ajila
Anamuk
Aray Mala
Arunthathiyar
Arwa Mala
Baira
Bakad
Bant (in Belgaum, Bijapur, Dharwar and North Kanara districts)
Bakuda
Balagai
Bandi

Banjara, Lambani
Bathada
Beda Jangam, Budga Jangam
Bellara
Bhangi, Mehtar, Olgana, Rukhi, Malkana, Halalkhor , Lalbegi, Balmiki, Korar, Zadmali
Bhambi, Bhambhi, Asadaru, Asodi, Chamadia, Chamar,
Chambhar, Chamgar, Haralayya, Harali, Khalpa, Machigar,
Mochigar, Madar, Madig, Mochi, Muchi, Telugu Mochi, Kamati Mochi, Ranigar
Rohidas, Rohit, Samgar
Bhovi
Bindla
Byagara
Chakkiliyan
Chalavadi, Chalvadi
Channayya
Chandala
Chenna Dasar, Holaya Dasar
Dakkal, Dokkalwar
Dakkaliga
Dhor, Kakkayya, Kankayya
Dom, Dombara, Paidi, Pano
Ellamalawar, Yellammalawandlu
Ganti Chores
Garoda, Garo
Godda
Gosangi
Halleer
Halsar, Haslar, Hulasvar Halasvar
Handi Jogis
Hasla
Holar, Valhar
Holaya, Holer, Holeya
Holeya Dasari
Jaggali
Jambuvulu
Kadaiyan
Kalladi
Kepmaris
Kolupulvandlu
Koosa
Koracha
Korama
Kotegar, Metri
Kudumban
Kuruvan
Lingader
Machala
Madari
Madiga
Mahar, Taral, Dhegu, Megu
Mahyavanshi, Dhed, Vankar
Maru Vankar
Maila
Mala
Mala Dasari
Mala Hannai
Mala Jangam
Mala Masti
Mala Sale, Netkani
Mala Sanyasi
Mang, Matang, Minimadig
Mang Gurudi, Mang Garodi
Manne
Mashti
Mavilan
Meghval, Menghvar
Moger
Mukri
Mundala
Nadia, Hadi
Nalkadaya
Nalakeyava
Nayadi
Pale
Pallan
Pambada
Panchama
Panniandi
Paraiyan, Paraya
Paravan
Reneyar
Samagara
Samban
Sapari
Sillekyathas
Sindhollu, Chindollu
Sudugadu Siddha
Thoti
Tirgar, Tirbanda
Valluvan

Kerala[27]
Adi Andhra
Adi Dravida
Adi Karnataka
Ajila
Arunthathiyar
Ayyanavar
Baira
Bakuda
Bandi
Bathada
Bellara
Bharatar

Boyan (excluding the areas comprising the Malabar district as specified by sub-section (2) of section 5 of the states Reorganisation Act, 1956 (37 of 1956)
Chakkiliyan
Chamar, Muchi
Chandala
Cheruman
Domban
Gavara
Godagali
Godda
Gosangi
Hasla
Holeya
Kadaiyan
Kakkalan
Kalladi
Kanakkan, Padanna
Karimpalan
Davara
Koosa
Kootan, Koodan
Kudumban
Kuravan, Sidhanar
Maila
Malayan (in the areas comprising the Malabar districts as specified by sub-section (2) of section 5 of the states Reorganisation Act, 1956 (37 of 1956)
Mannan
Mavilan
Moger
Mundala
Nalakeyava
Nalkadaya
Nayadi
Padannan
Pallan
Palluvan
Pambada
Panan
Panchama
Paraiyan, Parayan, Sambbavar
Paravan
Pathiyan
Peumannan
Pulayan, Cheramar
Pulaya Vettuvan
Puthirai Vannan
Raneyar
Samagara
Samban
Semman
Thandan
Thoti
Vallon
Valluvan
Vannan
Velan
Vetan
Vettuvan

Tamil Nadu[28]
Adi Andhra
Adi Dravida
Adi Karnataka
Ajila
Arunthathiyar
Ayyanavar (in Kanyakumari district and Shenkottah taluk of Tirunelveli district)
Baira
Bakuda
Bandi
Bellara
Bharatar (in Kanyakumari district and Shenkottah taluk of Tirunelveli district)
Chakkiliyan
Chalavadi
Chamar, Muchi
Chandala
Cheruman
Devendrakulathan
Dom, Dombara, Paidi, Pano
Domban
Godagali
Godda
Gosangi
Holeya
Jaggali
Jambuvulu
Kadaiyan
Kakkalan (in Kanyakumari district and Shenkottah taluk of Tirunelveli district)
Kalladi
Kanakkan, Padanna (in Nilgiris district)
Karim Palan
Kavara (in Kanyakumari district and Shenkottah taluk of Tirunelveli district)
Koliyan
Koosa
Kootan, Koodan (in Kanyakumari district and Shenkottah taluk of Tirunelveli district)
Kudumban
Kuravan, Sidhanar
Madari

Madiga
Maila
Mala
Mannan (in Kanyakumari district and Shenkottah taluk of Tirunelveli district)
Mavilan
Moger
Mundala
Nalakeyava
Nayadi
Padannan (in Kanyakumari district and Shenkottah taluk of Tirunelveli district)
Pagada
Pallan
Palluvan
Pambada
Panan (in Kanyakumari district and Shenkottah taluk of Tirunelveli district)
Panchama
Pannadi
Panniandi
Paraiyan, Parayan, Sambavar
Paravan (in Kanyakumari district and Shenkottah taluk of Tirunelveli district)
Pathiyan (in Kanyakumari district and Shenkottah taluk of Tirunelveli district)
Pulayan, Cheramar
Puthirai Vannan
Raneyar
Samagara
Samban
Sapari
Semman
Thandan (in Kanyakumari district and Shenkottah taluk of Tirunelveli district)
Thoti
Tiruvalluvar
Vallorl
Valluvan
Vannan (in Kanyakumari district and Shenkottah taluk of Tirunelveli district)
Vathiriyan
Velan
Vetan (in Kanyakumari district and Shenkottah taluk of Tirunelveli district)
Vettiyan
Vettuvan (in Kanyakumari district and Shenkottah taluk of Tirunelveli district)

Pondicherry[29]
Adi Andhra
Adi Dravida
Chakkiltyan
Jambuvulu
Kuravan
Madiga
Mala, Mala Masti
Paky
Pallan
Parayan, Sambavar
Samban
Thoti
Valluvan
Vetan
Vettiyan

Notes:

1. The Constitution (Jammu and Kashmir) Scheduled Castes Order, 1956.
2. The Scheduled Castes and Scheduled Tribes Orders (Amendment) Act, 1976 (No. 108 of 1976), dated the 18th September, 1976.
3. The Scheduled Castes and Scheduled Tribes Orders (Amendment) Act, 1976 (No. 108 of 1976), dated the 18th September, 1976.
4. The Scheduled Castes and Scheduled Tribes Orders (Amendment) Act, 1976 (No. 108 of 1976), dated the 18th September, 1976.
5. The Scheduled Castes and Scheduled Tribes Orders (Amendment) Act, 1976 (No. 108 of 1976), dated the 18th September, 1976.
6. The Scheduled Castes and Scheduled Tribes Orders (Amendment) Act, 1976 (No. 108 of 1976), dated the 18th September, 1976.
7. The Scheduled Castes and Scheduled Tribes List (Modification) Order, 1956.
8. The Scheduled Castes and Scheduled Tribes List (Modification) Order, 1956 and as added by Act 31 of 1966.
9. The Scheduled Castes and Scheduled Tribes Orders (Amendment) Act, 1976 (No. 108 of 1976), dated the 18th September, 1976.

10. The Scheduled Castes and Scheduled Tribes Orders (Amendment) Act, 1976 (No. 108 of 1976), dated the 18th September, 1976.
11. The Scheduled Castes and Scheduled Tribes Orders (Amendment) Act, 1976 (No. 108 of 1976), dated the 18th September, 1976.
12. The Scheduled Castes and Scheduled Tribes Orders (Amendment) Act, 1976 (No. 108 of 1976), dated the 18th September, 1976.
13. The Constitution (Sikkim) Scheduled Castes Orders, 1978 C.O. 110.
14. The Scheduled Castes and Scheduled Tribes Orders (Amendment) Act, 1976 (No. 108 of 1976), dated the 18th September, 1976.
15. The Scheduled Castes and Scheduled Tribes List (Modification) Order, 1956.
16. The Scheduled Castes and Scheduled Tribes Orders (Amendment) Act, 1976 (No. 108 of 1976), dated the 18th September, 1976.
17. The Scheduled Castes and Scheduled Tribes List (Modification) Order, 1956 and as inserted by Act 81 of 1971.
18. The Scheduled Castes and Scheduled Tribes Orders (Amendment) Act, 1976 and the Constitution (Scheduled Tribes) Order (Amendment) Act, 1987.
19. The Scheduled Castes and Scheduled Tribes Orders (Amendment) Act, 1976 (No. 108 of 1976), dated the 18th September, 1976.
20. The Scheduled Castes and Scheduled Tribes Orders (Amendment) Act, 1976 (No. 108 of 1976), dated the 18th September, 1976.
21. The Scheduled Castes and Scheduled Tribes Orders (Amendment) Act, 1976 (No. 108 of 1976), dated the 18th September, 1976.
22. The Constitution (Goa, Daman and Diu) Scheduled Castes Orders 1968, C.O. 81.
23. The Constitution (Goa, Daman and Diu) Scheduled Castes Orders 1968, C.O. 81.
24. The Constitution (Dadra and Nagar Haveli) Scheduled Castes Orders 1962, C.O. 64.
25. The Scheduled Castes and Scheduled Tribes Orders (Amendment) Act, 1976 (No. 108 of 1976, dated the 18th September, 1976.
26. The Scheduled Castes and Scheduled Tribes Orders (Amendment) Act, 1976 (No. 108 of 1976), dated the 18th September, 1976.
27. The Scheduled Castes and Scheduled Tribes Orders (Amendment) Act, 1976 (No. 108 of 1976), dated the 18th September, 1976.
28. The Scheduled Castes and Scheduled Tribes Orders (Amendment) Act, 1976 (No. 108 of 1976), dated the 18th September, 1976.
29. The Constitution (Pondicherry) Scheduled Castes Orders 1964, C.O. 68.

Appendix-V.7

Major Castes of the Scheduled Category Arranged in Descending Order of Numerical Strength at the All-India Level, 1981

Name of Caste	*Population*	*Name of Caste*	*Population*
Chamar/Chambhar	25,817,567	Pan/Pano	806,514
Adi Dravida	4,517,262	Adi Andhra	791,888
Pasi	3,981,796	Ad Dharmi	703,012
Madiga	3,885,325	Ganda/Gandi	624,896
Mehta/Balmiki	3,232,832	Banjara/Lambani	608,288
Mala	2,934,797	Bhavi	607,931
Dhoba/Dhobi	2,868,518	Chakkilingh	546,755
Dusad	2,836,748	Shilpkar	514,877
Kori/Koli	2,480,556	Arundhatiya/Arunthathiyar	504,903
Mahar	2,334,379	Halanga/Holer	450,677
Rajbanshi	2,258,760	Bairwa/Berwa	429,627
Adi Karnataka	1,927,700	Kandra	381,550
Namasudra	1,887,230	Madari	361,781
Bagdi/Duley	1,831,804	Thori	350,835
Pod/Poundra	1,536,196	Cheruman	294,823
Musahar	1,534,912	Kuravan	291,004
Mazhabi	1,527,055	Dhanak	269,436
Dom/Dum/Doom	1,311,747	Lohar	263,988
Balahi/Balai	1,258,212	Thandan	204,530
Bhambi	1,218,662	Julaha	179,845
Mang	1,211,335	Bazigar	179,630
Megh	1,180,035	Kanakkan/Padanna	144,210
Bauri	1,171,597	Dhor	93,384
Mahyavansi/Dhed/Dhedh	1,068,682	Mala Sale/Netkani	81,730
Meghva/Meghwal/Meghwar	1,065,817	Lingader	65,076
Paraiyan/Parayan	1,043,036	Senva/Shenva/Chenva	64,368
Paraiyan	1,043,036	Od	61,855
Pallan	1,039,540	Garoda/Garo	53,029
Bhuiya	952,025	Hali	20,022
Pulayan	852,185		
Total			91,759,810

Major Castes of the Scheduled Category Arranged in Descending Order of Numerical Strength by States of the Indian Union, 1981 Census

Himachal Pradesh
Koli
Chamar
Lohar
Julaha
Dom
Hali

Punjab
Mazhabi
Chamar
Ad Dharmi
Balmiki
Dom
Bazigar

Haryana
Chamar
Balmiki
Dhanak
Mazhabi
Bazigar
Od

Uttar Pradesh
Chamar
Pasi
Dhobi
Koli
Balmiki
Shilpkar

Rajasthan
Chamar
Megh
Balai
Bairwa
Thori
Koli

Madhya Pradesh
Chamar
Balai
Mahar
Koli
Balmiki
Ganda

Bihar
Dusadh
Chamar
Musahar
Bhuiya
Dhobi
Pasi

Orissa
Pan
Dom
Ganda
Dhobi
Bauri
Kandra

West Bengal
Rajbansi
Gagdi
Namasudra
Pod
Bauri
Chamar

Gujarat
Mahyavansi
Bhambi
Mehtar
Meghval
Benva
Garoda

Maharashtra
Mahar
Mang
Bhanbi
Mehtar
Dhor
Lingader

Tamil Nadu
Adi Dravida
Pallan
Paraiyan
Chakkillyan
Arunthathiyar
Madari

Andhra Pradesh
Madiga
Mala
Adi Andhra
Adi Dravida
Mala Sale
Arundhatiya

Karnataka
Adi Karnataka
Dhovi
Banjara
Adi Dravida
Holaya
Bhambi

Kerala
Pulayan
Cheruman
Kuravan
Thandan
Paraiyan
Kanakkan

Classification of Austric Languages, 1991

Branch	*Language*	*Speakers, 1991*	*Per cent of All Speakers*
Mon Khmer	Khasi	912,283	9.64
	Nicobarese	26,261	0.28
Munda	Santali	5,216,325	55.13
	Munda	413,894	4.37
	Mundari	861,378	9.10
	Bhumij	45,302	0.48
	Birhor Koda/Kora	28,200	0.30
	Ho	949,216	10.03
	Asuri	N.A.	N.A.
	Brijia	N.A.	N.A.
	Korku	466,073	4.93
	Kharia	225,556	2.38
	Juang	16,858	0.18
	Savara	273,168	2.89
	Gadaba	28,158	0.30
	Kharwari		
	Total Speakers	9,462,672	100.00

Source: Census of India, 1991, Series -1, India, Paper 1 of 1997, Table C-7, *Language*.

Classification of Tibeto-Burman Languages, 1991

Branch	*Group*	*Language*	*Speakers, 1991*	*Per cent of All Speakers*
Tibeto-Himalayan	Bhotia	Tibetan	69,416	0.86
		Balti	N.A.	N.A.
		Ladakhi	N.A.	N.A.
		Lahauli	22,027	0.27
		Sherpa	16,105	0.20
		Sikkim Bhotia	55,483	0.69
	Himalayan	Kinnauri	61,794	0.76
		Lepcha	39,342	0.49
		Lahauli*	—	—
North-Assam	NEFA	Aka	N.A.	N.A.
		Dafla	N.A.	N.A.
		Abor/Adi	N.A.	N.A.
		Adi	158,409	1.96
		Miri**	390,583	4.83
		Mishmi	29,000	0.36
		Mishing	N.A.	N.A.
Assam-Burmese	Bodo	Bodo***	1,221,881	15.10
		Kachari	N.A.	N.A.
		Lalung	33,746	0.42
		Dimasa	88,543	1.09
		Garo	675,642	8.35
		Koch	26,179	0.32
		Rabha	139,365	1.72
		Milir/Karbi	366,229	4.53
		Tripuri	694,940	8.59
	Naga	Angami	97,631	1.21
		Sema	166,157	2.05
		Rengma	37,521	0.46
		Khezha	13,004	0.16
		Ao	172,449	2.13
		Lotha	85,802	1.06
		Kabui	68,925	0.85
		Mao	77,810	0.96
		Tangkhul	101,841	1.26
		Konyak	137,722	1.70
		Pochury	11,231	0.14
		Phom	65,350	0.81
		Yin Chungre	47,227	0.58
		Khiemnungan	23,544	0.29

Branch	Group	Language	Speakers, 1991	Per cent of All Speakers
Kuki-Chin		Manipuri/Meitei	1,270,216	15.70
		Thado	107,992	1.33
		Paite	49,237	0.61
		Lushai	538,842	6.66
		Rangkhul	N.A.	N.A.
		Halam	29,322	0.36
		Hmar	65,204	0.81
		Total Speakers+	8,092,940	100.00

Source: Census of India, 1991, Series-1, India, Paper 1 of 1997, Table C-7, *Language*.

Notes:
* The census did not count Lahauli of Chamba separately, although it was other than the Lahauli mentioned under Bhotia group.

** includes Mishing.

*** includes Cachari, although total speakers of Cachari were separately shown as 11,588.

+ Total speakers of all languages of Tibeto-Burman family.

Classification of Dravidian Languages, 1991

Branch	*Language*	*Speakers, 1991*	*Per cent of All Speakers*
South Dravidian	Tamil	52,886,931	27.99
	Yerukala	63,133	0.03
	Malayalam	30,325,637	16.05
	Yerava	17,295	0.00
	Kannada	32,753,676	17.34
	Kuruba	N.A.	N.A.
	Coorgi/Kodaga	97,011	0.05
	Tulu	1,550,334	0.82
	Toda	N.A.	N.A.
	Kota	N.A.	N.A.
	Koda/Kota	27,703	0.01
Central Dravidian	Telugu	65,900,723	34.88
	Vadaga	N.A.	N.A.
	Kui	641,600	0.34
	Kolami	98,281	0.05
	Gondi	2,124,852	0.12
	Parji	44,001	0.02
	Koya	270,994	0.14
	Khond/Kondh	220,783	0.12
	Konda	17,864	0.01
North Dravidian	Kurukh-Oraon	1,426,618	0.76
	Malto	108,148	0.06
	Total Speakers	188,945,126	100.00

Source: Census of India, 1991, Series-1, India, Paper 1 of 1997, Table C-7, *Language*.

Classification of Indo-European Languages, 1991

Branch	Group	Language	Speakers, 1991	Per cent of All Speakers
Dardic	Dard	Dardi	N.A.	N.A.
		Shina	N.A.	N.A.
		Kohistani	N.A.	N.A.
		Kashmiri*	56,693	0.01
Indo-Aryan	Northwestern	Lahnda**	27,386	0.00
		Sindhi/Kachchi***	2,122,848	0.34
	Southern	Marathi	62,421,442	9.89
		Konkani	1,723,264	0.27
	Eastern	Oriya	27,586,476	4.37
		Bihari		
		(a) Maithili	7,766,597	1.23
		(b) Magadhi	10,566,842	1.67
		(c) Bhojpuri	23,102,050	3.66
		Bengali	66,552,894	10.54
		Assamese	12,962,721	2.05
	East Central	Awadhi	481,316	0.08
		Bagheli	1,387,160	0.22
		Chhattisgarhi	10,595,199	1.68
	Central	Hindi (Western Hindi)		
		(a) Bangaru		
		(b) Braj Bhaka	85,230	0.01
		(c) Bundeli	1,657,473	0.26
		(d) Kanauji		
		Urdu	43,406,932	6.88
		Punjabi/East Punjabi	23,085,063	3.66
		Rajasthani+	13,328,581	2.11
		(a) Marwari	4,673,276	0.74
		(b) Mewari	2,114,622	0.33
		(c) Mewati	102,916	0.02
		(d) Kurmali	236,856	0.04
		(e) Bagri Rajasthani	593,730	0.09
		(f) Banjari	887,632	0.14
	Northern	Eastern Pahari/Nepali	2,075,746	0.33
		Central Pahari		
		(a) Kumauni	1,717,191	0.27
		(b) Garhwali	1,872,578	0.30

Branch	Group	Language	Speakers, 1991	Per cent of All Speakers
		Western Pahari++		
		(a) Jaunsari	96,995	0.02
		(b) Sirmauri	370,558	0.06
		(c) Kului	152,442	0.02
		(d) Mandeali	440,421	0.07
		(e) Chameali	63,408	0.01
		(f) Bharmauri/Gaddi	18,919	0.00
		(g) Churahi	45,107	0.01
		Total Speakers	631,273,191	100.00

Source: Census of India, 1991, Series-1, India, Paper 1 of 1997, Table C-7, *Language*.

Notes:
* The numerical strength of the Kashmiri speakers shown here is incomplete as 1991 census was not conducted in Jammu and Kashmir. The figure includes 22,398 speakers of Siraji.

** Includes 20,589 speakers of Multani.

*** Sindhi 1,551,384; Kachchi 566,199.

\+ A total strength of 13,328,581 has been shown separately under Rajasthani.

++ A total strength of 2,179,832 has been shown separately under Pahari; eastern, western or central categories not indicated.

Languages of the Eighth Schedule, 1991

S. No.	*Languages*	*Speakers*	*Percentage of All-India Population*
1.	Hindi	337,272,114	40.22
2.	Bengali	69,595,738	8.30
3.	Telugu	66,017,615	7.87
4.	Marathi	62,481,681	7.45
5.	Tamil	53,006,368	6.32
6.	Urdu	43,406,932	5.18
7.	Gujarati	40,673,814	4.85
8.	Kannada	32,753,676	3.91
9.	Malayalam	30,377,176	3.62
10.	Oriya	28,061,313	3.35
11.	Punjabi	23,378,744	2.79
12.	Assamese	13,079,696	1.56
13.	Sindhi	2,122,848	0.25
14.	Nepali	2,076,645	0.25
15.	Konkani	1,760,607	0.21
16.	Manipuri	1,270,216	0.15
17.	Kashmiri*	56,693	0.01
18.	Sanskrit	49,736	0.01
	Total**	807,441,612	96.29

Source: Census of India, 1991, Series-1, India, Paper 1 of 1997, Table C-7, *Language*.

Note: * Excluding Kashmiri speakers in Jammu and Kashmir.

** Speakers of the Eighth Schedule languages excluding Jammu and Kashmir.

Degree of Concentration of Selected Scheduled Languages, 1991

Language	*Concentration Index (%)*	*State*
Assamese	99.07	Assam
Oriya	93.36	Orissa
Gujarati	92.92	Gujarat
Marathi	92.66	Maharashtra
Malayalam	92.49	Kerala
Tamil	91.38	Tamil Nadu
Kannada	90.94	Karnataka
Telugu	85..40	Andhra Pradesh
Bengali	84.12	West Bengal
Punjabi	80.01	Punjab

Source: Census of India, 1991, Series-1, India, Paper 1 of 1997, Table C-7, *Language.*

Dialects of Hindi

Hindi is the standardized form of a large number of dialects which serve the purpose of oral communication in the day-to-day life of the people. However, many of these dialects have a literary tradition which goes back to several centuries. For example, the literature produced in *Braj Bhasha* and *Awadhi* forms an integral part of the contemporary pedagogic tradition of Hindi literature. Poets such as Surdas, Tulsidas, Kabir and Rahim left behind a glorious poetic tradition which continues to inspire the Hindi poets even today. Other dialects, such as *Maithili* and *Marwari*, also have a rich literary tradition. The fact that all of them have subsumed under Hindi as its dialects leaves many questions open. The collection of data on mother tongues during the census operations confuses the issue further. It may not be very helpful if the census publishes data on mother tongues without subjecting the dialects to a scientific scheme of linguistic classification. The matter of classification cannot be left to the people who do not always know which branch or group the dialect they use belongs to. In the absence of the scientific criteria, anomalies arise which have serious implications. For example, at one census people claim *Maithili* as their mother tongue and at another census they claim Hindi as their mother tongue. An Indian linguist, L.M. Khubchandani described this phenomenon as 'fluidity'. A total of 48 dialects which have been subsumed under Hindi are listed along with the numerical strength of their speakers at the 1991 census arranged in a descending order.

Mother Tongues Grouped under Hindi

Mother Tongue	*Speakers**	*Mother Tongue*	*Speakers**
Bhojpuri	23,102,050	Bagheli/Baghelkhandi	1,387,160
Rajasthani	13,328,581	Harauti	1,235,252
Chhattisgarhi	10,595,199	Kortha/Khotta	1,049,655
Magadhi/Maghai	10,566,842	Surguja	1,045,455
Maithili	7,766,597	Dhundhari	965,006
Marwari	4,673,276	Banjari	887,632
Unspecified	4,642,964	Nagpuria	777,738
Malvi	2,970,103	Bagri Rajasthani	593,730
Pahari	2,179,832	Kangri	487,999
Mewari	2,114,622	Awadhi	481,316
Lamani/Lambadi	2,054,537	Mandeali	440,421
Garhwali	1,872,578	Surjapuri	370,558
Kumauni	1,717,191	Haryanavi	362,476
Bundeli/Bundelkhandi	1,657,473	Kurmali Thar	236,856
Sadan/Sadri	1,569,066	Pawari/Powari	213,874

Mother Tongue	*Speakers**	*Mother Tongue*	*Speakers**
Nimadi	1,420,051	Kulvi	152,442
Panch Pargania	151,599	Sondwari	37,958
Sugali	113,491	Bharmauri/Gaddi	18,919
Mewati	102,916	Sirmauri	18,280
Jaunsari	96,995	Pangwali	14,780
Braj Bhasha	85,230	Khairari	14,307
Lodhi	68,145	Labani	13,722
Laria	64,903	Sanori	11,537
Chambeali	63,408	Hindi	233,432,285
Churahi	45,107	Total Speakers	337,272,114

Source: Census of India, 1991, Series-1, India, Paper 1 of 1997, Table C-7, *Language.*

Notes: * Number of persons who returned the language as their mother tongue at the 1991 census. A perusal of above data leads to the identification of a number of anomalies. Some examples are cited below:

(a) Bagri Rajasthani, Kurmali Thar, Marwari and Mewati as well as Rajasthani are shown as separate dialects. In fact all these dialects are subsumed under Rajasthani which is a regional expression.

(b) Pahari is shown separately, while there are dialects, such as Juansari, Kangri, Kulvi, Kumauni, Garhwali, Mandeali, Chambeali, Bhirmauri/Gaddi etc. have been shown separately. They are all sub-groups of the Pahari and genetically related to it.

These anomalies make the use of census data on languages problematic.

Distribution of the Hindus, 1991

States/Union Territories	*Population*	*Concentration Index (%)*
States		
Andhra Pradesh	59,281,950	8.62
Arunachal Pradesh	320,212	0.05
Assam	15,047,293	2.19
Bihar	71,193,417	10.35
Goa	756,621	0.11
Gujarat	36,964,228	5.38
Haryana	14,686,512	2.14
Himachal Pradesh	4,958,560	0.72
Jammu and Kashmir	N.A.	N.A.
Karnataka	38,432,027	5.59
Kerala	16,668,587	2.42
Madhya Pradesh	61,412,898	8.39
Maharashtra	64,033,213	9.31
Manipur	1,059,470	0.15
Meghalaya	260,306	0.04
Mizoram	34,788	0.01
Nagaland	122,473	0.02
Orissa	29,971,257	4.36
Punjab	6,989,226	1.02
Rajasthan	39,201,099	5.70
Sikkim	277,881	0.04
Tamil Nadu	49,532,052	7.20
Tripura	2,383,934	0.35
Uttar Pradesh	113,712,829	16.54
West Bengal	50,866,624	7.40
Union Territories		
Andaman and Nicobar Islands	189,521	0.03
Dadra and Nagar Haveli	132,213	0.02
Chandigarh	486,895	0.07
Daman and Diu	89,153	0.01
Delhi	7,882,164	1.15
Lakshadweep	2,337	0.00
Pondicherry	695,981	0.10
All India Total	687,646,721	100.00

Source: Census of India, 1991, Table C-9, *Religion*.

Distribution of the Christians, 1991

States/Union Territories	Population	Concentration Index (%)
States		
Andhra Pradesh	1,216,348	6.19
Arunachal Pradesh	89,013	0.45
Assam	744,367	3.79
Bihar	843,717	4.30
Goa	349,225	1.78
Gujarat	181,753	0.93
Haryana	15,699	0.08
Himachal Pradesh	4,435	0.02
Jammu and Kashmir	N.A.	N.A.
Karnataka	859,478	4.38
Kerala	5,621,510	28.62
Madhya Pradesh	426,598	2.17
Maharashtra	885,030	4.51
Manipur	626,669	3.19
Meghalaya	1,146,092	5.84
Mizoram	591,342	3.01
Nagaland	1,057,940	5.39
Orissa	666,220	3.39
Punjab	225,163	1.15
Rajasthan	47,989	0.24
Sikkim	13,413	0.07
Tamil Nadu	3,179,410	16.19
Tripura	46,472	0.24
Uttar Pradesh	199,575	1.02
West Bengal	383,477	1.95
Union Territories		
Andaman and Nicobar Islands	67,211	0.34
Dadra and Nagar Haveli	2,092	0.01
Chandigarh	5,030	0.03
Daman and Diu	2,904	0.01
Delhi	83,152	0.42
Lakshadweep	598	0.00
Pondicherry	58,362	0.30
All India Total	19,640,284	100.00

Source: Census of India, 1991, Table C-9, *Religion.*

Districts Classified According to the Percentage of Christians in the Total Population of the District, 1991

Percentage Categories	Name of the District
Above 90	Tamenglong, Churachandpur, Ukhrul (Manipur)
	West Khasi Hills (Meghalaya)
	Aizawl (Mizoram)
	Phek, Zunheboto, Wokha, Mokokchung, Tuensang, Mon (Nagaland)
80-90	Senapati, Chandel (Manipur)
	East Garo Hills (Meghalaya)
50-80	Jaintia Hills, East Khasi Hills, West Garo Hills (Meghalaya)
	Lunglei, Chhimtuipui (Mizoram), Kohima (Nagaland)
20-50	Lower Subansiri (Arunachal Pradesh)
	North Cachar Hills (Assam)
	Gumla (Bihar)
	North Goa, South Goa (Goa)
	Wayanad, Thrissur, Ernakulam, Idukki, Kottayam, Alappuzha, Pathanamthitta (Kerala)
	Kanyakumari (Tamil Nadu)
10-20	Changlang, Tirap (Arunachal Pradesh)
	Karbi Anglong (Assam)
	Kannur, Kollam, Trivandrum (Kerala)
	Sundargarh (Orissa)
	Nilgiri, Chidembaranar, Tirunelveli-Katta (Tamil Nadu)
5-10	Krishna, Guntur (Andhra Pradesh)
	West Siang, East Siang, Dibang Valley (Arunachal Pradesh)
	Kokrajhar, Goalpara, Darrang, Sonitpur, Golaghat (Assam)
	Ranchi (Bihar)
	The Dangs (Gujarat)
	Bangalore, Dakshin Kannad (Karnataka)
	Kasargod (Kerala)
	Raigarh (Madhya Pradesh)
	Bishnupur (Manipur)
	Phulbani (Orissa)
	Gurdaspur (Punjab)
	Madras, Dindigul-Anna, Tiruchirappalli, Pasumpon Multhuram Thevar, Ramnathapuram (Tamil Nadu)
	Darjeeling (West Bengal)
2-5	West Godavari, Prakasam, Hyderabad (Andhra Pradesh)
	East Kameng, Lohit (Arunachal Pradesh)
	Bongaigaon, Lakhimpur, Sibsagar, Dibrugarh, Tinsukhia (Assam)
	Sahibganj, Dumka, Lohardaga, Pashchimi Singhbhum (Bihar)
	Bidar, Chikmagalur, Kodagu,Uttar Kannad (Karnataka)
	Kozhikode, Malappuram, Palakkad (Kerala)

Percentage Categories	Name of the District
	Surguja (Madhya Pradesh) Greater Bombay, Thane (Maharashtra) Imphal (Manipur) Sambalpur, Koraput, Ganjam (Orissa) North District, East District, South District, West District (Sikkim) Chengalpattvi-M.G., North Arcot, Ambedkarnagar, Tiruvannamalaisa, South Arcot, Coimbatore, Thanjavur, Pudukkottai, Madurai, Kamarajar (Tamil Nadu) North Tripura (Tripura) Jalpaiguri (West Bengal)
1-2	Visakhapatnam, East Godavari, Nellore, Cuddaphah, Kurnool, Rangareddy, Medak (Andhra Pradesh) West Kameng, Upper Subansiri (Arunachal Pradesh) Nalbari, Kamrup, Dhemaji, Jorhat, Hailakandi, Cachar (Assam) Palamau, Purbe Singhbhum (Bihar), Kheda (Gujarat) Kolar, Mysore, Shimoga (Karnataka) Jhabua, Bhopal (Madhya Pradesh) Sindhudurg, Pune (Maharashtra) Amritsar, Firozpur (Punjab) Dharmapuri, Salem, Periyar (Tamil Nadu) South Tripura (Tripura)
Below 1	No. of Districts = 296

Distribution of the Muslims, 1991

States/Union Territories	*Population*	*Concentration Index (%)*
States		
Andhra Pradesh	5,923,954	5.83
Arunachal Pradesh	11,922	0.01
Assam	6,373,204	6.27
Bihar	12,787,985	12.59
Goa	61,455	0.06
Gujarat	3,606,920	3.55
Haryana	763,775	0.75
Himachal Pradesh	89,134	0.09
Jammu and Kashmir	N.A.	N.A.
Karnataka	5,234,023	5.15
Kerala	6,788,364	6.68
Madhya Pradesh	3,282,800	3.23
Maharashtra	7,628,755	7.51
Manipur	133,535	0.13
Meghalaya	61,462	0.06
Mizoram	4,538	0.00
Nagaland	20,642	0.02
Orissa	577,775	0.57
Punjab	239,401	0.24
Rajasthan	3,525,339	3.47
Sikkim	3,849	0.00
Tamil Nadu	3,052,717	3.00
Tripura	196,495	0.19
Uttar Pradesh	24,109,684	23.73
West Bengal	16,075,836	15.82
Union Territories		
Andaman and Nicobar Islands	21,353	0.02
Dadra and Nagar Haveli	3,341	0.00
Chandigarh	17,477	0.02
Daman and Diu	9,048	0.01
Delhi	889,641	0.88
Lakshadweep	48,765	0.05
Pondicherry	52,867	0.05
All India Total	101,596,057	100.00

Source: Census of India, 1991, Table C-9, *Religion*.

Districts Classified According to the Percentage of Muslims in the Total Population of the District, 1991

Percentage Categories	*Name of the District*
Above 80	N.A.
50-80	Dhubri, Goalpara, Barpeta, Marigaon, Nagaon, Hailakandi, Cachar (Assam) Kishanganj (Bihar) Malappuram (Kerala) Murshidabad (West Bengal)
20-50	Hyderabad (Andhra Pradesh) Bongaigaon, Kamrup, Darrang, Karimanj (Assam) Paschim Champaran, Darbhanga, Purnia, Katihar, Sahibganj, Araria (Bihar) Gurgaon (Haryana) Kasargod, Kannur, Wayanad, Kozhikode, Palakkad (Kerala) Bhopal (Madhya Pradesh) Jaisalmer (Rajasthan) Bijnor, Moradabad, Rampur, Saharanpur, Hardwar, Muzaffarnagar, Meerut, Ghaziabad, Badaun, Bareilly, Pilibhit, Bahraich, Gonda, Barabanki, Siddharthnagar, Deoria (Uttar Pradesh) Koochbihar, West Dinajpur, Maldah, Nadia, North Twenty-Four Parganas, South Twenty-Four Parganas, Haora, Birbhum (West Bengal)
10-20	Guntur, Cuddapah, Anantapur, Kurnool, Rangareddy, Medak, Nizamabad (Andhra Pradesh) Kokrajhar, Nalbari, Sonitpur, Lakhimpur (Assam) Gaya, Nawada,Siwan, Gopalganj, Purbi Champaran, Sitamarhi, Muzaffarpur, Begusarai, Samastipur, Madhubani, Saharsa, Madhepura, Bhagalpur, Godda, Dumka, Deaghar, Dhanbad, Giridih, Hazaribagh, Palamau, Lohardaga, Ranchi (Bihar) Jamnagar, Kachch, Ahmedabad, Khera, Bharuch (Gujarat) Faridabad (Haryana) Bangalore, Belgaum, Bellary, Bidar, Bijapur, Dakshin Kannad, Dharwad, Gulbarga, Kodagu,Kolar, Raichur, Shimoga, Uttar Kannad (Karnataka) Thrissur, Ernakulam, Kollam, Trivandrum (Kerala) Ratlam, Ujjain, Shajapur, Dewas, Indore, East Nimar (Madhya Pradesh) Greater Bombay, Nashik, Jalgaon, Aurangabad, Jalna, Parbhani, Bid, Nanded, Latur, Akola, Amravati (Maharashtra) Thoubal (Manipur) West Garo Hills (Meghalaya) Bikaner, Churu, Alwar, Bharatpur, Sikar, Tonk, Jodhpur, Nagaur, Barmer (Rajasthan) Nainital, Bulandshahr, Aligarh, Agra, Firozabad, Etah, Shajahanpur, Kheri, Sitapur, Hardoi, Unnao, Lucknow, Rai Bareily, Farrukhabad, Kanpur Nagar, Fatehpur, Pratapgarh, Allahabad, Faizabad, Varanasi (Uttar Pradesh) Jalpaiguri, Calcutta, Hugli, Medinipur, Barddhaman (West Bengal)

Percentage Categories	*Name of the District*
5-10	Krishna, Prakasam, Nellore, Chittoor, Mahbubnagar, Adilabad, Karimnagar, Warangal, Nalgonda (Andhra Pradesh) Golaghat, Sibsagar (Assam) Patna, Nalanda, Bhojpur, Rohtas, Aurangabad, Jehanabad, Saran, Vaishali, Khagaria, Munger, Purbi Singhbhum (Bihar) South Goa (Goa), Rajkot, Surendranagar, Bhavnagar, Amreli, Junagadh, Banas Kantha, Sabar Kantha, Mahesana, Vadodra, Surat (Gujarat) Yamunanagar (Haryana) Chamba, Sirmaur (Himachal Pradesh) Bangalore rural, Chikmagalur, Chitradurga, Hassan, Mysore, Tumkur (Karnataka) Idduki, Kottayam, Alappuzha (Kerala) Gwalior, Mandsaur, Dhar, West Nimar, Rajgarh, Vidisha, Sihore, Raisen, Jabalpur, Seoni (Madhya Pradesh) Thane, Raigarh, Ratnagiri, Dhule, Ahmadnagar, Pune, Sangli, Solapur, Kolhapur, Osamanabad, Yavatmal, Nagpur (Maharashtra) Bishnupur, Imphal (Manipur) Sangrur (Punjab) Jhunjhunu, Dhaulpur, Sawai Madhopur, Jaipur, Ajmer, Pali, Bhilwara, Chittorgarh, Bundi, Kota, Jhalawar (Rajasthan) Madras, North Arcot-Ambed, Nilgiri, Thanjavur, Pudukkottai, Pasumpon, Multhuram Thevar, Madurai, Tirunelveli Kota (Tamil Nadu) West Tripura, North Tripura (Tripura) Dehradun, Mathura, Mainpuri, Etawah, Kanpur Dehat, Jalaun, Jhansi, Hamirpur, Banda, Gorakhpur, Jaunpur, Ballia, Mirzapur (Uttar Pradesh) Bankura, Puruliya (West Bengal)
1-5	Visakhapatnam, East Godavari, West Godavari (Andhra Pradesh) West Kameng, Lower Subansiri, West Siang, East Siang, Dibang Valley, Lohit (Arunachal Pradesh) Dhemaji, Jorhat, Dibrugarh, Tinsukhia, Karbi Anglong, North Cachar Hills (Assam) Gumla, Pashchimi Singhbhum (Bihar) North Goa (Goa) Gandhinagar, Panch Mahals, Valsad, The Dangs (Gujarat) Ambala, Kurukshetra, Karnal, Panipat, Sonipat (Haryana) Kangra, Una, Bilaspur, Solan (Himachal Pradesh) Mandya (Karnataka) Pathanamthitta (Kerala) Morena, Bhind, Datia, Shivpuri, Guna, Tikamgarh, Chhatarpur, Panna, Sagar, Damoh, Satna, Rewa, Shahdol, Sidhi, Jhabua, Betul, Hoshangabad, Narsimhapur, Mandla, Chhindwara, Balaghat, Surguja, Bilaspur, Rajnandgaon, Durg, Raipur (Madhya Pradesh) Sindhudurg, Satara, Wardha, Bhandara, Chandrapur, Gadchiroli (Maharashtra) Chandel (Manipur) East Khasi Hills (Meghalaya) Kohima (Nagaland) Sundargarh, Keonjhar, Mayurbhanj, Baleshwar, Cuttak, Puri (Orissa) Rupnagar, Patiala (Punjab) Ganganagar, Jalor, Sirohi, Udaipur, Dungarpur, Banswara (Rajasthan) East District (Sikkim) Chngalpattu-M.G., Dharmapuri, Tiruvannamalai-Sa, South Arcot, Salem, Periyar, Coimbatore, Dindigul Anna, Tiruchirappalli, Kamarajar, Chidambaranar, Kanyakumari (Tamil Nadu) South Tripura (Tripura) Garhwal, Lalitpur, Sonbhadra (Uttar Pradesh) Darjeeling (West Bengal)
Below 1	No. of Districts = 59

Districts Classified According to the Percentage of Muslims in the Rural Population of the District, 1991

Percentage Categories	*Name of the District*
50-80	Dhubri, Goalpara, Barpeta, Nagaon, Karimganj, Hailakandi (Assam) Kishanganj (Bihar) Malappuram (Kerala) Maldah, Murshidabad (West Bengal)
20-50	Kokrajhar, Bongaigaon, Kamrup, Darrang, Marigaon, Cachar (Assam) Pashchim Champaran, Darbhanga, Purnia, Katihar, Sahibganj, Araria (Bihar) Kachch (Gujarat) Gurgaon (Haryana) Kasaragod, Kannur, Wayanad, Kozikhode, Palakkad (Kerala) Thoubal (Manipur) Jaisalmer (Rajasthan) Bijnor, Moradabad, Rampur, Saharanpur, Hardwar, Muzaffarnagar, Meerut, Ghaziabad, Bareilly, Bahraich, Gonda, Siddharthnagar, Deoria (Uttar Pradesh) Koochbehar, West Dinajpur, Nadia, North Twenty-Four Parganas, South Twenty-Four Parganas, Haora, Barddhman, Birbhum (West Bengal)
10-20	Cuddapah, Kurnool (Andhra Pradesh) Nalbari, Sonitpur, Lakhimpur (Assam) Gaya, Nawada, Siwan, Gopalganj, Purbi Champaran, Sitamarhi, Muzaffarpur, Begusarai, Samastipur, Madhubani, Saharsa, Bhagalpur, Godda, Dumka, Deoghar, Dhanbad, Giridih, Hazaribagh, Palamau, Lohardaga (Bihar) Bharuch (Gujarat) Yamunanagar, Faridabad (Haryana) Bidar, Dakshin Kannad, Dharwad, Gulbarga, Kodagu (Karnataka) Thrissur, Ernakulam, Kollam, Trivandrum (Kerala) Aurangabad (Maharashtra) Imphal (Manipur) West Garo Hills (Meghalaya) Alwar, Bharatpur, Barmer (Rajasthan) Ramanathapuram (Tamil Nadu) North Tripura (Tripura) Dehradun, Bulandshahr, Badaun, Pilibhit, Shahjahanpur, Kheri, Sitapur, Lucknow, Farrukhabad, Fatehpur, Pratapgarh, Barabanki, Faizabad, Sultanpur, Maharajganj, Basti, Azamgarh (Uttar Pradesh) Jalpaiguri, Hugli, Medinipur (West Bengal)
5-10	Guntur, Prakasam, Nellore, Chittoor, Anantapur, Mahbubnagar, Rangareddy, Medak, Nizamabad, Adilabad (Andhra Pradesh) Golaghat, Sibsagar (Assam) Rohtas, Aurangabad, Jehanabad, Saran, Vaishali, Madhepura, Khagaria, Munger, Ranchi (Bihar)

Percentage Categories	*Name of the District*
	Jamnagar, Rajkot, Junagadh, Banas Kantha, Mahesana, Kheda, Vadodara (Gujarat)
	Chamba (Himachal Pradesh)
	Bangalore, Belgaum, Bellary, Bijapur, Chikmagalur, Kolar, Raichur, Shimoga, Uttar Kannad (Karnataka)
	Iddukki, Alappuzha (Kerala)
	Ujjain, Shajapur, Dewas, Indore, East Nimar, Vidisha, Bhopal, Sehore, Raisen (Madhya Pradesh)
	Raigarh, Ratnagiri, Jalgaon, Solapur, Jalna, Parbhani, Bid, Nanded, Osmanabad, Latur, Buldana, Akola, Amravati, Yavatmal (Maharashtra)
	Bishnupur (Manipur)
	Bikaner, Jhunjhunu, Sawai Madhopur, Ajmer, Jodhpur, Nagaur (Rajasthan)
	Nilgiri, Thanjavur, Pudokkottai (Tamil Nadu)
	West Tripura (Tripura)
	Nainital, Aligarh, Mathura, Etah, Hardoi, Unnao, Rae Bareilly, Kanpur Dehat, Jalaun, Jhansi, Banda, Allahabad, Gorakhpur, Mau, Jaunpur, Ghazipur, Varanasi, Mirzapur (Uttar Pradesh)
	Bankura, Puruliya (West Bengal)
1-5	West Godavari, Krishna, Karimnagar, Warangal, Khammam, Nalgonda (Andhra Pradesh)
	West Kameng, Lower Subansiri, East Siang, Dibang Valley (Arunachal Pradesh)
	Dhemaji, Jorhat, Dibrugarh, Tinsukhia, Karbi Anglong, North Cachar Hills (Assam)
	Patna, Nalanda, Bhojpur, Gumla, Purbi Singhbhum, Pashchimi Singhbhum (Bihar)
	North Goa, South Goa (Goa)
	Surendarnagar, Bhavnagar, Amreli, Sabar Kantha, Gandhinagar, Ahmadabad, Panch Mahals, Surat, Valsad (Gujarat)
	Kurukshetra, Karnal, Panipat, Sonipat, Jind (Haryana)
	Kangra, Una, Bilaspur, Solan, Sirmaur (Himachal Pradesh)
	Bangalore rural, Chitradurga, Hassan, Mandya, Mysore, Tumkur (Karnataka)
	Kottayam, Pathanamthitta (Kerala)
	Morena, Bhind, Gwalior, Datia, Shivpuri, Guna, Tikamgarh, Chhatarpur, Panna, Sagar, Damoh, Satna, Rewa, Shahdol, Sidhi, Mandsaur, Ratlam, Dhar, West Nimar, Rajgarh, Hoshangabad, Jabalpur, Narsimhapur, Chhindwara, Seoni, Balaghat, Surguja (Madhya Pradesh)
	Thane, Sindhudurg, Nashik, Dhule, Ahmadnagar, Pune, Satara, Sangli, Kolhapur, Wardha, Nagpur, Chandrapur, Gadchiroli (Maharashtra)
	Kohima (Nagaland)
	Sundargarh, Baleshwar, Cuttak, Puri (Orissa)
	Rupnagar, Patiala, Sangrur (Punjab)
	Ganganagar, Churu, Dhaulpur, Jaipur, Sikar, Tonk, Pali, Jalor, Sirohi, Udaipur, Chittorgarh, Banswara, Bundi, Kota, Jhalawar (Rajasthan)
	Chengalpattu-M.G., North Arcot-Ambed, Dharmapuri, Tiruvannamalai-Sa, South Arcot, Periyar, Coimbatore, Dindigul-Anna, Tiruchirappalli, Pasumpon Multhuram Thevar, Madurai, Kamarajar, Chidambaranar, Tirunelveli-Katta, Kanyakumari (Tamil Nadu)
	South Tripura (Tripura)
	Agra, Firozabad, Mainpuri, Etawah, Kanpur Nagar, Lalitpur, Hamirpur, Ballia, Sonbhadra (Uttar Pradesh)
	Darjeeling (West Bengal)
Below 1	No. of Districts = 83

Districts Classified According to the Percentage of Muslims in the Urban Population of the District, 1991

Percentage Categories	*Name of the District*
Above 80	N.A.
50-80	Malappuram (Kerala)
	Bijnor, Moradabad, Rampur, Bahraich, Barabanki, Mau (Uttar Pradesh)
40-50	Goalpara (Assam)
	Kishanganj (Bihar)
	Saharanpur, Muzaffarnagar, Badaun, Bareilly, Pilibhit, Shahjahanpur, Gonda, Azamgarh (Uttar Pradesh)
30-40	Kurnool, Hyderabad, Nizamabad (Andhra Pradesh)
	Dhubri (Assam)
	Nalanda, Araria (Bihar)
	Panch Mahals (Gujarat)
	Bidar, Gulbarga (Karnataka)
	Kasaragod, Wayanad, Kozikhode (Kerala)
	East Nimar (Madhya Pradesh)
	Parbhani (Maharashtra)
	Sikar, Tonk, Nagaur, Dungarpur (Rajasthan)
	Meerut, Bulandshahr, Aligarh, Etah, Kheri, Sitapur, Hardoi, Rai Bareilly, Fatehpur, Faizabad, Siddharthnagar, Jaunpur, Ghazipur (Uttar Pradesh)
	Murshidabad (West Bengal)
20-30	Cuddapah, Anantapur, Mahbubnagar, Medak, Adilabad (Andhra Pradesh)
	Nalbari, Lakhimpur, Hailakandi (Assam)
	Rohtas, Aurangabad, Jehanabad, Nawada, Siwan, Pashchim Champaran, Purbi Champaran, Darbhanga, Madhubani, Khagaria, Bhagalpur, Godda, Sahibganj, Lohardaga (Bihar)
	Jamnagar, Sabarkantha, Bharuch (Gujarat)
	Bangalore Rural, Belgaum, Bellary, Bijapur, Chitradurga, Dharwad, Kodagu, Kolar, Raichur, Tumkur, Uttar Kannad (Karnataka)
	Kannur, Palakkad, Idduki (Kerala)
	Mandsaur, Ratlam, Shajapur, West Nimar, Rajgarh, Bhopal, Sehore, Raisen (Madhya Pradesh)
	Ratnagiri, Nashik, Aurangabad, Jalna, Bid, Nanded, Osmanabad, Latur, Buldana, Akola, Amravati (Maharashtra)
	Baleshwar (Orissa)
	Churu, Jhunjhunu, Dhaulpur, Banswara, Jhalawar (Rajasthan)
	North Arcot-Ambed, Ramanathapuram (Tamil Nadu)
	Nainital, Hardwar, Agra, Firozabad, Unnao, Lucknow, Farrukhabad, Etawah, Kanpur Dehat, Kanpur Nagar, Jalaun, Hamirpur, Pratapgarh, Allahabad, Sultanpur, Basti, Varanasi (Uttar Pradesh)
	South Twenty-Four Parganas, Haora (West Bengal)

Percentage Categories	*Name of the District*
10-20	Krishna, Guntur, Prakasam, Nellore, Chittoor, Rangareddy, Karimnagar, Warangal, Khammam, Nalgonda (Andhra Pradesh) Kamrup, Darrang, Marigaon, Nagaon, Golaghat, Sibsagar, Dibrugarh, Cachar (Assam) Patna, Bhojpur, Gaya, Saran, Gopalganj, Sitamarhi, Muzaffarpur, Vaishali, Begusarai, Samastipur, Saharsa, Madhepura, Purnia, Katihar, Munger, Deogarh, Dhanbad, Giridih, Hazaribagh, Palamau, Gumla, Ranchi, Purbi Singhbhum (Bihar) South Goa (Goa) Rajkot, Surendarnagar, Bhavnagar, Amreli, Junagadh, Kachch, Banas Kantha, Mahesana, Ahmadabad, Kheda, Vadodra, Surat (Gujarat) Bangalore, Chikmagalur, Dakshin Kannad, Hassan, Mandya, Mysore, Shimoga (Karnataka) Thrissur, Ernakulam, Kottayam, Alappuzha, Pathanamthitta, Trivandrum (Kerala) Morena, Datia, Shivpuri, Guna, Tikamgarh, Chhattarpur, Panna, Sagar, Damoh, Rewa, Ujjain, Dewas, Jhabua, Indore, Vidisha, Hoshangabad, Jabalpur, Chhindwara, Seoni (Madhya Pradesh) Greater Bombay, Thane, Raigarh, Dhule, Jalgaon, Ahmadnagar, Satara, Sangli, Solapur, Kolhapur, Yavatmal, Nagpur (Maharashtra) Chandel, Thoubal (Manipur) Bikaner, Sawai Madhopur, Jaipur, Jaisalmer, Jodhpur, Pali, Bhilwara, Udaipur, Chittorgarh, Bundi, Kota (Rajasthan) Dharmapuri, Tiruvannamalai-Sa, Nilgiri, Dindigul-Anna, Tiruchirappalli, Thanjavur, Pudukkotai, Pasumpor Muthuram, Thevar, Tirunelveli-Katta (Tamil Nadu) Garhwal, Ghaziabad, Mathura, Mainpuri, Jhansi, Lalitpur, Banda, Maharajganj, Gorakhpur, Deoria, Ballia, Mirzapur, Sonbhadra (Uttar Pradesh) Maldah, Calcutta, Hugli, Medinipur, Barddhaman, Birbhum (West Bengal)
5-10	West Godavari (Andhra Pradesh) Lower Subansiri, East Siang, Lohit (Arunachal Pradesh) Bongaigaon, Barpeta, Sonitpur, Jorhat, Tinsukhia, Karbi Anglong, Karimganj (Assam) Dumka, Pashchimi Singhbhum (Bihar) North Goa (Goa) Valsad, The Dangs (Gujarat) Gurgaon (Haryana) Bilaspur, Sirmaur (Himachal Pradesh) Bhind, Gawalior, Satna, Shahdol, Sidhi, Betul, Narsimhapur, Mandla, Balaghat, Surguja, Bilaspur, Rajnandgaon, Durg, Raipur, Bastar (Madhya Pradesh) Sindhudurg, Pune, Wardha, Bhandara, Chandrapur, Gadchiroli (Maharashtra) Bishnupur (Manipur) Kohima (Nagaland) Sundargarh, Keonjhar, Cuttack (Orissa) Ganganagar, Ajmer, Barmer, Jalor, Sirohi (Rajasthan) North District, West District (Sikkim) Madras, Chingalpattu-M.G., South Arcot, Salem, Periyar, Coimbatore, Madurai, Chidambaranar, Kanyakumari (Tamil Nadu) Dehradun, Almora (Uttar Pradesh) Koochbehar, North Twenty-Four Parganas, Puruliya (West Bengal)
1-5	Srikakulam, Vizianagaram, East Godavari (Andhra Pradesh) West Kameng, West Siang, Dibang Valley, Tirap (Arunachal Pradesh) Kokrajhar, Dhemaji, North Cachar Hills (Assam) Gandhinagar (Gujarat) Yamunanagar, Panipat, Sonipat, Faridabad (Haryana) Chamba, Mandi, Shimla, Solan (Himachal Pradesh) Raigarh (Madhya Pradesh)

Percentage Categories	Name of the District
	Imphal (Manipur) East Khasi Hills, East Garo Hills, West Garo Hills (Nagaland) Sambalpur, Mayurbhanj, Dhenkanal, Phulbani, Bolangir, Kalahandi, Koraput, Ganjam, Puri (Orissa) Alwar, Bharatpur (Rajasthan) East District, South District (Sikkim) Kamarajar (Tamil Nadu) West Tripura, North Tripura, South Tripura (Tripura) Uttarkashi, Chamoli, Tehri Garhwal, Pithoragarh (Uttar Pradesh) Jalpaiguri, Darjeeling, West Dinajpur, Nadia, Bankura (West Bengal)
Less than 1	No. of districts = 32

Distribution of the Sikhs, 1991

States/Union Territories	Population	Concentration Index (%)
States		
Andhra Pradesh	21,910	0.13
Arunachal Pradesh	1,205	0.01
Assam	16,492	0.10
Bihar	78,212	0.48
Goa	1,087	0.01
Gujarat	33,044	0.20
Haryana	956,836	5.88
Himachal Pradesh	52,050	0.32
Jammu and Kashmir	N.A.	N.A.
Karnataka	10,101	0.06
Kerala	2,224	0.01
Madhya Pradesh	161,111	0.99
Maharashtra	161,184	0.99
Manipur	1,301	0.01
Meghalaya	2,612	0.02
Mizoram	299	0.00
Nagaland	732	0.00
Orissa	17,296	0.11
Punjab	12,767,697	78.52
Rajasthan	649,174	3.99
Sikkim	375	0.00
Tamil Nadu	5,449	0.03
Tripura	740	0.00
Uttar Pradesh	675,775	4.16
West Bengal	55,392	0.34
Union Territories		
Andaman and Nicobar Islands	1,350	0.01
Dadra and Nagar Haveli	20	0.00
Chandigarh	130,288	0.80
Daman and Diu	101	0.00
Delhi	455,657	2.80
Lakshadweep	1	0.00
Pondicherry	29	0.00
All India Total	16,259,744	100.00

Source: Census of India, 1991, Table C-9, *Religion*.

Bibliography

Ahmad, Aijazuddin (1999): 'Social Geography' in G.S. Gosal (ed.), *A Survey of Research in Geography*, 1976-82, Indian Council of Social Science Research, New Delhi: pp. 249-309.

Ahmad, Aijazuddin (1999): *Social Geography*, New Delhi: Rawat Publications.

Ahmad, Aijazuddin (2009): *Geography of the South Asian Subcontinent: A Critical Approach*, New Delhi: Concept Publishing Company Pvt. Ltd., New Delhi.

Ahmad, Aijazuddin (1979): 'Language and Dialect' in Moonis Raza (ed.) *A Survey of Research in Geography*, 1969-72, Indian Council of Social Science Research, Bombay: Allied Publishers, pp. 110-14.

Ahmad, Aijazuddin (1985): 'Regional Development Process and Redistribution of Tribal Population in Mid-India' in Leszek A. Kosinski and K. Maudood Elahi (eds.), *Population Redistribution and Development in South Asia*, Dordrecht: D. Reidel Publishing Company, pp. 65-78.

Ahmad, Aijazuddin (1988): 'Cultural Roots of Tribals in India', *Contemporary Affairs*, Vol. II, No. 2, April-June, pp. 50-60.

Ahmad, Aijazuddin (1993): 'Social Structure and Regional Development: An Introduction' in Aijazuddin Ahmad (ed.) *Social Structure and Regional Development: A Social Geography Perspective*, Jaipur: Rawat Publications.

Ahmad, Aijazuddin (1993): *Muslims in India*, Vol. I, Bihar, New Delhi: Inter-India Publications.

Ahmad, Aijazuddin (1993): *Muslims in India*, Vol. II, Rajasthan, New Delhi: Inter-India Publications.

Ahmad, Aijazuddin (1993): *Muslims in India*, Vol. III, Delhi, New Delhi: Inter-India Publications.

Ahmad, Aijazuddin (1993): *Muslims in India*, Vol. IV, Uttar Pradesh: Urban, New Delhi: Inter-India Publications.

Ahmad, Aijazuddin (ed., 1984):'Social Geography' in Manzoor Alam, *A Survey of Research in Geography*, 1972-75, Indian Council of Social Science Research, New Delhi: Concept Publishing Company Pvt. Ltd. New Delhi, pp. 67-84.

Ahmad, Aijazuddin and M. Ishtiaque (1994): 'Dialect Regions of Bihar: Some Issues in Methodology' in N.H. Itagi (ed.) *Spatial Aspects of Language*, Mysore: Central Institute of Indian Languages, pp. 111-21.

Ali, S.M. (1969): *The Geography of the Puranas*, Delhi: Peoples Publishing House.

Ali, Syed Ashfaq (1972): *Tribal Demography in Madhya Pradesh*, Bhopal: Jai Bharat Publishing House.

Allchin, Bridget and Raymond (1968): *The Birth of Indian Civilisation*, Hammondsworth: Penguin Books Ltd.

Ambrose, John (1980): 'Micro-scale Language Mapping: An Experiment in Wales and Brittany', *Discussion Papers in Geo-linguistics*, No. 2, Stoke-on-Trent: Department of Geography and Sociology, North Staffordshire, Polytechnic.

Anas, M. (1983): 'An Aspect of the Linguistic Geography of India', *The Geographer*, Vol. XXX, No. 2, pp. 14-16.

Bagchi, D. (1970): 'Ali Rajpur: A Study in Urban—Tribal Relationship', *The Deccan Geographer*, Vol. VIII, Nos. 1-2, pp. 129-39.

Barai, D. and Sudarshan Mukerjee (1975): 'The Karen of Middle Andaman', *Indian Geographical Journal*, Vol. L, No. 1, pp. 1-5.

Barber, C. L. (1965): *The Story of Language*, London: The English Language Book Society and Pan Books Ltd.

Barpujari, H.K. (1970): *Problem of the Hill Tribes of North-East Frontier, 1822-42*, Vol. I, Guahati: Lawyers' Book Stall.

Bennet, Charles Jr. (1980): 'The Morphology of Language Boundary: Indo-Aryan and Dravidian in Peninsular India' in David E. Sopher (ed.) *An Exploration of India*, London: Longman, pp. 234-51.

Berreman, Gerald (1960): 'Caste in India and the United States', *American Journal of Sociology*, Vol. LXVI, pp. 120-27.

Berreman, Gerald (1965): 'The Study of Caste Ranking in India', *Southwestern Journal of Anthropology*, Vol. XXI, pp. 115-29.

Beteille, A. (1969): *Caste, Class and Power: Changing Patterns of Stratification in a Tanjore Village*, Bombay: Oxford University Press.

Beteille, A. (1977): 'Caste and Social Status' in Romesh Thapar (ed.), *Tribe, Caste and Religion in India*, Delhi: The Macmillan Company of India Ltd., pp. 59-65.

Beteille, Andre (1977): 'The Definition of Tribe' in Romesh Thapar (ed.), *Tribe, Caste and Religion*, Delhi: The Macmillan Company of India Ltd., pp. 7-14.

Beteille, Andre (1992): *Society and Politics in India: Essays in a Comparative Perspective*, Delhi: Oxford University Press.

Bharadwaj, S.M. and Harvey, M.E. (1975): 'Occupational Structure of the Scheduled Castes in General Population of Punjab: A Comparative Multi-Variate Analysis', *National Geographical Journal of India*, Vol. XXI, No. 2, pp. 75-97.

Bharadwaj, S.M. (1973): *Hindu Places of Pilgrimage in India*, Berkeley: University of California Press.

Bhatt, B.L. (1977): 'The Religious Geography of South Asia: Some Reflections', *The National Geographical Journal of India*, Vol. XXIII, Part 1-2, pp. 26-39.

Bhattacharaya, N.N. (1991): 'The Contemporary Geo-Political Problems of North-East India', *North-Eastern Geographer*, Vol. XXIII, Nos. 1-2, pp. 1-5.

Bose, A., T. Nongbri and N. Kumar (eds., 1990): *Tribal Demography and Development in North-East India*, Delhi: B.R. Publishing Corporation.

Bose, A., U.P. Sinha and R.P. Tyagi (eds., 1990): *Demography of Tribal Development*, Delhi: B.R. Publishing Corporation.

Bose, N.K. (1968): *Calcutta, 1964: A Social Survey*, Calcutta: Lalvani Publishing House.

Bose, N.K. (1969): 'The Tribal Situation', *Man in India*, Vol. XLIX, No. 3, pp. 217-24.

Bose, N.K. (1971): 'Land-Man Ratio in Tribal Areas', *Man in India*, Vol. LI, No. 4, pp. 267-74.

Bose, N.K. (1971): 'Some Aspects of Indian Civilisation', *Man in India*, Vol. LI, No. I, pp. 1-15.

Bose, N.K. (1977): 'India's Eastern Tribes' in Romesh Thapar (ed.), *Tribe, Caste and Religion*, Delhi: The Macmillan Company of India Ltd., pp. 54-58.

Buttimer, A. (1969): 'Social Space in Interdisciplinary Perspective', *Geographical Review*, Vol. LIV, pp. 417-26.

Caruso, S. and Risa Palm (1973): 'Social Space and Social Pace', *Professional Geographer*, Vol.XXV, pp. 221-22.

Cater, John and Trevor Jones (1989): *Social Geography: An Introduction to Contemporary Issues*, London: Edward Arnold.

Chandna, R.C. (1972): 'Scheduled Caste Population in Haryana: A Geographical Analysis', *National Geographical Journal of India*, Vol. XVIII, Nos. 3-4, pp. 177-86.

Chattopadhyaya, Deviprasad (1959): *Lokayata: A Study in Ancient Indian Materialism*, New Delhi: Peoples Publishing House.

Chib, S.S. (1987): 'Tribal Population of Himachal Pradesh', *Geographical Review of India*, Vol. XLIX, No. 3, pp. 33-37.

Cohn, B.C. and Milton Singer (ed., 1968): *Structure and Change in Indian Society*, Chicago: Aldine Publishing Company.

Deddee, Jaymala and B.B. Ahir (1988): 'Seasonal Movements in the Sahyadrian Rainshadow of Two Pastoral Groups: The Dhangars and Banjaras', *Transactions of the Institutes of Indian Geographers*, Vol. X, No. 2, pp. 1-14.

Desai, A.R. (1969): *Rural Sociology in India*, Bombay: Popular Prakashan.

Desai, A.R. (1977): 'Tribes in Transition' in Romesh Thapar (ed.), *Tribe, Caste and Religion*, Delhi: The Macmillan Company of India Ltd., pp. 15-28.

Desai, Anjana (1988): 'Seasonal Movements of Tribes: An Issue in Regional Planning', *The Indian Geographical Journal*, Vol. LXIII, No. 1, pp. 39-43.

Desai, I.P. (ed., 1988): *Division and Hierarchy: An Overview of Caste in Gujarat*, Delhi: Hindustan Publishing Corporation.

Deshpande, C.D. (1973): 'The Naga Village: A Reconnaissance Study', *Geographical Outlook*, Vol. IX, pp. 15-18.

Dube, Saurabh (1993): 'Caste and Sect in Village Life: Satnamis of Chhattisgarh, 1900-1950', Shimla: Indian Institute of Advanced Studies, *Occasional Paper* 5.

Dumont, Louis (1988): *Homo Hierarchicus: The Caste System and its Implications*, Delhi: Oxford University Press.

Dutt, A.K. and A.G. Noble (1977): 'Diffusion of Hinduism in South East Asia with Special Reference to Indo-China', *The National Geographical Journal of India*, Vol. XXIII, Part 1-2, pp. 86-94.

Dutt, A.K. and S. Devgun (1977): 'Diffusion of Sikhism and Recent Migration Patterns of Sikhs in India', *Geographical Journal*, Vol. I, No. 5, pp. 81-89.

Dutt, N.K. (1986): *Origin and Growth of Caste in India*, Calcutta: Firma Kim Pvt. Ltd.

Eyles, John (1981): 'Social Geography' in R.J. Johnston, *et. al.*, *The Dictionary of Human Geography*, Oxford: Basil Blackwell, pp. 309-12.

Eyles, John (1983): *Social Geography in International Perspective*, London and Sydney: Croom Helm. Of particular interest is chapter ten by Robert W. Bradnock, 'Research in Social Geography: South Asia', pp. 275-95.

Gautam, Alka (1984): 'The Hill Saoras of Orissa—A Study in Tribal Geography', *The Geographical Observer*, Vol. XX, pp. 21-26.

Ghurye, G.S. (1950): *Caste and Class in India*, Bombay: Popular Book Depot.

Ghurye, G.S. (1963): *The Scheduled Tribes*, Bombay: Popular Prakashan.

Ghurye, G.S. (1969): *Caste and Race in India*, Bombay: Popular Prakashan.

Gill, Mehar Singh (1987): 'Urbanisation of Scheduled Caste Population in Punjab', *Geographical Review of India*, Vol. XLIX, No. 1, pp. 71-84.

Goel. N.P. (1981): 'Changes in the Distribution Pattern of Hindi Speaking Population, 1951-71', *Doab Geographer*, Vol. I, Nos. 1-2, pp. 55-63.

Gosal, G.S. and A. B. Mukerji (1972): 'Distribution and Relative Concentration of Scheduled Caste Population in India', *Economic and Socio-cultural Dimension of Regionalisation*, Census Centenary Monograph, No. 7, New Delhi: Office of the Registrar-General, India.

Gosal, G.S. and A.B. Mukerji (1970): 'The Religious Composition of India's Population: A Spatial Analysis', *Tijdschrift voor economic en sociale geografie*, Vol. LXI, No. 2, pp. 91-101.

Goswami, B.B. (1973): 'Tribes of North-East India: A Few Comments on their Social and Cultural Ties with the Non-Tribals', *North-Eastern Research Bulletin*, Vol. IV, pp. 41-48.

Haimendorf, Christoph Von-Furer (1969): 'Apatani Tribe on the Road to Prosperity', *Geographical Magazine*, Vol. LII, No. 3, pp. 216-21.

Haimendorf, Christoph Von-Furer (1977): 'Tribal Problem in India' in Romesh Thapar (ed.), *Tribe, Caste and Religion*, Delhi: The Macmillan Company of India Ltd., pp. 1-6.

Haimendorf, Christoph Von-Furer (1982): *Tribes of India: The Struggle for Survival*, New Delhi: Oxford University Press.

Hashmi, Sohail (1977): 'Some Socio-economic and Demographic Characteristics of Muslims in an Industrial Setting: A Case Study of Eight Wards of Ahmedabad', Unpublished M. Phil. Dissertation, Centre for the Study of Regional Development, Jawaharlal Nehru University, New Delhi.

Hassan, M.S.R. (1978): 'Agricultural Economy of the Santals of Bihar—A Study in Tribal Geography', *Geographical Bulletin of India*, No. 3, pp. 61-68.

Hutton, J.H. (1963): *Caste in India: Its Nature, Function and Origin*, Bombay: Oxford University Press.

Indrapal and A.K. Pareek (1984): 'Geo-Economic Prospects for Tribal Upliftment: A Case Study of Banswara District', *Annals of the Association of Rajasthan Geographers*, Vol. IV, pp. 101-7.

Itagi, N.H. (1994): 'Spatial Variation in the Incidence of Bilingualism in the Tribal Population of India' in N.H. Itagi (ed.) *Spatial Aspects of Language*, Mysore: Central Institute of Indian Languages, pp. 175-85.

Jain, Ashok Lata (1972): 'Tribal Territories in India: An Exploratory Analysis', Unpublished M. Phil. Dissertation, Centre for the Study of Regional Development, Jawaharlal Nehru University, New Delhi.

Jambholkar, G.L. (1976): 'Levels of Socio-economic Deprivation among the Scheduled Castes in Rural India', Unpublished M. Phil. Dissertation, Centre for the Study of Regional Development, Jawaharlal Nehru University, New Delhi.

Jones, E. (ed., 1975): *Readings in Social Geography*, Oxford: Oxford University Press.

Jones, E. and John Eyles (1977): *An Introduction to Social Geography*, Oxford and New York: Oxford University Press.

Joshi, Y. G. (1982): 'Spatial Impact of Tribal Development Block on the Agricultural Development—A Study of the Jhabua District, M.P.', *Geographical Review of India*, Vol. XLIV, No. 4, pp. 52-62.

Khan, Rasheeduddin (1977): 'The Changing Role of Religious Minorities' in Romesh Thapar (ed.) *Tribe, Caste and Religion*, New Delhi: The Macmillan Company of India Ltd., pp. 143-60.

Khan, W. and Sudhir Wanmali (1972): 'Impact of Linguistic Reorganisation of States on City-size Distribution in Peninsular India' in A. Chandra Sekhar (ed.) *Economic and Socio-cultural Dimensions of Regionalisation*, Census Centenary Monograph No. 7, New Delhi: Office of the Registrar General, India, pp. 451-72.

Khatana, Ram Parsad (1985): 'The Transhumance Economy of the Gujjar Bakarwals of Jammu and Kashmir', Unpublished Ph.D. Thesis, Centre for the Study of Regional Development, Jawaharlal Nehru University, New Delhi.

Khosla, Romi (1971): 'End of an Era for Ladakh Monastries', *The Geographical Magazine*, Vol. XLIII, No. 5, pp. 333-41.

Khubchandani, M.L. (1972): 'Mother Tongue in Multilingual Societies' in A. Chandra Sekhar (ed.) *Economic and Socio-cultural Dimensions of Regionalisation*, Census Centenary Monograph No. 7, New Delhi: Office of the Registrar General, India, pp. 427-50.

Khubchandani, M.L. (1973): *Social Stratification and Language Behaviour*, Shimla: Indian Institute of Advanced Study.

Khubchandani, M.L. (1983): *Plural Languages, Plural Cultures: Communication, Identity and Socio-political Change in Contemporary India*, Honolulu: East-West Centre.

Khubchandani, M.L. (1988): *Language in a Plural* Society, Delhi: Motilal Banarasidas; Shimla: Indian Institute of Advanced Study.

Khubchandani, M.L. (1993): 'India as a Socio-linguistic Area' in Aijazuddin Ahmad (ed.) *Social Structure and Regional Development: A Social Geography Perspective*, Jaipur: Rawat Publications, pp. 101-13.

Khubchandani, M.L. (1994): 'India as a Socio-linguistic Area' in N.H. Itagi (ed.) *Spatial Aspects of Language*, Mysore: Central Institute of Indian Languages, pp. 33-43.

Knight, D.B. (1982): 'Identity and Territory: Geographical Perspectives on Nationalism and Regionalism', *Annals of the Association of American Geographers*, Vol. LXXII, pp. 514-531.

Kosambi, D.D. (1962): *Myth and Reality: Studies in the Formation of Indian Culture*, Bombay: Popular Prakashan.

Kosambi, D.D. (1972): *The Culture and Civilisation of Ancient India in Historical Outline*, Delhi: Vikas.

Kosinski, Leszek A. and K. Maudood Elahi (eds., 1985): *Population Redistribution and Development in South Asia*, Dordrecht: D. Reidel Publishing Company.

Krishan, Gopal (1971): 'Distribution of Sikhs Outside Punjab', India, *The Indian Geographical Journal*, Vol. XLVI, Nos. 1-2, pp. 36-41.

Krishan, Gopal (1971): 'Distribution of Sikhs Outside the Punjab, India', *The Sikh Review*, Vol. XIX, No. 208, pp. 24-30.

Krishan, Gopal and Neela Thapar (1994): 'Cultural Diversity and Development in India', *Annals of the National Association of Geographers, India*, Vol. IV, No.2, pp. 27-44.

Krishna, Gopal (1977): 'Framework of Minority Politics' in Romesh Thapar (ed.) *Tribe, Caste and Religion*, New Delhi: The Macmillan Company of India Ltd., pp. 161-68.

Lollen, Tumter (1995): 'Tribal Communities of Arunachal Pradesh: A Geographical Perspective on Ethnicity and Territoriality', Unpublished M. Phil. Dissertation, Centre for the Study of Regional Development, Jawaharlal Nehru University, New Delhi.

Luithui, Luingam (1977): 'Political Economy of Forestry in Manipur', Unpublished M. Phil. Dissertation, Centre for the Study of Regional Development, Jawaharlal Nehru University, New Delhi.

Mandavdhare, S.M. (1986): 'Spatial Patterns of Caste Distribution and Land Relations in Marathwada', Unpublished Ph. D. Thesis, Centre for the Study of Regional Development, Jawaharlal Nehru University, New Delhi.

Mandelbaum, D. G. (1968): 'Family, Jati, Village' in B.S. Cohn and Milton Singer (eds.) *Structure and Change in Indian Society*, Chicago: Aldine Publishing Company, pp. 29-31.

Mandelbaum, D. G. (1970): *Society in India*, Bombay: Popular Prakashan.

Mazumdar, K. (1973): 'Distribution of Tribal Population in Eastern Gujarat', *The National Geographical Journal of India*, Vol. XIX, Parts 3-4, pp. 177-92.

Meinig, D. W. (ed., 1979): *Interpretation of Ordinary Landscapes*, Ithaca: Cornell University Press.

Mikesell, Marvin W. (ed., 1973): 'Geographers Abroad: Essays on the Problems and Prospects of Research in Foreign Areas', *Research Paper* No. 152, Chicago: Department of Geography, University of Chicago.

Miller, E. J. (1954): 'Caste and Territory in Malabar', *American Anthropologist*, Vol. LVI, pp. 410-20.

Mitra, S. (1976): 'The Lapchas of Darjeeling District—A study in Acculturation', *Geographical Review of India*, Vol. XXXVIII, No. 2, pp. 123-39.

Mitra, S. (1977): Development Problems of Tribal Agriculture in India', *Geographical Review of India*, Vol. XXXIX, No. 2, pp. 107-116.

Mitra, S. (1978): 'The Tribal Culture of West Bengal', *Geographical Review of India*, Vol. XL, No. 3, pp. 219-27.

Mohammad, Noor (1994): *Caste and Primary Occupations: A Geographical Analysis*, New Delhi: Concept Publishing Company Pvt. Ltd. New Delhi.

Mohapatra, A.C. (1981): 'Spatial Dimensions of Tribal Development: A Regional Approach', *Indian Journal of Regional Science*, Vol. XIII, No. 2, pp. 113-23.

Mukerji, A. B. (1964): 'Cultural Landscape of a Telangana Village: A Morphogenetic Study', *Geografia*, Vol. III, pp. 11-42.

Mukerji, A. B. (1964): 'Succession of Cultural Landscapes in Telangana Reddy Villages', *Indian Geographical Journal*, Vol. XXXIX, pp. 42-58.

Mukerji, A.B. (1973): 'The Muslim Population of Uttar Pradesh, India: A Spatial Interpretation', *Islamic Culture*, Vol. XLVII, No.3, pp. 213-30.

Mukerji, A.B. (1979): 'Tribe' in Moonis Raza (ed.), *ICSSR Survey of Research in Geography*, 1969-72, New Delhi: Allied Publishers, pp. 97-107.

Mukerji, A.B. (1980): *The Chamars of Uttar Pradesh—A Study in Social Geography*, Delhi: Inter-India Publications.

Mukherjee, S. (1977): 'Nagaland—A Regional Study', *Deccan Geographer*, Vol. XV, pp. 209-34.

Nigam, R.C. (1972): *Handbook on Mother-Tongue in Census*, New Delhi: Office of the Registrar General, India.

Nolan, Mary Lee (1987): 'Christian Pilgrimage Shrines in Western Europe and India: A Preliminary Comparison', *The National Geographical Journal of India*, Vol. XXXIII, No. 4, pp.370-78.

O' Malley, L.S.S. (1975): *Indian Social Heritage*, London: Curzon Press.

Omvedt, Gail (ed., 1982): *Land, Caste and Politics in Indian State*, Delhi: Authors Guild Publications.

Palanisamy, R. (1981): 'Spatial Analysis of Ecological Setting, Occupational Structure and Socio-Economic Transformation of the Scheduled Tribes in Three Southern States of Tamil Nadu, Kerala and Karnataka', Unpublished M. Phil. Dissertation, Centre for the Study of Regional Development, Jawaharlal Nehru University, New Delhi.

Pandey, S. (1972): 'A Note on Physical and Social Factors and Settlement Types in the Thar' in R.L. Singh (ed.) *Rural Settlements in Monsoon Asia*, Varanasi: National Geographical Society of India, pp. 334-48.

Panikkar, K.M. (1955): *Geographical Factors in Indian History*, Bombay.

Patil, T.P. (1975): 'Spatial Distribution of Scheduled Caste Population in Bhima-Siva Interfluve of Sholapur District', *Geographical Review of India*, Vol. XXXVII, No. 3, pp. 221-34.

Piggott, Stuart (1950): *Pre-Historic India*, Harmondsworth: Penguin Books.

Prasad, M. (1977): 'Internal Structure of a Tribal Village of Chhotanagpur, India', *Geoscope*, Vol. VIII, No. 1, pp. 58-74.

Prasad, Maheshwari (1979): *Tribal Geography: An Introductory Bibliography*, New Delhi: Classical Publications.

Ramachandran, Janani (1985): 'Performance of an Innovation in the Warli Tribal Community—A Critical Analysis of Agencies Involved and the Relative Influence of Factors Affecting Adoption Process', *Annals of the National Association of Geographers, India*, Vol. V, No. 2, pp. 16-43.

Ramachandran, Janani (1988): 'The Warli Tribal Community: Economic Realities and the Warlis' Viewpoint', *Annals of the National Association of Geographers, India*, Vol. VIII, No. 2, pp. 1-9.

Raza, Mehdi (1970): 'Ethno-Botany of the Ranchi Plateau' *The Geographer*, Vol. XVII, pp. 21-27.

Raza, Mehdi (1971): 'Structure and Function of Rural Markets in Tribal Bihar', *The Geographer*, Vol. XVIII, pp. 17-25.

Raza, Mehdi (1973): 'Genre de vie: A Case Study', *The Geographer*, Vol. XX, No. 1, pp. 49-54.

Raza, Moonis (1979): 'Defining the Area of Social Geography' in Moonis Raza (ed.) *ICSSR Survey of Research in Geography*, 1969-72, New Delhi: Allied Publishers, pp. 63-65.

Raza, Moonis (ed., 1979) *A Survey of Research in Geography*, New Delhi: Indian Council of Social Science Research, pp. 63-65.

Raza, Moonis and Aijazuddin Ahmad (1990): *An Atlas of Tribal India*, New Delhi: Concept Publishing Company Pvt. Ltd.

Raza, Moonis, Aijazuddin Ahmad and Nafis Ahmad Siddiqui (1973): 'Muslims of India: A Regional Demography' in Zafar Imam (ed.) *Muslims in India*, New Delhi: Orient Longman, pp. 113-32.

Raza, Moonis, Aijazuddin Ahmad, Ashoklata Jain and C.K. Chauhan (1977): 'The Tribal Population of India—Spatial Patterns of Clustering and Concentration', *Occasional Papers*, No. 5, Centre for the Study of Regional Development, Jawaharlal Nehru University, New Delhi.

Roy Burman, B.K. (1972): 'Distribution of Scheduled Tribes of India: An Explanatory Geo-Cultural Appraisal', *Economic and Socio-cultural Dimension of Regionalisation*, Census Centenary Monograph No. 7, New Delhi: Office of the Registrar General, India, pp. 483-538.

Roy Burman, B.K. (1972): 'Tribal Demography: A Preliminary Appraisal' in K.S. Singh (ed.), *Tribal Situation in India*, Shimla: Indian Institute of Advanced Study, pp. 39-50.

Roy, B.K. (1987): 'Census Count of Religions of India, 1901-81 and Contemporary Issues', *The National Geographical Journal of India*, Vol. XXXIII, No. 3, pp. 239-52.

Sakharov, I.V. (1972): 'Ethno-linguistic Geography of India: Facts and Problems' in A. Chandra Sekhar (ed.) *Economic and Socio-cultural Dimensions of Regionalisation*, Census Centenary Monograph No. 7, New Delhi: Office of the Registrar General, India, pp. 387-426.

Sankalia, H.D. (1962): *Pre-history and Proto-history of India and Pakistan*, Bombay: University of Bombay.

Sastri, K.A. Nilakanta (1976): *A History of South India*, Madras: Oxford University Press.

Schwartzberg, J.E. (1965): 'The Distribution of Selected Castes in the North Indian Plain', *The Geographical Review*, Vol. LV, No. 4, pp. 477-95.

Schwartzberg, J.E. (1967): 'Prolegomena to the Study of South Asian Regions and Regionalism' in Robert I. Crane (ed.) *Regions and Regionalism in South Asian Studies: An Exploratory Study*, Durham: Duke University, pp. 89-111.

Schwartzberg, J.E. (1968): 'Caste Regions of the North Indian Plain' in B.S. Cohn and Milton Singer (ed.) *Structure and Change in Indian Society*, Chicago: Aldine Publishing Company, pp. 81-113.

Schwartzberg, J.E. (1993): 'Caste and the Study of Regional Development' in Aijazuddin Ahmad (ed.) *Social Structure and Regional Development: A Social Geography Perspective*, Jaipur: Rawat Publications, pp. 21-49.

Schwartzberg, Joseph E. (ed., 1978, 1994): *A Historical Atlas of South Asia*, Chicago, London: The University of Chicago Press.

Sengupta, A. (1980): 'Distribution of Linguistic Groups in Calcutta Metropolitan District', *Man in India*, Vol. LX, No. 2, pp. 27-37.

Sharma R.S. (ed., 1974): *Indian Society: Historical Probings*, New Delhi: Peoples Publishing House.

Sharma, A.K. (1989): 'Growth of Muslim Population in India: Some Policy Issues', *The Eastern Anthropologist*, Vol. XLII, No. 4, pp. 353-64.

Sharma, A.K. (1994): 'Muslim Fertility in Urban U.P.: A Qualitative Study', *Demography India*, Vol. XXIII, Nos. 1-2, pp. 41-49.

Shastri, P.S. (1985): 'Patterns of Tribal Literacy in Vidarbha', *Population Geography*, Vol. VII, Nos. 1-2, pp. 40-48.

Siddqui, N.A. (1973): 'Religious Groups in Kerala: Growth (1951-61) and Distribution (1961)', *The Geographer*, Vol. XX, No. 1, pp. 55-74.

Sil, Ajit K. (1990): 'Adaptation of the Migrant Oraons in their Present Habitat in Sundarbans', *Geographical Review of India*, Vol. LII, No. 1, pp. 89-90.

Singh, A.P. (1979): 'Tribes of Uttrakhand: Some Aspects of Cultural Ecology', *Journal of Himalayan Studies and Regional Development*, Vol. III, pp. 51-54.

Singh, B.N. and B.K. Misra (1976): 'Tribes of Orissa—A Geographical Analysis', *Geographical Review of India*, Vol. XXXVIII, No.2, pp. 167-78.

Singh, K.S. (1978): 'Colonial Transformation of Tribal Societies in Middle India', *Economic and Political Weekly*, Vol. XIII, No. 30, July 29, pp. 1221-32.

Singh, K.S. (1985): '*Tribal Society in India: An Anthropo-Historical Perspective*', New Delhi: Manohar Publications.

Singh, K.S. (ed., 1972): '*Tribal Situation in India*', Simla: Indian Institute of Advanced Study.

Singh, Kashi N. (1968): 'The Territorial Basis of Medieval Town and Village Settlement in Eastern U.P., India', *Annals of the Association of American Geographers*, Vol. LVII, pp. 203-14.

Singh, Kashi N. (1972): 'An Approach to the Study of the Morphology of the Indian Village' in R.L. Singh (ed.) *Rural Settlements in Monsoon Asia*, Varanasi: National Geographical Society of India, pp. 203-214.

Singh, Kashi N. (1979): 'Caste', in Moonis Raza (ed.) *A Survey of Research in Geography: 1969-72*, New Delhi: Allied Publishers.

Singh, Kashi N. (1993): 'Caste and Clan in the Indian Rural Settlement System' in Aijazuddin Ahmad (ed.) *Social Structure and Regional Development: A Social Geography Perspective*, Jaipur: Rawat Publications, pp. 51-75.

Singh, L.R. and Dina Nath (1981): 'Spatial Patterns of Scheduled Caste Population in the Saryupar Plain', *Geographical Review of India*, Vol. XLIII, No. 4, pp. 311-25.

Singh, R.L. (1974): 'Evolution of Clan Territorial Units Through Land Occupance in the Middle Ganga Valley', *National Geographical Journal of India*, Vol. XX, pp. 1-19.

Singh, R.L. and R. B. Singh (1972): 'Spatial Diffusion of Rajput Clan Settlements in a Part of Middle Ganga Valley' in R.L. Singh (ed.) *Rural Settlements in Monsoon Asia*, Varanasi: National Geographical Society of India, pp. 152-70.

Singh, R.A. (1994): 'Historical Atlas of Indian Languages: A Case Study of Migration of Indo-Aryan through the Ages' in N.H. Itagi (ed.) *Spatial Aspects of Language*, Mysore: Central Institute of Indian Languages, pp. 187-95.

Singh, R.B. (1975): *Rajput Clan Settlements in Varanasi District*, Varanasi: National Geographical Society of India.

Singh, R.L. (1955): 'Evolution of Rural Settlements in Middle Ganga Valley', *National Geographical Journal of India*, Vol. X, No. 1, pp. 1-44.

Singh, R.L. and Kashi N. Singh (1963): 'Evolution of the Medieval Towns in the Saryupar Plain of the Middle Ganga Valley: A Case Study', *National Geographical Journal of India*, Vol. X, No. 1, pp. 1-11.

Singh, R.P. and N.G. Sunitikala Devi (1975): 'Meities of Manipur: A Study in Human Ecology', *Geographical Review of India*, Vol. XXXVII, No. 1, pp. 53-61.

Singh, Rana P.B. (1974): 'Clan Settlements in the Saran Plain, Middle Ganga Valley', Unpublished Ph. D. Thesis, Banaras Hindu University, Varanasi.

Singh, Rana P.B. (1975): 'Distribution of Caste and Search for a New Theory of Caste Ranking: Case of the Saran Plain', *National Geographical Journal of India*, Vol. XXI, No. 1, pp. 20-40.

Singh, Rana P.B. (1975): 'Mechanism of the Diffusion of the Clan Settlements in the Saran Plain', *National Geographical Journal of India*, Vol. XXI, Nos. 3-4, pp. 172-96.

Singh, Rana P.B. (1987): 'Emergence of the Geography of Belief System: A Search of Identity in India', *The National Geographical Journal of India*, Vol. XXXIII, No. 2, pp. 184-204.

Singh, Rana P.B. (1987): 'Religious Fair, Spatial Affinity and Economics in India: Case of Dadri Mela (Ballia District)', *The National Geographical Journal of India*, Vol. XXXIII, No. 3, pp. 277-304.

Singh, Rana P.B. (1987): 'Towards Myth, Cosmos, Space and Mandala in India: A Search in Geography of Belief Systems', *The National Geographical Journal of India*, Vol. XXXIII, No. 3, pp. 305-26.

Singh, Savinder (1971): The Naga Problem—A Geographical Appraisal, *National Geographer*, Vol. VI, pp. 47-55.

Sinha, Surajit (1982): 'Rethinking about Tribes and Indian Civilisation' in Budhadeb Choudhuri (ed.), *Tribal Development in India: Problems and Prospects*, New Delhi: Inter-India Publications, pp. 3-14.

Smith, David M. (1979): *Where the Grass is Greener: Living in an Unequal World*, Victoria: Penguin Books Australia Ltd.

Sopher, D.E. (1973): 'Toward a Rediscovery of India: Thoughts on Some Neglected Geography', in M.M. Mikesell (ed.) *Geographers Abroad: Essays on the Problems and Prospects of Research in Foreign Areas*, Chicago: Department of Geography, University of Chicago, Paper No. 153, pp. 110-32.

Sopher, D.E. (1974): 'Indian Pastoral Castes and Livestock Ecologies: A Geographical Analysis' in L.S. Leshnik and G.D. Sontheimer (eds.) *Nomads and Pastoralists in South Asia*, Wiesbaden.

Sopher, D.E. (1977): 'Rohelkhand and Oudh: An Exploration of Social Gradients across a Political Frontier' in Richard C. Fox (ed.) *Realm and Region in Traditional India*, N.C. Chapel Hill.

Sopher, David E. (1987): 'The Message of Place in Hindu Pilgrimage', *The National Geographical Journal of India*, Vol. XXXIII, No. 4, pp. 353-69.

Sopher, David E. (ed., 1980): *An Exploration of India: Geographical Perspectives on Society and Culture*, London: Longman.

Spencer, G.W. (1969): 'Religious Network and Royal Influence in Eleventh Century South India', *Journal of the Economic and Social History of the Orient*, Vol. 12, pp. 42-56.

Srinivas, M.N. (1962): *Caste in Modern India and Other Essays*, Bombay: Asia Publishing House.

Srinivas, M.N. (ed. 1981): *Studies in Sociology and Social Anthropology*, Delhi: Hindustan Publishing Corporation.

Srinivas, M.N. (1986): *India: Social Structure*, Delhi: Hindustan Publishing Corporation.

Subbarao, B. (1958): *The Personality of India*, Baroda: M.S. University.

Sukhwal, B.L. (1985): *Modern Political Geography of India*, New Delhi: Sterling Publishers Pvt. Ltd.

Thapar, Romila (1977): *A History of India*, Vol. 1, Hammondsworth: Penguin Books Ltd.

Thapar, Romila (1990): *From Lineage to State*, Delhi: Oxford University Press.

Tripathi, R.S. and J.P. Vishwakarma (1990): 'Castes in Rural Areas of Bundelkhand—A Study of Major Characterstics and Process of Change', *Geographical Review of India*, Vol. LII, No. 1, pp. 84-88.

Weber, Max (1965): *The Sociology of Religion*, London: Methuen & Co.

Williams, Colin H. (not dated): 'On Measurement and Application in Geolinguistics', *Discussion Papers in Geolinguistics*, No. 8, Stoke-on-Trent: Department of Geography and Recreation Studies, North Staffordshire Polytechnic.

Williams, Stephen Wyn (not dated): 'Language Maintenance, Erosion and Ethnic Identity', *Discussion Papers in Geolinguistics*, No. 6, Stoke-on-Trent: Department of Geography and Recreation Studies, North Staffordshire Polytechnic.

Index